Conservation Song

Wapulumuka Oliver Mulwafu

Conservation Song

A History of Peasant–State Relations and the
Environment in Malawi, 1860–2000

The White Horse Press

Copyright © Wapulumuka Oliver Mulwafu
First published 2011 by
The White Horse Press, 10 High Street, Knapwell, Cambridge, CB23 4NR, UK

Set in 10 point Adobe Garamond Pro
Printed by Lightning Source

All rights reserved. Except for the quotation of short passages for the purpose of criticism or review, no part of this book may be reprinted or reproduced or utilised in any form or by any electronic, mechanical or other means, including photocopying or recording, or in any information storage or retrieval system.

British Library Cataloguing in Publication Data
A catalogue record for this book is available from the British Library

ISBN   978-1-874267-77-5

To my mother and my late father

Contents

1. Introduction... 1
2. Pre-Colonial Environment and Production Systems, 1860s–1900 . 18
3. Christian and Colonial Attitudes Towards the Environment...... 40
4. Scientific Networking, Ideology and the Rise of Conservation
   Discourse in Colonial Malawi............................. 59
5. The Natural Resources Board and the Soil Conservation
   Campaign in Colonial Malawi, 1946–1964 81
6. Colonial Intervention into African Trust Lands, 1939–1964 106
7. State Intervention into Private Estate Production in the
   Shire Highlands 118
8. Conservation and Politics, 1952–1964..................... 143
9. The Religious Dimension to the Campaign against Soil Erosion
   in Colonial Malawi...................................... 166
10. Ecological Change, Gender Relations and Peasant Resistance
    in Zomba District....................................... 187
11. Post-colonial Environmental Discourses, 1964–2000......... 215
12. Conclusion.. 235
Bibliography... 239
Index 261

List of Illustrations and Tables

Figure 1.1. Photo showing soil conservation works in Thyolo district. . 5

Figure 1.2. Map of Malawi. 11

Figure 4.1. Relationship between key natural resources linked by soil (erosion) 63

Table 4.1. Nyasaland Colonial Staff Trained at the IFI 73

Table 4.2. Key Staff of the IFI 75

Figure 5.1. Structure of the Natural Resources Board 86

Figure 5.2. Chiefs attending a briefing meeting on a land improvement scheme as part of the soil conservation programme. In the background, there is an example of properly managed land. 90

Figure 5.3. Training of agricultural field staff at Colby in 1956. 99

Figure 5.4. Controlling gully erosion with stone check dams, 1953 . 101

Figure 5.5. Strip rotation on a village land improvement scheme in Central Province, 1956 101

Table 5.1. Impact of the Bunding Campaign, 1951–1955 103

Table 6.1. Status of Village Forest Areas in 1931 111

Figure 6.1. Vingonyeka Traditional Method of Soil Conservation . . 114

Figure 6.3. Garden showing how Vingonyeka technique is used. . . . 115

Figure 6.5. Gully erosion in Misuku hills 115

Figure 6.2. An improved Vingonyeka traditional method of soil conservation 115

Figure 6.4. Another garden showing Vingonyeka technique in the making 115

Figure 7.1. Mulanje tea experimental station during opening ceremony in 1954. 138

Figure 8.1. Level used for making ridges. 149

Figure 8.2. Example of a well managed garden 150

Figure 10.1. Map of Zomba district 188

Table 10.1. Relationship between Napolo and Geomorphological Changes 194

Figure 10.2. Peasants filling in one of the eroded gullies at Domasi in the early 1950s 199

Figure 10.3. Student accommodation and farm at the Jeanes training school, Domasi, 1936. Note the soil conservation layout of the fields with ridge and furrow cultivation along the contour. 199

Table 11.1. Land Use and Vegetation 225

Figure 11.1. Cultivation extending on the fringes of a forest reserve in the Misuku Hills. 228

Acknowledgements

This book is a product of many years of research into environmental changes and their relationships with humans under different institutional regimes in Malawi's history. I began my research in 1996, initially as part of doctoral studies supported by a grant from the Rockefeller Foundation. Since then I have received various kinds of support that have allowed me to conduct additional research on a number of themes. I wish to single out the USAID-funded BASIS collaborative research project into promoting equitable access to land and water resources in southern Africa. In addition, WaterNet, a regional network for capacity building in integrated water resources management in southern Africa, is hereby acknowledged for the opportunity to interact and share ideas at its annual symposia. All the studies and contacts enriched immensely my knowledge and understanding of environmental issues in the region and beyond.

I am grateful to my doctoral supervisor, Allen Isaacman, and all the professors I worked with at the University of Minnesota, especially Stuart Schwartz, Jean Allman and the late Susan Geiger. My cohorts in the MacArthur Interdisciplinary Programme for the Study of Peace and Justice (now known as the Programme for the Study of Global Change) deserve commendation for cultivating a friendship that has endured to this day. In particular, I wish to thank Marissa Moorman, Derek Peterson, Guy Thompson, Jacob Tropp and the late Ana Margarita Gomez, who shared a lot as we braved the chilly winters of the land of a thousand lakes. Phil and Sandie Johnson of Brooklyn Park, Minnesota, have for years remained very good family friends.

I owe a debt to numerous people and institutions – too many to mention each by name – that have worked with me over the years. Let it be known that your advice gave me the necessary intellectual stimulus to move on. I was, however, encouraged to pursue the book project because of fruitful discussions with and constant support from Bill Adams, Peter Alegi, William Beinart, Lewis Dzimbiri, Harri Englund, Laura Fair, James Fairhead, Anne Ferguson, Kingsley Jika, Linley Karltun-Chiwona, Peter Limb, Elias Mandala, Wellington Masamba, John McCracken, Alister Munthali, Pauline Peters, Derek Peterson, Prof. Kings Phiri, Megan Vaughan, Liz Watson and Ruth Watson. All my colleagues in the History Department at Chancellor College of the University of Malawi are gratefully acknowledged for sharing the heavy teaching responsibilities when I had to take some time off to work on my own research. I also wish to thank John Wilson for kindly sharing some family pictures which I have used in this book.

One of the greatest challenges of teaching in Malawi, and indeed in most African countries, is the disproportionate amount of pressure placed on the few well qualified scholars. Faculty members are often burdened with administrative responsibilities among which time for sustained professional development becomes a scarce commodity. The sabbatical leave I spent in Michigan and Cambridge proved to be the most fruitful part of my professional development. Getting away after ten years of continuous teaching and administrative service gave me an opportunity to concentrate on my research and writing. In the USA, I am greatly indebted to the History Department and the African Studies Centre at Michigan State University in East Lansing for the hospitality and institutional support. I would probably not have completed this book as quickly as I have done had it not been for the time and resources generously provided by the Centre of African Studies and Wolfson College at the University of Cambridge. The Visiting Research Fellowship under the Cambridge/Africa Collaborative Research Programme facilitated an exchange of ideas at workshops and seminars on the theme of Public Understanding of Science in Africa. It was great to interact with my colleagues in the programme – Verki Fanso, Muza Gondwe, Joseph Kariuki and Olufunke Adeboye and Dorian Addison, who deserve special thanks for the good company during the unusually cold and snowy winter.

Research for this book was conducted in many places and various people assisted me in getting the required data. At the Malawi National Archives in Zomba, the staff have always been friendly and ready to assist. I acknowledge in particular the dedication of Joel Thaulo and James Mindozo. I also thank all staff at the Society of Malawi in Blantyre, at the Malawiana Collection, Chancellor College library and at the documentation centres of all government departments I visited in the country. I am equally grateful to staff at the National Archives of the UK at Kew as well as to the staff at Rhodes House at Oxford University for the additional sources I consulted. A significant part of my study benefited from data collected through interviews with informants in villages throughout Malawi. I am deeply grateful to those rural men and women who unconditionally spent hours away from their busy schedules recounting events either as they themselves experienced them or as they were passed down by their parents.

Two chapters in this book have come from articles previously published in journals. I therefore wish to thank Taylor and Francis for permission to publish chapter seven, which is a modified version of the paper that came out in the *Journal of Southern African Studies* 28/1 (2002): 25–43 (http://www.informaworld.com); and Brill for chapter three, which initially came out in the *Journal of Religion in Africa* 34/3 (2004): 298–319 (www.brill.nl).

This book is especially dedicated to my late father, Oliver Katepela Mulwafu, who, with his own disciplinarian approach, always encouraged the spirit of hard work and the love of education. My mother, Dailess Jane Nachiwona, created a fertile environment for our upbringing and always reminded us to have faith in the Lord. I thank all the members of my family who have made sacrifices to see me accomplish what I have done so far. My wife, Levis, children – Emmanuel, Wapu Jr and Watipaso – and all my brothers and sisters will be delighted to see this book as a reflection of their intangible input into my growth as an academic member of their family.

The conclusions and interpretations contained in this book do not reflect the ideas or views of the publisher or the people who provided information. All such ideas remain the responsibility of the author.

AUTHOR BIOGRAPHY

Wapulumuka Oliver Mulwafu is Associate Professor of Environmental History and SADC–WaterNet Professorial Chair of Integrated Water Resources Management at Chancellor College, University of Malawi. He is a Guest Editor of the Water and Society theme for the *Journal of Physics and Chemistry of the Earth* as well as a member of the Advisory Board of the *Journal of Southern African Studies*. During his recent sabbatical leave in 2009–2010, he was a Visiting Research Fellow at the Centre of African Studies and Wolfson College, University of Cambridge (UK) and Visiting Professor in the Department of History at Michigan State University (USA). His work has appeared in various publications including the *Journal of Southern African Studies, Journal of Religion in Africa, Journal of Physics and Chemistry of the Earth, Malawi Journal of Social Science, Malawi Journal of Science and Technology* and *Society of Malawi Journal*.

1

Introduction

Struggle for sustainable societies

In 1924, Captain A.J.W. Hornby, one of Nyasaland's long serving agricultural scientists, argued that soil was the most important asset of the territory and called on future trustees to prevent the loss of soil capital. Nearly a decade later, Paul Topham, the country's first soil erosion officer, bemoaned degradation of the environment due in large measure to soil erosion and consequently launched a country-wide campaign to arrest the problem. African peasants who were obliged to reform their farming practices to conform to the new ideas viewed the situation very differently. The ensuing soil conservation policies, laws and programmes became very unpopular and some scholars have even questioned the scientific basis of these ideas. In 1994, the National Environmental Action Plan (NEAP) identified soil erosion as the most serious of the nine environmental problems facing the post-colonial state of Malawi. Policy-makers, scholars and non-governmental organisations have been working frantically to develop suitable policies and programmes to help curb the problem. As in colonial days, African peasants have again been the main target of state-induced conservation policies and programmes. In the meantime, agricultural scientists continue to adapt their ideas, which reinforce modern conservationist thinking and policies. These two episodes are not simple renditions of state intervention separated by time; they represent a history of engagement with peasants whose lives and practices did not rest on scientific criteria or solely on the measure of production. There were a variety of religious, cultural and social engagements with farming, which were not purely economic in nature.

Environmental degradation in Southern Africa represents one of the major challenges facing post-colonial states trying to create sustainable societies. By sustainability, we mean communities where individuals and states interact with the environment in ways that ensure adequate reproduction and renewal of human and natural resources. Although scholars disagree on the precise definition of 'sustainability', the term nonetheless offers a useful way to explore the interrelationship between power, poverty and environmental degradation over time.[1] As such it

---

1. See, for example, K. Amanor and S. Moyo (eds.) *Land and Sustainable Development in Africa* (London and New York: Zed Publications, 2008); O. Ukaga and A.G. Afoaku (eds.) *Sustainable Development in Africa: a Multifaceted Challenge* (Trenton, NJ: Africa World Press, 2005); S. Lele, 'Sustainable Development: a Critical Review', *World Development* 19/6 (1991): 607–21; T. O'Riordan, 'The Politics of Sustainability', in R.K. Turner (ed.) *Sustainable*

Introduction

moves beyond the presentist assumptions and biases current in most discussions about development and offers a strategic entry point to explore the historical roots of Africa's social and ecological problems. This book is an attempt to show how contemporary policies and practices of soil conservation are produced out of historical contexts. We begin from the premise that many of the present environmental crises in Africa are integrally connected to past policies and practices and, in turn, have far-reaching implications for the future.[2] In the Southern African region, the challenge of sustainability is particularly acute in Malawi, where a combination of land shortage, population density, drought, commercial farming and refugee influxes has resulted in the rapid destruction of natural resources. Foremost among these problems is soil erosion, which has degraded land on a perennial basis.[3]

Setting the state's conservation policies against the ways peasants adapted to the multiple threats of soil erosion, overgrazing, and deforestation over time provided me with a strategic entry into the larger social and environmental history of Malawi. This type of historical inquiry can provide valuable insights into the contradictions, negotiations, tensions and struggles in rural society that must necessarily be at the centre of any discussion of sustainability. Because sustainability is a desired state goal and because conservation programmes are still a vital element of agricultural production techniques in the countryside the study illuminates current debates about the development process in Malawi. In the statement of its goals and priority programmes, the Malawi post-colonial state has emphasised the sustainable use of resources as one of the key components of its development policy objectives.[4]

Environmental Economics and Management: Principles and Practice (London and New York: Belhaven Press, 1993), pp. 37–69; M.A. Toman, 'The Difficulty of Defining Sustainability', *Resources* 106 (1992): 3–6; David Hulme and Marshall Murphree (eds.) *African Wildlife and Livelihoods: the Promise and Performance of Community Conservation* (Portsmouth NH: Heinemann, 2001).

2. For a detailed discussion on continuities and changes between colonial and post-colonial state policies, see Allen Isaacman, 'Historical Amnesia, or, the Logic of Capital Accumulation: Cotton Production in Colonial and Post-Colonial Mozambique', *Environment and Planning D: Society and Space* 15 (1997): 757–790. M. Tiffen, M. Mortimore and F. Gichuki, *More People, Less Erosion: Environmental Recovery in Kenya* (London and New York: John Wiley, 1994).

3. J.R. Ngoleka Mlia, 'History of Soil Conservation in Malawi' in *History of Soil Conservation in the SADCC Region* (SADCC, March 1987); E.J. Mwendera, 'A Short History and Annotated Bibliography on Soil and Water Conservation in Malawi', *SADCC Report* No.20 (September, 1989), pp. 1–6; Lincoln W.S. Singini, 'Soil Erosion and its Control in Malawi', *Dziko: The Geographical Magazine* 8 (1980): 10–18.

4. For details, see Malawi Government, *Vision 2020: National Long-Term Perspective Study*, Vol.1 (1998) and the *Environmental Management Act* of 1996. Recently the government developed the Malawi Growth and Development Strategy as its overarching policy framework for poverty reduction. The strategy focuses on accelerated economic growth, social development, good governance and environmental sustainability. Malawi Government, *Malawi Growth and Development Strategy, 2006–2011* (Lilongwe: Ministry of Economic Planning and Development, Feb 2007).

Issues and arguments of the book

Current debates over conservation are framed largely by colonial science's prescriptive efforts to reform the adaptable and innovative practices of African peasants.

Issues and arguments of the book

Conservation Song: A History of Peasant–State Relations and the Environment in Malawi, 1860–2000 explores ways in which colonial relations have shaped meanings and conflicts over control and management of the environment in a land we now call Malawi. It examines the origins and effects of policies on issues of soil conservation, which required an integrated approach to the use and management of such natural resources as land, water and forestry, and their legacies in the post-colonial era. The overall colonial approach to issues of the environment has a fundamental contemporary significance and is not simply a phenomenon created in the colonial period. For instance, like other countries in the region, post-colonial Malawi has been bedevilled with increasing rates of environmental degradation due, in part, to the expansion of human and animal populations, commercial crop production, drought and the consequent deforestation. These factors were as critical six to seven decades ago as they are today. They are in a sense part of an endless lyric of a conservation song with a long chequered history. To use a metaphor of music, the song of conservation was initially composed and first performed in the colonial period when Malawi was Nyasaland and a British Protectorate, modified during the immediate post-colonial period and further refashioned in the post-dictatorship period to suit the evolving political climate. But the basic lyrics and the underlying tune remain essentially the same. The book attempts to trace the development of this conservationist idea; at the same time it demonstrates changes and continuities in peasant–state relations under different political systems.

While the dominant narrative posits conservation as a progressive movement aimed at re-organising and protecting natural resources from destruction, it is shown in this work that the idea was itself contested and was deeply embedded in colonial power relations and scientific ethos.[5] In other words, conservation emerged as an important tool of colonial state intervention into and control of people and scarce resources. *Conservation Song* thus shows the specific ways in which the idea of conservation was rooted in and driven by a particular type of science regarding the organisation of space and landscapes. It offers a strategic entry point to understanding the historical roots of Africa's social and ecological problems over time, problems that are also intertwined with relationships of power and poverty.

In the post-colonial period – i.e. the period after 1964 – the conservation tempo subsided and became, at some points, almost non-existent in the public discourse, only to re-emerge in the 1990s as a result of the democratisation move-

---

5. R.W. Kettlewell, *Agricultural Change in Nyasaland, 1945–1960* (Stanford, 1965); P. Topham, 'Land Conservation in Nyasaland: an Attempt at Widespread Control, 1937–1940', in *Farm and Forest* Vol.6 (Ibadan, 1945), pp. 5–8.

Introduction

ment. In the period after 1964, when Nyasaland attained independence, the state focused on the strategies of persuasion, demonstration, and the promotion of *achikumbe*, a rebranding of the colonial progressive farming system. But, unlike in the colonial period when technical expertise was predominantly European, in the post-colonial period, a cadre of African technical staff assumed responsibility for the implementation of soil conservation policies which, not surprisingly, did not generate any overt resistance from peasants. The expansion of commercial crop production, particularly tobacco, which required not only the opening up of new fields but also the use of valuable natural resources such as trees for curing the crop, brought the ruling elite into complicity with key agents for increased environmental degradation. This reflected contradictions in the state's approach as well as the nuanced understanding of the issue of soil conservation.

Conservation Song raises four central arguments. First, it contends that early colonial state policies irreversibly transformed both the economy and land tenure systems in Malawi but, in the process, placed additional burdens on the land. It shows that the economy shifted from one primarily based on subsistence and exchange of food crops to an export-oriented cash economy system with distinct peasant and plantation sectors. The peasant sector produced food crops such as maize, beans and groundnuts on customary land, while the plantation sector, run by European settlers, produced mainly export crops such as tobacco, tea, coffee and cotton, either on freehold or leasehold land.[6] Evidence from this period suggests that the increasing loss of fertile lands, combined with some environmentally destructive practices of both Africans and European settlers and coupled with overcrowding on the lands Africans retained, produced an ecological crisis by the 1930s.[7] In response, the colonial state initiated a major, and highly controversial, conservation scheme only a few years before the outbreak of the Second World War. Colonial authorities intervened on an unprecedented scale at the point of production: they forced peasants to allocate precious time and labour to contour ridging, box ridging, bunding and terracing.[8] Many scholars have suggested that this intervention in the late 1930s marked the ascendancy of the ideology of conservation and social engineering. Proponents of this thesis hold that, while state officials had been aware

---

6. Leroy Vail, 'The State and the Creation of Malawi's Colonial Economy', in R. Rotberg (ed.) *Imperialism, Colonialism and Hunger* (Lexington, 1983) pp. 39–86.
7. A.J.W. Hornby, *Denudation and Soil Erosion in Nyasaland* (Zomba: Government Printer, 1934) Bulletin No.11; P.H. Haviland, *Report on Soil Erosion Prevention and Reclamation of Eroded Arable Land in Nyasaland* (1930); P. Topham, 'Land Conservation in Nyasaland'; F. Dixey et al. *The Destruction of Vegetation and its Relation to Climate, Water Supply, and Soil Fertility* (Zomba: Government Printer, 1924); J.R. Ngoleka Mlia, 'History of Soil Conservation in Malawi'; E.B. Worthington, *The Ecological Century: a Personal Appraisal* (London: Oxford University Press, 1983).
8. R.W. Kettlewell, *An Outline of Agrarian Problems and Policy in Nyasaland* (Zomba: Government Press, 1955); R.W. Kettlewell, *Agricultural Change in Nyasaland*; *Report of the Postwar Development Committee*.

Issues and arguments of the book

Figure 1.1. Photo showing soil conservation works in Thyolo district

of many of the ecological problems in the colonies,[9] the devastating experience of the Dust Bowl in the Great Plains of the United States propelled them to act.[10] While conventional scholarship continues to emphasise the role of the American Dust Bowl in prompting British colonial intervention, this work shows that the influence of the Imperial Forestry Institute (IFI) at Oxford University has grossly been underestimated. It is argued that the IFI, whose establishment predated the Dust Bowl, played a unique role in training colonial service staff as well as in generating scientific ideas about conservation, not only in Malawi but also in the British Empire as a whole.

---

9. Richard Grove, *Green Imperialism: Colonial Expansion, Tropical Island Edens and the Origins of Environmentalism, 1600–1860* (Cambridge, 1995).
10. David Anderson, 'Depression, Dust Bowl, Demography, and Drought: the Colonial State and Soil Conservation in East Africa During the 1930s', *African Affairs* 83/332 (1984): 321–44; William Beinart, 'Soil Erosion, Conservationism and Ideas about Development: a Southern African Exploration, 1900–1960', *Journal of Southern African Studies (JSAS)* 11 (1984): 52–83; John K. McCracken, 'Experts and Expertise in Colonial Malawi', *African Affairs* 81/322 (1982): 101–116.

Introduction

Conservation Song also demonstrates that the introduction of the colonial conservation project transformed the longstanding interaction between peasant producers and their environment. Implementation of these laws meant a fundamental restructuring of the peasant sector in ways that created new forms of conflict between the state and the peasantry. Both oral and archival evidence suggest that colonial authorities and the peasantry held quite different views on the organisation of space and time, views that in turn precipitated intense conflicts in the countryside. Conservation measures required a substantial labour input from peasants between the months of June and November, a period that coincided with important post-harvest religious and social ceremonies. While Europeans observed the movement of the calendar, Africans followed the cycles of nature and these different cultural constructions of time were critical in shaping the intense rural reactions to the new laws.[11] Struggles also ensued over the meaning of land, specifically over who owned it and how it should be used.

The third argument analyses what happened when the state intensified its campaign as further ecological changes took place in some parts of the country with equally transformative effects on African values and attitudes towards land use and ownership. African knowledge of and practices on the environment were neither static nor unresponsive to changes brought about by non-human factors; they were part of the dynamic and ever-changing landscape. *Conservation Song* argues that, in the period of increased state intervention in the management of natural resources in the 1940s and 1950s, little space was given to consideration of alternative modes of thought, including indigenous systems of knowledge, while scientifically-backed conservation ideas had to be implemented in order to transform the structures of African societies and their activities affecting the environment. That notwithstanding, state policies and practices on conservation were begrudgingly mediated. This opened up space for contests among various groups in the African and European communities. Conservation, which inevitably meant state intrusion into the private spaces of peasants and commercial land users, was but one area where silent warfare was conducted for much of the colonial period in British Africa. African peasants were neither passive victims nor indifferent bystanders; they responded in many ways including cooperation, adaptation and the use of both hidden and violent forms of resistance. This book discusses the largely

---

11. Keletso Atkins, *The Moon is Dead! Give Us Our Money! The Cultural Origins of an African Work Ethic, Natal, South Africa, 1843–1900* (Portsmouth, NH: Heinemann, 1993); Steve Feierman, *Peasant Intellectuals: Anthropology and History in Tanzania* (Madison: University of Wisconsin Press, 1990); Richard Grove, 'Scottish Missionaries, Evangelical Discourses and the Origins of Conservation Thinking in Southern Africa, 1820–1900', *JSAS* 15/2 (1989): 163–187; Elias Mandala, *Work and Control in a Peasant Economy: a History of the Lower Tchiri Valley in Malawi, 1860–1960* (Madison: University of Wisconsin Press, 1990); Kate B. Showers, 'Soil Conservation in the Kingdom of Lesotho: Origins and Colonial Response, 1830s–1950s', *JSAS* 15/2 (1989): 263–286; L. White, '"They Could Make Their Victims Dull": Gender and Genres, Fantasies and Cures in Colonial Southern Uganda', *American Historical Review* 100/5 (1995): 1379–1402.

Theoretical context

unexplored area of religious opposition to conservation, a development that not only questioned the moral value of conservation but also helped to undermine the entire colonial project. But such actions also illustrate contradictions inherent in Christian attitudes to and interpretations of the African environment.

The final argument, and it is related to one presented in the preceding paragraph, attempts to explain the smouldering tensions and violence that erupted in 1953 in many rural areas such as Domasi, Ntcheu and Thyolo when rural growers boycotted the implementation of conservation measures.[12] Peasant women, who were forced to do much of the labour for the conservation schemes, played a critical insurgent role. Thus these protests were as much about the politics of gender as they were responses to state intervention at the point of production. The colonial state conservation policies were codified into three successive laws in 1946, 1949 and 1951, locally known as *malimidwe*. By highlighting *malimidwe* as one of the grievances against colonial rule, nationalist leaders were able to gain the support of peasants in the struggle against colonialism. However, scholars who have seen these rural protests through the nationalist lens have tended to lose sight of the essence of the conflict, which was about the meaning of land and the control of labour.

Theoretical context

The increasing scholarly interest in sustainability has had surprisingly little impact on agrarian research in Malawi. The literature suffers from several problems. First, it fails to appreciate how local environmental factors have long contributed to soil erosion. Second, most research is devoid of any serious exploration of the problems of land degradation in the pre-colonial period and of the ways Malawians have historically sought to conserve soil resources through such practices as intercropping, *matuto*, *makusa*, *vingonyeka*, building stone lines and planting contour banana strips on the edges of food gardens. Third, the literature ignores the ways in which peasant actions, both coping and struggling, transformed state conservation practices during the colonial period. That most scholars have conceptualised peasant experiences largely through a nationalist paradigm, in which rural farmers were presumed to have been led from above or from outside, explains this gap in the literature.

The study of the Shire Highlands benefits from insights derived from both political ecology and political economy in order to examine what have been previ-

---

12. See Robert I. Rotberg, *The Rise of Nationalism in Central Africa: The Making of Malawi and Zambia, 1873–1964* (Cambridge, Mass: Harvard University Press, 1965); Roger Tangri, 'The Rise of Nationalism in Colonial Africa: the Case of Colonial Malawi', *Comparative Studies in Society and History* 10/2 (1968): 142–161; Zimani D. Kadzamira, 'Agricultural Policy and Change During the Colonial Period in Malawi' (Chancellor College: History Seminar Paper, 1975/76); Joey Power, *Political Culture and Nationalism in Malawi: Building Kwacha* (Rochester: University of Rochester Press, 2010).

Introduction

ously defined as 'natural calamities'.[13] Until recently, the question of environmental conservation has been the domain of natural scientists, often leading to overly scientific approaches that marginalise the socio-cultural dimensions of the struggle over the land. But recent research demonstrates that environmental issues can no longer be treated as purely natural phenomena.[14] A number of scholars have stressed that the issue of sustainability cannot be extrapolated from political and economic forces operating at the local, national and transnational levels.[15] Indeed, the very notions of conservation and sustainability raise several questions: Sustainability for whom? Who sets the development agenda? In whose interest is this agenda? How does it affect gender relations? The idea of foregrounding power relations in discussions of conservation and sustainability lies at the centre of this book.[16]

A careful reading of earlier anthropological works on Central and Southern Africa offers some valuable insights into ways in which changes in ecology have affected land use practices and settlement patterns. In the case of neighbouring Zambia, population pressure and shifting agriculture (*chitemene*) led to land degradation and a reduction in output. Peasants responded by adopting ploughs to open up larger tracts of land, which then required a dramatic leap in labour and time to plant and weed the crops. These changes in turn affected land tenure and agrarian

---

13. See Paul Robbins, *Political Ecology: A Critical Introduction* (Blackwell Publishing, 2004); Elizabeth E. Watson, *Living Terraces in Ethiopia: Konso Landscape, Culture and Development* (London: James Currey, 2009); Piers Blaikie, *The Political Economy of Soil Erosion* (London and New York: Longman, 1985); P. Blaikie and H. Brookfield (eds.) *Land Degradation and Society* (London and New York: Methuen, 1987); Paul Richards, 'Ecological Change and the Politics of African Land Use', *African Studies Review* 26 (1983): 1–72.

14. Kate B. Showers, K. and G. Malahlela, 'Oral Evidence in Historical Environmental Impact Assessment', *JSAS* 18 (1992): 277–95; M. Tiffen, M. Mortimore and F. Gichuki, *More People, Less Erosion: Environmental Recovery in Kenya* (London & New York: John Wiley, 1994); Shula Marks, *The Imperial Lion: Human Dimensions of Wildlife Management in Central Africa* (Boulder, CO: Westview Press, 1984).

15. William M. Adams, *Green Development: Environment and Sustainability in the Third World* (London and New York: Routledge, 1990); Sara Berry, *No Condition is Permanent: the Social Dynamics of Agrarian Change in Sub-Saharan Africa* (Madison: University of Wisconsin Press, 1993); Fred Cooper and Randall Packard, 'Introduction: Development Knowledge and the Social Sciences' (Unpublished Paper, 1996); Arturo Escobar, *Encounter Development: the Making and Unmaking of the Third World* (Princeton, NJ: Princeton University Press, 1995); Allen Isaacman, *Cotton is the Mother of Poverty: Peasants, Work, and Rural Struggle in Colonial Mozambique, 1938-1961* (Portsmouth, NH: Heinemann, 1996); Henrietta L. Moore and Megan Vaughan, *Cutting Down Trees: Gender, Nutrition and Agricultural Change in the Northern Province of Zambia, 1890-1990* (Portsmouth, N.H: Heinemann, 1994); James C. Scott, *Weapons of the Weak: Everyday Forms of Peasant Resistance* (New Haven: Yale University Press, 1985); Michael Watts, 'Idioms of Land and Labor', in T. Bassett (ed.) *Land Tenure in Africa* (Madison: University of Wisconsin Press, 1992) pp.159–196.

16. W. Adams, *Green Development*; Judith Carney, 'Struggles over Land and Crops in an Irrigated Rice Scheme', in J. Davison (ed.) *Agriculture, Women and Land: the African Experience* (Boulder, CO: Westview Press, 1988), pp. 59–78; Watts, 'Idioms of Land and Labor'; Chambers, *Rural Development*.

Theoretical context

systems in ways that were very different from previous forms of organising land, labour and production.[17] In Malawi, Clyde Mitchell argued that the social structure of the Yao-speaking people obstructed the successful implementation of the colonial state's community development scheme in the Zomba district. In particular, he noted that the emphasis on the principles of uxorilocal marriage and matrilineal primogeniture adversely affected the land tenure system and inheritance patterns.[18]

The study also benefits from several pioneering environmental studies in other parts of Africa, which have explored the origins, nature and impact on African peoples in general of conservation policies within the colonial context.[19] More recent studies emphasise the different understandings of the African environment, which demonstrate the creativity and sophistication of indigenous peoples in the use and management of such environmental resources as land, water, soil and vegetation.[20] For Malawi, Beinart, Mandala, and McCracken respectively have examined the impact of conservation laws but have limited their discussions to the colonial period.[21] These works provide an important starting point for a more systematic and longer view of conservation and sustainability. The works also show that African peasants had developed their own ways of managing the land resources.

Peasant opposition to betterment schemes and the ways in which this opposition was gendered represent another critical aspect of my study. Studies in other parts of Africa demonstrate that peasants not only resisted state authorities but also developed various coping strategies to minimise the effects of state intervention. The studies also show that the imposition of betterment schemes had a differential impact on peasant communities, including such factors as gender, age and social status in society. For example, anti-erosion measures were particularly opposed by

---

17. William Allan, *The African Husbandman* (New York: Barnes and Noble, 1967); Norman Long, *Social Change and the Individual: a Study of the Social and Religious Responses to Innovation in a Zambian Rural Community* (Manchester: Manchester University Press, 1968).

18. See J. Clyde Mitchell, *The Yao Village: a Study in the Social Structure of a Nyasaland Tribe* (Manchester: Manchester University Press, 1956).

19. See, for example, James Giblin, *The Politics of Environmental Control in Northeastern Tanzania, 1840–1940* (Philadelphia, 1992); James McCann, *People of the Plow: an Agricultural History of Ethiopia, 1800–1990* (Madison: University of Wisconsin Press, 1995); David Anderson and Richard Grove (eds.) *Conservation in Africa: People, Policies and Practice* (Cambridge: C.U.P, 1987); Grove, *Green Imperialism*; John M. Mackenzie, *The Empire of Nature: Hunting, Conservation and British Imperialism* (Manchester, 1988); Tiffen *et al. More People, Less Erosion*.

20. See Melissa Leach and Robin Mearns (eds.) *The Lie of the Land: Challenging Received Wisdom on the African Environment* (Portsmouth, NH: Heinemann, 1996); James Fairhead and M. Leach, *Misreading the African Landscape: Society and Ecology in a Forest-Savanna Mosaic* (Cambridge and New York: Cambridge University Press, 1996); Jacob Tropp, *Natures of Colonial Change: Environmental Relations in the Making of the Transkei* (Athens: Ohio University Press, 2006); Nancy J. Jacobs, *Environment, Power and Injustice: a South African History* (Cambridge: 2003); and Emmanuel Kreike, *Re-creating Eden: Land Use, Environment, and Society in Southern Angola and Northern Namibia.* (Portsmouth, NH: Heinemann, 2004).

21. See W. Beinart, 'Soil Conservationism'; E. Mandala, *Work and Control*; and J. McCracken, 'Experts and Expertise'.

Introduction

women because they entailed the elimination of the only land available to them and a reduction in time for them to work in their fields.[22]

Methodology and Sources

The main area of research for this book is the Shire Highlands region in southern Malawi, an area that has been experiencing serious environmental degradation for a long time. Both oral and written sources point to the occurrence of land degradation in many parts of the region from as early as the 1920s. This was exacerbated by two main factors. The first relates to the influx of large numbers of people into the region and the farming practices of both European settlers and Africans. The increase in population put heavy pressure on land resources as some African communities were relocated to areas that were susceptible to degradation.

These social factors were magnified by the structure and properties of soils in this region. The soils are mostly laterites, which vary from coarse sandy, to sandy loam, to sandy clay soils and are generally very susceptible to erosion. According to A.J.W. Hornby, the Agricultural Chemist and Assistant Director of Agriculture, the soils of the Shire Highlands contained a high percentage of iron and alumina which had an important bearing on their chemical and physical properties. This meant that the soils did not have a high content of phosphates and potash, which, in turn, accounted for lower rates of fertility and water-holding capacity. When it rained, the water could not percolate to the water table because of the existence of an impervious pan beneath the soil.[23] The failure of these soils to absorb rainwater resulted in surface run-off, which caused both sheet and gully erosion.[24]

---

22. See Allen Isaacman, 'Peasants and Rural Social Protest in Africa' in Frederick Cooper *et. al. Confronting Historical Paradigms: Peasants, Labor, and the Capitalist World System in Africa and Latin America* (Madison: University of Wisconsin Press, 1993), pp. 235–242; Anne Mager, '"The People Get Fenced": Gender, Rehabilitation and African Nationalism in the Ciskei and Border Region, 1945–1955', *JSAS* 18/4 (1992): 761–782; Joan McGregor, 'Conservation, Control and Ecological Change: the Politics and Ecology of Colonial Conservation in Shurugwi, Zimbabwe', *Environment and History* 1 (1995): 257–79; Donald S. Moore, 'Clear Waters and Muddied Histories: Environmental History and the Politics of Community in Zimbabwe's Eastern Highlands', *JSAS* 24/2 (1998): 377–402; Pamela A. Maack, '"We Don't Want Terraces!" Protest and Identity under the Ulugulu Land Usage Scheme', in G. Maddox *et al.* (eds.) *Custodians of the Land: Ecology and Culture in the History of Tanzania* (Athens, OH: Ohio University Press, 1996) pp. 152–74.

23. A.J.W. Hornby, 'The Erosion of Arable Soil in Nyasaland and Methods of Prevention', in F. Dixey, J.B. Clements and A.J.W. Hornby, *The Destruction of Vegetation and its Relation to Climate, Water Supply, and Soil Fertility* (Zomba: Government Printer, 1924) Bulletin No.1, p. 10.

24. Sheet erosion means the removal of a small amount of soil material from different parts of the field; and gully erosion means the removal of soil material from the field in the form of streams along depressions. Both types of erosion are easily accelerated by human activity and can result in environmental degradation.

Methodology and Sources

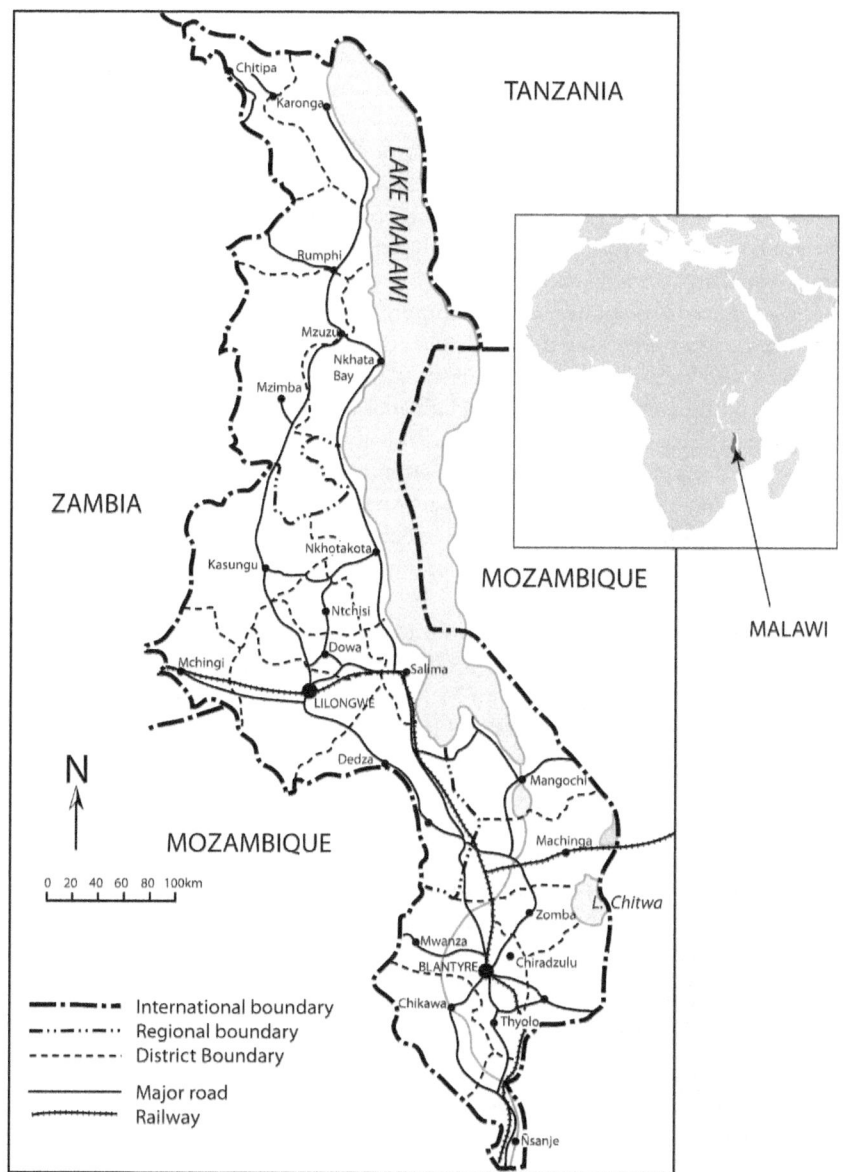

Figure 1.2. Map of Malawi. Source: National Statistical Office.

Introduction

Although the book focuses mainly on the colonial period, I also attempt to reconstruct pre-colonial (1860s–1891) forms of environmental conservation and to understand the local practices and systems of knowledge that came under attack in the colonial period. In the modern usage of the word, it may appear anachronistic to suggest that the idea of conservation ever occurred in immediate pre-colonial times. But I argue that such farming practices as inter-cropping and rituals for clearing forest land are living conservation traditions which date back to the pre-colonial period.[25] In adopting this longer perspective, I reject the artificial pre-colonial and colonial divide in order to explore the many common challenges that rural growers faced over time. An appreciation of the *longue durée*[26] has also enabled me to explore how the rural poor reconstruct, interpret and use the past, which, I would contend, has far-reaching contemporary implications. Megan Vaughan pointed out that the Shire Highlands area was sparsely populated in the mid-nineteenth century when the British missionaries and traders first arrived. To escape the effects of the slave trade, rural communities had fled to fortified mountain places, thus increasing population pressure on those erosion-susceptible lands. The imposition of colonial rule in 1891 exacerbated this problem as European settlers, aided by the state, appropriated much of the best land that the African population could have returned to.[27]

This book also directly speaks to the literature on indigenous systems of knowledge that sustained African production systems. The spread of Western scientific knowledge and practices into Malawi is but one part of the story explored. Local land management practices and indigenous systems of knowledge and the way they clashed with European prescriptions are another central component of this project.[28]

Conservation Song draws on a rich collection of written and oral data gathered by the author over a period of nearly fifteen years. Detailed interviews in form of life histories and key informant interviews have been carefully analysed to reconstruct the experiences of peasants in the face of state intervention. Although the study is

---

25. See Paul Richards, *et al.* 'Indigenous Knowledge Systems for Agriculture and Rural Development: The CIKARD Inaugural Lectures', *Studies in Technology and Social Change* 13 (1989): 1–40; Paul Richards, *Indigenous Agricultural Revolution: Ecology and Food Production in West Africa* (London: Hutchinson, 1985); Robert Chambers, *Rural Development: Putting the Last First* (London: Longman Scientific and Technical, 1983); S. Feierman, *Peasant Intellectuals*; Fiona Mackenzie, 'Political Economy of the Environment, Gender and Resistance under Colonialism: Murang'a District, 1910–1950', *Canadian Journal of African Studies* 25/2 (1991): 226–56.
26. F. Braudel, *On History* (London, 1980).
27. Megan Vaughan, 'Social and Economic Change in Southern Malawi: a Study of Rural Communities in the Shire Highlands and Upper Shire Valley from Mid-Nineteenth Century to 1915' (Ph.D. dissertation, University of London, 1981) and *The Story of an African Famine: Gender and Famine in Twentieth-Century Malawi* (Cambridge: Cambridge University Press, 1987).
28. See S. Marks, *The Imperial Lion*; and E. Mandala, *Work and Control*.

Methodology and Sources

primarily situated in the Shire Highlands region of southern Malawi, data from other parts of the country have been harnessed to show the wider impact of state intervention. The study has been enriched by primary written sources obtained from the National Archives of Malawi in Zomba, the British National Archives at Kew and the Rhodes House Library in Oxford.

This book draws on insights and methodological advances derived from scholars working both in social history and environmental studies. Through a critical examination of the problem of soil erosion, viewed from the lived experiences of Malawian peasants, I demonstrate the ways in which social history can illuminate an understanding of ecological and environmental change. Social history allows us to recount the experiences and struggles of rural women and men as well as to raise questions of power relations when examining ecological issues such as soil erosion. Recent studies of soil erosion in South Africa, Lesotho and Kenya underscore the significance of interdisciplinary analysis in environmental research.[29]

This project has used a wide array of sources to reconstruct the complex social and environmental history of rural Malawi. First, archival material is critical to understanding the nature of colonial discourse and practices in terms of policies, legislation, implementation of programmes and interpretation of the response of peasants.

The rich written records notwithstanding, the study of the late pre-colonial and colonial past would be impossible without detailed oral testimonies from rural growers. Without oral sources including life histories, songs and proverbs, it becomes impossible to reconstruct the lived experiences of ordinary men and women, particularly in such areas as household relations and labour organisation. Feeley-Harnik, Feierman, Isaacman, Moore and Vaughan, Watts and White in their respective works point to new methodological avenues to understand the complex and often ambiguous relationships between colonial state structures and Africans. By reading both oral and written sources critically against each other, these scholars have opened up new ways of thinking about the colonial encounter.[30]

Oral interviews yielded important insights into matters relating to local systems of knowledge, land use practices, household relations and peasant reaction to colonial conservation laws. Interviews with a number of elderly persons, both

---

29. Kate B. Showers, 'Soil Erosion in the Kingdom of Lesotho and Development of Historical Environmental Impact Assessment', *Ecological Applications* 6/2 (1996): 653–664; K. Showers, 'Soil Erosion in the Kingdom of Lesotho: Origins and Colonial Response'; Tiffen *et al. More People, Less Erosion*; W. Beinart and J. McGregor (eds.) *Social History and African Environments* (James Currey, 2003); William Beinart, *The Rise of Conservation in South Africa: Settlers, Livestock, and the Environment 1770–1950* (Oxford: Oxford University Press, 2003).

30. G. Feeley-Harnik, *A Green Estate* (Washington: Smithsonian Institute Press, 1991); S. Feierman, *Peasant Intellectuals*; A. Isaacman, *Cotton is the Mother of Poverty*; H.I. Moore and M. Vaughan, *Cutting Down Trees*; M. Watts, 'Idioms of Land and Labor'; and L. White, '"They Could Make Their Victims Dull"'; Louise White, *et al.* (eds.) *African Words, African Voices: Critical Practices in Oral History* (Bloomington: Indiana University Press, 2001).

Introduction

male and female, who had participated in the conservation measures of the 1940s and 1950s demonstrated that the differential impact of conservation policies was also reflected in gender relations, especially in regard to labour organisation and use of resources. The elders described in vivid detail how and why they tried to subvert colonial ridging policies and how they drew on knowledge of prior practices to survive in times of poor harvest or famine.[31] They also described how they cleared land for cultivation, carefully examining the type of vegetative cover to determine the soil quality.[32]

Lastly, field observations are important for collecting baseline data to make maps of land use and erosion features. The vast collection of pictorial material in the National Archives and in the Society of Malawi on such aspects of the conservation programmes as terracing and ridging allowed the author to compare archival material to contemporary conditions in the field. This also enabled the reconstruction of environmental changes that have taken place over time.

Despite the availability of all these sources, there are some problems in reconstructing the environmental history of Malawi in the late nineteenth and early twentieth centuries. First, there is a problem with the nature of sources themselves. Although travel accounts of the early missionaries, traders and settlers provide us with detailed information about production systems, the idea of conservation was not mentioned explicitly in the literature. Thus, it remains one of the greatest challenges for scholars to critically read the travel accounts alongside oral material for information that can illuminate our understanding of the subject. Nonetheless, African communities in many areas actually knew and practised indigenous forms of conservation.[33] Second, racial prejudice tends to colour most of the writings about African peoples and their interaction with the environment. Given that the late nineteenth century was a period of heightened intellectual fascination with the application of Social Darwinism, few Europeans, including the missionaries, were immune from assimilating these prejudices.[34] Third, the image of the African interior as the jungle or heathen place inhabited by backward and uncivilised peoples tended to captivate the minds of many travellers and settlers. Indeed,

---

31. See Charles Ambler, *Kenyan Communities in the Age of Imperialism: the Central Region in the Late Nineteenth Century* (New Haven and London: Yale University Press, 1988); M. Vaughan, *The Story of an African Famine*.

32. Group interview: Mr Dexter Jobo, Mr Handson Mzengeza and Mr Frank Likome, Chalunda Village, TA Nsabwe, Thyolo district, dated 11 June 1997; Mr Simon Benson Chimpeni of Joliji Village, TA Mpama, Chiradzulu district, dated 5 June 1997; and Mr Kimu Mbatata of Malemia Village, TA Malemia, Zomba district, dated 19 May 1997.

33. Interview, Mai Estery Edward Phiri, Ndaona Village, TA Nsabwe, Thyolo district, dated 29 May 1997; Mai Linley Kambwiri, Ntogolo Village, TA Malemia, Zomba district, dated 16 May 1997. The informants gave the examples of *matuto* and *makusa* as some of the ways in which Africans cultivated the land to avert the excessive washing away of the soil.

34. Many works by missionaries such as the Rev. Duff MacDonald, described Africans in very prejudiced ways: see *Africana or The Heart of Heathen Africa* (London, 1882) and Donald Fraser, *Winning a Primitive People* (London, 1914).

there was a strong belief among some Europeans in the existence of a virgin world somewhere in the 'East' where the local people lived in harmonious relationship with nature. Newly discovered tropical colonies were described in vivid images and symbols as 'paradises', the 'Garden of Eden' or even the 'promised land.'[35] In the case of Malawi, the works of Donald Fraser and Duff Macdonald exemplify this particular mindset.[36] Thus, encountering people in the interior of Africa became a vindication of theories and imaginings. These encounters were as symbolic as they were a fulfilment of reality. The African world had been portrayed as exotic, a wilderness and unexploited land, the ideal Eden where man was supposed to live in a harmonious relationship with nature. For example, the works of Elspeth Huxley, Ernest Hemingway and Karen Blixen fall within this tradition.

Oral sources, too, have their limitations. Given the fact that the period under discussion is far removed from the lived experiences of most of our informants, some gaps exist in the data. Even where traditions exist, the problem of loss of memory often obscures more than it illuminates the events and landscape features that prevailed over a century ago. In addition, there was a common tendency among some informants to romanticise the past. It was not unusual to find expressions to the effect that things were better then than they are today.

Outline of the book

Although the chapters are organised chronologically, they also reflect a thematic approach. The introductory chapter provides a background to the book, discussing the theoretical influences, sources of data and broader methodological issues. It contextualises the book in terms of the broader literature on soil conservation and environmental history in southern Africa. It is followed by Chapter Two, which examines the pre-colonial environment and production systems. This chapter analyses land use and production systems in late nineteenth century Malawi and the consequences of the encounter between the indigenous peoples and various immigrant groups. It also examines African use and perceptions of environment and changes in these over time. The chapter argues that differences in the use of resources and the attitudes and perceptions held by Europeans and Africans produced tensions that would later develop into violent peasant resistance against the colonial state.

Chapter Three builds on this to analyse the ways in which religious ideas influenced attitudes to and perceptions of conservation. It demonstrates that, although there was no uniform religious policy on conservation, some Christian

---

35. This idea is discussed extensively in D. Anderson and R. Grove, 'The Scramble for Eden: Past, Present and Future in African Conservation' in D. Anderson and R. Grove (eds.) *Conservation in Africa: People, Policies and Practice* (Cambridge, 1987) pp. 1–12; and R. Grove, *Green Imperialism*.

36. Donald Fraser, *African Idylls: Portrait and Impressions of Life on a Central African Mission Station* (London: Seeley, Service and Co. 1923); and D. Macdonald, *Africana*.

religious groups took unique positions on the issue. These ideas also influenced early colonial state policies including missionary and early colonial attitudes to African environment.

The next two chapters examine the science, ideology and rise of conservation discourse in colonial Malawi. Chapter Four discusses the emergence of the ideology of conservation and argues that, although such ideas were influenced by the American Dust Bowl, the specific role played by the Imperial Forestry Institute has been less acknowledged. It was the scientific ideas and activities of the staff at Oxford that propelled the conservation movement in Malawi. The chapter outlines the major shifts in colonial policy on conservation and shows that there was a change in preoccupations, from preservation of forests and wildlife to soil conservation and land use practices. In the later part of the colonial period, as the state became more intrusive and coercive, peasants became more recalcitrant. The following issues are discussed: impact of the Dust Bowl ideology, the role of the Imperial Forestry Institute and colonial scientific ideas and the people behind the crusade for conservation. Chapter Five focuses on the establishment and impact of the Natural Resources Board. The chapter examines the legal and institutional framework established to implement soil conservation polices in the colony. Special focus is placed on the Natural Resources Board and ways in which it interfaced with the African peasants in the closing years of the colonial period.

At the height of the anti-erosion campaign, the state attempted to intervene in both African and European production systems. Chapters Six and Seven demonstrate the ways in which the state intervened at different points of the production systems. Chapter Six shows that, as in other African countries, state intervention in African Trust Lands was not just high-handed but also went beyond implementation of the conventional programme of soil conservation. The state used the opportunity to restructure African rural societies in ways that reflected the modernist approach. Chapter Seven looks at the story of state intervention into private estates. This chapter shows that, although peasant production remained the major focus of state intervention into conservation, some abortive attempts were made to control environmental degradation on private estates. Through the agency of the Natural Resources Board, the state began, in the 1950s, to apply conservation measures on private estates that it had long been implementing on African Trust Land. But this generated great controversy and the state was forced practically to abandon the campaign.

Chapter Eight is about the relationship between conservation and certain religious groups. In particular, the chapter examines the response of the religious groups to state-driven conservation initiatives. It focuses on the activities of two Christian religious leaders – Pastor Wilfred Gudu of the Sons of God Church and Reverend Michael Scott of the Anglican Church – who used their religious positions to champion opposition to soil conservation in colonial Malawi. Dismissed by state authorities as fanatics, schizophrenic psychics or political malcontents, their actions

Outline of the book

not only exposed some injustices in the manner in which state dealt with the African peasants but also undermined the moral authority of state intervention project.

Chapter Nine provides a case study of ecological change, gender relations and peasant resistance in Zomba District during the late colonial period. In this chapter, the aim is to demonstrate the ways in which ecological change intersected with gender relations in a largely matrilineal area of southern Malawi. While the state intervened in order to promote soil conservation and rural development by giving power and resources to men, this did not chime well with the customs and traditions of the area. Against the background of an area plagued by a history of frequent ecological disasters, peasants reacted to state intervention with a bloody riot in October 1953. The chapter argues that the state's attempts to reorganise and transform land use practices precipitated resistance from the women and men who fought to retain the traditionally female-controlled land tenure system.

Chapter Ten looks at the broader issue of the connection between conservation and politics in the period between the imposition of the Federation in 1953 and the attainment of independence in 1964. While a lot of scholarship has linked resistance to conservation to the rise of African nationalism, it remains an under-appreciated fact that peasants championed the cause for their own reasons. Aggrieved by land dispossession and coercive labour regimes, state intervention provided peasants with a weapon to challenge the erstwhile impenetrable colonial state. Apart from overt resistance, peasants used a range of hidden forms of resistance. The chapter argues that peasant resistance must be understood not only from the point of view of nationalism but from that of their daily protests and struggles against the intrusive colonial state. By using case studies of Thyolo and Chiradzulu, the chapter provides an in-depth understanding of local factors that fuelled peasant resistance.

The final chapter examines the way in which the post-colonial state has dealt with soil conservation, an issue that had previously polarised relations between peasants and the state. It further shows that, while the concept of conservation has been broadened to encompass the environment more generally, the conservationist spirit disappeared for many years and the idea became amorphous. It has only been in the post-dictatorship era from the early 1990s that the idea has resurfaced but with a new set of issues and challenges. The chapter discusses the following issues: the disappearance of the conservation crusade, the impact of population growth, the influence of civil society organisations and the resurgence of conservation and the impact of public policy reform and environmentalism. This concluding chapter summarises the main arguments raised in the monograph and reflects on the current state of conservation in Malawi.

2

Pre-Colonial Environment and Production Systems, 1860s–1900

> In Nyasaland, where agriculture is the only industry and the export crops are very few, it behoves the trustees of the greatest asset of the country, the soil, to adopt all the measures which are economically possible to prevent the loss of soil capital. (A.J.W. Hornby, 1924).[1]

Introduction

This chapter examines the history of the late nineteenth century colonial encounter between the indigenous Nyanja-speaking people of the Shire Highlands in Southern Malawi and various immigrant groups and its ecological consequences. From the 1840s, the region experienced an unprecedented influx of immigrants such as the Ngoni, the Yao, the Lomwe and the British, most of whom began to exert a disproportionate amount of pressure on natural resources. As competition over use and control of resources intensified, so too did the rate of the resultant ecological degradation. Based on an analysis of travel accounts and oral interviews, sources that have hitherto not been thoroughly utilised, the chapter demonstrates that cultural differences between Europeans and Africans in perceptions of and attitudes to production and the use and management of resources produced tensions and misunderstandings that would later shape the development of conservationist thinking in the territory. The chapter is divided into two main sections, the first of which looks at indigenous production systems in the Shire Highlands economy, paying particular attention to peasant knowledge about the environment and the social relations that governed the use and management of natural resources. The second section explores the local conservation practices that were used to sustain the production systems of the region.

The chapter argues that, although Africans knew a great deal about environmental conservation in the pre-colonial period, such knowledge did not give them full control over the environment. Some aspects were beyond human control and others lay within the purview of their management capacity. But whether they exercised any measure of control over environmental resources or not, one thing is clear: their knowledge was closely tied to matters of production and survival. Consequently, most ideas about the environment revolve around these issues. Fur-

---

1.   A.J.W. Hornby, 'The Erosion of Arable Soil in Nyasaland and Methods of Prevention', p. 16.

Malawi's key natural resources

thermore, the chapter shows that, at the time the encounter between Europeans and Africans took place, from the middle part of the nineteenth century, new forms of contestation and adaptation emerged in the way natural resources could be used and managed in the territory. This was partly due to the different perceptions of the environment held by the two groups and partly due to the changing nature of the landscape. While the primary focus of this chapter is on the period before colonial rule in 1891, it also passingly addresses some issues in the early colonial period, mainly as a way of foregrounding the subsequent discussion.

Malawi's key natural resources

Although literature abounds on the nature and kind of natural resources that existed in pre-colonial Malawi, we know relatively little about the notions of environment or ways in which Africans conserved their environment at different points in time. Apart from general geographically-oriented studies and the accounts of early European travellers and settlers, there has been no study systematically examining Malawi's pre-colonial environmental history.[2] Thus, a good starting point is the re-examination of chronicles of the late nineteenth century, since a few of them contain invaluable information on the country's resources and their use.[3] One caveat, though, is that in some cases the descriptions are coloured by the state of knowledge at the time, especially theories of Social Darwinism which sought to classify people along racial lines and by their stages of civilisation. But by reading these sources alongside oral traditions, a more balanced picture emerges in our understanding of Malawi's pre-colonial environmental history.

The most vital resources for Malawi are those related to land and water. The significance of these resources is better appreciated when one considers the fact that the country has no exploitable mineral resources that might have attracted investment in its economic sector. In 1924, Hornby argued that 'in Nyasaland, where

---

2. See, for example, Swanzie Agnew, 'Environment and History: the Malawian Setting' in B. Pachai (ed.) *The Early History of Malawi* (London: Longman, 1972), pp. 28–48; and J.G. Pike and G.T. Rimmington, *Malawi: A Geographical Study* (London: 1965). See also Elias Mandala's book, *Work and Control in a Peasant Economy: A History of the Lower Tchiri Valley in Malawi, 1859–1960* (Madison: University of Wisconsin Press, 1990).

3. For example, I have found the following travel accounts to be useful as sources of information in writing the environmental history of pre-colonial Malawi: David Livingstone, *Narratives* (1865); A.C.P. Gamitto, *King Kazembe and the Marave, Cheva, Bisa, Bemba, Lunda and other Peoples of Southern Africa, being the Diary of the Portuguese Expedition to that Potentate in the years 1831 and 1832* Vol.1, trans. by I. Cunnison (Lisbon: 1960); Harry Johnston, *British Central Africa* (1897); H.L. Duff, *Nyasaland Under the Foreign Office* (London: George Bell and Sons, 1903) and Alice Werner, *Natives of British Central Africa* (New York: 1906); John Buchanan, *The Shire Highlands (East Central Africa) as a Colony and Mission* (London: 1885); Henry H. Rowley, *The Story of the Universities Mission to Central Africa* (London: 1867); Walter A. Elmslie, *Among the Wild Ngoni* (Edinburgh, 1899); Horace Waller (ed.) *Last Journals of David Livingstone* [London: 1874] (Connecticut: 1970 – a reprint of the original), Vol. 1, pp. 111–158.

Pre-colonial environment and production systems

agriculture is the only industry and the export crops are very few, it behoves the trustees of the greatest asset of the country, the soil, to adopt all the measures which are economically possible to prevent the loss of soil capital'.[4] Thus, the basis of the economy was land, to be used for producing crops or obtaining resources such as timber and rubber. As part of the Great Rift Valley system which links Lake Malawi with the Rukwa rift in the north and the Urema trough in the south, Malawi has a diverse geographical configuration.[5] Most of the plateaus and mountains are located in the northern and southern parts of the country while the central region is generally plains and contains very fertile soils. It is this geographical factor that allowed many people to settle in the central and southern parts of Malawi, at least by the late nineteenth century. The major lake runs parallel to the plateau from north to south. Other lakes and rivers traverse the country and served as important sources of water for both human and animal life.[6] In addition, water-based food like fish formed an important occupation for some inhabitants of the country. The land itself, of which one third is arable and the rest either mountainous or unsuitable for agricultural production, has various soil characteristics of which Africans had come to acquire knowledge in order to survive.

As regards fish resources, data indicate that pre-colonial Malawi had many types of fish in most of its lakes and rivers. Communities living in the surrounding areas used fish for food as well as for exchange with neighbouring groups in the mountains. The harvest season was often determined by the weather conditions. For example, when *mwera* or south-east winds blew over the lakes from about May to August, people generally refrained from fishing. During this time, they would switch to other activities and return in September when the waters had calmed down.[7] Every individual participating in fishing activities was expected to comply with these conditions. Defaulters would either face reprimand by chiefs or risk their lives through courting misfortunes like being eaten by water-based animals such as crocodiles, hippos or even snakes. In extreme cases, however, these violations were believed to have wider effects on society like the occurrence of illnesses, famines and droughts. In most societies in Malawi, such occurrences were almost invariably attributable to human agency, resulting from the people's neglect of their obligations to nature. In other words, these were believed to be manifestations of the wrath of God.

Vegetation is yet another important resource for the country. Ranging from savannah to woodland and rainforests, vegetative cover was as essential to human survival as other resources. Grasses, trees and their fruits, for example, were used

---

4.   A.J.W. Hornby, 'The Erosion of Arable Soil in Nyasaland', p. 16.
5.   J.G. Pike, *Malawi*, pp. 3–52.
6.   S. Agnew, 'Environment and History: the Malawian Setting', pp. 28–48; Frank Debenham, *Nyasaland: The Land of the Lake* (London: 1955).
7.   Interview: Village Headman (Mr Stewart G. Mabvumbe) of Namasalima Village, TA Kuntumanji, Zomba district, dated 2 April 1997.

Production and land use systems in the Shire Highlands, 1860–1900

for building houses, medicine and food for people and domesticated animals. Much of the extant literature shows that no major geological transformations have affected the landscape in recent years.[8] It is further argued that we must look for explanations elsewhere for those changes that have occurred on the environment, for example in human activity or climatic influence. In the pre-colonial period, the vegetative cover was being transformed by human-induced activities but the major ecological crises were those relating to drought, famine and disease.

Production and land use systems in the Shire Highlands, 1860–1900

European observers had long identified the Shire Highlands as a viable economic zone for the production of both food and cash crops. Travellers in the mid-nineteenth century expressed admiration at the range and level of agricultural production carried out by Africans in the region.[9] David Livingstone, one of the earliest British travellers in the area, noted that 'the country is exactly the same as I found the middle of the continent: exceedingly fertile, and abounding in running streams: ... [the mountains] are all green and well wooded, and one, Zomba, 6,000 feet high at least, is inhabited, and has a top about 15 miles broad.'[10] Many of the subsequent European settlers and colonial officials who carried out investigations of the soils and vegetation of the country before 1900 came to the conclusion that agricultural production had to be encouraged as the backbone of the country's economy.[11] For example, Hector Duff, a senior administration official with long experience in colonial service, described Zomba district in the following terms: 'a copious perennial supply of water is at hand; the climate is favourable; the soil rich; almost everything will grow there – in fact, no gardener could wish for a better field.'[12] Thus, it is no surprise the good soils and favourable climatic conditions that prevailed there made the Highlands a preferred area of European settlement and economic production.

---

8. J.G. Pike, *Malawi*, pp. 3–22.
9. Of course, the earliest contacts between Europeans and the Nyanja-speaking people go as far back as the 17th century when Portuguese traders visited the Maravi Kingdom. But it was not until the 19th century that the British came in to settle and colonise the country. See, for example, A.C.P. Gamitto, *King Kazembe*.
10. Livingstone's letter to Shelborne of 9 August 1859, appearing as Reference No. FO 84/1082, quoted in A.J. Hanna, *The Beginnings of Nyasaland and North-Eastern Rhodesia, 1859–95* (Oxford: Clarendon University Press, 1956), p. 4.
11. See, for example, John Buchanan, *The Shire Highlands (East Central Africa) as a Colony and Mission* (London, 1885); H. Johnston, *British Central Africa*; A. Werner, *The Natives of British Central Africa*; Hector L. Duff, *Nyasaland Under the Foreign Office* (London, 1906); and P.T. Terry, 'African Agriculture in Nyasaland, 1858–1894', *The Nyasaland Journal* 15, (1962).
12. H. L. Duff, *Nyasaland Under the Foreign Office*.

Pre-colonial environment and production systems

Thus, extant written documentation demonstrated convincingly that, by the mid-nineteenth century the Shire Highlands had a well developed economy.[13] The economy itself was based on the production of food and cash crops as well as long-distance trade. The Nyanja-speaking people, as the local inhabitants were called, produced a variety of crops. In the 1850s and 1860s, Livingstone, described and commended the way in which Africans produced their crops, which included cotton, cassava, sweet potatoes, maize, groundnuts, sorghum, millet, beans, pumpkins, cucumbers, yams, gourds, tobacco, bananas and peas. In addition, he saw many animals that were domesticated. Such animals included chickens, goats, pigs and cattle.[14] Although he is best known for his missionary impact, Livingstone also made a significant contribution to publicising the economic potential that the Shire Highlands offered for the production of cash crops. He described the Shire Highlands as a 'cotton country of unlimited extent, which really seems superior to the American, for, here we have no frosts to cut off the crops'.[15] He was particularly interested in opportunities for the production of cash crops like cotton and sugar. Influenced by the capitalist idea of creating a British cotton growing empire, Livingstone hoped that the increased production of cotton in Nyasaland could open up markets for the crop that would in the end undermine the American industry, based on slavery. His obsession with cotton production also led him to appeal for European settlement, which would help fight against the slave trade and in its place promote agricultural production and legitimate trade. Later travellers and settlers made similar observations about the fertile nature of the land and the ways local farmers effectively used their environment. Writing in the 1880s, John Buchanan, a former employee of the Blantyre Mission and prominent farmer in Zomba, observed that:

> The crop which the natives on the Shire Highlands grow chiefly is *chimanga* – Indian corn. It is grown extensively, and thrives luxuriantly ... In the month of January you take a walk out through the more thickly populated places, and you see garden upon garden of splendid *chimanga*, an infallible proof that the country is good.[16]

On the suitability of the land for agricultural production, the Reverend Henry Rowley observed, 'Setting aside other difficulties, with a little outlay and much

---

13. For example, see J. Buchanan, *The Shire Highlands*; H. Johnston, *British Central Africa*; and H. Rowley, *The Story*.
14. H. Waller (ed.) *Livingstone: Last Journals*, Vol. 1, pp.111–158. David Livingstone wrote repeatedly that he was simply a forerunner of many traders and merchants that would come later to the country. And, as is reflected in the composition of his team, economic interests also loomed large. With him at the head was Norman Bedingfeld as the second in command; John Kirk, the botanist; Charles Livingstone, his brother; Richard Thornton, the geologist; Rae, the engineer; Baines, the storekeeper; and Walker, the quartermaster.
15. Livingstone's letter to W.C. Oswell, dated 1 November 1859, No. 29 in David Livingstone, *Letters and Documents, 1841–1872*, ed. by Timothy Holmes, (London: James Currey, 1990), p.64.
16. J. Buchanan, *The Shire Highlands*, p. 118.

Production and land use systems in the Shire Highlands, 1860–1900

care you might make the country produce enough for the wants of moderate men, sufficient therefore for the wants of the Christian Missionary. More than this my experience will not let me say.'[17] When British colonial rule was formally imposed in 1891, the production of maize had been so well established that it appeared to be indigenous to the region. For example, when asked to mention some of the indigenous crops that their ancestors used to grow, my informants stated, among others, bananas, cassava, sorghum, maize, *khobwe* [cowpeas], *nzama* [groundbeans], pumpkins and *mphonda* [edible gourds].[18] Few peasants realised that maize was an exotic crop. In the meantime, Africans had developed numerous ways and creative adaptations for the production and use of maize. But although maize and most other crops were widely grown in the region, they had been introduced in earlier centuries by either the Swahili or the Portuguese.

The Nyanja-speaking people maintained longstanding contacts with Portuguese and Swahili traders as far away as the Indian Ocean coast.[19] They had established trade contacts with those local groups of people that demanded their commodities such as the Yao, the Mang'anja and the Ngoni. For Livingstone, that situation was perfectly in line with his missionary objective of establishing a basis for legitimate trade to replace the slave trade. He had in mind the production of such crops as cotton and sugar – then in high demand in industrialising Britain. Given the strength of the Abolitionist movement in Britain in the nineteenth century, Livingstone's ideas and accounts of the encounter did much to attract British attention and sympathy, resulting in the arrival of numerous missionary parties by the late 1880s. These missionaries also served as harbingers of colonisation in the sense that they prepared the way for the eventual imposition of colonial rule in the territory.

Nyanja cultivation methods were ideally suited for the environment. The Nyanja people often established their principal gardens close to their homes. This had the major advantage of easing protection of the planted crops from the marauding animals.[20] Iron hoes fixed to a wooden handle were the principal agricultural implements. In addition, the Nyanja used a variety of tools like sickles for cutting grass and axes for cutting down trees. Maize, cassava, *nandolo* [pigeon peas], sorghum,

---

17. Rev. Henry Rowley, *The Story of the Universities Mission to Central Africa* (London, 1867), p. 337.
18. Interview: Mr Marko Kanjedza and Irina Wilson of Ng'ombe Village, TA Malemia, Zomba district, dated 16 May 1997.
19. See Kings Phiri, 'Production and Exchange in Pre-Colonial Malawi', in *Malawi: an Alternative Pattern of Development* (Edinburgh: Centre of African Studies, 1985) pp. 3–32; B. Pachai, 'Christianity and Commerce in Malawi: Some Pre-Colonial and Colonial Aspects', in G.W. Smith, B. Pachai and R.K. Tangri (eds.) *Malawi: Past and Present* (Blantyre, C.L.A.I.M., 1972), pp. 37–68. See also A.C.P. Gamitto, *King Kazembe*.
20. Interview: Mr William Maluwa, Malemia Village, TA Malemia, Zomba district, dated 8 May 1997.

pumpkins and beans constituted the major food crops, while tobacco and cotton were grown for domestic use as well.[21]

Peasants used three different methods to plant their crops in the pre-colonial period. The first was known as *matuto* or *katuto* [mound cultivation]. This system was commonly used for planting crops like sweet potatoes and cassava. The Nyanja people and indeed many other groups in the country made flat mounds of about four to six feet in diameter on which these two crops were grown, sometimes interplanted with a variety of leguminous plants such as beans and groundnuts. As an indigenous farming technique, the mound system proffered some advantages to the farmers. Peasant elders recalled that their grandparents had taught them that mounds were easy to make and relied on the use of basic tools like hoes and axes. Moreover, mounds helped to control soil erosion, particularly in the hilly areas. Run-off water would go round and round the mounds and this would reduce its erosive strength.[22] Another reason for making mounds was that the soil so heaped provided enough space for crops to grow with relative ease and especially for tubers to produce bigger roots.

The second significant agricultural technique was known as *kulima pansi*[23] or *chitipula*.[24] This was a practice whereby farmers tilled the ground and removed all grasses before planting crops like maize, sorghum, cow peas, *nandolo* and *mphonda*. This system was particularly useful for farming on flat lands. But even in hilly areas where this technique was used, peasants would plant crops like sorghum and millet by broadcasting seeds. Werner made some reference to this system of farming when she described 'regular gardens' as another method by which Africans planted their crops.[25] This method did not require much labour, since peasants simply tilled land that had been cleared of shrubs and grasses through burning. It is a method that was often associated with wet season cultivation as production tended to rely on rainfall.

A third method of planting crops was called *makusa*.[26] As a form of shifting cultivation, this was a farming technique by which farmers collected grass and tree branches, burnt them and then covered the ash with soil.[27] At the start of the rainy season, farmers would plant crops like maize, pumpkins, *mphonda* and *zipwete*

---

21. Detailed information on how each of these crops were grown is readily available in both written and oral sources but more difficult is to establish in what ways their production may have engendered land degradation.
22. Interview: Mai Estery Edward Phiri of Ndaona Village, TA Nsabwe, Thyolo district, dated 13 June 1997.
23. Interview: Mai Estery Edward Phiri.
24. Interview: Village Headman (Mr Stewart G. Mabvumbe) of Namasalima Village, TA Kuntumanji, Zomba district, dated 2 April 1997.
25. Alice Werner, *The Natives of British Central Africa*, pp. 180–86.
26. In other parts of the country, a variant of this practice is known as *visoso*.
27. Interview: Mr James Lupoka, Geography Department, Chancellor College, Zomba, dated 17 April 1997.

Production and land use systems in the Shire Highlands, 1860–1900

[cucumbers] in the ash mix. The value of this system has been amply examined by Moore and Vaughan in their study of the efficacy of the *chitemene* system in the Northern Province of Zambia.[28] Thus, despite the fact that colonial accounts often dismissed the technique as retrogressive shifting cultivation, it had far-reaching ecological and economic implications for growers in the Shire Highlands.

Many of the available written sources point to the widespread use of the agricultural practice of shifting cultivation in the Shire Highlands. This farming practice has often been viewed as backward and wasteful to the environment. But the importance of shifting cultivation can only be appreciated when one considers the fact that it developed as an adaptive strategy to deal with the unsuitable environments of tropical Africa. There are two main factors that explain why shifting cultivation came to be widely used by Africans in this region. First, it helps to increase soil fertility through the replenishment of the soil with phosphorus. It has been established scientifically that burning vegetation facilitates the release of phosphorus, an important plant nutrient, from vegetation to the soil.[29] It also added soil fertility in the form of ash and humus. Second, shifting cultivation maximised the use of labour in situations where the land–labour ratio was highly skewed. But some sources make a direct link between shifting cultivation and environmental degradation, particularly deforestation. Expressing her disappointment at the absence of forests in late nineteenth century Malawi, Werner wrote, 'Large trees, growing close together, are just what one does not find, as a rule, in the country we are thinking of. The Bush (*tengo, or chire*) usually consists of small trees, thinly scattered, with tufts of grass, small bushes, and various herbaceous plants growing between them, and here and there a large tree standing by itself.'[30] But the early debates neglected discussion of soil erosion or overgrazing as also contributing to environmental degradation. It should be emphasised that the practice of shifting cultivation or slash-and-burn became quite widespread in communities that were often on the move. In many countries in Central and Southern Africa, this practice is variously known as *visoso, makusa, chitemene, matematema or ndemela*.[31] *Visoso*, for example, maximised the harvest output with little effort and time. The system developed in response to the abundance of land and the shortage of labour in many places.

Furthermore, the longstanding association between the cultivation of millet and sorghum, the staple crops at the time, with the slash-and-burn practice

---

28. H. Moore and M. Vaughan, *Cutting Down Trees*.
29. See E.N Chidumayo, 'Environment and Development in Zambia' in David S. Johnson and Wolf Roder (eds.) *Proceedings of the National Seminar on Environment and Development* (Lusaka: Zambia Geographical Association, 1979), p. 14.
30. A. Werner, *The Natives of British Central Africa*, p. 9.
31. A thorough discussion of this practice can be found in several works, such as J.B. Clements, 'The Cultivation of Finger Millet (*Eleusine coracana*) and its Relation to Shifting Cultivation in Nyasaland', *Empire Forestry Journal* 12 (1933): 16–20; and H. Moore and M. Vaughan, *Cutting Down Trees*.

had practical benefits for the peasants. First, neither millet nor sorghum required much labour input when compared to other crops such as maize or rice and yet they yielded much more produce per unit of labour. Sorghum or millet required only one weeding whereas maize had to be weeded twice before the crop could be ready for harvest.[32] According to Buchanan, sorghum had the other advantage of being a biennial crop. Moreover, the grain is much easier to convert into flour than maize. In addition, 'the plant will yield a fair return in shingly soil that would not support maize. This is due to the fact that the roots of sorghum are of stronger character and tend to spread farther in search of food.'[33] Because of these considerations, peasants continued to grow sorghum even though maize was increasingly becoming the major food and cash crop in the country.

Peasants farmed in fragmented gardens without a fixed and permanent tenure system, although there was a certain measure of security to the land. The idea of cultivating such fragmented gardens helped Africans to minimise the effects of poor harvest. It was a strategy aimed at minimising food shortages. While Africans had the freedom to establish gardens anywhere, they still had to get permission from chiefs who were the ceremonial owners of the land. The significance of this point was clearly seen in cases where immigrants had just arrived in a village. It was the responsibility of chiefs to give them land and the attendant usufructory rights. In doing so, they also made sure that the land was outside the immediate use of other local inhabitants.

The process of acquiring and preparing new land for cultivation was carefully calibrated to fit the rainy season. According to both Johnston and Werner, this activity proceeded in different phases. First of all, a peasant in search of new land would 'betroth the ground', whereby the farmer would tie bunches of grass into knots or tie the grass round the tree trunk as a sign that someone had already chosen a particular place for cultivation. For as long as the knot was in place, no inhabitant or passer-by would attempt to use the land. The task of felling trees would follow. Towards the end of the dry season, all the grass and stumps in the field were burnt. When the rains began in November or December, cultivation of the land would start. All the ash from the burnt grass was hoed into the soil for manure. If it was an old garden in which maize had been grown the previous year, the dry stalks were carefully burnt for manure too. As soon as the rains had fallen, crops would be planted.

Inter-cropping was also a critical feature of the indigenous farming system in the Shire Highlands. It is perhaps one of the oldest indigenous techniques of crop production in tropical Africa.[34] It involves planting different crops on the same

---

32. Oral Interview: Mr Dexter Jobo, Mr Handson Mzengeza and Mr Frank Likome of Chalunda Village, TA Nsabwe, Thyolo, dated 11 June 1997.

33. J. Buchanan, *The Shire Highlands*, p. 122.

34. See, for example, Paul Richards, 'Ecological Change and the Politics of African Land Use', *African Studies Review* 26 (1983): 1–72; Allen Isaacman, *Cotton is the Mother of Poverty:*

Production and land use systems in the Shire Highlands, 1860–1900

piece of land. For example, Nyanja people planted maize together with pumpkins and beans. This farming technique was meticulously done as Werner wrote:

> 'Maize is sown in rows of about six feet apart, the soil being gathered into heaps, and three or four grains sown on the top of each. I have seen a man and his wife doing this together, one making the holes with a pointed stick, while the other dropped the grains in. Pumpkins and gourds are sown on the same heaps with the maize, and spread out between the rows.'[35]

As an indigenous farming technique, inter-cropping had several advantages. First, the growing of different crops in one garden served as an important means of ensuring food security. Since different crops responded differently to climatic conditions, farmers would at least harvest something in times of drought or locust infestation. Inter-cropping reduced the risks of crop failure because different crops required different soil nutrients and matured at different times. Second, inter-cropping enhanced soil fertility, even though few peasants could explain exactly how this farming technique helped to accomplish this. Most of them simply said that it improved *chajira* [fertility] when maize was planted with pumpkins or beans. In fact, leguminous plants like groundnuts helped to add nitrogen to the soil, which could then be used by other plants like maize. Third, inter-cropping helped to maximise labour use since peasants could plant different crops on one piece of land that had already been cleared. Fourth, crops provided a cover of plants for the soil, which protected the land from wind and water erosion. At the same time, the moisture thus preserved could be effectively used by the plants. Fifth, inter-cropping reduced the growth of weeds and, in the process, reduced the amount of labour required. Mai Gemu Kapalamula of Chiradzulu district said the advantage of inter-cropping was that 'all these crops [maize, beans, pigeon peas, groundnuts and pumpkins] were grown on the same piece of land and were producing bumper yields. We did not have to spend much of our labour cultivating many gardens.'[36]

To further increase food security and reduce threats of famine, the Nyanja developed two different farming regimes, which enabled them to produce crops all year round. *Dimba* or wetland cultivation went on throughout the year. During the rainy season, gardens were prepared for growing such crops as maize, pumpkins and beans. On the other hand, *dimba* cultivation in the dry season involved furrow irrigation for planting crops. Crops planted during this time included maize, *nandolo* and different varieties of vegetables. However, *mphala* or upland farming was undertaken during the rainy season and grew crops like maize, millet and beans. Mandala has discussed these issues in great detail in his analysis of the Mang'anja

---

Peasants, Work, and Rural Struggles in Colonial Mozambique, 1938–1961 (Portsmouth, NH: Heinemann, 1996), pp. 31–51.

35. A. Werner, *The Natives of British Central Africa*, p. 181.
36. Interview: Mai Gemu Kapalamula, Kapalamula Village, TA Mpama, Chiradzulu district, dated 3 June 1997.

Pre-colonial environment and production systems

production systems in the Lower Shire valley.[37] This type of farming became the main bone of contention among early conservationist thinkers in colonial Malawi. Mai Mbebua and Mr S. Likome of Thyolo district said their parents used to 'cultivate hilly areas and were not making ridges at all. Instead, they were just tilling the land, *kutipula pansi*. When the whitemen came, they introduced the system of making ridges which are so easily eroded. So to prevent erosion of the soil, they began to prohibit cultivation of hilly areas.'[38]

Work in this complex agricultural system was divided according to gender. Many peasants used family labour, which invariably meant husband, wife and children. The writings of many nineteenth century travellers and settlers provide, in very general terms, information on the roles played by women and men. The Rev. Rowley succinctly summarised gender roles and the position of women within the Nyanja-speaking society:

> The position of the [women] in the Mang'anja and Ajawa was in no way inferior to that of the man. It is imagined that among the Africans generally the woman is but the drudge, the slave of the man. It may be so to a certain extent among tribes which are pastoral ... but with the people we were with, who were essentially agricultural, no such disparity existed; men and women worked together in the fields, and the special occupations of the women were thought to be no more degrading than the specialties of our women are to our own women at home[39]

While Rowley's observation may be correct in explaining the position of women *vis-a-vis* the men, he did not take into account the gendered ways in which the specific tasks were performed in society. Indeed, although families tended to work together in their gardens, some tasks were divided along gender lines. Interviews with several informants also indicated that differentiation existed not just by gender but also by age. Children were taken to the fields from an early age and taught different kinds of agricultural work. Their participation in the labour process was not insignificant. For example, the labour process involved clearing, burning and tilling the land by men; planting seeds by women and children; weeding the gardens by men and women; harvesting and transporting the produce by men, women and children; processing the grains by women and children; storing the produce by women and men. Mai Gulaye of Thyolo district pointed out that 'farming was generally done by both men and women. In fact, garden work consisted of many activities such as land preparation, planting, weeding and harvesting. But depending upon the amount of work available, even children would go out to work.'[40] In the context of contemporary Malawi, gendered analysis of labour and production processes has

---

37. E. Mandala, *Work and Control*.
38. Interview: Mai Mbebua and Mr S. Likome, Chalunda Village, TA Nsabwe, Thyolo district, dated 11 June 1997.
39. H. Rowley, *The Story*, p. 208.
40. Interview: Mai Gulaye, Khozombe Village, TA Nsabwe, Thyolo district, dated 29 May 1997.

Limits to production

been undertaken by many scholars, including Vaughan and Hirschmann and Jean Davison. The general thrust of the argument is that labour tasks are so gendered that women tend to shoulder the bulk of the agricultural work.

Apart from clearing and tilling the land, weeding was the most labour-intensive exercise that fell on the shoulders of both men and women. For example, when the maize plant had reached a height of six inches the whole garden had to be hoed to get rid of weeds. Having observed the way in which Africans weeded their gardens, Buchanan wrote approvingly that 'their method of dealing with grass is a good one, and in fact the only one I have found to be of any use during the wet season.'[41] He went on to explain that what Africans actually did was to collect all the hoed-out weeds and grass and bury them so that they could not sprout. At other times, they would put them into heaps so that they could wither away in the sun. In most cases, a second weeding was not necessary. But when a second weeding took place, the maize would have reached the height of three feet. At that time, Buchanan wrote, 'The earth is pulled to the root of the plant, which enables it to support itself against the wind, and also affords its adventitious roots a medium of supplying it with the necessary sustenance.'[42] These weeding techniques further illustrate the creative adaptations that the peasants in the Shire Highlands made in producing their crops and managing the environment.

Limits to production

Despite the fact that Africans had developed many innovative ways of growing crops, they still faced several problems in their production. The principal challenge appears to have been that of labour shortage. Dependent largely on family labour, many African households could not easily expand their production with only a few individuals working the land. Second, increased agricultural production was also limited, to some extent, by the absence of proper storage facilities. During harvest, most farmers removed maize cobs from the stalks and took them to the *nkhokwe* or granaries. According to Werner, the *nkhokwe* commonly used were quite vulnerable to attacks by rats and weevils. Furthermore, the *nsanja* or rafters in houses, which tended to offer more protection, were too small to store the harvested crops in large quantities.[43] Thus, in some cases, crops left over from previous years were burnt in the field. Some informants said that they had participated as children in burning these old surplus crops.[44]

Recurring threats of war compounded the problem of food security. The late nineteenth century was a period of great political insecurity in the country,

---

41. J. Buchanan, *The Shire Highlands*, p. 120.
42. *Ibid.*
43. A. Werner, *The Natives of British Central Africa*, p. 181.
44. Interview: Mr James Anusa Nkupata, Ng'ombe Village, TA Malemia, Zomba district, dated 16 May 1997.

largely due to the activities of the slave trade and internecine wars, and these factors made it difficult for some farmers to produce more than what they needed for a single agricultural year.[45] Human settlements tended to be concentrated around fortified areas and even though people preferred lowland areas for their farming activities, largely because of the existence of fertile soils, the changing political and socio-economic climate in the area made this increasingly difficult.[46] The prospect of external invasions, which increased with immigration and movements of different groups of people, undermined production as farmers lived in constant fear and did not work freely in their gardens. Owing to these conditions, permanent settlements were not very common and Africans practised shifting cultivation which, according to John Buchanan, could be justified by the fact that they were often on the move. Buchanan observed that, when asked about production, the Africans did not hesitate to explain that,

> it is of no use their planting bananas and other fruits for no sooner will they have come to the point of enjoying the rewards of their labour than some change takes place which necessitates their removal to another district. They are thus regardless of anything toward the public good and provision for the future.[47]

The other problem affecting production in the region was the occurrence of famines. The famines of the 1860s and 1890s made life even more difficult for the peasants dependent on agricultural production.[48] Many people fled to hilly areas where they established settlements and also opened up gardens. However, cultivation of hilly areas had the major disadvantages of being dependent on rainfall and more labour demanding. With the arrival and settlement of many European settlers and the immigration of Africans from neighbouring areas in the last quarter of the nineteenth century, African population distribution was further distorted in the region. There was a relocation of farming areas and more land was put to cultivation. The effects of increased human cultivation of the marginal lands in no small measure contributed to deforestation and soil erosion, a situation contemporary chroniclers observed and often described in graphic terms.[49]

---

45. Interview: Mr Kimu Mbatata, Malemia Village, TA Malemia, Zomba district, dated 19 May 1997. See also Leroy Vail, 'Ecology and History: the Example of Eastern Zambia', *Journal of Southern African Studies* 3/2 (1977): 129–155; and Megan Vaughan's doctoral thesis, 'Social and Economic Change in Southern Malawi'.
46. Interview: Village Headman Mjojo, Mjojo Village, TA Mlumbe, Zomba district, dated 21 May 1997.
47. J. Buchanan, *The Shire Highlands*, pp. 121–2.
48. In his book, *The Story*, the Rev. Henry Rowley estimated that about nine out of ten people died during the famine of 1862/63. See also Elias Mandala, *The End of Chidyerano: a History of Food and Everyday Life in Malawi, 1860–2004* (Portsmouth, NH: Heinemann, 2005).
49. See, for example, H.H. Johnston, *British Central Africa*; and A. Werner, *The Natives of British Central Africa*.

Limits to production

For their part, early European conservationists argued that African farming systems were ruinous to the environment in the sense that they encouraged deforestation and soil erosion.[50] They charged that Africans wantonly cut down trees and that their cultivation of the land was improper. However, a reading of some oral accounts gives a different perspective. Evidence from oral interviews with elderly peasants in the region maintains that some of the farming practices used by the Nyanja people actually contributed to the fertility of the soil and a reduction in erosion. This variation in interpretations not only points to differences in perceptions and attitudes that had been developing over time but also provides a basis for the narratives of environmental degradation that would dominate the rest of the colonial period.

In terms of agriculture, therefore, the basic ways in which Africans conserved their land included general tilling before planting, raising mounds, mixed cropping and planting protective grasses like *nsenjere* and *thadzi*.[51] Before the increase in population, these practices were effective in controlling soil erosion. However, the situation began to change in the late nineteenth century when population pressure, due to immigration and land alienation, further aggravated land shortage problems in the area. In response to these changes, peasants adapted their farming techniques and in some cases adopted new ones brought in by immigrant groups.

The agricultural calendar served as the main organising principle of work and labour distribution for the African peasants. The counting of years was often based on the agricultural calendar so that significant events or catastrophes served as important landmarks to remembering past history. So too were years themselves divided into seasons. A specific example of seasons will be given here to highlight the relationship between agricultural production and environmental management. Three main seasons were identified in a year but the range of activities varied considerably. First, *dzinja*, the wet season, often starts in November or December and lasts for four to five months, depending on the altitude of a particular place. This is the time when most *mphala* crops are grown, as agriculture under this regime is primarily dependent on rainfall. Africans associated the climatic term *dzinja* with the production of food so that the start of rains signalled symbolically a period of plenty. It was a time when people took to work in the fields in response to nature's benevolence for giving them rains.[52]

The rainy season itself was often a period of starvation for those who could not produce enough food crops. That situation has not changed much in recent years and, as Mandala demonstrates, *dzinja* is still associated with food shortag-

---

50. See F. Dixey *et al. The Destruction of Vegetation*.
51. Interview: Mr Katchenga of Chalunda Village, TA Nsabwe, Thyolo district, dated 11 June 1997.
52. Matthew Schoffeleers, 'The Chisumphi and Mbona Cults in Malawi: a Comparative History', in J.M. Schoffeleers (ed.) *Guardians of the Land: Essays on Central African Territorial Cults* (Gwelo: Mambo Press, 1978) pp. 147–186.

es.[53] In such cases, a system of *kusuma/kupempha* existed whereby a member of a household would go to another place to ask for food. Food would be given in exchange for commodities like chickens, goats or crops that were not produced in those areas. In extreme cases, where a family did not have anything to exchange, children would be given temporarily to the family supplying food. As a kind of pawnship, the child had to work for the family that had helped his/her parents until the next harvest season.[54] The second season, *pfuko*, runs from April to June. This is a period when crops are harvested from the fields and sometimes leguminous crops like beans are planted in the *mphala* and *dimbas*. The season is characterised by light rains and the temperature tends to be generally cooler. The third season, *mwamvu* or *chirimwe* [dry season] lasts from July until November. This was post-harvest time and a number of celebratory activities took place. It was supposed to be a time of plenty and people thanked nature for being good to them through various festivities, such as traditional dances, libations and sacrifices.

Faced with an unpredictable environment, Africans sought to manage their land through both material and spiritual means. They viewed human beings as forming an integral part of nature and believed that it was their responsibility to care for land so that harmony could be maintained between nature and society. 'When you are good to the land, the land will also be good to you. That is why we give offerings to our ancestral spirits so that they can in turn give us good things like fertile soils, good rains and good harvest.'[55]

In this particular region, peasants also relied on the intervention of ancestral spirits and the Mbona territorial cult to ensure land fertility and food security.[56] They gave offerings to their ancestral spirits periodically in order to maintain order in society. Sacred places existed throughout the Shire Highlands region such as at Namvula Hill in Thyolo, Malabvi Hill in Chiradzulu and Sakata Hill in Zomba. In times of drought or poor harvest, peasants prepared flour that was poured under a *mpoza* tree with the following prayer being uttered:

Ambuye kumandako	Our forefathers there in the graves
ndiwo kuno zasowa	we do not have relish
ana akuvutika	your children are suffering

Upon acceptance of the offering by the ancestor spirits, the people would say the following words:

---

53. E. Mandala, *Chidyerano*.
54. Interview, Mai Linley Kambwiri, Ntogolo Village, TA Malemia, Zomba district, dated 16 May 1997.
55. Interview: Mr Billiot Mlaliki, Nzundo Village, TA Nsabwe, Thyolo district, interviewed on 29 May 1997.
56. M. Schoffeleers, 'The Chisumphi and Mbona Cults in Malawi'.

Limits to production

Katundu uja tamulandira   *We have received those things.*[57]

There were also some trees and animals that were not willingly destroyed, for they were treated as sacred. Megan Vaughan has noted that one of her informants told her that there was no indiscriminate cutting down of trees: 'In those days the elders made clear distinctions between which trees could be cut down and those which were to be left'.[58] Similarly, Mai Mbebua and Mr S. Likome of Chalunda Village in Thyolo district said that people were not allowed to cut down some types of trees like *tsangwa* and *mpoza* because these were 'specially chosen for the purpose of *kutsira nsembe* ... In addition, trees like *mbawa*, *mlombwa* and *tchonya* were restricted because they helped to bring about rainfall. Whenever somebody was found tampering with these trees he would be taken to the Group Village Headman for interrogation.'[59] Authority had to be obtained from traditional rulers before cutting down special trees or killing animals. A whole set of rules and regulations existed that governed the use and management of a range of natural resources. It was expected that every member of the society would comply with these rules; failure to do so would not only result in a punishment but also in undesirable consequences such as misfortunes and sudden illnesses. In some cases, chiefs had to consult oracles of *ufa* [flour] before granting permission to their people to undertake certain activities like farming, fishing and hunting.[60] If the result of the oracle was positive, people would be allowed to use resources but if it was negative they could not. One informant told me, 'when you see a man starting to build a house at a time when the rains are expected, know that that person may be accused of withholding the rains.'[61] Such an individual would be reported to the chief who would in turn summon him to explain why he did not observe the customs of society. These beliefs are still commonly held in some parts of the country, as reported by the media.[62]

---

57. Group Interview: Mr Dexter Jobo, Mr Handson Mzengeza and Frank Likome, Chalunda Village, TA Nsabwe, Thyolo district, dated 11 June 1997.
58. Megan Vaughan, 'Uncontrolled Animals and Aliens: Conservation Mania in Malawi' (Unpublished History Seminar Paper, University of Malawi, 1977/78).
59. Interview: Mai Mbebua and Mr S. Likome, Chalunda Village, TA Nsabwe, Thyolo district, dated 11 June 1997.
60. Interview: Mai Agnes Nyambi & Mai Emma Juliyo, Nchocholo Village, TA Likoswe, Chiradzulu district, dated 17 August 1997.
61. Interview: Mr Katchenga, Chalunda Village, TA Nsabwe, Thyolo district, dated 11 June 1997.
62. For example, in the *Daily Times* of 22 February 2010, under the caption 'Chief Selling Rain in Chiradzulu', Village Headman Maleta of Traditional Authority Kadewere was reportedly believed to have powers to ask ancestral spirits to bring about rains. In another incident, a magistrate's court in Mulanje district on 4 February 2010 sentenced Mr Chikumbeni Mwanatheu to two months imprisonment with hard labour for admitting to using magical powers to block rains from falling in his area. *Daily Times* of 12 February 2010.

Pre-colonial environment and production systems

Indigenous systems of knowledge, conservation practices and food security

Well before the imposition of colonial rule, peasants in the Shire Highlands had developed a complex system of environmental knowledge. While additional data need to be collected in different parts of Malawi, the discussion here is based mainly on the research conducted in the Shire Highlands region. In this respect, examples have been drawn from peasant knowledge about climate and soils, two aspects that provide an interesting dimension to African perceptions of the environment. This discussion has chosen to focus on these concepts for two reasons: first, because of the prevalence of beliefs and ideas in discussions of the environment in the local Chichewa language and also to some extent in the early travellers' accounts; second, these notions are valuable as instruments to gain a deeper understanding of the lived experiences of the peasants and the historical changes associated with their complex interaction with the environment.

Peasants devised and practised a variety of measures to conserve their land. Indigenous systems of knowledge were built on decades of practice and experience transmitted from one generation to the next. Individual peasants used local knowledge and techniques on their gardens as they saw fit and necessary and have adapted them with the passage of time. Their methods of farming simply required the use of basic tools like the hoe and the axe and not much labour. Peasants were aware that undertaking conservation helped to prevent erosion and increase soil fertility and therefore increase the yield.[63]

Elders related that one particularly common conservation strategy was the practice of putting grass or tree branches on top of the outer ridge of the *dimba* gardens. At other times, the outer ridge would be planted with sugar cane or some other type of grass to reinforce it. This technique helped to block the surface run-off water that could easily erode the soil in the garden. Peasants mentioned that this method could be used for hilly areas too. With gardens that were established in hilly areas, different types of plants such as bananas, sugar canes, cassava, pineapples and oranges would be planted around the perimeter. The planting of grasses like *nsenjere* and elephant grass also served as livestock feed apart from being used for thatching houses. In addition, the crops planted in such gardens would be used to scare away marauding animals. The other advantage is that, when ready, the crop would be harvested and used for food. Peasants said this technique did not demand much labour.[64]

Other elders recalled that their grandparents used to plant bananas on the edges of gardens. Banana is one of the crops that has been grown by Africans for a long time and has many utilitarian functions. It grows fairly well in different climatic conditions and especially in moderately cold areas. It is also a crop that is

---

63. Interview: Village Headman Khozombe, Khozombe Village, TA Nsabwe, Thyolo district, dated 13 June 1997.
64. Interview: Mr H.M. Selemani and Mai Garaundi, Jekete Village, TA Mpama, Chiradzulu district, dated 4 June 1997.

Indigenous systems of knowledge, conservation practices and food security

good during times of drought and famine since it does not dry up easily. The banana has also been used to protect the land from soil erosion. In gardens that were close to the home, peasants planted bananas at the top edge. They would then dispose of any organic refuse under the banana stems. That refuse provided fertility to the bananas and the banana trees themselves acted as a hedge against run-off water which might erode the soil in the garden beneath it. This method was commonly practised in the Thyolo district where bananas are grown widely and have, in recent years, superseded maize and cassava production.[65] Bananas were also planted in gardens situated further away from peasants' homes.

A third method involved peasants' use of stones as a conservation aid. Normally, stones were piled up to form a wall or ridge running across the slope in order to block water from eroding the soil. They would trap trash and prevent water from being washed down the slope. In the Thyolo district, this method was widely used, owing to the hilly terrain of the area. The method was also particularly suited to the area because of its stony nature.[66] A variation of this method, called *vingonyeka*, was widely used in the northern part of the country and this spatial spread may show the antiquity of the technique.[67]

One other method of controlling erosion used in the pre-colonial period was the diversion of water flow from its natural course. This was usually done above the garden or from the source of a river to where the garden was to be made. The water running through a furrow would be used to irrigate the plants in the gardens. In cases where the water flow was very strong, this method helped to reduce the speed and control erosion down the slope. Occasionally, small earth dams would also be made to store water for irrigating crops in the gardens.[68] These techniques were used in areas where intensive farming had developed and where societies produced crops for both subsistence use and exchange in markets.

Peasants also possessed knowledge about the soils that enabled them to use land meaningfully. Apart from simply distinguishing between different types of soils, the people also had different names to denote different values of land. Vegetative cover was a significant indicator of soil fertility so that cultivation of crops depended on the type of trees or grass in a particular locality. For example, an area where grasses like *sonthe* and *khumbwi* and trees like *mwanga*, *mombo*, *mpalisa* and

---

65. Interview: Mr Katchenga, Chalunda Village, TA Nsabwe, Thyolo district, dated 11 June 1997.
66. Interview: Mr Lekisemu, Nzundo Village, TA Nsabwe, Thyolo district, dated 28 May 1997.
67. For more details on this, see W.O. Mulwafu, 'The Development of the Coffee Industry in the Misuku Hills of Northern Malawi, 1924–1964', *Malawi Journal of Social Science* 18 (2004): 1–16; and J. McCracken, 'Conservation and Resistance in Colonial Malawi: the "Dead North" Revisited', in William Beinart and Joann McGregor (eds.) *Social History and African Environments* (Oxford: James Currey, 2003), pp. 155–174.
68. Interview: Mr Katchenga, Chalunda Village, TA Nsabwe, Thyolo district, dated 11 June 1997.

napini grew was regarded as having fertile soil.[69] When planting crops, Africans took into account these different soil characteristics, bearing in mind that different crops required different types of soils. Settlement and agricultural production were, among other factors, dependent on the nature of the soils in a particular locality. However, many peasants noted that, over time, there has been a substantial change in the quality of the soil. The types of soils they used to know when they were young were generally darkish in color and tended to be very fertile; they were known as *chuluwadaka* or *kafukufuku*. Nowadays, such soils have been replaced by *nthaka-ya-ulongo* or *katondo*, reddish soils that are not very good for agricultural production. On such poor soils trees like *chinomba* or *chisoso* grow.[70]

Elders stressed that the type and quality of soil essentially determined land use in a given area as shown in the case of the peasant communities in the Shire Highlands area. The fact that the local Nyanja language has a rich collection of descriptive terms for different types of soils is testimony to the value placed on knowledge of soils.[71] *Mtsilo* is a type of soil found on hill slopes and it is usually black in color and of friable texture. Soils of this type are found in most hilly parts of the country such as Mulanje, Zomba and the Northern Region and are generally good for thick forest growth. *Chigugu* is a type of soil often found on shallow surfaces of valleys, especially those overlying hard basic gneiss rock, such as most plains in the central and southern regions. Such soils are good for the growth of grasses and shrubs. *Katondo* or *katondwe* soil is found on lower slopes, forms a thin layer over compact red soil and is generally not good for agricultural production. *Chifukankululu* is a type of soil remarkable for its porosity; its name comes from the word *nkululu*, meaning an insect that burrows in the soil. The soil is good for growing a variety of crops. Another kind of soil is *ntapo*, which refers to deposits of clay. These soils have no agricultural value, except for use in making pots for domestic purposes. *Mtsilo wa nchenga* is land that has dry and sandy margins and tends to be fertile because of its high silt and moisture content and be good for rice and cotton growing. The Lower Shire and most lakeshore areas of Malawi have this kind of soil. *Makande* are sandy clay soils and are very poor for crop production.[72]

---

69. Interview: Mai Mbebua and Mr S. Likome, Chalunda Village, TA Nsabwe, Thyolo district, dated 11 June 1997.

70. Interview: Messrs Dexter Jobo, Handson Mzengeza, Frank Likome, Chalunda Village, TA Nsabwe, Thyolo district, dated 11 June 1997. Also interview with Mr Katchenga, Chalunda Village, TA Nsabwe, Thyolo district, dated 11 June 1997.

71. A good starting point for the soils of Malawi include the works of A.J.W. Hornby, *Soil Survey of Nyasaland* (Zomba: Agricultural Department, Bulletins No. 2 of 1924 and 1 of 1925); and Veronica Berry and Celia Petty (eds.) *The Nyasaland Survey Papers, 1938–1943 Agriculture, Food and Health* (London: Academy Books, 1992), pp. 11–57.

72. In almost all the areas I visited, peasants provided detailed information on the different types of soils. The words for the soil types are more or less the same with minor variations existing in the pronunciations.

Indigenous systems of knowledge, conservation practices and food security

Knowledge of all these kinds of soils was part of the ecological repertoire of the peasant economy. As producers, they constantly assessed the quality of the soil before establishing new settlements or opening up new fields. Their knowledge of soils corroborated scientific descriptions carried out in the 1920s by the Department of Agriculture. For instance, Hornby, the Agricultural Chemist, noted that 'the chief point is that the percentage of iron and alumina is high in all the soils of the Shire Highlands, which has an important bearing on the chemical and physical properties'. He further observed that the soils were 'mostly laterites which vary from coarse sandy, sandy loam to sandy clay soils and that the colour too varied from red to grey and black'.[73]

Peasants in the Shire Highlands also used the idea of *chire*, which literally means bush or forest, to protect trees. *Chire* was an area of forest set aside by chiefs or elders to provide refuge for game when the annual bush fires had begun. As the surrounding grassland areas were fired, it was expected that the animals would run into the *chire*. Once they were in the *chire*, the hunters would go in to them, which was easy to do because they knew the forests well. Some individuals established *chire* primarily for the value of trees or fruits.[74] In this sense, *chire* were different from sacred places used for shrines or the graveyards as the word is more commonly used in recent times. The system of *chire*, which were often controlled by chiefs and elders, had a reciprocal function to society. In fact, the colonial state tried to use this idea of *chire* as a basis for promoting village forest areas in the country. From the early 1920s, the state encouraged the establishment of forests in the villages, which were under the control of the village headmen.[75]

As soon as the British had declared Protectorate rule over Malawi in 1891, conflicts arose with the local people over the use and management of the environment. Some of these conflicts were clearly articulated while others were not. But as David Anderson and Richard Grove have pointed out, Europeans coming from an environmentally different society hoped to create an Eden in Africa, an ideal place where humans could live in harmony with nature.[76] They came with their own ideas about the environment and wanted to apply them in the colonies, often with little consideration for indigenous systems. African land use systems were described as primitive or retrogressive and had to be replaced by scientifically-based knowledge, which entailed the transformation of structures of African societies and their activities affecting the environment. In light of this position, this discussion argues that, through an understanding of European ideas and constraints about the environment, we are able to see not only their perceptions in Africa but also

---

73. A.J.W. Hornby, *Soil Survey of Nyasaland* (Zomba: Agricultural Department, Bulletin No. 2 of 1924), p. 10.
74. Interview: Mr Joliji, Joliji Village, TA Mpama, Chiradzulu district, dated 5 June 1997.
75. For details, see MNA S1/969/26 and J.B. Clements, *A Communal Forest Scheme in Nyasaland*; Alice Werner also made some reference to this idea. See *The Natives of British Central Africa*.
76. D. Anderson and R. Grove, 'The Scramble for Eden'.

the African side of the story. This is reflected in the writings which, while quite critical of African land use systems, also tell us much about what they thought was the right way to use the environment.[77] In some cases, Europeans introduced new crops and methods of farming that required new ways of looking at and using the environment. This meant that some of the crops that had been produced for a long time, e.g. millet, could no longer be grown using the old methods in the face of new market conditions. Fruitless efforts were made to have such crops grown in new ways. Indeed, for the greater part of the early colonial period, officials had difficulties getting Africans to grow crops, particularly food crops, by new ways and methods that had been introduced by Europeans, such as contour and box ridging, terracing and bunding. In some areas, the settlers, aided by the colonial state, began to force Africans to grow cash crops like tobacco, tea, coffee and tung oil using new conservation measures. But the full impact of this policy was not felt until the late 1930s.

Conclusion

The foregoing discussion has highlighted different aspects of production and conservation in the Shire Highlands region. It has shown that there was an indigenous logic to the conservation practices undertaken by the Nyanja people, that there were different means of conservation and that soil conservation techniques intersected with the social and political order. Even though most Europeans were impressed by the variety of crops grown by Africans, they invariably decried their land use practices and particularly the method of shifting cultivation. Often described as destructive and ruinous to the environment, the shifting cultivation or slash-and-burn system became one of the major targets of the European fight for conservation of natural resources. It was persistently argued, and often in alarmist terms, that unless such practices were curtailed, Nyasaland would become a deforested country with the possibility of degenerating into a desert. Similar ideas were propagated in colonial Zambia where the *chitemene* system of shifting cultivation came under heavy attack from the colonial state. It was argued that the system was primitive and wasteful.[78] Oral interviews confirmed this view about the practice of shifting cultivation. Africans used farming techniques suited to the circumstances under which they lived. They made mounds and sometimes tilled the ground to plant their crops. They also planted protective grass and reeds in areas considered prone to erosion. Informants in Thyolo and Chiradzulu districts noted that various types of shifting cultivation were practised to mitigate the problems of labour shortage.[79]

---

77. See A. Werner, *The Natives of British Central Africa*, Chs 6 and 8; and H.L. Duff, *Nyasaland under the Foreign Office*, Chs 6, 7, 8 and 16.
78. H. Moore and M. Vaughan, *Cutting Down Trees*.
79. Interview, Mr Yakobe, Joliji Village, TA Mpama, Chiradzulu district, dated 5 June 1997; Interview, Mr Lekisemu, Nzundu Village, TA Nsabwe, Thyolo district, dated 28 May 1997.

Conclusion

These farming techniques were in tune with the actual living conditions prevalent at the time. Both missionary and colonial accounts offer new insights for examining the question of the colonial encounter in order to understand the particular circumstances in which the Africans lived and interacted with the environment.

3

Christian and Colonial Attitudes Towards the Environment

Introduction

The relationship between Christianity and conservation in Malawi is not easy to establish, partly because there was no official policy on conservation and partly because missionaries did not actively participate in this endeavour. Moreover, in the modern usage of the word, it may appear anachronistic to suggest that the idea of conservation ever occurred in the immediate pre-colonial times. But this chapter argues that, through the study of farming practices and use of trees and wildlife resources, we can tease out information and reconstruct a history of conservation in Malawi. Early missionaries produced a plethora of primary sources and it is only fair that we look more closely at these in order to get a sense of the missionaries' attitudes and their perceptions of the African people and their environment. In order to do so, I raise two critical questions in an attempt to understand the nature of the relationship between Christianity and conservation. First, what were the attitudes and perceptions of the missionaries in the area of conservation? Were there any Christian ideas and beliefs that influenced nineteenth-century missionaries' thinking about conservation? Second, how much influence did the early missionaries have on the evolution of colonial conservation campaigns? And how did Africans respond to these state initiatives?

This chapter focuses on representations of the colonial encounter and the European disdain for African agriculture and environmental practices, built on misinformation and cultural arrogance, as exemplified in the writings of Harry Johnston and his contemporaries. Since the Europeans did not speak in one voice, it is important to explore missionary perspectives that differed from the colonial regime's. The views of early colonial officials were critical in forming the basis for subsequent state intervention in the 1930s. The missionaries, too, contributed to discussions on conservation. But the differences between the two groups lay in the fact that they had different aims and methods in trying to reform peasant production. The state sought to create rational peasants while the missionaries looked for a restored Eden.

While both sets of writings were quite critical of African land use systems, they also tell us much about what colonial officials thought would be the right

Missionaries, sources and the African environment

way to use land resources.[1] The Europeans sought to introduce new cash crops and methods of farming, which required equally new ways of looking at and using the environment. This meant that, in the face of new market conditions, some of the crops that had been produced for a long time, such as millet, sorghum and bananas, could no longer be grown using the old methods of farming and conservation.

This chapter is divided into four sections. The first examines the challenges of writing an environmental history of Malawi. Special attention is paid to the problem of sources used. Section two looks at Edenic beliefs and how these influenced early Christian views of the African environment. Section three is concerned with the ways in which Christian beliefs influenced colonial policies on the environment. The last section provides a discussion of the impact of African traditional religion on conservation.

Missionaries, sources and the African environment

The major sources of information for this chapter are travel accounts, official commentaries and oral interviews. An extensive reading of missionary accounts has been done to understand their perceptions of African peoples and the local environments they came into contact with. Despite relegating African peoples to objects of study, travel accounts and diaries were particularly useful for the richness of detail about what was observed at that time of the encounter. The works of Elspeth Huxley, Ernest Hemingway and Karen Blixen fall within this tradition whereby encountering people in the interior of Africa became a vindication of metropolitan theories and imaginings.

Oral traditions provide not necessarily an alternative source of information but a complementary one. If a researcher asks the right questions, oral traditions can yield valuable information about the lived experiences of the African people and their interaction with the environment. But they too have their limitations. Given the fact that the period under discussion is far removed from what most of my informants could easily remember, some gaps exist in the data.

Although not all missionaries were conservationists and their ideas were by no means uniform, there can be little doubt that the attitudes and perceptions held by many early missionaries indirectly shaped the country's colonial policies on African agriculture and conservation of natural resources. Given the fact that early Christian missionaries played multifarious, and sometimes quite controversial, roles in their encounters with the people of Africa, their writings helped prepare the ground for subsequent colonial policy on conservation. While their primary objective was to spread Christianity, they also indulged in numerous other activities that were integral to the overall realisation of that objective, such as the promotion

---

1. See, for example, Richard Grove, 'Scottish Missionaries, Evangelical Discourses and the Origins of Conservation Thinking in Southern Africa, 1820–1900', *Journal of Southern African Studies* 15/2 (1989): 163–87; also D. Anderson and R. Grove, 'The Scramble for Eden'.

of agricultural production and trade and the provision of health and educational services.[2] In fact, the arrival of Christian missionaries in Malawi in the nineteenth century heralded the dawn of a new era with the introduction of western forms of thought and practice in almost all walks of life. So significant was the transformational effect of this encounter that Christianity became the basis of many of the colonial state's policies and programmes.[3]

In the field of agriculture, however, the role of Christianity appears to have been much less pronounced than in other areas like education and health. That notwithstanding, the campaign for conservation of resources invariably invoked biblical references that showed the influence of religious thinking and perceptions on the management of the African environment. The emphasis on agricultural production in this chapter is part of an effort to unravel those images and references that hitherto have not been considered in the literature but were crucial to the initial understanding of environmental conservation.[4]

This chapter suggests that missionaries initially paid little attention to conservation, not because the subject was unimportant but, rather, because they had other, more pressing, issues to deal with – the suppression of the slave trade, pacification of the area, education and evangelisation. Given the precarious situation they had to deal with, all these issues were seen as necessary conditions for the realisation of the overall goal of 'civilising' and Christianising the Africans. For example, the key objectives of the Universities' Mission to Central Africa (UMCA) were summarised as follows:

(a) to raise the natives into spiritual fellowship with ourselves by the preaching of the gospel;

(b) to raise them in the scale of civilization by the encouragement of agriculture and a lawful commerce, and the ultimate extinction of the slave trade.[5]

---

2. See, for example, Jean Allman, 'Making Mothers: Missionaries, Medical Officers and Women's Work in Colonial Asante, 1924–1945', *History Workshop Journal* 38 (1994): 23–47; John McCracken, *Politics and Christianity in Malawi, 1875–1940: the Impact of the Livingstonia Mission in the Northern Province*, Kachere Monograph No. 8 (Blantyre, 2000); Terence Ranger, 'Godly Medicine: the Ambiguities of Medical Mission in Southeastern Tanzania, 1900–1945', in S. Feierman and J. Janzen (eds.) *The Social Basis of Health and Healing in Africa* (London, 1992); and Robert Strayer, 'Mission History in Africa: New Perspectives on an Encounter', *African Studies Review* XIX/1 (1976): 3–15.

3. At Magomero, for instance, the missionaries faced opposition from some local chiefs and the ever-looming threat of Yao raids. What is more, in 1863, the UMCA was compelled to withdraw from the territory partly because of the death of their leader, Bishop Mackenzie, and partly because of the hostile conditions they experienced.

4. It should be noted that agriculture was not necessarily the only area in which conservation as an analytical concept was negotiated and contested. Great controversy also raged over the meaning, use and management of forests and wildlife. For example, several regulatory rules were imposed in the first thirty years of colonial rule, such as the Game Ordinances of 1891, 1897, 1911, 1926 and the Forest Ordinances of 1911 and 1926.

5. H. Rowley, *The Story*, p. 1.

Missionaries, sources and the African environment

Thus, throughout the first thirty years of the encounter, missionaries made a painstaking effort to achieve these objectives. While their success varied from place to place and at different periods, their contribution to the creation of general security cannot be doubted.[6]

Second, the missionaries had come to realise that African land use practices were not as ecologically destructive as they had originally thought. While African agriculture could not be described as the best, it could also not be dismissed as completely backward, since it was particularly suited to the conditions in which Africans operated at the time. This view was corroborated by Rev. Henry Rowley, one of the leading members of the UMCA, when he noted that it was presumptuous for any European to teach Africans how to farm.

> Yet with regard to agriculture we soon discovered that the natives could teach us more than we could teach them, and that we could offer them little inducement to grow more of anything than they needed for themselves. So another part of our programme, the encouragement of agriculture, was virtually a dead letter.[7]

John Buchanan, one of the earliest staff members at the Blantyre Mission and later a planter in Zomba, made a similar observation on this issue:

> It is of no use an English agriculturalist going to the Shire Highlands to teach the natives agriculture. This, in a certain sense, is true; in another sense it is not true. They grow their own crops very well in their own way; but then their way would not suit an English agriculturalist, nor be adopted by any intelligent colonist. Their system as at present does comparatively little harm to the country; but were the country densely populated, then their style of agriculture would have to be changed, or the country would become ruined.

Both Buchanan's and Rowley's statements raise a number of important issues regarding the initial encounter between Europeans and Africans. First, it is difficult to generalise about European views of Africans. Similarly, African forms of knowledge and practices cannot be homogenised. Indeed, some Europeans realised that Africans used different farming methods but not necessarily inferior ones. This view challenges the argument raised by some commentators that African interaction with the environment was inherently destructive, a point that I discuss in detail later in this chapter. But scholars need to get beyond such generalisations in order to understand the particular circumstances in which the Africans lived and worked.

---

6. In many instances, mission stations provided sanctuary to war victims and runaway slaves as well as food for destitutes in times of famine. For details on the activities of missionaries in Malawi and its neighbouring countries, see the works of D. Livingstone and C. Livingstone: *The Narrative of an Expedition to the Zambezi and its Tributaries and of the Discovery of Lakes Shirwa and Nyassa* (London, 1865); D. Livingstone, *Missionary Travels and Researches in South Africa* (London, 1857); and E.D. Young, *Mission to Nyassa* (London, 1977).
7. H. Rowley, *The Story*, p. 65.

Christian and colonial attitudes towards the environment

Data gathered in interviews helps to support this position.[8] Before the advent of colonialism, not all the farming methods were completely ruinous to the environment. Africans made mounds or sometimes tilled the ground to plant protective grass and reeds in areas considered prone to erosion. Such practices were particularly suited to the local conditions of specific areas, though, and we cannot generalise, on the basis of a few examples, that all Africans practised environmentally friendly methods of production. The story of African use and management of the environment is much more complicated and therefore requires a complex analysis.

Upon realising the viability of African agriculture, the missionaries immediately began to redirect their energies and limited resources to other fields like church-building, education and health. One may also argue that missionaries perhaps understood their own limitations as far as promotion of agricultural production was concerned. It is instructive to note that the first missionary party to the country included an agriculturalist by the name of Alfred Adams who advised the team on the agricultural conditions of the areas they visited. Missionaries did not give up farming completely but created small gardens around the mission stations and schools. Similarly, they did not actively promote conservation of resources. The production of crops on a commercial basis remained the responsibility of individual European settlers and companies. Yet when the colonial state had established control over the area, conservation began to emerge as an important terrain of colonial interaction and contestation with the Africans.

Impact of the Edenic mythology

Biblical mythology was important in shaping the development of conservationist thinking among Europeans who came to the interior of Eastern and Southern Africa in the nineteenth century. In Genesis, particularly in the first three chapters, we read the story of God's creation and man's relationship with other creatures. God gave man custodianship of all of His creation: '[Then God said], "Let us make man in our image, in our likeness, and let them rule over the fish of the sea and the birds of the air, over the livestock, over all the earth, and over all the creatures that move along the ground"' (Genesis 1:26). Having done this, 'The Lord God took the man and put him in the Garden of Eden to work it and take care of it' (Genesis 2:15). Furthermore, we read that the Garden of Eden had beautiful trees, good fruit and flowing rivers. Everything seems to have been perfect and man lived in a state of harmony with other creatures: 'Now the Lord God had planted a garden in the east, in Eden; and there he put the man he had formed. And the Lord God made all kinds of trees grow out of the ground – trees that were pleasing to the eye and good for food. In the middle of the garden were the tree of life and the tree of the knowledge of good and evil.' (Genesis 2:8–9) These images are important

---

8. Interview: Mr Yakobe, Joliji Village, TA Mpama, Chiradzulu, dated 5 June 1997; Interview: Mr Lekisemu, Nzundu Village, TA Nsabwe, Thyolo, dated 28 May 1997.

Impact of the Edenic mythology

in understanding subsequent European encounters with Africa and other parts of the world. In a large measure, they not only defined perceptions of the 'other' but also dictated the terms of the relationship with the peoples and environments encountered.[9]

In the case of Malawi, many missionaries used these biblical images to describe the African environment they met with. For example, the Rev. Duff MacDonald quoted the Rev. Horace Waller as describing Mulanje Mountain as a 'Land of Promise'[10] because of its beautiful topography and weather. Another missionary wrote that 'the country we passed through was as wild as the most enthusiastic lover of uncultivated nature could desire – the real thing, an African waste, but certainly not a desert'.[11] In the case of Malawi, many missionaries used these biblical images to describe the African environment they met with. This was quite consistent with age-old western tradition of viewing the tropics as paradises that offered delight and immense opportunities for human beings. Explorers and travellers were driven by the urge to find such new places, characterised by fertility of the land, fruitfulness, pleasant scenery, lack of seasonality and humans living in harmony with nature.[12]

These initial European perceptions of Africa and African peoples did to a large extent shape the nature of the colonial relationship that was to evolve later. According to Richard Grove, Europeans imposed an image of Africa 'as a special kind of "Eden", for the purposes of the European psyche, rather than as a complex and changing environment in which people have actually had to live'.[13] In addition, Africa has been portrayed 'as offering the opportunity to experience a wild and natural environment which was no longer available in the domesticated landscapes of Europe'.[14] Even the flowers of Africa offered a unique experience to the minds of missionaries. 'God might have made the world and not have made the flowers; or have limited them to the localities where alone they would be appreciated'.[15] Abundance of trees and flowers was among the natural features that embodied the aesthetic beauty of the newly discovered lands. This was a carry-over from the eighteenth century trope of earthly paradise fantasies that had developed in the European literary and scholarly imagination: missionaries and other travellers entertained Edenic visions even though the belief in the finding a real Eden had

---

9.   D. Anderson and R. Grove, 'The Scramble for Eden'.
10. D. MacDonald, *Africana*, p. 148.
11. H. Rowley, *The Story*, p. 101.
12. See R. Drayton, *Nature's Government: Science, Imperial Britain, and the Improvement of the World* (New Haven: Yale University Press, 2000); S. Johnson, 'Views in the South Seas: Nature, Culture and Landscape in Pacific Travel Accounts, 1700–1775', unpublished Ph.D. dissertation (University of Cambridge, 2005).
13. D. Anderson and R. Grove, 'The Scramble for Eden', p. 4.
14. *Ibid*. p. 5.
15. H. Rowley, *The Story*, pp. 355–6.

by that time significantly diminished.[16] Considering Africa from this Western mythological viewpoint, Europeans thought it their unfettered responsibility to intervene in the way the environment had been managed in Africa. They had to protect and conserve the rich natural resources that were perceived to be under threat of destruction by the Africans.

This brings us to the issue of the spoliation of this Garden of Eden and the consequences for human nature. In the Bible, we note that the power that God gave to man was not absolute, for any abuse of it resulted in admonition, as indeed we read in Chapter Three of Genesis when Adam and Eve have eaten the prohibited fruit. Against the background of an 'ecologically destroyed Europe', human activity was perceived as a constant threat to the idealised garden of Eden and some of the clearest signs of this spoliation included deforestation, desertification and famine. Thus, in view of this situation, western experts seized the occasion to intervene and impose their preferred solutions.[17] The basis of intervention derived from both technological superiority and also biblical reference to God's devolution of human stewardship over nature (Genesis 1:26). Ironically, the same references gave Europeans licence to exploit resources in ways they thought were good and rational. This also explains why African interaction with the environment was often described as ruinous or destructive. Europeans invariably linked environmental degradation with moral decadence, both of which were perceived to have occurred in Africa at the time of the encounter. Consequently, many restrictive laws were imposed in order to make sure the environment was properly used and managed by the Africans.

In an attempt to devise a framework for explaining the role of missionaries in conservation, Grove proposed the idea of 'Evangelical Mentality'.[18] This mindset, supposedly held by many missionaries, maintained that African indigenous systems of knowledge and land use practices were fundamentally inferior to those of Europeans. Through his study of South Africa, Grove observed that missionaries there viewed Africans as morally wicked people who lacked the responsibility to take care properly of the environment. In the Pacific islands and several parts of the New World, native peoples were similarly viewed as culturally and technologically backward. Examining historical and literary accounts of early modern travellers, Sarah Johnson has shown that the island of Tahiti, for instance, was depicted as a paradise but one inhabited by savages (however noble) – a people who were described as morally depraved due to their sexual laxity. As with biblical Eden, it was shameless sexual activities that led to the downfall of the glorious pre-lapsarian era through the onset of diseases such as syphilis.[19] The missionaries further dismissed any African explanations of environmental change and processes in their society.

---

16. See R. Drayton, *Nature's Government*, pp. 1–25; S. Johnson, 'Views in the South Seas', p. 24.
17. D. Anderson and R. Grove, 'The Scramble for Eden', p. 7.
18. See R. Grove, 'Scottish Missionaries'.
19. See R. Drayton, *Nature's Government*, pp. 3–8; S. Johnson, 'Views in the South Seas', pp. 48–54.

Christianity, conservation and the colonial state

They described them as 'savages', 'heathen' people who lacked conceptions of right and wrong and were in need of white man's guidance. Although there was no single authentic missionary voice, many of them broadly subscribed to this portrayal.[20] It is clear that moral and political influences on conservation emanated from the activities of the missionaries. In the case of South Africa, Grove maintained that such ideas propelled John Croumbie Brown, a renowned botanist and evangelist, to begin writing extensively on the destructive tendencies of Africans who were described as 'savages', morally bankrupt and destructive animals. The implications of these phrases were particularly important when applied to the African use and management of natural resources. Similarly, the missionary Robert Moffat played an important role in the conservation debate in South Africa and even set up a demonstration centre at Kuruman.[21] However, their missionary counterparts in Malawi played a less than salutary role in conservation – even though a few of those spent some time in South Africa before coming to Malawi.[22] A number of them never went beyond the mere description of the African farming practices they observed.

Some Europeans saw things differently. Daniel Rankin, an explorer and part-time trader, noted that, 'it is to the credit of the Scottish Missions that they afforded every encouragement for the promotion of the tentative agricultural development of the country. One of their number became the first and largest coffee grower in the district, and is at the present time one of the most successful planters.'[23] This statement, apparently referring to Buchanan in Zomba, suggests the need for us to recognise the uneven successes of the missionaries in different areas. What is more, a number of missionary groups appear to have realised that agricultural production had to be propelled by independent planters. In fact, Rankin went further to argue that it was unrealistic to expect priests to engage seriously in agriculture or trade: 'this eccentric attempt to combine the heterogeneous offices of priest and trader met with little success financially, and the enterprise gradually devolved into a transport agency for the various local missions'.[24] In the area of transport, the African Lakes Company conducted business on behalf of the missionaries.

Christianity, conservation and the colonial state

As precursors to colonial rule, the missionaries made a significant contribution to understanding the environmental conditions of the people and areas they came

---

20. See D. Fraser, *Winning a Primitive People*; and D. Macdonald, *Africana*.
21. John Croumbie Brown, *Management of Crown Forests of the Cape of Good Hope* (Edinburgh, 1877) and *The Hydrology of Southern Africa* (London, 1875).
22. For example, James Stewart worked for some years in South Africa, and David Livingstone also spent some time with the family of Robert Moffat, his father-in-law, before coming to Malawi. For more details on Robert Moffat's activities see R. Grove, 'Scottish Missionaries'.
23. Daniel Rankin, *Zambezi Basin and Nyasaland* (Edinburgh, 1893), p. 258.
24. *Ibid.* p. 257.

Christian and colonial attitudes towards the environment

into contact with. They also called for their government at home to intervene and colonise the territory so that they could carry out their work smoothly and successfully. At the same time, as European imperialism in Africa reached its *apogée* in the late nineteenth century, ideas about conservation had been embodied in the larger scheme of colonisation. Tropical colonies increasingly came to be viewed as paradises where natural wilderness akin to the Garden of Eden was perceived to have existed. In many island colonies, for example, the missionaries and medical doctors established botanical gardens as an attempt to recreate nature in its unfallen perfection.[25] Drayton has argued that botanical gardens were part and parcel of the process of consolidating newly occupied lands. In these gardens, travellers and settlers introduced new plants and species in order to add beauty to the environment but also to improve agricultural production which was construed as central to societal development.[26] After the establishment of colonial rule in Malawi, the state began to campaign for conservation, not because it was driven by any conservationist ideals but rather because of the growing influence of the evangelical mentality and the writings of the Scottish missionaries.

For example, in his book written after sixteen years of work among the Ngoni, Tumbuka and Nsenga people, the Rev. Donald Fraser noted that:

> unless the present wasteful methods are mended, the land will be deforested, and the soil become sterile, and the people will of necessity be forced every few years to flit to new and richer lands. Every such flitting puts back the tribe several years in moral and general progress. So long too, as the natives are allowed to cut down trees when they would open new gardens, and to consider the land free for their new migrations, none will take the trouble to learn better methods of fertilisation, and cultivation, and we shall soon see this well-wooded land as bare as the wild veldts of South Africa.[27]

John McCracken has offered perhaps the most convincing explanation of the way in which missionaries were able to shape colonial policies on conservation. He shows that a small group of Scottish missionaries played a key role in influencing state conservation policies. Focusing on the *visoso* (a kind of shifting cultivation) system for producing millet, the missionaries attacked it for environmental and moral reasons. They argued that the system not only led to deforestation but also encouraged production of a crop used for beer brewing. Missionaries tended to regard beer drinking as a social evil, rather like polygamy, worthy of condemnation. Their concerns were accepted and taken up by state officials like A.J.W. Hornby and R.W. Kettlewell during their anti-erosion campaigns in the 1930s and 1940s.[28]

---

25. R. Grove, *Green Imperialism*.
26. See R. Drayton, *Nature's Government*, pp. 106–28.
27. D. Fraser, *Winning a Primitive People*, p. 306.
28. J. McCracken, 'Conservation and Resistance in Malawi'.

Christianity, conservation and the colonial state

One of the questions arising from this discussion is: when did spoliation of the environment begin and when did it reach the level that necessitated the introduction of state conservation campaigns? This is not easy to establish. Both written and oral accounts suggest that some forms of degradation had taken place before the arrival of Europeans. African farming systems, particularly shifting cultivation and slash-and-burn, resulted in the long-term deforestation or desiccation of the country. Many contemporary travellers observed this situation and described it in vivid terms. Two explanations have been advanced here. First, there is an argument that degradation of proportionate levels took place after the arrival of nineteenth-century conquerors and settlers. Many groups of people were involved in this: missionaries, traders, settlers and the Africans themselves. But, for Leroy Vail, great emphasis should be placed on the Ngoni intrusion, whose impact in northern Malawi led to the creation of an ecological disequilibrium. This conclusion is based on the fact that Ngoni invasion disrupted trade and encouraged concentration of settlements, and cattle keeping, activities that increased the carrying capacity of the area in question. Elsewhere, European efforts to promote commercial farming resulted in the opening up of many areas to cultivation, including ecologically fragile ones. Thus the rapid and extensive degradation of the environment was certainly exacerbated by the commercialisation of production.[29] The missionaries wanted to introduce 'legitimate' trade to replace the slave trade, which invariably meant production of those crops required by British industrial capitalism.[30] Apart from putting a commercial value on such crops as cotton and tobacco, Africans had to adopt new farming techniques, such as ridging and terracing. Even though it has now become quite fashionable to relate environmental degradation to population growth, this does not seem to have had much weight in the case of Malawi. Buchanan clearly argued that population pressure was not an important factor on land in the nineteenth century.[31] In fact, the rapid growth in population is really a post-independence phenomenon: before 1964 the population of the country was fairly small (less than 2 million) in relation to the land available (94,080 sq.km). Certainly, it could not by itself have resulted in the substantial destruction of the environment. The Malawi experience is not unique in this regard. In Kenya, it has been established that, rather than population growth leading to degradation, it actually enhanced the need for people to develop ways that reduced erosion of the

---

29. Leroy Vail, 'The Making of the "Dead North": a Study of the Ngoni Rule in Northern Malawi, c. 1855–1907', in J.B. Peires (ed.) *Before and After Shaka: Papers in Nguni History* (Grahamstown: Institute of Social and Economic Research, 1981), pp. 230–65. See also Leroy Vail, 'Ecology and History: The Case of Eastern Zambia', *Journal of Southern African Studies* 3/2 (1977): 129–55.
30. D. and C. Livingstone, *The Zambezi and its Tributaries*.
31. J. Buchanan, *The Shire Highlands*.

soil.³² The tenuousness of this argument suggests that factors leading to degradation must be sought elsewhere.

The second argument is the desiccationist theory. Although there may well have been other people who propounded this idea prior to the 1890s, Johnston, the first Commissioner and Consul-General, was probably the first person in Malawi to present it in a more refined and unambiguous manner.³³ Johnston's ideas had significant ramifications for understanding the intentions and actions of colonial officials on African agriculture and conservation of natural resources. First, he emphasised what has been described as the 'exotic factor' by suggesting that Africans had until recently subsisted on hunting and gathering and that crops like maize and millet and domestic animals had only been introduced in the few decades before the establishment of colonial rule.³⁴ He further argued that Africans in the region had failed to improve the cultivation of crops, whether indigenous or imported from outside by Arabs or Europeans.³⁵ By drawing comparisons with other countries in Europe or Asia, he contended that, in Africa, little effort had been made to domesticate most of the plants and increase their intensive production. It was this failure that had resulted in the slash-and-burn system that was deemed so destructive to the environment. Drayton has advanced the idea that cultivation of land was part of the responsibility that had been bestowed on man after the biblical Fall. Hence, societies that did not practice agriculture were viewed as abdicating their God-given duty. Improving the use of the land was not just necessary for human existence but it also helped to recreate the lost glory. Failure to do so was considered environmentally destructive and culpable in the eyes of God.³⁶ Johnston also maintained the view that the country had once been covered with dense forest but that man had gradually destroyed all that, replacing it with vegetation better suited to resist the action of bush fires. For him, man had been and continued to be the greatest factor in environmental degradation. By studying the rainfall patterns, the river systems and the vegetative cover, he concluded that man had played a significant role in the deforestation of the region:

> It is scarcely an exaggeration to say that had British Central Africa been left for another couple of hundred years simply and solely to the black man and the black man had continued to exist without thought for the future as he does at present, this country would have become treeless, as many portions of it were becoming when we embarked on its administration.³⁷

---

32. M. Tiffen et al. *More People, Less Erosion: Environmental Recovery in Kenya* (New York, 1994).
33. For details on this, see H. Johnston, *British Central Africa* (London, 1897).
34. Hector L. Duff, *Nyasaland Under the Colonial Office* (London, 1906), p. 298.
35. H. Johnston, *British Central Africa*, pp. 428–9.
36. See R. Drayton, *Nature's Government*, pp. 50–66.
37. *Ibid.* p. 37.

Christianity, conservation and the colonial state

Johnston took a very strong position on the destructive impact of man on the environment, and particularly on the use of bush fires for preparing land for farming:

> the natives make clearings for their plantations. They cut down trees, leave them to dry and then set fire to them and sow their crops amongst the fertilizing ashes. The same type of forest never grows up again ... Besides this wanton destruction of forest for the growing of food crops (and as a rule the native merely grows one crop of corn and then moves off to another patch of virgin soil, leaving the old plantation to be covered with grass and weeds) the annual bush fires play a considerable ... part of the disforesting of the country.[38]

Second, Johnston maintained that the lack of tenure over land offered no incentive for the proper use and management of land resources. Africans had no idea of manuring the ground and that explained why they could not continue to cultivate the same piece of land for a long time. Instead, they were completely dependent on every year clearing virgin land that offered better yields. 'One of the great lessons we have to teach the Central African negro is fixity of tenure, the need of settling permanently on one piece of land, and, by careful manuring, the constant raising of crops from within a certain definite area.'[39] Ten years later, Hector Duff, another colonial official, complained about the persistence of this problem and opined that,

> I do not know whether we shall ever succeed in getting the natives to realise and put into practice the idea of permanent title to land ... but it is pretty certain that until they make some steps in this direction, their general position in the scale of mind and morals will remain very much what it is at present.[40]

The significance of these ideas was clearly noticed in the 1890s when, soon after the declaration of Protectorate rule in Malawi, a series of restrictive measures were introduced in an effort to actualise Johnston's and the missionaries' ideas about conservation. At that point, the major environmental concerns for Malawi included the increasing rates of deforestation, wildlife depletion and soil erosion. The missionaries recorded these events extensively in their travel accounts, memoirs and reports. By the turn of the twentieth century, perceptions of and increased levels of information on these issues enabled the colonial state to intervene, though selectively, with an assortment of rules and regulations on various aspects of environmental conservation. One area in which these measures were implemented was game resources. This is also an area that received a lot of attention from contemporary chroniclers. Almost every account one comes across mentions numerous kinds of animals that European travellers came into contact with. Indeed, both oral and

---

38. *Ibid.* p. 37.
39. *Ibid.* p. 425.
40. H. Duff, *Nyasaland*, p. 297.

written sources show the variety of wildlife: lions, elephants, hyenas, zebras, hippopotamus, rhinoceros, kudu, buffaloes and so on.[41]

Contrary to Alice Werner's argument that hunting was not an important feature of African life in Malawi, oral accounts in the country and indeed research findings elsewhere do indicate that hunting was a complex activity that played a vital role in the lives and economies of particular African societies.[42] Werner had stated that 'none of the tribes of British Central Africa can be said to live by hunting, or even to make it one of their principal occupations'.[43] This observation may hold true for some ethnic groups, especially those that had agriculture as their primary occupation. But, even then, the distinction appears not to have been so simple throughout the pre-colonial period. It obscures the fact that some groups, for example the Nyanja, Mang'anja and Tumbuka, combined the activities of hunting and agriculture. Moreover, hunting was often done by special clans or families, although no hard and fast restrictions were placed on others wishing to do so.[44] Since animals had several functions to human beings, such as being sources of food, hides and medicine, there is a high likelihood that hunting must have formed an important but not necessarily central feature of Malawi's pre-colonial domestic economy. Hunting as an occupation had its own rituals that tended to regulate the killing of animals.

According to Vaughan, who has conducted extensive research on the socio-economic history of the Shire Highlands, 'in the pre-colonial period conservation had been an integral part of hunting, and hunting an integral part of society. Now these connections no longer existed.'[45] The challenge now is to establish the point at which hunting became an integral part of society and when it ceased to be so and to understand the extent to which conservation had been part of the remit of hunting. Moreover, there is the question of what Africans did in place of, or as a supplement to, hunting. These questions may shed some light on the situation in the late nineteenth century when game hunting – its use and management – became a highly charged issue between Africans and Europeans. However, the idea of conservation was still in its nascent stage during this period. Europeans generally blamed Africans for their recklessness in the use of game resources. They charged that Africans simply killed animals without any consideration for the preservation of the species. Consequently, the first attempt to regulate African hunting came soon after the establishment of colonial rule in 1891. In that year, gun control measures were introduced in the form of a gun tax, followed by another regulation making

---

41. *Ibid.* pp. 140–160.
42. Interview: Mai Linley Kambwiri, Ntogolo Village, TA Malemia, Zomba, dated 16 May 1997.
43. A. Werner, *The Natives of British Central Africa*, p. 185.
44. Interview: Mai Linley Kambwiri.
45. Megan Vaughan, 'Uncontrolled Animals and Aliens: Colonial Conservation Mania in Malawi' (Chancellor College, History Seminar Paper, 1977/78).

Christianity, conservation and the colonial state

it illegal to sell guns and gunpowder to Africans.[46] Those who already possessed guns were required to obtain licences. The aim was to limit the number of Africans in possession of firearms which, so colonial officials argued, were responsible for the depletion of animals as well as the frequent internecine wars. But not many Africans could afford to pay these taxes. Nonetheless, hunting of animals continued in ways that could not be easily noticed by the colonial officials. At the same time, Africans argued that hunting was necessary as a way of protecting themselves and their livestock from the depredations of wild animals. Even though guns were not readily available, most of them continued to hunt using traditional methods, such as traps and snares, poison, dogs, fires and pitfalls.[47]

Similar experiences were observable in cutting down trees and tilling land. The early colonial state accused Africans of wantonly cutting down trees, largely as part of the shifting cultivation farming practice. They also blamed Africans for not digging the ground deeply enough but only scratching the surface. To remedy this situation, the colonial state promoted the idea of fixity of tenure and the making of ridges. Unfortunately, no serious efforts were made to implement these ideas until the 1930s when the state began to intervene seriously in African production systems.[48] But Africans had their own ways of conserving resources. As one of the informants in Chiradzulu reminisced:

> there were no specific rules as such on the cutting down of trees. But restrictions came about when people agreed to dedicate a chosen tree for *kutsira nsembe* [to give offerings to ancestors]. They would choose a particular type of tree and a big one for that matter. Such a tree would be regarded as sacred and not to be cut by anyone in the village. Restrictions were also imposed on trees that were used for making useful things is society such as mortars, canoes and extracting medicine.[49]

Despite the fact that missionaries in Malawi did not play as active a role in conservation as their counterparts in South Africa, they at least helped in documenting the conditions and problems that they experienced in various stations throughout the country. For example, they were well aware of the limitations facing Nyasaland as a nation in establishing a viable economic system. Among these problems was a shortage of the labour essential for the successful development of

---

46. See H. Duff, *Nyasaland*.
47. Interview, Mr Sandaramu Michael Kholopete, Mkanda Village, TA Mlumbe, Zomba, dated 21 May 1997.
48. See J. McCracken, 'Experts and Expertise in Colonial Malawi', *African Affairs* 81/22 (1982): 101–116, and 'Conservation and Resistance in Malawi': 155–174; and W.O. Mulwafu, 'The State, Conservation and Peasant Response in Colonial Malawi: Some Preliminary Observations, 1920s–1964', in Alan H. Jeeves and Owen J.M. Kalinga (eds.) *Communities at the Margin: Studies in Rural Society and Migration in Southern Africa, 1890–1980* (Pretoria: University of South Africa Press, 2002), pp. 201–215 and 'Soil Erosion and State Intervention into Estate Production in the Shire Highlands Economy of Colonial Malawi, 1891–1964', *Journal of Southern African Studies* 28/1 (2002): 25–44.
49. Interview: Mr Yakobe, Joliji Village.

the growing of coffee and other cash crops.[50] Second, some missionaries complained that the farming practices of Africans, and especially the methods of slash-and-burn and shifting cultivation, posed a major threat to the economic development of the country.[51] All these problems militated against the desired goals of both the church and the colonial state. Both wanted to create a society in which the people were healthy and able to produce effectively for themselves and colonial demands.

By the 1930s, conservation had become one of the most important policy issues in colonial Malawi. The accumulation of vast amounts of knowledge about the country and awareness of external environmental problems, such as the American Dust Bowl, all contributed immensely to the rekindling of interest in conservation of natural resources.[52] The interventionist state launched a campaign for conserving vast amounts of land. It was particularly concerned about the problem of soil erosion. In 1939 a new policy on soil conservation came into being and agricultural staff across the country were instructed to implement it vigorously and relentlessly. The state encouraged the adoption of such conservation measures as box-ridging, terracing and bunding. In the process of implementing this policy, the state came into direct conflict with many sections of the African community: peasants, nationalist politicians and some sects of the Christian churches.[53]

While the episode about religious opposition illustrates the progressive feelings of the 'new men' and religious independence of conservation, it also complicates the role of Christianity. Certainly the attitude of Christians towards conservation was not the same throughout the colonial period. Some groups tended to support conservation measures while others opposed them. Those missionaries who supported conservation wanted to see the ending of the *visoso* technique of production for reasons explained earlier. On the other hand, critics of conservation, particularly sectarian churches like the Sons of God and the Jehovah's Witnesses (Watch Tower movement), attacked the idea on apocalyptic grounds. Like most other new men (missionary educated Africans who had adopted some aspects of western culture and thus found they could not fit properly into traditional African societies), these radical Africans increasingly came to realise the difficulties and impact of colonial conservation campaigns as regarded their farming practices and the labour process.

---

50. D. Rankin, *Zambezi Basin*, pp. 260–2.
51. See D. Fraser, *Winning a Primitive People*, p. 306 and H. Rowley, *The Story*.
52. For more details on external factors, see J. McCracken, 'Experts and Expertise in Colonial Malawi', pp. 101–116. Mandala also discusses this issue within the context of the Lower Shire Valley. See Chs 4 and 5 of his *Work and Control in Peasant Economy*.
53. See Roger Tangri, 'The Rise of Nationalism in Colonial Africa: the Case of Colonial Malawi', *Comparative Studies in Society and History* 10/2 (1968): 142–161; and J.C. Chakanza, *Voices of Preachers in Protest: The Ministry of Two Malawian Prophets, Elliot Kamwana and Wilfrid Gudu* (Zomba, 1998).

Conservation and African religious beliefs

A small but significant amount of literature is now emerging on the relationship between African beliefs and practices and the environment in general. Omari has argued that, in most African societies, natural resources were preserved largely in the name of religion. Writing in the context of Tanzania, he noted that religious values and taboos were critical in providing a repertoire of rules and regulations for preserving natural resources. Although Africans may not have planned to practice conservationist ideas, their religious beliefs and values resulted in the development of ecological and environmental concerns. Positive values concerning the use of natural resources were passed from generation to generation through songs, proverbs and stories.[54]

Writings by Mwase, Schoffeleers, Mandala, Vaughan and Potter provide some good pointers to this subject and one of the issues raised is that Africans too had beliefs that governed the use and management of natural resources.[55] For example, rain cults played important social and political functions in society. In times of drought, plagues and epidemics, chiefs worshipped at the shrines controlled by spirit mediums. According to Schoffeleers, cult organisations do not just 'preserve ... forest areas. They also prescribe forms of behaviour which seemingly have nothing to do with the environment, but which are nevertheless said to have a profound effect on it.'[56] Every member of the community observed societal norms and rules regarding the use of natural resources, such as cutting trees or opening a new garden for cultivation. Thus, Traditional Authorities had a crucial role in predicting and interpreting ecological irregularities in society. For example, they could make pronouncements on misbehaviour and other malpractices in society. They could also organise rain-calling ceremonies in their respective communities.

The intrusion of colonial rule and the immigration of large groups of people into the country led, in some cases, to the destruction of these rain cults. Colonialism affected people's attitudes towards nature and natural resources in various ways. Traditional value systems, which treated resources as belonging to the community and being subject to individual responsibility to care were replaced with capitalist values emphasising profit and selfish attitudes. Natural resources now came to be

---

54. See C.K. Omari, 'Traditional African Land Ethics', in J.R. Engel and S.G. Engel (eds.) *Ethics of Environment and Development* (London, 1990), pp. 167–175.
55. George S. Mwase, *Strike a Blow and Die: a Narrative of Race Relations in Colonial Africa*, ed. by Robert Rotberg (Cambridge, Mass. 1967); E. Mandala, *Work and Control in a Peasant Economy*, p. 229; Matthew Schoffeleers, *Guardians of the Land: Essays on the Central African Territorial Cults* (Gwelo, Zimbabwe, 1978); Matthew Schoffeleers, *Religion and the Dramatization of Life: Spirit Beliefs and Rituals in Central and Southern Malawi*, Kachere Monograph No. 5, (Zomba, 1977); M. Vaughan, 'Uncontrolled Animals and Aliens: Colonial Conservation Mania in Malawi'; John R. Potter, '*Mizimu*, "Demarcated Forests" and Contour Ridges: Conservation in Malawi from 1800 to 1964' (BA Thesis: Williams College, Massachusetts, 1987).
56. M. Schoffeleers, *Religion and the Dramatization of Life*, pp. 14–15.

seen as objects for exploitation and profit-making. In the Shire Highlands region, the expansion of commercial farming has been associated with the destruction of such forest areas as Malabvi, Chiradzulu, Namvula, Kalulu and Zomba mountains. It became difficult for Africans to conduct their rain-calling ceremonies in these denuded areas. The consequence of all this was the belief that the ancestral spirits had either moved to other places or no longer felt at home when being propitiated at these sites.

Thus, during the introduction of *malimidwe* [conservation rules], Africans in the Shire Highlands also resisted partly because of the fear that their rain cults were being threatened. Because of the increase in population, a number of areas in the region fell under cultivation and this accelerated the process of land degradation. In response, the colonial state introduced *malimidwe*, which involved the use of various conservation measures in areas that were deemed susceptible to erosion. In some cases, hill-slope areas had either to be closed to cultivation or protected with bunds and storm drains. The colonial authorities also instituted forest reserves in different areas based on their scientific understanding of the environment. The colonial authorities maintained that deforestation resulted in desiccation. Consequently, the state began, as early as the 1890s, to place restrictions on the use of forest products as well as to introduce legislation on the general protection of forest reserves. On the other hand, Africans established rain cults in forested areas based on their cultural understanding of the value of rain and the spirit world. For example, they declared some places sacred for the burial of their deceased relatives. It was believed that the dead would communicate with their ancestral spirits who would, in turn, provide for the needs and requirements of people in the living world. Such areas could not be cleared of forests because to do so would be to send off their ancestral spirits.[57]

Peasants thought that they had to resist the destruction of their forests at all costs. These were forests that had been created by the peasants themselves for *chire* (bush deliberately left to grow for ritual activities), *kudzinja* [deserted settlement area or graveyard] and other functions. Writing about the influence of the Mbona cult on the Mang'anja people in Southern Malawi, which is the lower side of the Shire Highlands, Schoffeleers notes that, in the 1930s, the spirit medium issued a prophecy against the adoption of ridge cultivation. In explaining the role of the Mbona cult in peasant resistance to *malimidwe*, both Mandala and Schoffeleers argue that peasants took into consideration the movement of the Mbona himself who was the giver of rains.[58] Incarnated as a snake, the Mbona needed to move on land that did not have any obstructions, such as ridges and contour bunds. Schoffeleers throws a clearer light on African resistance by observing that

---

57. Interview: Mr Simon Benson Chimpeni, Joliji Village, TA Mpama, Chiradzulu district, dated 5 June 1997.
58. See E. Mandala, *Work and Control in a Peasant Economy*, p. 229; and M. Schoffeleers (ed.) *Guardians of the Land*, pp. 4–7.

Conclusion

it was 'couched in nativistic terms stressing the observance of the ancestral ways as a condition of securing the continuous protection by the ancestral spirits of the land and the population'.[59] Thus, securing a good passage for the Mbona was one of the principal obligations that peasants had to undertake in return for protection and the provision of rains.

Conclusion

This chapter has shown that, although conservation was never an explicit objective of the early missionaries, it nonetheless constituted an important base for subsequent images and religious representation of the African environment. A great many late nineteenth and early twentieth century writings used biblical images that depicted the African environment in reference to religious tropes, ranging from the original Garden of Eden to the fallen world of industrial Europe. In the process, missionaries indirectly influenced the colonialist perception of African natural resources.

The introduction of conservation laws by the colonial state in Malawi sparked differences with the local people over the notion of environment. This was manifested at different levels, such as in questions of the use and value of resources and in methods of their management. While some of these differences were highly charged, others were not. As Anderson and Grove have pointed out, Europeans coming from an environmentally different society had hoped to create an Eden in Africa, an ideal place where humans could live in harmony with nature.[60] They came with their own ideas about the environment and wanted to apply them in the colonies with little consideration for the indigenous systems of knowledge.[61] But the full impact of these contending attitudes and perceptions came to be felt after the 1930s when population pressure and extensive utilisation of resources created land shortages and degradation in some parts of the country.

The missionaries were among the European settlers who acquired large amounts of land in the early years of colonialism.[62] For the most part, they used their land to build mission stations and schools and for a range of other activities. Although few missions directly participated in agricultural production, a number of individuals attached plantations to these missions where they grew a variety of cash crops like coffee, cotton tea and tobacco. In fact, individuals like John Bucha-

---

59. M. Schoffeleers, *Religion and the Dramatization of Life*, p. 105.
60. D. Anderson and R. Grove, 'The Scramble for Eden'.
61. In light of this position, I argue that, through a scrutiny of European writings, we are able to understand not only their own perceptions of the African environment but also the African perceptions of and attitudes towards the Europeans.
62. For example, the Church of Scotland Mission owned more than 3,000 acres in Blantyre and Zomba districts; the Rev. Horace Waller owned the Chiradzulu Estate with about 5,441 acres; and John Chilembwe's Providence Industrial Mission owned 93 acres at Mbombwe in Chiradzulu district. See also B. Pachai, *Land and Politics in Malawi, 1875–1975* (Kingston, Ont: Limestone Press, 1978).

nan of the Blantyre Mission are credited with the introduction of coffee farming in the country. Buchanan promoted coffee production with great enthusiasm so that the land under cultivation increased steadily until the turn of the century. For example, in 1891, about 1,600 acres had been planted with coffee trees and that number rose to 5,700 acres in 1896 and then to 17,000 acres in 1900.[63] However, the coffee industry collapsed at the turn of the century due to poor prices on the world market, and instead three other crops entered the picture: tea, cotton and tobacco. In total, Buchanan owned more than 200,000 acres of estate land in different parts of the country, such as Lunzu and Michiru in Blantyre and Mulunguzi and Malosa in Zomba.

As I discuss in subsequent chapters, from the early days of the encounter to the late colonial period, an overzealous campaign was conducted to have cash crops grown in new ways. Indeed, for the greater part of the early colonial period, many officials had difficulties getting Africans to grow crops, particularly food crops, using new methods introduced by Europeans, such as contour and box ridging, terracing and bunding. Some peasants argued that these exotic methods had the major disadvantage of requiring heavy capital investment and also using a lot of time and labour.[64] In many areas of the Shire Highlands, the settlers, aided by the colonial state, began to persuade and, in some cases, force Africans to grow cash crops like tobacco, tea, coffee and tung using new conservation measures.[65]

European colonialism sought to reform African agriculture in a variety of ways, including the introduction of contour ridging, terracing and new land use practices. Drawing on Protestant beliefs about cultivation and the ideology of improvement, changing African agriculture became vital to the global process of Enlightenment and imperialism. At the centre of all this was the belief that since the relationship between man and nature had changed over time, it was necessary to transform the modes of cultivation. Nature, in its older form alone, could no longer sustain human life.[66]

These ideas clashed with the African production systems and conservation strategies I have just described and led to struggles I will analyse in the subsequent chapters. The next chapter looks at emergence of colonial conservation policies and practices and how these affected peasant production in the Shire Highlands region.

---

63. Colin Baker, 'Malawi's Exports: an Economic History', in G.W. Smith, B. Pachai and R.K. Tangri (eds.) *Malawi: Past and Present* (Blantyre: C.L.A.I.M., 1971), pp. 89–90.

64. Interview: Mr Billiot Mlaliki, Nzundu Village, TA Nsabwe, Thyolo district, dated 29 May 1997.

65. Interview: Mr Billiot Mlaliki, Nzundu Village, TA Nsabwe, Thyolo district, dated 29 May 1997; also interview: Mai Nangozo, Ndaona Village, TA Nsabwe, Thyolo district, dated 11 June 1997. In the Thyolo district, the conservation campaign was led by the agricultural staff based at Masambanjati in chief Changata's area. In the 1950s, it was people like W. V. Rose, the agricultural supervisor, and Gifford Guga, his assistant, who carried out their conservationist ideas in the gardens of peasants throughout the district.

66. See R. Drayton, *Nature's Government*, pp. 50–66; S. Johnson, 'Views in the South Seas'.

4

Scientific Networking, Ideology and the Rise of Conservation Discourse in Colonial Malawi

> Knowledge is power ... By extension, the continuing ignorance and occlusion of alternative knowledges (local knowledge and other narratives) allows the globalizing institutions ... to uphold hegemonic and normalising discourses ... Academics need to penetrate these discourses in multiple contexts and at different levels.[1]

Introduction

Science and politics were central to the rise of conservationist discourse in southern Africa in the first half of the twentieth century. Although colonial science has earned itself a bad name in some circles, its influence in policy formulation and state intervention in natural resource conservation cannot be ignored; besides there are some key lessons to be learnt from specific contexts. In a recent thought-provoking article by Beinart *et al.* an examination of the role of colonial science shows the value of paying attention to specific contexts in which events take place or in which ideas are produced.[2] At the risk of oversimplifying issues, the article calls for a reassessment of the critique of colonial science, which has all too often failed to transcend parochial identities as scholars have been preoccupied with demonstrating the subject's failures or ill-effects rather than continuities and interactions in the development of knowledge. Using the case of veterinary medicine in South Africa, for instance, Beinart *et al.* show the complex ways in which knowledge developed by drawing on ideas and experiences across time and space. Their study further shows that colonial scientists did not operate in a closed environment; in fact, many of them had wider experience that transcended their localised research sites and circulated their findings widely to influence public decision-making process.

Colonial Malawi was part of the southern African region where such ideas were generated and where strenuous efforts were made to implement them in the late colonial period. As McCracken has shown, the terrain was wide and varied, ranging from tsetse-fly control, livestock management and forestry to soil conser-

---

1. Sian Sullivan, 'Getting the Science Right, or Introducing Science in the First Place? Local "Facts", Global Discourse- "Desertification" in North-west Namibia' in P. Stott and S. Sullivan (eds.) *Political Ecology: Science, Myth and Power* (London: Arnold, 2000), p. 34.

2. William Beinart, Karen Brown and Daniel Gilfoyle, 'Experts and Expertise in Colonial Africa Reconsidered: Science and the Interpenetration of Knowledge' *African Affairs* 108/432 (2009): 413–433.

vation. Colonial technical staff formulated their policies based on observations, reading of travel accounts, surveys and scientific theories as well as adapting ideas from other parts of the world. On the issue of soil conservation, it is argued that much of the inspiration and support came from the Oxford School of Imperial Ecology and the Imperial Forestry Institute at the University of Oxford, which became the engine for the conservation drive that peaked and generated conflicts in the 1940s and 1950s.[3]

Scholarship on soil conservation in eastern and southern Africa is now available in relative abundance. We know a great deal about the impulse and reasons for conservation, the key actors and strategies used and the mixed reactions of groups of people who were the targets of state intervention – the Africans in Malawi and commercial farmers in South Africa and Southern Rhodesia. What is less known, however, is the way in which the idea of conservation itself was rooted in and driven by a particular kind of science about the organisation of space and natural resources. Conservation, which usually meant state intrusion into the spaces of the peasants, is perhaps one area more than any other where struggles and contestations took place for much of the late colonial period.

The chapter begins from the premise that, while scientific ideas on conservation provided authoritative knowledge, their implementation was highly contested. Both state officials and Africans constantly negotiated and redefined what conservation meant, how it should be implemented, by whom and when. These issues loomed large in both official accounts and peasant narratives. Recent scholarship in many parts of Africa has demonstrated the limits and contestations of scientific ideas and their efficacy.[4] In some cases, scientific knowledge has been challenged as having been inappropriately formulated;[5] in others, it was wrongly implemented.[6] The rest of this chapter discusses the origins of scientific ideas about conservation and ways in which they were implemented in colonial Malawi.

---

3. See the role of research institutes in Helen Tilley, 'African Environments and Environmental Sciences: the African Research Survey, Ecological Paradigms and British Colonial Development, 1920–1940' in W. Beinart and J. McGregor (eds.) *Social History and African Environments* (James Currey, 2003), pp. 109–130.

4. See the work of C.A.M. Attwell and F.P.D. Cotterell, 'Postmodernism and African Conservation Science', *Biodiversity and Conservation* 9 (2000): 559–577; James Fairhead and Melissa Leach, 'False Forest History, Complicit Social Analysis: Rethinking Some West African Environmental Narratives', *World Development* 23/6 (1995): 1023–1036; M. Leach and R. Mearns (eds.) *The Lie of the Land: Challenging Received Wisdom on the African Continent* (Oxford: International African Institute, 1996).

5. S. Sullivan, 'Getting the Science Right'; Katherine Homewood and W.A. Rodgers, 'Pastoralism, Conservation and the Overgrazing Controversy' in D. Anderson and R. Grove (eds.) *Conservation in Africa* (Cambridge, 1987), pp. 111–128.

6. Lucy Jarosz, 'Defining and Explaining Tropical Deforestation: Shifting Cultivation and Population Growth in Madagascar (1896–1940)', *Economic Geography* 69/4 (1993): 366–79; M. Leach and R. Mearns (eds.) *The Lie of the Land*; K. Showers, 'Soil Erosion in the Kingdom of Lesotho: Origins and Colonial Response'.

Origins of conservationist thinking in colonial Malawi, 1936–43

The idea is not to discard or challenge the authority of science but rather to present a more balanced account, since discourses have great policy implications. As Sullivan has argued, we recognise the fact that 'objective understandings of environmental and socio-economic phenomena arrived at by science are themselves constrained by historically located cultural ideals peculiar to all aspects of Western Enlightenment thought'.[7] This discussion specifically focuses on three main issues: the impact of the Dust Bowl in propagating the idea of conservation, the role played by the Imperial Forestry Institute of Oxford University in training and providing a scientific basis for ideas on conservation and the special activities of men on the spot who spoke, wrote and implemented the policies. In addition, the role of the Natural Resources Board as a specially created state institution responsible for implementing policies is highlighted. This chapter benefits from a substantial amount of data collected by the author over the years in the form of oral testimonies and archival sources.

Origins of conservationist thinking in colonial Malawi, 1936–43

The debate on conservation and management of natural resources in Malawi has a long history. As early as the 1890s, newly appointed colonial officials began to talk about the need to preserve the territory's natural resources, which were perceived to be under threat of further degradation. Driven by the idea that Africans were incapable of using resources wisely and efficiently, the colonial state introduced a number of regulatory policies and laws that came to characterise much conservationist thinking right through to the early 1930s. For the most part, these policies concerned game control and use of forest resources, issues that had already received a considerable amount of attention among scholars.[8]

Although soil conservation measures were imposed initially in the late 1930s and extended countrywide in the two decades that followed, their origins went back to the 1920s. As early as 1924, the Department of Agriculture published a bulletin addressing the general problem of soil erosion and deforestation and suggesting remedial measures.[9] Ten years later, the colonial administration issued

---

7. S. Sullivan, 'Getting the Science Right', p.34.
8. John McCracken, 'Colonialism, Capitalism and Ecological Crisis in Malawi: a Reassessment' in D. Anderson and R. Grove (eds.) *Conservation in Africa: People, Policies and Practice* (Cambridge: C.U.P. 1987) pp. 63–78; Brian Morris, 'Conservation Mania in Colonial Malawi: Another View' *Nyala*, 19 (1996): 17–36; David Njaidi, 'Towards an Exploration of Game Control and Land Conservation in Colonial Mangochi, 1891–1964', *The Society of Malawi Journal* 48/2 (1995): 1–25; W. Mulwafu, 'The Interface of Christianity and Conservation in Colonial Malawi, 1891–1930', *Journal of Religion in Africa* 34/3 (2004): 298–319; M. Vaughan, 'Uncontrolled Animals and Aliens'.
9. F. Dixey *et al. The Destruction of Vegetation and its Relation to Climate, Water Supply, and Soil Fertility.*

another report with a more detailed assessment of the same conditions.[10] Although officials were concerned about environmental degradation at this early stage and had many suggestions for reversing it, no concerted effort to implement remedial measures occurred until after 1938. Thereafter, a conservationist drive took hold and issues of proper land use and management featured prominently in most policies and programmes.[11]

Prior to the 1930s, soil conservation had been discussed and considered in colonial circles but not as part of the general development of the territory. It was mainly restricted, as noted above, to forestry and wildlife resources. In fact, until 1927, Forestry was simply a division of the Department of Agriculture. Even after the creation of the Forestry Department conservation was still seen in a narrow sense of game and forestry resources. The Department of Agriculture itself focused mainly on crop production and paid little attention to issues of soil conservation. Only in the 1930s did the government begin to examine the issue of soil conservation in a broader perspective and that marked a watershed period in Malawi's conservation history. One important development concerned the initiative to conduct agricultural surveys in different parts of the country with the aim of providing 'profiles of soil types, land utilisation maps, and economic development potential of the areas'.[12] In a letter sent to the Chief Secretary on 11 May 1933, the Director of Agriculture stated that he had urged the surveyors to pay particular attention to the different types of erosion taking place in the country.[13]

Meanwhile, at the suggestion of the Secretary of State for Colonies, Governor Harold Kittermaster established the Native Welfare Committee in 1935 with the express purpose of promoting the welfare of natives by general material development along social, economic and political lines.[14] In fact, this policy was in tandem with the British colonial system of trusteeship under which the Africans too had to have a share, albeit a controlled one, in the development of the territory. It was generally believed that the Native Welfare Committee was to be advisory in nature and not simply executive. It would coordinate the work of various departments, including the medical, education, forestry, veterinary and agriculture. From its inception, the committee was concerned with a variety of issues such as health and tsetse-fly control but it was agriculture that came to prominence throughout its operation.

---

10. A.J.W. Hornby, *Denudation and Soil Erosion in Nyasaland*.
11. Beinart dubbed this trend the ideology of conservationism while Vaughan, in her unpublished paper, noted that there was a mania for wildlife conservation in the 19th century, which came to be overshadowed by soil erosion in the 1930s. W. Beinart, 'Soil Erosion, Conservationism and Ideas about Development: a Southern African Exploration, 1900–1960', *Journal of Southern African Studies* 11 (1984): 52–83; M. Vaughan, 'Uncontrolled Animals and Aliens'.
12. MNA: A3/2/11
13. *Ibid.*
14. MNA: S1/148/35.

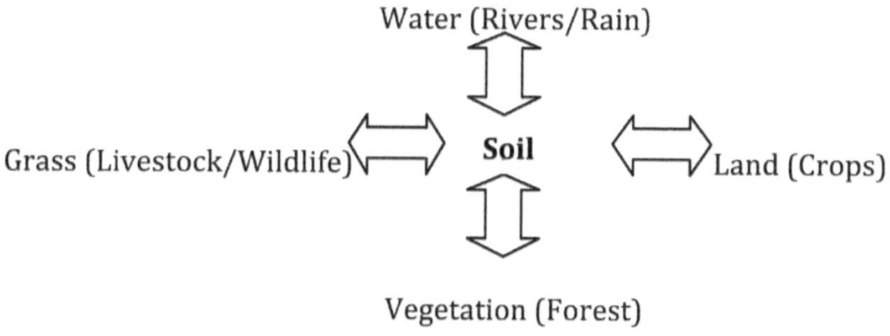

Origins of conservationist thinking in colonial Malawi, 1936–43

```
                    Water (Rivers/Rain)
                            ⇅
Grass (Livestock/Wildlife) ⇄   Soil   ⇄ Land (Crops)
                            ⇅
                    Vegetation (Forest)
```

Figure 4.1. Relationship between key natural resources linked by soil (erosion)

Another important change that occurred at that time was the creation of the Agronomic subcommittee of the Native Welfare Committee, which recommended a multi-sectoral approach to dealing with the issue of conservation. Thus, from that point onwards, the Agriculture, Veterinary and Forestry Departments began to work closely together. After two years of development, the major achievements of the Native Welfare Committee included (a) the recognition of the nature and extent of the problem of soil erosion in the Protectorate and bringing it to the national level for the first time; (b) the recommendation in 1936 to appoint a Soil Erosion Officer whose primary duty was 'to study the problem of soil erosion in its widest aspects and in conjunction with the Agricultural Department and the Native Administration, to prepare and operate long range plans for its control';[15] (c) the recognition that an ecological approach was needed to deal with the problem of soil erosion. As a precursor to the modern ecological approach, there was growing realisation that the problem was complicated and required a multi-disciplinary approach, which many ecologists including Jan Smuts and Edward Roux later came to advocate, although with emphasis on different perspectives.[16]

At this point, John Burton Clements, the Conservator of Forests, argued that

> an ecological approach to [the problem] is to be recommended and the affected areas must be divided and classified into regions for complete study not only of their present condition and of their normal erosion but also of the best means of ensuring as large a measure of control as may be possible. Present erosion must be checked and new erosion must be obviated, and the work is likely to entail administrative measures of a drastic nature.'[17]

---

15. MNA: FE 1/4/1
16. Peder Anker, 'The Politics of Ecology in South Africa on the Radical Left', *Journal of the History of Biology* 37/2 (2004): 303–331.
17. MNA: A3/2/162: Minutes of the Fifth Meeting of the Native Welfare Committee of 12 February 1936.

Scientific networking, ideology and the rise of conservation discourse

Writing as he did in 1936, this was a sharp warning about the coercive approach that would come into force in a few years' time. The initial responsibility was to be left with the soon to be appointed Soil Erosion Officer. Owing to the scantiness of qualified staff, little work was done in this area other than the mere passing of a series of legislative measures that were rarely reinforced until the late 1940s. Again, back in 1936, J.B. Clements had cautioned that

> it has to be recognised that scientific knowledge on the subject of tropical soils is at present insufficient to indicate as to what extent artificial amelioration is capable of adjusting that delicate balance, between soil formation and soil destruction, which exists under natural tropical vegetation and which is so rapidly upset when land is cultivated. Widespread research is therefore essential for ascertaining how to ensure the proper vegetation and humus conditions for the preservation of tropical soils. Only intensive studies of the problem, the ecological as well as other standpoints, are likely to reach a solution, and it is hoped that the work of the Soil Erosion Officer will contribute.[18]

Clements' views reflect the flexibility with which some colonial experts working on various aspects of Africa dealt with scientific knowledge.[19] It further shows that, while their ideas were not sacrosanct, they clearly understood their limits and looked up to other sources of knowledge while at the same time seeking the most appropriate models. At times, though, the ideas were shrouded in the prejudicial language and stereotypes of the time. Having recognised the problem, the state began, through the agency of the NWC, to put in place measures for its control. Although the NWC was supposed to work in African Trust Lands, it remained dominated by Europeans; the majority of members were white government officials and settlers. The only African who served briefly on the committee was George Simeon Mwase. He was appointed in February 1941 but relinquished his position a year later when he ran into conflicts with state authorities over a range of issues including racial discrimination.[20] In the next section, an examination of the scientific and ideological factors that facilitated colonial intervention in soil conservation will be presented.

In terms of export agriculture, Africans had to be encouraged to grow cash crops so that they could benefit from the wealth generated. The irony to all this is that during the same period, Sir Frank Stockdale, the Agricultural Adviser to the Secretary of State for Colonies, was busy promoting the idea that cash crop production was responsible for soil erosion: 'crops such as cotton, maize and tobacco must be regarded as highly erosive crops. Severe erosion dates from the period when high prices for cotton resulted in an attempt to produce as much cotton as possible.'[21]

---

18. MNA: FE 1/4/1
19. W. Beinart *et al.* 'Experts and Expertise'.
20. For further information on Mwase and his relations with the state, see his autobiography, *Strike a Blow and Die: A Narrative of Race Relations in Colonial Africa*.
21. MNA: NS 1/2/4: folio no.9.

Origins of conservationist thinking in colonial Malawi, 1936–43

By underscoring the impact of commercial agricultural production, Stockdale effectively subscribed to the argument raised in the case of the USA that careless farming and lack of state regulation were responsible for the cause of soil erosion in the Great Plains. Subsequent analyses of the Dust Bowl have also attributed this to capitalist interests. The solution often suggested for this was promoting small-scale farming, mixed farming and animal husbandry, use of compost or farm manure and training in anti-erosion methods.[22] This development represents contradictions in official policy-making and heralded the challenges that would be encountered later, at the point of implementation.

The continued publication of excoriating reports on land degradation went a long way towards sensitising colonial authorities to the gravity of the situation.[23] Many colonial officials maintained the perception that Africans were ignorant or inefficient with regard to use of natural resources. As late as the 1940s, Clements, the Conservator of Forests, wrote: 'It is universally recognised that, left to himself, the African will destroy his environment before he will learn conservation, and that such an event would be a catastrophe causing untold misery.'[24] Perceptions and representations such as these did nothing but ignite interest in conservation and the consequent intervention. Clements had also promoted the idea of community forests as a strategy to increase the rapid growth of forest cover in the colony. As we shall see in Chapter Six, a programme of village forest schemes, to be managed by village headmen and supervised by the District Commissioners in liaison with forestry staff, was launched in 1926. Second, the desire to promote African production, which also required restructuring land use practices, was no less influential in the minds of the conservationists. Realising that African production could no longer be ignored, the colonial agriculturalists did all they could to introduce new ways of production. Peasants were frequently accused of practising farming methods that encouraged land degradation. In 1936, for example, Capt. Hornby wrote, 'My eventual aim in cooperation with others through the Native Welfare Committee, is better hygiene and sanitation, better food, better animal husbandry as well as better agriculture, and the increase of the growing of cash crops, especially cotton.'[25] Realisation of this ideal entailed intensive use of land resources that were already considered degraded. It also required a multi-sectoral approach, which drew on knowledge and expertise from various disciplines.

---

22. See Donald Worster, 'The Dirty Thirties: A Study in Agricultural Capitalism', *Great Plains Quarterly* (1986): 107–116 and Harry C. McDean, 'Dust Bowl Historiography', *Great Plains Quarterly* (1986): 117–126.
23. Apart from the Agricultural Survey reports mentioned previously, see also the earlier work by F. Dixey et al. *The Destruction of Vegetation and its Relation to Climate, Water Supply, and Soil Fertility*.
24. MNA: S 47/1/5/1: J.B. Clements' memo of 11 February 1944.
25. MNA: A3/2/226.

Scientific networking, ideology and the rise of conservation discourse

By the late 1930s, conservation had become one of the most important policy issues in colonial Malawi, transcending all the parochial and independent activities that had hitherto been carried out by the Departments of Game and Forestry. The accumulation of vast amounts of knowledge about the country's environment and the influence of external factors and scientific networks all contributed immensely to the rekindling of interest in the debate on conservation of natural resources.[26] It was against this background that the interventionist state launched an impassioned campaign for conservation in which vast amounts of land had to be conserved or protected, particularly to arrest the problem of soil erosion. In 1939 a new policy on soil conservation came into effect and agricultural staff in all parts of the country were instructed to implement it with vigour and relentlessness.[27] The state encouraged Africans throughout the territory to use such conservation measures as box-ridging, terracing and bunding in their farming operations.

The Dust Bowl syndrome

Increased interest in soil conservation in colonial Malawi was also greatly influenced by conservation ideas and land use practices in the United States of America. It was in the USA that the idea of conservation as a progressive and scientific practice emerged in the last quarter of the nineteenth century, spurring a great deal of debate on the use and management of natural resources. The conservation movement there came to a climax at the turn of the century, spearheaded by such well-known personalities as Theodore Roosevelt, Gifford Pinchot, Frederick Newell and later Victor Shelford, Aldo Leopold and Frederick Clements.[28] One of the major characteristics of the movement was the emphasis placed on the rational use of resources, with a focus on efficiency, planning for future use and the application of expertise to broad national problems.[29] For many years, orthodox scholarship held the view that it was from the USA that most conservation ideas spread to former British colonies in eastern and southern Africa, including Malawi. Beinart has, however, since revisited that idea and now emphasises the hybridity of scientific knowledge,

---

26. For more details on external factors, see J. McCracken, 'Experts and Expertise in Colonial Malawi'. Mandala also discusses this issue within the context of the Lower Shire Valley. See Chs. 4 and 5 of his *Work and Control in Peasant Economy*.

27. See Nyasaland Government, *Land Conservation Policy*, Circular No. 1 of 1939, dated 25 January 1939.

28. See, for example, Theodore Roosevelt, 'Conservation' in T. Roosevelt, *The New Nationalism*, ed. by W.E. Leuchtenburg (Prentice-Hall, 1961) pp. 49–76; Aldo Leopold, *A Sand County Almanac* (New York, 1949); Donald C. Swain, 'Conservation in the 1920s', in Roderick Nash, *American Environmentalism* (New York: McGraw-Hill, 1990) pp. 117–25.

29. See, for example, Samuel B. Hays, *Conservation and the Gospel of Efficiency: the Progressive Conservation Movement, 1890-1920* (Cambridge, Mass: Harvard University Press, 1959).

The Dust Bowl syndrome

with much of the empirical data coming from South Africa itself.[30] While the conservation discourse had already been set up by the travel literature of the colonial encounter it was the Dust Bowl that amplified ecological concerns. Generally, it was assumed that degradation was a given fact and that it was a logical outcome of destructive land use practices. Although, in some cases little scientific evidence was presented, travel accounts warned that such a trend was likely to continue unless necessary measures were taken.

That the Dust Bowl ideology affected Africa is neither new nor contested. Indeed many scholars have written on the connections and how they helped to prop up support for governments in the British Empire to intervene with conservation crusades.[31] The American experience provided them with an opportunity to see change in a different way, a way that assumed its necessity sooner rather than later. In many ways, the late colonial interventions in Africa's natural resources mirrored America's struggle to arrest an ecological decline. Such experiences were to be transferred and implemented in the former British colonies. The power of ideology was also critical in lending support to local scientific initiatives on conservation. Reports by scientists and colonial technical staff corroborated the ideology that had been set in motion. This explains why the crusade continued even in the most difficult of times, when considerable opposition from both the Africans and some European settlers and state officials developed. Images of the Dust Bowl were quite strong and its shadows were being seen everywhere in British eastern and southern Africa.[32]

Although several scholars have attributed the change in British colonial thinking about conservation to the Dust Bowl, I would suggest that it was a particular combination of both local factors and external influences that led to the emergence of conservation consciousness in colonial Malawi. It was the unique constellation of very able men at a particular moment in time, aided by the necessary legislation and institutional framework, that propelled the establishment of a nascent conservation network.[33] The network had no formal structure as such but was ideologically very strong in terms of the issues discussed and the passions involved, the goal it sought to achieve and the character of the individuals behind

---

30. See W. Beinart, 'Soil Erosion, Conservationism and Ideas about Development'. Beinart has since revisited the argument and advocated hybridity of ideas: *The Rise of Conservation in South Africa: Settlers, Livestock, and the Environment 1770–1950* (2003). See also P. Anker, 'The Politics of Ecology in South Africa'.

31. See Belinda Dodson, 'A Soil Conservation Safari: Hugh Bennett's 1944 Visit to South Africa', *Environment and History* 11/1 (2005): 35–53; Sarah Phillips, 'Lessons from the Dust Bowl: Dryland Agriculture and Soil Erosion in the United States and South Africa, 1900–1950', *Environmental History* 4/2 (1999): 245–266; and J.M. Powell, 'The Empire Meets the New Deal: Interwar Encounters in Conservation and Regional Planning', *Geographical Review* 43/4 (2005): 337–360.

32. See W. Beinart, 'Soil Erosion, Conservationism and Ideas about Development'.

33. Between 1930 and 1960, the most active people in conservation included P. Topham, R.W. Kettlewell, G.F.T. Colby, J.B. Clements and A.J.W. Hornby.

it. Driven by the desire to achieve an ecological balance between human beings and nature, the conservationists looked to the United States of America and the two settler colonies in the region as the models for implementing their ideas.

Although colonial Malawi was under British direct administration, South Africa had a significant influence on developments in the territory. From the early days of the establishment of protectorate rule, John Cecil Rhodes provided an annual grant of £10,000 to assist the new administration. In later years, some of the investors and scientific experts also tended to be drawn from those who had previously worked in South Africa or Southern Rhodesia. Little wonder then that Malawi's conservationist ideas, including the legislation and strategies, were to a large extent modelled on what had been introduced in the two territories. A case in point is the introduction of betterment schemes, which were initially experimented with in South Africa in the 1930s and later applied to Southern Rhodesia and Nyasaland in the 1940s. Technical experts like Frank E. Kanthack, Director of Irrigation in South Africa, had on a number of occasions provided advice to the northern British colonies of Malawi and Kenya and so had P.H. Haviland who carried out some agricultural studies in colonial Malawi and Southern Rhodesia.

Externally, the role of the Dust Bowl in the United States cannot be over-emphasised. Indeed, during the reign of Dr Hugh H. Bennett, Director of the United States Soil Conservation Service, the Colonial Office in London was inundated with literature and training opportunities for colonial staff, which were in turn despatched to former colonial possessions. At the same time, pressure was mounting from Southern Rhodesia and South Africa for Nyasaland to act quickly and before the situation developed into a crisis. Most of the interaction appears to have been among technical experts, with South Africans visiting Nyasaland, but there is at the moment no evidence of any people from Nyasaland travelling to South Africa. In addition, Beinart (1984, 2007) and Anderson (1984) maintain that conservation was a product of the emergence of western scientific thinking about ecology in the colonies.[34] A few years earlier, McCracken argued that conservation programmes were part of wider official policies to reorganise the peasant economy and in this respect the state was heavily influenced by the growth of interest in environmental science throughout the Western world.[35] As part of the effort to reorient technical staff to matters of soil conservation, the SCS organised study tours for people responsible for soil erosion in British colonies. Accordingly, before assuming his duties as Soil Erosion Officer, Paul Topham undertook a visit to the USA in 1936. Under the sponsorship of the Carnegie Foundation, he visited several states in the Great Plains that had been affected by the Dust Bowl. The purpose

---

34. See W. Beinart, 'Soil Erosion, Conservationism and Ideas about Development in Southern Africa'; David Anderson, 'Depression, Dust Bowl, Demography and Drought: the Colonial State and Soil Conservation in East Africa during the 1930s', *African Affairs* 83 (1984): 321–43; and John R. Potter '*Mizimu*, "Demarcated Forests" and Contour Ridges'.

35. K.J. McCracken, 'Experts and Expertise in Colonial Malawi'.

The torchbearers of conservation

of the tour was described as being 'to enable him to see the latest developments in the work of the United States Soil Conservation Service'.[36] Afterwards, he wrote an elaborate report that was eventually serialised by Oxford University as part of the Imperial Forestry Institute Papers.

The torchbearers of conservation

The interest in soil conservation in Malawi could not have proceeded very far without the commitment of a group of individuals whose shared vision propelled the movement. Although many of the colonial technical staff we discuss here may not have considered themselves conservationists as such, a scrutiny of their ideas, beliefs and activities undoubtedly justifies their description as Malawi's foremost colonial conservationists. They include Paul Topham, J.B. Clements, Richard Kettlewell, A.J.W. Hornby and Geoffrey Colby, who acted as torchbearers of the incipient conservation movement. Granted that their influence was exercised at different times and in the various forums in which they sat, such as the Native Welfare Committee, the Postwar Development Committee, and the Natural Resources Board, their collective impact was nonetheless significant. As senior government employees, these individuals influenced others immensely inasmuch as they also helped to influence policy formulation. Their commitment ensured that their vision of creating a conservation-conscious nation did not lose its purpose and direction. This is the vision they worked for and by means of which, in 1952, the Director of Agriculture was able to report boastfully that the whole country had become conservation-conscious.

    A closer look at the background and experiences of each of these conservationists allows us to gain insights into why they worked so relentlessly against the tide of opposition. The first figure to note here is Paul Topham. Born in India, where his father had worked as a civil engineer, Topham attended Emmanuel College, Cambridge where he obtained a BA in Forestry. He immediately began a colonial service career in Nyasaland and, between 1926 and 1936, attended about four training courses at the Imperial Forestry Institute at Oxford , one of which led to his attainment of BSc degree in 1933. He wrote a thesis entitled 'The Physiography of Nyasaland and its Effects on the Forest Flora of the Country' under the guidance of Prof. R.S. Troup who subsequently remarked that 'as one of the examiners I can testify as to the thoroughness and capacity shown by Mr Topham in presenting his facts and conclusions. This type of work is of greatest value from the economic as well as from the scientific point of view and its encouragement in different colonies is much to be desired.'[37] Topham's fourth refresher course at Oxford coincidentally focused on issues of soil erosion, soil science and ecology and, as soon as he came back from that course, he proceeded on a study tour to the USA.

---

36. MNA: F1/3/1
37. MNA A3/2/198 – personal file, Topham 312.AII/Vol. II.

Scientific networking, ideology and the rise of conservation discourse

There he visited North Carolina, Mississippi, the Tennessee Valley Authority and Cornell University. He also had a chance to meet Dr Bennett, the Director of the US Soil Conservation Service. This prepared him intellectually and practically for the role he was to play in Malawi, particularly in defining the issues of erosion and in preparing documents for the incipient policies on soil conservation.[38] In 1937, Topham was seconded to the Agronomic Subcommittee of the NWC and became the first Soil Erosion Officer in the country – thus becoming the key link person on ecological conservation. For two years, he worked tirelessly to study the soil conditions of the country as well as to implement measures in selected areas of the country. However, in 1939, he went back to the Forestry Department as Assistant Conservator of Forests, a position he held until 1946. Thereafter, he worked briefly at Michiru Estate before leaving the country to assume a teaching position at Oxford University. Intellectually, he held the view that the true agricultural lands in Nyasaland were insufficient to support the existing population as well as to supply crops for export and for that reason it was necessary to work on maintaining the soil fertility in all cultivated areas. He further believed that, since land of temporary value is normally more difficult to protect than true agricultural land, it was important for Africans to cultivate defined arable land that could be easily protected.[39] An extract from one of his writings is quite instructive about his beliefs on forestry:

> The needs of individual species and of forest types were correlated with soils and their apparent age. This depends to a great extent on the physiography. The patchwork of soils of various ages and their correlation with vegetation presents very serious difficulties in accepting monoclimax and climax theories of succession. Useful data of 'what might have been', without fire or mankind, are generally unobtainable and can only be of academic interest so far as forests are concerned. A polyclimax philosophy, recognizing also that succession has almost everywhere been deflected, is of more practical value.[40]

These ideas – the protection and maintenance of arable lands and the consolidation of land holdings – were to become critical to the conservation crusade. Local observations captured in official reports of the 1920s and 1930s made frequent allusion to these issues, demonstrating ways in which knowledge and ideas about conservation transcended territorial boundaries.

Richard Kettlewell was another influential conservationist, providing expertise in the field of agriculture. Equipped with a BSc degree from Reading and a diploma in Agriculture from Cambridge, he began his career in Nyasaland in 1934; he rose through the ranks of the colonial service until he became the Direc-

---

38. Paul Topham, 'Land Conservation in Nyasaland: An Attempt at Widespread Control, 1937 to 1940', in *Farm and Forest* (Ibadan, 1945), Vol.6, pp.5–8 and another paper, 'Notes on Soil Erosion in the United States', Paper No.6 (Oxford: IFI, 1937).
39. MNA: S1/66/36.
40. P. Topham, Nyasaland Government, Forestry Department Annual Report, 1935.

The torchbearers of conservation

tor of Agriculture in 1951 and Minister of Lands, Natural Resources and Surveys in 1959. Under the governorship of Colby, he became closely associated with and responsible for the highly controversial *malimidwe* policies. As a top agricultural officer, he launched a strenuous campaign to conserve the country's natural resources, which were assumed to be in danger of being overwhelmed by an alarming growth in population and the consequent threats of serious soil erosion.[41] Kettlewell had amassed experience by serving all over the country, especially the northern and central parts. During the Second World War, he served in the military in Ceylon for three years and was released in March 1943 to return to Nyasaland. He was also the author and principal architect of Malawi's postwar agricultural policy and many other articles on agricultural production.[42]

Geoffrey Colby also played a key role in the promotion of soil conservation policies. After graduating from Cambridge, he joined the colonial administrative service in Nigeria from 1925 to 1948. He came to Malawi in 1948 as Governor of the Protectorate. Dubbed the 'development governor', Colby presided over the most turbulent period in colonial Malawi's agrarian history.[43] It was during his administration, 1948 to 1956, that important laws and policies on the conservation of natural resources were passed and implemented. And these laws gave rise to peasant resistance in many rural areas of the territory.[44]

Another person who contributed to the collection and documentation of data was A.J.W. Hornby. Initially employed, in 1924, as the country's Agricultural Chemist in charge of Soil and Tobacco Investigations, he rose to become an Assistant Director of Agriculture and Agricultural Chemist by 1934 and then Acting Director of Agriculture in 1940. A holder of a BSc degree, he was later honoured with the title of Member of the British Empire (MBE) for his outstanding service. Hornby wrote quite extensively on agricultural issues of the country in the late 1920s and early 1930s, including on tea production, tobacco marketing and tung production. His writings are particularly important when one considers the fact that, apart from travel accounts, there was little work produced by technocrats in the early years of colonial rule.[45]

The history of conservation in colonial Malawi would not be complete without the name of John Burton Clements, a man who promoted conservationist ideas in the early years of British colonial rule. Having joined the colonial service in Malawi in 1920 after completing a BSc degree in Forestry at Edinburgh University,

---

41. See his obituary, which appeared in *The Times*, London, dated Monday, 2 December 1994.
42. R.W. Kettlewell, *Agricultural Change in Nyasaland: 1945–1960* (Stanford: Food Research Institute, 1965), Vol.5 pp. 229–285; also *An Outline of Agrarian Problems and Policy in Nyasaland* (Zomba: Govt Printer, 1955).
43. See Colin Baker, *Development Governor: a Biography of Sir Geoffrey Colby* (London: British Academy Press, 1994).
44. G.F.T. Colby, 'Recent Developments in Nyasaland', *African Affairs* 55/21 (1956): 273–282.
45. See A.J.W. Hornby, *Denudation and Soil Erosion in Nyasaland*.

he rose to become head of the forestry unit in the Department of Agriculture. He worked hard to move Forestry out of Agriculture, a process that came to fruition in 1929. As part of the small bureaucracy living close together in the colonial capital of Zomba, Topham worked with many of the leading conservationists including Kettlewell. He believed firmly in the rational and effective use of land resources and worked hard to protect the rich forest resources of the territory until his retirement in 1946. He also published quite extensively on forestry matters as well as on land use in the country.[46] He was one of the longest serving officers, with twenty six years of service, seventeen as head of the Forestry Department. After 1946, the man who provided expertise in forestry was R.G.M. Willan who, like Kettlewell, had served in the military during the Second World War. He acted as Chief Conservator of Forests for some years but effectively took charge of the department in 1950.

From the early 1930s until the late 1950s, these individuals worked tirelessly in their different portfolios to conserve the country's natural resources. As pointed out earlier, the issues of soil erosion and land utilisation did not receive much attention in the initial years and were carried out by the Forestry unit in the Department of Agriculture. By the early 1940s, there was a new focus on what in modern terminology we might call as integrated land use management and not just crop production. It is to the credit of these individuals that much research into and documentation of Malawi's ecological history began to be carried out. They made the subject of soil conservation feature prominently in the overall policy documents of the colony as well as allowing it to assume a multi-sectoral dimension, involving the Agriculture, Forestry and Veterinary Services Departments. In the absence of any trained ecologist at the time – after all, the field of ecology was in its infancy – they may be considered the harbingers of Malawi's modern environmentalism who set the stage for the rise of a conservation network.

Scientific research and training institutions

In order to appreciate the value and significance of the scientific ideas that conservationists in Nyasaland promoted we need to understand the role played by the Universities of Oxford and Cambridge. Many of the technical staff received all or part of their training at one of the two universities. The Imperial Forestry Institute at Oxford also served to provide practical experience to colonial officials and it was a unique training ground for many people who ended up championing conservation in colonial Southern Africa.[47]

---

46. See, for example, his article, 'Land Use in Nyasaland', *Imperial Forestry Institute Paper No.9* (Oxford, 1935).

47. David Anderson has noted that some of the agricultural staff who joined the colonial service in East Africa had received their training in tropical agriculture from the Imperial College of Tropical Agriculture in Trinidad.

Scientific research and training institutions

Table 4.1. Nyasaland Colonial Staff Trained at the IFI

Name	Training at IFI	Position
Clements, BSc (Edinburgh)	July 1930 refresher course Oct–Nov 1933 at IFI 1937: refresher course	Conservator of Forests
Topham, BA (Cantab), BSc (Oxon)	1926 1930 Hilary Term – Systematic Botany, Forest Management, Colonial Land Tenure 1933 Forest Ecology, Systematic Botany, Forest Management 1936 IFI for 8 weeks – emphasis on soil erosion	Assistant Conservator of Forests Soil Erosion Officer
Carver	1928 Trinity Term – studied Tropical Silviculture, Systematic Botany Apr–May 1935 Forest Management, Ecology, Soil Science	Assistant Conservator of Forests
Townsend, BA Dip.For (Oxon)	1936 Trinity Term – focus on soil problems, regional and vegetation surveys	Assistant Conservator of Forests

So, what did these conservationists in colonial Malawi have in common? Almost all the senior forestry staff who served in Malawi between 1924 and 1950 had attended some of the refresher courses at the Imperial Forestry Institute at Oxford (see table above). Established in 1924 at the recommendation of the British Empire Forestry Conferences of 1920 and 1923 and the Interdepartmental Committee on Imperial Forestry Education in 1921, the Institute became a *de facto* provider of ideas and theories about conservation of colonial natural resources. The first Director of the Institute, Prof. R.S. Troup, was a keen supporter of short-term refresher courses for colonial forestry staff. It is well to remember that, until the 1940s, the issue of soil conservation was under the purview of the Forestry Department in Nyasaland. Perhaps one factor that helped the Forestry Department take a lead in the drive for conservation of natural resources was the role played by Clements and Topham, two of colonial Malawi's prominent forestry officials. These individuals made sure that the issue of conservation received as much attention as possible within the colonial set-up. It was only much later, and particularly with the arrival of Kettlewell, that the Department of Agriculture began to take a more active role.

The Imperial Forestry Institute was primarily intended as a research and training organisation for the British Empire and was headed by a full Professor of forestry. In fact, until the mid 1940s, Oxford remained the only university offering higher training and research in forestry in England and therefore played a key role in providing forestry education to officers in the colonial forest service. The fame and status of the Institute were not admired by all. On a few occasions, IFI was accused of monopolising postgraduate training in forestry, using state resources.[48] It offered a variety of courses that were tailored to meet the diverse needs of the colonial empire, including Silviculture, Tropical Systematic Botany, Structure and Properties of Wood, Utilisation of Tropical Forest Products, Forest Management, Colonial Land Tenure, Ecology, Soil Science, Surveying and Engineering and Practical Instruction. Almost every member of the Forestry Department, which was initially responsible for soil conservation, attended some of these training courses at Oxford. When J. Oliphant took over the headship of the Institute in 1936, he sought support from the Carnegie Foundation of New York to sponsor study tours to the US Soil Conservation Service. It was in this connection that, on 21 November 1936, the Secretary of State wrote to the Governor of Nyasaland that, at the suggestion of Oliphant, Director of IFI, Mr Topham travels to the USA together with an officer from Palestine to study soil conservation work there. Oliphant and his staff were particularly interested in monitoring the practical implementation of conservation ideas learned at the Institute. Correspondence between Nyasaland colonial staff and IFI corroborates this point.

The IFI was viewed in very positive terms by the Nyasaland colonial service. On 26 February 1934, J.B. Clements observed: 'I consider that a sound knowledge of soil science is highly desirable in forest officers appointed to Africa, and I suggest that some acquaintance with the subject is necessary before the final year spent at the IFI, even if only to afford a proper appreciation of the close relations between soils, plant ecology and silvicultural practice.'[49] Similarly, in response to a questionnaire sent by Director Oliphant, Clements wrote in 1946, 'in postgraduate training of officers nominated to African colonies, it is suggested that a short course on native agricultural systems and economic usage of land would be of great value. These subjects are of vital political and scientific importance. Forest officers work in very close cooperation with political officers and are constantly advising on land policy generally.'[50] At the same time, the Institute also made available resources for colonial forestry staff to publish their works in the *Empire Forestry Journal* (*EFJ*). Between 1926 and 1940, the *EFJ* published papers by several key personnel in Malawi's conservation campaign such as Clements, Topham, Carver, Willan and Townsend.[51]

A close scrutiny of the published papers, annual reports and other writings shows that the conservationists were greatly influenced by Frederick Clements' theory

---

48. Although the Universities of Cambridge and Edinburgh ran some degree courses in Forestry, they complained about the dominance of Oxford and wanted an open door policy to run similar programmes. See *Nature* 119/2988 (5 February 1927): 197.
49. MNA F1/3/1
50. MNA F1/3/1
51. For example, see the works of Clements (1926 & 1933), Topham (1930), R.G.M. Willan (1940), Carver and Webb, all of which appeared in this journal.

Scientific research and training institutions

of plant succession and grassland ecology.[52] Clements had argued that, 'succession is inherently and inevitably progressive. As a developmental process, it proceeds as certainly from bare area to climax as does the individual from seed to mature plant.'[53] A succession of plant groups went through a staged sequence to become the final adult form or terminal formation. In relation to natural resources, the theory maintained that vegetation is critical for the conservation of water and land resources. In working for the conservation of resources in colonial Malawi, many technocrats sought to put into practice some aspects of this theory. They believed that most of the plant successions had actually reached their terminal point and hence required conservation. On the other hand, the areas that had been denuded of vegetation had to be afforested. In particular, hilly areas were identified as suitable for the regeneration of grass and forest cover. During their training at IFI, forestry staff from Nyasaland were exposed to this theory and used it to explain ecological conditions in the territory. For example, in his application for a training course at Oxford, Carver, another forestry official, had specifically mentioned the climax theory as one of the topics he wished to learn more about. It is to the activities of the Institute, which had sowed early seeds of conservation, rather than to the Dust Bowl that we must look for a deeper understanding of the science and practice of conservation, at least in the case of Nyasaland.

Table 4.2. Key Staff of the IFI

Name	Position	Period
Robert Scott Troup	Director of IFI	1924–1935
Joseph Burtt Davy	Head of Systematic Botany	1925–1940
John Ninian Oliphant	Director of IFI	1936–1944
H.G. Champion	Director of IFI	1944–early 1950s

The conservation movement was aided by training and professional support provided by the IFI. The cordial relations established with Institute's staff certainly encouraged colonial experts to link up their ideas with practical work on the ground. Two individuals were particularly influential in this regard. Joseph Burtt Davy was a Systematic Botanist who began his career in the Department of Botany at the University of California. He later joined the US Department of Agriculture in Washington as an Assistant Curator before moving on to work as an Agrostologist and Botanist in the Department of Agriculture in Pretoria, South Africa from 1903–1913. While there, he collected about 14,000 specimens of different plant species in the Transvaal province and was also credited with the establishment of the

---

52. For detailed information on grassland ecology, see Frederick Clements; also James C. Malin, *The Grasslands of North America: Prolegomena to its History* (Lawrence, Kansas: James C. Malin, 1947), especially pp. 120–168.
53. F. Clements, 'Plant Succession: an Analysis of the Development of Vegetation', *Carnegie Institute Publications* 242 (1916): 1–512, 82

Division of Botany, the precursor to the current South African National Biodiversity Institute. He was instrumental in the establishment of a maize-breeding centre at Vereeniging as well as in the introduction of plants and seeds from different parts of the world such as the forage crop, *teff* and the lawn grass, *kikuyu*. In 1925, after obtaining a PhD from Cambridge he joined Oxford University where he became Head of the Department of Systematic Botany at IFI until his death in 1940. He was very influential in the development of tropical forest botany and ecology in the empire and published extensively on the subject. In 1929, he visited Nyasaland to study the forest flora of the territory and had a joint publication with Topham in the *Kew Bulletin* of 1930/31.

Robert Scott Troup was a great exponent of the idea of scientific forestry in the British Empire. He began his career in 1897 by joining the Indian Forest Service with a posting to Burma. In 1906, he was stationed at the Forest Research Institute and College at Dehra Dun. Subsequently, he was promoted to the position of Assistant Inspector-General of Forests to the government of India where he served until 1915. In 1920, he became Professor of Forestry at Oxford University, succeeding the distinguished German forester, and his mentor, Sir William Schlich. In 1924, he became Director of the IFI, a position he relinquished in 1936, to be succeeded by Prof. H.G. Champion. Although his initial interests lay in the Indian subcontinent, he later broadened his scope through various tours to study forestry in many parts of the colonies, including Africa. He died in 1939 at the age of 64. He is particularly renowned for championing ideas of scientific forestry to postgraduate probationers and research courses. He published extensively and one of his booklets on colonial forest administration, *Save Our Soil*, was widely used to promote soil conservation in Nyasaland.[54] Perhaps the chief landmark of his career was the publication of a monumental three-volume work on *Silviculture of Indian Trees* in 1921–22. These books, which contain valuable information on the propagation and management of Indian species, were widely used to train government forest officers, personnel from wood based industries and individuals in cultivating forest trees using scientific methods. He laid a strong foundation for research in systematic forestry in India and was consequently honoured with the Most Distinguished Order of Saint Michael and Saint George (CMG) in 1934 for his outstanding service in the advancement of forestry in the colonies.

Scientific networking and hybridity of knowledge

The focus on hybridity of knowledge shows that previous scholarship may have over-emphasised the influence of the American Dust Bowl. We should use a much broader perspective and look at developments taking place elsewhere at the same time, for example in India and Nazi Germany where strong forestry scholarship

---

54. MNA PCN 2/3/1

Scientific networking and hybridity of knowledge

had been established.⁵⁵ But we also need to look at South Africa which had a viable research tradition in botany, ecology and veterinary medicine.⁵⁶ Although different conditions existed in all these areas, the ideas were circulated widely, not just to inform the colonial world about what was happening but also to present the possibility of adopting such ideas in local situations to conserve natural resources.

Throughout the colonial period, contacts were maintained between London and her various colonial possessions. In the first place, almost all the IFI professors had at one time or the other worked in the colonies in Africa or Asia. Both Burtt-Davy and Troup had extensive work experience in South Africa, the USA and India while H.G. Champion worked in India as a silviculturist. Like Troup, Champion published extensively on the preliminary classification of the main types of forests occurring in India (including parts of Burma and Pakistan). Oliphant had been Director of Forestry in Malaya before assuming the position of Chief Conservator of Forests in Nigeria.⁵⁷

One of the lessons learnt from the First World War was the plight of timber supply in the UK and the need of developing large resources in tropical forests of the colonies. To this effect, schools of forestry, which had been established in Edinburgh, Cambridge and Oxford at the turn of the century, increasingly began to play a central role in training personnel. Elsewhere, in the Dominion territories such as India, Canada and Australia, efforts were made towards establishing training and research centres. Hence, the IFI was financed by grants from the Colonial Office and the UK Forestry Commission as well as contributions from some of the dominions and empire territories. Apparently, an understanding had been reached with Colonial Office that all forestry graduates recruited to the Colonial Forestry Service should spend a postgraduate year on a special course designed to meet the special conditions of the colonial forests. In terms of research, what was to be done in the forests concerned such areas as preparation of preliminary forest floras and the systematic study and identification of timbers. The IFI also served as an information centre on forest literature of the world and the experience of specialists. In 1938, the IFI underwent some structural reorganisation. It was merged with the School of Forestry and became a University Department under a professor. By 1950, the Institute reported that nearly 220 officers in the colonial forest service had attended a postgraduate course at Oxford. Training was also opened to forest officers from India and Pakistan as well as Australia, New Zealand, South Africa, Southern Rhodesia and the Sudan and Canada and the United States.

---

55. See R. Grove, *Green Imperialism*; William H. Rollins, 'Whose Landscape? Technology, Fascism, and Environmentalism on the National Socialist Autobahn', *Annals of the Association of American Geographers*, 85/ 3 (1995): 494–520; and Raymond H. Dominick, 'The Nazis and the Nature Conservationists', *Historian* 49/4 (1987): 508–38.

56. See W. Beinart, *The Rise of Conservation in South Africa*; and P. Anker, 'The Politics of Ecology in South Africa'.

57. See Peter Vandergeeste and Nancy Lee Peluso, 'Empires of Forestry: Professional Forestry and State Power in Southeast Asia', Part 2, *Environment and History* 12 (2006): 359–93.

Scientific networking, ideology and the rise of conservation discourse

By 1950, the IFI was actively involved in research and networking. It had published over 400 research papers in technical journals such as *Empire Forestry Journal*, *Quarterly Journal of Forestry* and the *Journal of Ecology*. The Institute also published 'Checklists of Forest Trees and Shrubs' for Uganda, Nyasaland, Gold Coast, Ceylon and Tanganyika. The Institute exchanged correspondence and publications with forest technocrats in the colonies and elsewhere and in some cases made frequent field visits to forest reserves and botanical gardens. In fact, Champion, one time Director of the Institute, noted that 'breadth of view is further ensured by contact with the foresters of continental countries during tours which are arranged in France and Switzerland (and formerly, also Germany, Austria, and Czechoslovakia) regularly, and periodically, in Sweden, Denmark, Norway, Belgium, and Holland. Study tours have also been arranged in Italy, Finland, Portugal, and even further afield.'[58]

South Africa also made a contribution to the rise of conservationism and the development of a new thinking on the management of the environment. From 1929, a serious debate emerged and for many years came to be dominated by the ideas of ecological holism and mechanism, representing two competing brands of ecology. Championed by Jan Christian Smuts and John Phillips, ecological holism theory was premised on the idea that, since there was a diversity of environments and peoples, the purpose of ecology was to discover the essential natural relationships between species and their environments as a basis for colonial social organisation and control.[59] The political implication of this theory was to naturalise racial differences – in an ecological society people of different racial groups would naturally find their places in the landscape. The distribution of political rights and opportunities would follow from one's racial standing in the hierarchy of beings. On the other hand, the competing theory of ecological mechanism was espoused by Lancelot Hogben of the University of Cape Town and Edward Roux. In the UK, Arthur George Tansley of the Oxford School of Imperial Ecology emerged as one of its greatest exponents. The theory sought a paternally managed ecological economy that understood nature as a malleable social resource. Its exponents held the view that science should be used to ease the plight of the poor and that there was a need for total reconstruction of science education to reflect a practical and more socially responsible science.

These debates placed more pressure on governments to formulate postwar policies on conservation. For British colonies in southern Africa, ecological holism smacked of segregation and hence could not be adopted. The other problem was that it had a rather idealist foundation. By not stressing the material basis, it was of little practical value to deal with the problems of society and supply a foundation

---

58. H.G. Champion, 'The Silver Jubilee of the Imperial Forestry Institute', *Journal of Forestry* 49/7 (1951): 486.

59. P. Anker, 'The Politics of Ecology in South Africa on the Radical Left', *Journal of the History of Biology* 37/2 (2004): 303–331.

for science. It seems plausible to argue that the British colonial government opted for the ecological mechanism theory of the Oxford School and this may explain why many technical staff went to the IFI in the UK. Based on scientific research in botany, ecology, forestry, animal ecology and veterinary studies, the mechanist theory emphasised intervention to avoid further destruction of resources. There was also the idea of patronage of networks.

The notion of conservation was also influenced by ideas prevalent in some European countries at the time. In the 1920s and 1930s, for example, organised scientific studies of soil in Europe were part of the fascist movement to address problems of mechanisation, which also began to question the role of capitalism in an imperial fascist movement. In Germany, environmental consciousness soared under the Nazis and was driven by scientific ecology, aesthetic desirability, the influence of Eastern philosophies, public health, promises of economic benefits, empathy for non-human life forms and respect for God's creation. Although it did not initiate conservation, the National Socialist government has been credited with the development of environmental policies that represented a continuation of a tradition of German conservationism. In particular, it passed the Reich Nature Protection Law (RNG) which provided for the protection of wild birds, regulation of outdoor advertising, establishment of city planning, combating water pollution, creation of a conservation bureaucracy and citizen participation in the protection of nature. The Nazi ideology did not promote conservation *per se* but its emphasis on racialism and nationalism meshed with key aspects of progressive environmentalism, such as the concepts of natural monuments and nature protection areas.[60] Conservation was critical to demonstrate *voelkisch* nationalism as well as the power and greatness of Germany. They both focused on man-in-nature rather than emphasising nature alone. To understand why the conservationists supported the Nazis, Raymond Dominick argues that the two were not congruent 'but where their arguments converged, intellectual vortices began to spin, generating currents that swept a considerable portion of the conservationists toward the Nazi camp'.[61] The German conservation movement was much more complicated than much extant scholarship would have us believe. In a recent paper, Frank Uekötter has argued that conservationists did not necessarily share the ideological plane of the Nazis but used the latter's platform to advance their conservationist agenda. Unlike National Socialism, they did not find causes of nature destruction in racist or anti-Semitic ideas but rather attributed it to urbanisation and industrialisation. Conservationists had a pragmatic relationship with Nazis through which they gained power and influence to do what they could not before, such as creating nature reserves

---

60. R.H. Dominick, 'The Nazis and the Nature Conservationists'.
61. *Ibid*: 510.

without compensation to property owners. In the process they ended up violating the civil rights of the people.[62]

To the extent that conservation became a central aspect of the late colonial development policy, one can cogently argue that a strong network of conservationists, albeit not of the order reached in the USA, was in the making in colonial Malawi. It was a group of well-informed technocrats who interacted with the wider community of conservationists and developed interest in and promoted the study of natural resources of the country. The network was loosely organised, operated largely within government structures and had no elected leaders. However, this network did not last long, owing to the emergence of nationalist politics that polarised many activities of the movement. As conservationists sought to protect the natural resources of colonial Malawi by coercing Africans to carry out conservation measures, they met a lot of peasant resistance in the process.

Conclusion

In this chapter, attempts have been made to demonstrate ways in which the idea of conservation was constructed and represented in colonial Malawi. It has shown that although the sources of ideas were diverse, it was the activities of the IFI at Oxford that played a central role in framing and supporting the men on the ground who championed the conservationist cause. To the extent that IFI provided such training, literature and the general scientific knowledge colonial Malawi was well poised to move forward with its campaign for soil conservation.

---

62. See F. Uekötter, 'The Nazis and the Environment – a Relevant Topic?' in T. Myllyntaus (ed.) *Thinking Through the Environment: Green Approaches to Global History* (Cambridge: White Horse Press, 2011), pp. 40–60.

5

The Natural Resources Board and the Soil Conservation Campaign in Colonial Malawi, 1946–1964

> It would be no exaggeration to say that the Protectorate is now conservation conscious and much progress in this direction achieved in the past three years may be credited to the Provincial and District Natural Resources Boards. (Director of Agriculture, Government of Nyasaland, 1952).

Introduction

This chapter examines the legal and institutional arrangements created by the state to implement soil conservation policies in the postwar period. First, the chapter demonstrates that postwar colonial policies on conservation intensified the process of restructuring the African peasantry in ways that had never been done before. This involved the introduction of new meanings of resources and their organisation and use by African peasants. Through the agency of the Natural Resources Board (NRB), the state intervened at the point of peasant production with an assortment of conservation works, the most important of which included bunding, terracing and contour ridging. Such social engineering practice had significant ramifications for rural farmers. It brought about tensions and conflicts between the state and the peasantry just as it raised concerns about the suitability and efficacy of scientific and agricultural modernisation policies. As was the case elsewhere in the southern African region, the state backed its policies with an array of coercive laws that, as some scholars have argued, lacked a human face.[1] Imposing criminal penalties, fines and imprisonment and uprooting of crops only worked to provoke the wrath of the peasants. In many instances, peasants refused to comply with these harsh measures or, where they cooperated, did so only when they could derive benefits for themselves. Indeed, apart from open protest, as happened in Thyolo, Ntcheu and Domasi districts, many peasants engaged in hidden forms of resistance, involving refusal to undertake conservation measures, illicit destruction of conservation works

---

1. Matembo Nzunda, 'Of Law on Soil Conservation' (Paper presented at the Research and Publications Committee Conference, Chancellor College, 1993); Joan McGregor, 'Conservation, Control and Ecological Change: The Politics and Ecology of Colonial Conservation in Shurugwi, Zimbabwe', *Environment and History* 1 (1995): 257–79; Pamela Maack, 'We Don't Want Terraces! Protest and Identity under the Ulugulu Land Usage Scheme', in G. Maddox, J. Giblin and I. Kimambo (eds.) *Custodians of the Land: Ecology and Culture in the History of Tanzania* (London: James Currey, 1996) pp. 152–169.

The Natural Resources Board and the soil conservation campaign

and desertion from work.² In addition, the discussion explores in detail the role played by the NRB in shaping the lives of Malawi's peasants and their production processes. Between 1946 and 1962, the Natural Resources Board came to symbolise a tower whose authority radiated to every peasant farming community in colonial Malawi. The role of the NRB is highlighted as a specially created state institution responsible for implementing policies that created conflicts and tensions across the country. It is clear that, even with such wide powers and institutional support, the capacity of the Board to implement fully its rules and regulations was compromised by prevailing local conditions and African resistance.

The Postwar Development Committee, 1943–1946

In the preceding chapter, it was demonstrated that conservationists worked initially within the framework of the Agronomic subcommittee of the Native Welfare Committee. When this subcommittee ceased its operations in 1943, much of the soil conservation work was taken up by the newly formed Postwar Development Committee, a precursor of the NRB. In order to appreciate fully the role and functions of the NRB in colonial Malawi, it is important first to examine general agricultural policy in the immediate postwar period. This provides a broader context in which to study the circumstances leading to the emergence of ideas and strategies about conservation of soil and natural resources in general. It is important to note that, even before the War came to an end, British colonial officials had been promoting soil conservation as part of the larger postwar agricultural development policy in colonial possessions.³ In 1941, the Colonial Office established the Committee on Postwar Problems to look at ways of addressing a range of challenges generated by the War. For the most part, this meant economic development and for Nyasaland it entailed increasing agricultural production. In line with the wishes of the colonial office in 1943, the Governor appointed a Postwar Development Committee with as broad a mandate as the Native Welfare Committee of the preceding decade.⁴ One important feature of this development programme was the incorporation of conservation of natural resources and land use matters into its overall develop-

---

2. Interview: Mr Billiot Mlaliki of Nzundu Village, TA Nsabwe, Thyolo district, dated 28 May 1997. See also J. McCracken, 'Conservation and Resistance in Colonial Malawi'; and W.O. Mulwafu, 'Soil Erosion and State Intervention into Estate Production'.

3. David Anderson and William Beinart have argued separately that the official colonial mind began to change in the 1930s. See W. Beinart, 'Soil Erosion, Conservationism and Ideas about Development in Southern Africa'; and D. Anderson, 'Depression, Dust Bowl, Demography and Drought'.

4. The Agronomic Subcommittee of the Native Welfare Committee ceased its operations in 1943. The composition of the new committee was as follows: the Chief Secretary (Chair), the Financial Secretary (official member), and Sir William Tait-Bowie, M.P. Barrow, H.G. Duncan, A.F. Barron, Rev. J.J.D. Stegmann, J.A. Lee and J. Marshall as members.

The Postwar Development Committee, 1943–1946

ment strategy. Technical staff succeeded in convincing government to include soil conservation as one of the key activities for the future development of the territory.

Although by 1946 both Paul Topham, the Soil Erosion Officer and Assistant Conservator of Forests, and John Burton Clements, the Conservator of Forests, had retired from the Nyasaland colonial service, their absence on the ground did not in any way weaken the conservationist movement. At that time, Kettlewell had already emerged as a potent force and a *de facto* successor to these two on soil conservation issues. Significant institutional reforms also took place during this period. First, through the Land Usage Scheme of the Postwar Development Committee, the conservationists moved natural resources matters to the Department of Agriculture and, in order to give full attention to the issue of soil erosion, a Soil Conservation Unit was also established within the department. In 1945, the Postwar Development Committee reported in rather neo-Malthusian language that 'the facts of rapidly increasing population and rapidly declining soil fertility have already been sufficiently emphasized to make it clear that the country's capacity for supporting its own people is under an increasing strain'.[5] Second, it was in 1946 that the conservationists made a major recommendation, namely to introduce legislation for the conservation of natural resources in the country. This marked the birth of Natural Resources Ordinance of 1946, the enabling legislation for the establishment of the Natural Resources Board. In all these instances, conservationists wanted to give meaning and expression to their cherished ideals of protecting the country's natural resources while at the same time operationalising the scientific and ideological knowledge that had by that time become hegemonic.

The main objectives of Nyasaland's postwar agricultural policy were: first, conservation of natural resources; second, production of ample food for all; third, increased and more economical production of cash crops or increased output and quality of cash crops; and finally, promotion of the improved systems of land use.[6] In other words, emphasis was placed on programmes to ensure that not only was there 'a sufficiency of food and an adequate supply of cash crops for a growing population, but also that the natural resources, on which the country so vitally depends, are not destroyed in the process of increasing the production of crops'.[7] In many respects, this would prove a difficult objective to achieve. Although the peasants were not mentioned specifically in policy statements, government officials increasingly began to look to them for the realisation of these objectives. This reflected a shift in Nyasaland's agricultural policy from the initial pre-Depression emphasis on European settler production to a deliberate effort at promoting peasant production.[8]

---

5. *Report of the Postwar Development Committee* (Zomba: Government Printer, 1946), p. 111.
6. R.W. Kettlewell, *Agricultural Change in Nyasaland: 1945–1960* Vol.5, pp. 229–285.
7. Nyasaland Government, *Colonial Reports: Annual* (Zomba: Government Printer, 1953).
8. It is important to note that both the issue of natural resource conservation and food production were critical to peasant production. The state's agricultural intensification programmes added more pressure on peasants to produce food for the markets. See, for example, Elias

The Natural Resources Board and the soil conservation campaign

An important question in this discussion centres on what exactly caused the state in Malawi to begin placing so much emphasis on conservation of natural resources and food production in the postwar period. State interest in conservation and rural production appear to have been sparked by a combination of several factors. First, cumulative knowledge from numerous reports and surveys on the ecological status of the country had been published since the 1920s.[9] Some of these reports highlighted cases of environmental degradation, although the evidence for the same would be a source of contestation. The majority of reports were based on observations by colonial technical staff. Secondly, the effects of the Great Depression cannot be easily discounted for the European plantation sector had suffered severely and the colonial state sought to redirect its energies into the peasant sector, which tended to be more resilient.[10] But, for that to be done, a proper policy on the use of natural resources was deemed necessary. Third, Paul Topham, the Assistant Conservator of Forests and Nyasaland's first Soil Erosion Officer, together with J.B. Clements and Dick Kettlewell, played a vital role in sensitising and steering the territory towards the development of legislation and an institutional framework for the conservation of natural resources. They were men of vast experience and, during long careers spanning more than twenty years in the territory, they had collected a lot of data and published numerous reports and articles.[11] Fourth, Western scientific ideas about conservation were gaining greater currency throughout the eastern and southern African region and governments were compelled to intervene sooner rather than later.[12] Soil conservation was viewed as a necessary means of increasing production as well as achieving rural development.

Mandala, '"We Toiled for the White Man in Our Own Gardens": the Conflict Between Cotton and Food in Colonial Malawi', in Allen Isaacman and Richard Roberts (eds.) *Cotton, Colonialism, and Social History in Sub-Saharan Africa* (Portsmouth, NH: Heinemann, 1995); J. McCracken, 'Peasants, Planters and the Colonial State: the Case of Colonial Malawi, 1905–1940', *Journal of Eastern Africa Research and Development* 12 (1982): 21–33; L. Vail, 'The State and the Creation of Malawi's Colonial Economy', in R. Rotberg (ed.) *Imperialism, Colonialism and Hunger* (Lexington: D.C. Heath and Co. 1983).

9. J.B. Clements, 'Land Use in Nyasaland'; A.J.W. Hornby, *Denudation and Soil Erosion in Nyasaland*; P.H. Haviland, *Report on Soil Erosion Prevention and Reclamation of Eroded Arable Land in Nyasaland, 1930*.

10. C.A. Baker, 'Depression and Development in Nyasaland, 1929–1939', *The Society of Malawi Journal* 27/1 (1974): 7–26.

11. P. Topham, 'Land Conservation in Nyasaland: An Attempt at Widespread Control and 'Notes on Soil Conservation in the United States'; J.B. Clements, 'The Cultivation of Finger Millet'; R.W. Kettlewell, *Agricultural Change in Nyasaland* and *An Outline of Agrarian Problems and Policy in Nyasaland* (Zomba: Govt Printer, 1955).

12. W. Beinart, 'Soil Erosion, Conservationism and Ideas about Development: a Southern African Exploration; and D. Anderson, 'Depression, Dust Bowl, Demography and Drought'.

The role of the Natural Resources Board, 1946–1964

The role of the Natural Resources Board, 1946–1964

Prior to 1946, no comprehensive policy or legislation existed on the conservation of natural resources in the Protectorate. The laws already in place tended to be parochial and superficial in nature. They were often limited to sectoral issues of game, tsetse-fly control and forestry only – for these were key aspects of conservation that the colonial state preoccupied itself with in the first four decades after the establishment of colonial rule. However, as more interest developed in soil conservation in the 1930s, coupled with the viability of peasant economies, the understanding of natural resources also broadened. The Natural Resources Ordinance of 1946 defined natural resources as (a) the soils and waters of the Protectorate and (b) the trees, grasses and vegetable products of the soil. Land resources had come to occupy a central place in this definition, so that controlling soil erosion and maintaining soil fertility inevitably dominated the activities of the NRB.

Conservationists in Malawi were also greatly influenced by trends and developments elsewhere in the region. For instance, the promulgation of the 1946 Ordinance was based on the Southern Rhodesian Natural Resources Act of 1941, which had in turn been derived from the South African and American conservation laws of the 1930s. In the American case, conservation laws had been passed to deal with the harsh effects of the Dust Bowl in the agricultural areas of the Great Plains. A lot is also to be learnt from the South African experience of betterment schemes of the 1930s whereby a programme for the conservation of natural resources and agricultural development was implemented before the apartheid regime. The betterment schemes, which involved the forced relocation of Africans and the rehabilitation and planning of areas so as to provide for separate residential, grazing and farming, in many ways became a model for the territories north of the Limpopo River.[13] In order to reach out to the farmers, the American government created the Soil Conservation Service, a body that disseminated information and organised lectures and demonstrations on the use and management of natural resources.[14] Similar ideas were subsequently adopted in the Southern Rhodesian context.[15] In colonial Malawi, the ideas were not accepted without opposition; indeed debate ensued about the relevance and suitability of the American conservation laws. Lockhart-Smith, the Attorney-General at the time, minced no words in cautioning government about the wholesale adoption of the American model. He observed that 'the legislation is reported to have worked satisfactorily in the U.S.A., but of

---

13. See W. Beinart, *The Rise of Conservation in South Africa: Settlers, Livestock, and the Environment, 1770–1950* (Oxford University Press, 2008), pp. 332–366.
14. R. Douglas Hurt, *The Dust Bowl: an Agricultural and Social History* (Chicago: Nelson-Hall, 1981).
15. Ian Phimister, 'Discourse and the Discipline of Historical Context: Conservationism and Ideas about Development in Southern Rhodesia, 1930–1950' *JSAS* 12/2 (1986): 263–275.

The Natural Resources Board and the soil conservation campaign

course the financial resources and trained personnel at the disposal of the States of the Union are vastly in excess of those available here'.[16]

Many of the problems discussed later vindicate Lockhart-Smith's concerns. That notwithstanding, the law was enacted and a Board was established. But what is striking about the 1946 Ordinance is that, for the first time ever, it brought together various organs of the country's main natural resource sectors: game, forests, soil (land) and livestock.[17] The state had recognised the significance of legislating on the conservation and utilisation of all these natural resources.

One of the most important aspects of the Natural Resources legislation was contained in section 3(1) which provided for the creation of the Natural Resources Board. The Board itself had both advisory and executive powers. Its functions included general dissemination of natural resources propaganda to stimulate interest in conservation, promotion of conservation projects, recommendation of legislation on conservation, approval of works and apportionment of costs for conservation projects. The Board also had the power to make recommendations in relation to forest reserves and stock limitations, to set up local Conservation Councils and to carry out any other functions the Governor required.

The newly appointed Board consisted of three official members, with the Director of Agriculture as its executive officer, the Provincial Commissioner as its Chairman and the Conservator of Forests as a member. Three unofficial members were to be appointed by the Governor but with no representation from the African community. In spite of its small size and budget, the Board was mandated to deal with all matters of conservation of natural resources at a Protectorate level. This was undoubtedly a gargantuan amount of work.

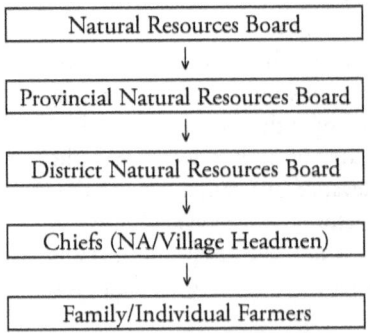

Figure 5.1. Structure of the Natural Resources Board

---

16. MNA S12/2/3/1: Natural Resources Board, February 1946–April 1949.

17. The issue of underground water resources was not part of the conservation crusade at this time. The state had primarily been concerned with the creation and protection of forest reserves in major catchment areas.

The role of the Natural Resources Board, 1946–1964

Barely a year after being constituted, the NRB issued an extremely alarming picture of the condition of natural resources in the country. It maintained that,

> if things are allowed to go on as they are, if people continue to ill-treat their soil which gives them everything they have, if soil is allowed to go on pouring down our rivers, if crops continue to be grown year after year on the same soil, if cattle are allowed to graze grassland bare- then there is no future for Nyasaland. There will be less and less to eat and there will be lower and lower yields from cash crops. The people will become poorer and poorer and hungrier and hungrier. The time will come when Nyasaland is a bare desert capable of supporting neither human beings nor animals and once this has happened nothing on earth can bring it back again.[18]

As of the late 1940s, that statement may have been presented with a degree of exaggeration; certainly the image of a bare desert resonated with fears that had been expressed in both South Africa and the USA and it is rather unlikely that the quality of the soil had declined to the extent of justifying such doom-saying. But it pointed to a trend that had been set and that future generations would wrestle with, particularly in the post-colonial period. As we demonstrate in Chapter Eleven, the success of the post-colonial agricultural-based economy was in many ways dependent on the exploitation of natural resources.

Although the conclusions of the report were meant to reflect the situation in all parts of the country, in the end they only identified six districts as being ecologically degraded and in need of immediate intervention. These were Thyolo, Zomba, Chiradzulu, Mzimba, Ntcheu and Fort Hill and, as elsewhere in the region, Africans were held responsible for this. In all cases, however, the general list of problems included unsuitable farming methods of agriculture, destruction of catchment areas, shifting cultivation, the burning of grass and inefficient animal husbandry practices. Establishing the cause and extent of environmental degradation has remained a controversial matter. Oral testimony presents rather different reasons for degradation. For instance, in the south, Lomwe immigration and pressure as a result of land alienation are presented as the major factors while, in the north, peasants in Fort Hill attributed degradation to the introduction of coffee production.

At any rate, it was against this background that the NRB sought to control soil erosion through the introduction of an assortment of preventive and regulatory measures directed against peasant producers. First, cultivation on steep slopes had to be discontinued. Hillsides were to be cultivated only if preserved by planting trees and grasses. Those slopes experiencing heavy water run-off after severe rains had to be protected with storm drains. Second, all farmers had to make box-ridges across the slope for planting annual crops. In areas where a slope was very steep, the cultivated land had to be bunded as well as box-ridged. Bunds had to be made at least eighteen inches high with a base of four feet. Except for grasses, no crops could be planted on these bunds. In areas that were very steep, the land had either

---

18. MNA PAM 650: *Soil Conservation in Nyasaland*, issued by the Nyasaland Natural Resources Board, (Zomba: Government Printer, 1947), p. 1

to be bench-terraced or put out of cultivation altogether. The Board prohibited any stream bank cultivation within a distance of eight yards from the river. Uncultivated areas had to be left to the growth of grass or planted with bananas, trees and bamboos. Anti-erosion measures also applied to paths leading to gardens and boundaries. These had to be bunded at intervals and planted with grasses. Similarly, compounds and buildings had to be protected with properly constructed water channels and the grounds planted with flat growing grasses. Creeping grasses had to be planted on all roadsides.

Where large quantities of livestock existed, the Board ordered the splitting up of herds into smaller units and bunding around kraals, dipping tanks and water holes. Cattle tracks had equally to be confined by fencing with hedges and bunding. Overgrazed areas had to be controlled by bunding of pasture-land and adoption of rotational grazing. There was to be no grazing on hillslopes, while *dimba* areas had to be used for production of dry season crops only. These measures were quite similar to those applied during the same period in other former British colonies in the region such as Southern Rhodesia, Lesotho and Tanzania and Kenya.[19]

In order to maintain soil fertility, the Board recommended the use of cattle manure, artificial fertilisers or compost. Farmers had to abandon shifting cultivation and instead adopt crop rotation or controlled shifting cultivation methods, since 'modern science has ... evolved a modification of the old system – this is to cultivate [land] for 3 to 4 years and then to rest [it] under grass'.[20] All these measures were to be achieved in the name of scientific ideology, which apparently provided a justification for intervention in and transformation of African land use practices. Progressive means were also used. For instance, a film, *Mangwende and the Trees*, was produced and used to propagate some of these ideas across the country.

One of the most important achievements of the Board in the initial years of its existence was the identification of what were considered local problem areas faced by Protectorate at the time in relation to conservation of natural resources. These included destocking, as in Ntcheu district, and erosion caused by storm water from roads, as in Thyolo district. The latter issue was more problematic in the sense that it required either the owners/occupiers of land adjoining public roads to be responsible for the disposal of storm water or the state to take responsibility through its Public Works Department. Related to this was the question of erosion in the vicinity of dipping tanks. Many Board officials had received reports from

---

19. Literature on this subject is extensive. Refer to W. Beinart, 'Soil Erosion, Conservationism and Ideas about Development in Southern Africa'; K. Showers, 'Soil Erosion in the Kingdom of Lesotho: Origins and Colonial Response'; J. McGregor, 'Conservation, Control and Ecological Change'; P. Maack, '"We Don't Want Terraces!"'; Ian Phimister, 'Discourse and the Discipline of Historical Context: Conservationism and Ideas about Development in Southern Rhodesia, 1930-1950', *JSAS* 12/2 (1986): 263–275; Fiona Mackenzie, 'Political Economy of the Environment, Gender and Resistance under Colonialism: Murang'a District, 1910–1950', *Canadian Journal of African Studies* 25/2 (1991): 226–56.
20. MNA PAM 650: *Soil Conservation in Nyasaland*, p.3.

veterinary staff, complaining that cattle going to and from the dipping tanks created tracks that contributed to soil erosion, a situation that had similarly raised a lot of controversy in Lesotho.[21] Finally, Board officials noted that the destruction of timber, particularly in tobacco producing areas in Central Province, reduced the supply of fuelwood, while at the same time exposing the land to erosive forces. Beyond the official reports, the details and extent of these problems were never elaborated until the Board was reorganised in 1949.

Another area where the Board achieved some degree of success was in disseminating conservation information throughout the countryside. In 1947, the NRB published an informational bulletin on soil conservation which, written in simple and straightforward language, attempted to explain the causes of erosion and the methods of controlling it. It was meant to be used by the Board's agents for propaganda purposes and it appeared in English and vernacular. The Board also unsuccessfully attempted to use postmark stamps bearing suitable slogans for propaganda purposes. By 1948, the only other achievement reportedly made by the Board at the local level was the implementation of destocking laws in the Livulezi area of the Ntcheu district. Aided by the Ntcheu District Conservation Council, the Board instructed Africans there to dispose of nearly 1,000 herds of cattle in four surrounding villages. This decision was part of the state effort to control overgrazing and erosion caused by overstocking.[22] Unlike in South Africa, where the state sustained a short but successful period of culling enforcement, no efforts were put in place to follow up and ensure lower stocking numbers over the longer term.

One of the thorniest problems the Board wrestled with in the initial years of its operation concerned soil conservation on private estates. In particular, it was about determining who should undertake conservation measures on land owned by private individuals or companies. Estate owners expressed the difficulty of persuading their tenants to carry out necessary soil conservation work. Under section 12(4) of the Ordinance the Board had power to order the owner or occupier of land to carry out such work as it might deem fit and, if the order were not complied with, to have the work carried out and debit the cost to the owner or occupier in question. But this was no easy task to achieve. In the first place, the Board was heavily understaffed to deal with the large number of tenants across the country. Furthermore, it was not feasible for the Board to recover the cost of undertaking conservation measures from every individual tenant or owner. While acknowledging its limited capacity, in 1947 the Board recommended that the government amend the law to provide instead for the eviction of tenants who refused to carry out soil conserva-

---

21. See K. Showers, 'Soil Erosion in the Kingdom of Lesotho: Origins and Colonial Response'; A. Mager, '"The People Get Fenced"'; W. Beinart and C. Bundy, *Hidden Struggles in Rural South Africa: Politics and Popular Movements in the Transkei and Eastern Cape, 1890–1930* (London: James Currey and Berkeley: University of California Press, 1987).

22. MNA S12/2/3: Minutes of Meeting of the Natural Resources Board for Nov. 1946. This issue is discussed in greater detail in Ch. 9.

tion measures as directed by the estate owner. The Board further recommended that the Conservation Council of the concerned district should advise the District Commissioner in each case as to whether an order for eviction was justified or not.

Figure 5.2. Chiefs attending a briefing meeting on a land improvement scheme as part of the soil conservation programme. In the background, there is an example of properly managed land. (Source: Dept of Agriculture Annual Reports, 1952–1955)

Despite these accomplishments, when measured against its statutory powers, the Protectorate Board's performance during the three years of its existence left much to be desired. It would be contended that it suffered from general ineptitude since virtually no action was taken on any of the crucial sections of the Ordinance. In terms of human capacity, it was badly handicapped and also lacked financial resources to implement decisions on the ground. Thus, most of its directives tended to operate at the level of propaganda. In some senses this reflected the limits of state power at a time when uncoerced policy implementation seems to have been more appropriate. Perhaps its greatest shortcoming was the limited contact it established with the peasants, the main target group for conservation. All members of the Board were either senior government officials working in Blantyre and Zomba or planters settled in the Thyolo and Lilongwe districts.[23] Hence, the Board tended to rely on Native Authorities and honorary Conservation Officers who lived in close proximity with the peasants. Chiefs too were involved but they

---

23. Members of the Board appointed on 17 May 1947 were: Mr D.W. Saunders-Jones, Provincial Commissioner, Central Province, as Chairman; the Conservator of Forests as an official member; the Director of Agriculture as its executive officer; and the Hon. G.G.S.J. Hadlow, OBE, of Cholo, Maj. F.D. Warren, MC, of Lilongwe and Mr L.J. Rumsey of Thyolo as unofficial members. See Government Notice No. 85/46.

The role of the Natural Resources Board, 1946–1964

had a rather controversial role to play. The Board had worked on the assumption that chiefs would cooperate and support their efforts in implementing the objectives of the Natural Resources Ordinance – a thing the chiefs did not always do.[24] Experience all over Africa shows that chiefs did not always act in the way the state expected them to; they were calculating individuals who could sometimes cooperate to benefit from the state and sometimes oppose it if they saw no benefits. In any case, some colonial government officials had already doubted the role of chiefs. As the Attorney-General complained, 'Native Authorities as administrative bodies are in their infancy, are sometimes incompetent, often idle and occasionally definitely obstructive'.[25] On the peasantry, the same official was unequivocally cynical: 'The peasant is notoriously conservative, and in one District at least a Native Authority has so far declined to make rules requiring its people to carry out methods of cultivation which it clearly regards as new-fangled and foolish'.[26] The relationship between peasants and chiefs vacillated according to the mutual interests of the two groups. But their conservative attitude and resistance to new ideas raises questions about the ideological differences and interpretations underlying the campaign for conservation. From the point of view of the colonial state, the display of a conservative attitudes necessitated more forceful intervention.

The second major weakness was that, although its principal mandate was to coordinate and supervise the conservation of natural resources among Africans, there was no African representative on the Board.[27] The reliance on European honorary conservation officers did not make matters any better. To begin with, none of them had any training in conservation work but were appointed under section 18(1) of the Ordinance ostensibly to 'provide the Board with representations throughout the Protectorate who will be able to bring to the Board's notice any pertinent matters which may come to their notice in the vicinity in which they reside'.[28] The appointed individuals appeared on paper as conservation officers but their real work never made any substantial impact on the ground. It might be argued that

---

24. Interview: Mai Gladys Nthyola and Mai Emmie Mbulaje of Nkuzang'ombe village, TA Malemia, Zomba district, dated 14 May 1997.
25. MNA S12/2/3/1: Attorney-General's Report on the 'Legal Aspect of Soil Conservation', p.6.
26. MNA S12/2/3/1: Attorney-General's Report on the 'Legal Aspect of Soil Conservation', p.6. For comparative experiences on the attitude of chiefs, see Grace Carswell, 'Soil Conservation Policies in Colonial Kigezi, Uganda: Successful Implementation and an Absence of Resistance' in W. Beinart and J. McGregor (eds.) *Social History and African Environments* (James Currey, 2003) pp. 131–154.
27. The complete list of Conservation Officers for the entire country consisted of the following: in Blantyre district, Mr J. Sibbald, Maj. A.J.W. Hornby, MBE, and Mr J. Kaye-Nicol; in Zomba district, Mr T.W. Williamson, Mr G.V. Thorneycroft; in Lilongwe district, Hon. R. McFadyen, and Mr Widdas; in Thyolo district, Mr J.W. Pryor, the Hon. M.P. Barrow and Mr G.D. Hayes; in Mulanje district, Mr J. Ramsden and Mr C.E. Snell; in Mzimba district, Mr C.E. Boardman; and in Karonga district, Mr W.A. Maxwell. None of these individuals was ever employed as a full-time member of staff of the Board.
28. MNA S12/2/3/1: Natural Resources Board, February 1946–April 1949.

The Natural Resources Board and the soil conservation campaign

these Soil Conservation Officers were appointed mainly for political expediency. It was assumed that, since they were important figures in local politics, they would necessarily be able to influence their own people to practise soil conservation works. Although in many territories educated Africans were beginning to be incorporated into the lower ranks of the civil service, there were very few of them in colonial Malawi. The issue of loyalty to the state also appeared to have been taken into account before appointing Africans to decision-making positions.

The fourth weakness of the Board was that, writ large, the entire approach to conservation was ill-conceived. The Board had adopted ideas from the American experience with the Dust Bowl which focused on propaganda, mainly through lectures and demonstrations. For British colonies in Africa, the assumption was that propaganda would similarly arouse public interest in the adoption of conservation measures. That could well have been effective if economic resources had been readily available. For Nyasaland, however, lack of financial resources and poor communication networks hampered the effective dissemination of information to all parts of the country. The Board used a trickle-down approach dependent on very thin staffing on the ground. Yet all ideas generated by the Board were supposed to be disseminated to the peasants through conservation officers as well as staff of the Departments of Agriculture, Forestry and Veterinary Services and the office of the District Commissioner. Moreover, it is quite clear that a disproportionate amount of time was spent discussing the implementation of physical conservation measures, such as making contour ridges, terraces and bunds, while little attention was paid to the interests and concerns of the peasants for whom all these bodies and rules were instituted.

Finally, the Board's application of the objects of the Ordinance was not impartial either. The Board focused on African peasant production but ignored the environmentally destructive practices of European settlers. The government defended this position by arguing that any extension of conservation measures to private estates would be seen as an intrusion into the private property of planters and an interference with the liberty of subjects according to English law. Until independence in 1964, few of the private estates owned by European settlers or companies were made targets of the conservation drive.[29] This was a very different situation from other colonies in the region. Unlike South Africa or Southern Rhodesia, where a thriving and vibrant commercial sector existed and where the state sustained a campaign for soil conservation measures in order to reshape settler agriculture, the limited experimental work embarked on in the late 1940s was abandoned after meeting severe opposition from the settlers.

Partly due to the increased wave of criticism that had been levelled against the Ordinance of 1946 and the incompetence of the NRB, the government decided to amend the Ordinance in order to make it more efficient and effective. In

---

29. For details on this, see W.O. Mulwafu, 'Soil Erosion and State Intervention into Estate Production in the Shire Highlands'.

Reforms in the conservation campaign, 1948–1951

addition, Geoffrey Colby, often described as one of Nyasaland's most progressive Governors (1948 to 1956), and Richard Kettlewell, a senior official of the Agriculture Department who later became its Director and Minister of Natural Resources and Surveys, began to exert a significant amount of influence in the area of conservation of natural resources. These two individuals played a critical role in reshaping Nyasaland's agricultural and conservation policies in the period after 1948.

Reforms in the conservation campaign, 1948–1951

The main purpose of the revised 1949 Ordinance was basically to decentralise the operations of the Board so as to make it more effective. As soon as the legislation came into operation, the issue of conservation and improvement of natural resources of the Protectorate fell under the control of the newly established Provincial and District Natural Resources Boards. Stressing the significance of the revised Ordinance and Board, the Chief Secretary advised all Provincial Commissioners that 'the ultimate aim must be Protectorate-wide coordination and progressive action on all aspects of the conservation, improvement and development of natural resources and the practice hitherto of indulging in isolated schemes must cease'.[30]

Unlike the repealed Ordinance which had very general objectives, the new legislation mandated the Provincial Boards to fulfil the following functions: (a) to make orders for the conservation of natural resources; (b) to recommend to the Governor any legislation deemed necessary for this purpose; (c) generally to supervise all natural resources; (d) to examine all conservation proposals submitted to them by the District Boards and executive officers; and (e) to stimulate by propaganda and such other means as deemed expedient a public interest in the conservation and improvement of natural resources. These specific functions of the Board had to be dealt with at Provincial level.[31]

Naturally, the government had high hopes for the new Board. Immediately before the appointment of the three Provincial Boards, the Chief Secretary again expressed the hope that, since the Boad's operations had been decentralised, with wide powers being given to Provincial Boards, these would be expected to meet much more regularly. Furthermore, the Boards were required to come up with more effective conservation measures by virtue of the specific and intimate knowledge supposedly possessed by their members in their areas of influence. And, in a radical departure from past practice, the Chief Secretary declared: 'it is also

---

30. MNA S38/2/3/1: Letter by Chief Secretary to Provincial Commissioners, dated 27 May 1949.
31. The Board consisted of the following: Provincial Commissioner as Chairman, Chief Soil Conservation Officer, Provincial Officers of the Departments of Agriculture, Forestry and Veterinary, the Provincial Soil Conservation Officer who served as the Executive Officer of the Board or any member to be appointed by the Provincial Commissioner as Executive Officer and three other persons that the Provincial Commissioner could appoint with the approval of the Governor.

The Natural Resources Board and the soil conservation campaign

desirable that the African community should be represented on the Boards though special care must be taken to ensure that Africans so appointed possess the necessary intelligence and sufficient qualities of forceful leadership, to enable them to impose the policy of the Board upon the area they represent'.[32] Thus, in the early 1950s, several prominent Africans were, for the first time, appointed to sit on the Provincial Boards. These included Inkosi M'Mbelwa II and E. Alex Muwamba in the North, J.R.N. Chinyama and H. Kanduna in the Centre and Ellerton K. Mposa and Stephenson Kumakanga in the South. These members were expected to support and implement the new legislation in their local areas at all costs. Wearing the face of government put them in direct conflict with the peasants, especially as nationalist consciousness began to spread across the territory. A new form of indirect rule appeared to have been put in place, only this time an educated class of Africans was drafted into the colonial system.

At the district level, the Natural Resources Boards were to be constituted as follows: the District Commissioner (DC) as Chairman; officers representing the Departments of Agriculture, Forestry and Veterinary Services (one of whom would be nominated by the District Commissioner as the Executive Officer of the Board); and three other persons or representatives of institutions to be appointed by the DC with the approval of the Provincial Commissioner. The principal functions of the District Boards were (a) to cooperate and assist the Provincial Board in carrying out the provisions of the 1949 Ordinance; (b) to formulate, for submission to its Provincial Board, conservation schemes to be executed in the given district; (c) on the authority of the Provincial Board, to undertake the construction works and other measures for the conservation of natural resources in given district; and (d) to take such measures for the prevention and control of bush fires as might be prescribed.[33]

From 1950 onwards, District Natural Resources Boards were established in many parts of the country but few functioned effectively. Among the few exceptions was the Domasi District Natural Resources Board which between 1952 and 1957 organised a relentless campaign on soil conservation that was celebrated as a model case for the country. The Domasi project was designed as an integrated programme in community development, involving, among other aspects, hygiene, sanitation, crop and livestock production and soil conservation.[34] The Domasi District Board was hailed particularly because of the way in which peasants had been coerced to implement soil conservation measures in order to achieve the objectives of the Natural Resources Board. Ironically, within a few years of its pronounced success, conflicts developed in the district between the state and the peasants in surrounding

---

32. MNA S38/2/3/1: Natural Resources: Preservation, May 1949–June 1953.
33. See the Nyasaland Government, *Natural Resources Ordinance of 1949*.
34. See Megan Vaughan, 'Better, Happier and Healthier Citizens: The Domasi Community Development Scheme, 1949–1954' (Unpublished Paper: Chancellor College, University of Malawi, History Staff Seminar, 1983).

Reforms in the conservation campaign, 1948–1951

villages.[35] Different interpretations prevail as to the causes and nature of the riot and this issue is the subject of Chapter Ten. However, peasant narratives point to the fact that the experimental project had almost completely ignored the ideas of Africans about the management of the local landscape. Being a flat area, some of the conservation measures that were being promoted such as ridge cultivation and bunding reduced yields as a result of waterlogging and destruction of plants by termites. Conflicts also developed in the Lower Tchiri valley where the Mang'anja speaking people opposed the forced introduction of ridging on the grounds that ridges obstructed the free movement of their Mbona ancestral spirits.[36]

Unless the state intervened more vigorously, the Ordinance of 1949 offered little hope for success. Provincial Boards employed soil erosion rangers, forest guards and agricultural instructors who went out into the villages to mark out areas for the construction of bunds and other measures. If there is any aspect of the Board that peasants today remember vividly, it is the penalties that the Ordinance of 1949 contained. Mr H.M. Selemani and Mai Garaundi of Jekete Village in Chiradzulu district remembered that one of the difficulties Africans faced when undertaking conservation measures was that they 'worked from the morning to sunset without any type of payment. Intimidation was used too. Those who failed to complete the assigned portions of work were fined or sent to prison ... The white men employed their African workers who were moving up and down to supervise the work and one of them in this area was Mr Sabola.'[37] The methods used for enforcing conservation rules and orders were extremely harsh and so were the penalties for noncompliance. Offenders were liable to a fine of £50 or to imprisonment for a period not exceeding six months or both. For recalcitrant offenders who refused to obey court orders requiring them, as owners or occupiers of land, to carry out conservation works within a specified time, there was a penalty of £50 and a further fine of £2 for each day they remained in default after conviction. Finally, section 18(3) provided for the uprooting of any crop planted by those 'natives' who disobeyed any rule prescribed by the Ordinance.[38]

Provincial Boards implemented many of the provisions of the 1949 Natural Resources Ordinance, usually accompanied with some degree of coercion, but whether or not they actually succeeded in improving the conservation of natural resources remains a matter of debate. At this time, a new cadre of officials, consisting largely of ex-soldiers who had spent a stint in the military during the Second World War, took charge of policy implementation. It might be asserted that, in addition to the desirability of implementing the measures, the military experience

---

35. Interview: Mr A.W. Chitenje of Ngwale village, TA Malemia, Zomba district, dated 15 May 1997. See also MNA NSG 1/2/2 on Domasi District Natural Resources Board.
36. See E. Mandala, *Work and Control in a Peasant Economy*.
37. Interview: Mr H. M. Selemani and Mai Garaundi, Jekete Village, TA Mpama, Chiradzulu district, dated 4 June 1997.
38. Nyasaland Government, *Natural Resources Ordinance, 1949*.

facilitated the practical and coercive implementation approach. Colonial state officials periodically reported that the interventions were achieving the desired goal. However, the Provincial Boards' notable achievements include the fact that the decentralisation process had been extended to the district level in order effectively to implement natural resources laws. In addition, Provincial Boards attempted to bring Africans into the decision making process, even though their relationship with and impact on the peasants was somewhat limited given that they were perceived as agents of the intrusive state. Finally, unlike the Protectorate Board, all the three Boards promulgated specific rules, which were enforced on the peasants in various parts of the country with different degrees of success. The Ordinance targeted mainly peasants on native trust land or tenants on private estates. As in the past, the practices of European-owned estates were virtually ignored. Apart from the government's reluctance to interfere with the rights of individual landowners, it was assumed that they would be able to take care of their land by themselves.[39]

At the height of the conservation crusade, a controversial issue cropped up in the Central Province, where the practice of visiting tenancy had developed over the years. Unlike labour tenants who resided on the estates and paid rent, visiting tenants lived on African Trust Lands and did not think it their responsibility to undertake conservation measures on the estates owned by Europeans. The Ordinance did not have any specific provision for visiting tenants and perhaps the closest clause was section 11 which required 'native' tenants on private estates to undertake conservation works applied to resident 'natives' only. When the Provincial Commissioner for the Centre brought this matter to the attention of the government, the Chief Secretary, acting on the advice of the Attorney-General, responded that, since tenants 'build a house and a barn of sorts and cultivate allotted pieces of land both for economic and food crops, they could be considered resident'.[40] This interpretation applied to all visiting tenants, regardless of whether they built houses or not. And, as time went on, this issue became an important source of peasant discontent and opposition to conservation measures in the Central and Southern Provinces. Tenants generally detested the idea of undertaking conservation measures on land that did not belong to them. This also reflected the contradictions inherent in the process and nature of policy formulation and interpretation.

By 1955, the Board began to discuss the question of development in its much wider context. For example, it observed that, while ridging and bunding had almost become synonymous with soil conservation, such measures had merely scratched the surface of the problem. Fragmentation of gardens and the lack of title deeds to individual plots on African Trust Land, maldistribution of population and the absence of mixed farming were far more serious problems that had not as yet been

---

39. W.O. Mulwafu, 'Soil Erosion and State Intervention into Estate Production in the Shire Highlands'.
40. MNA S38/2/3/1: Letter by Chief Secretary to Provincial Commissioner, Central Province, dated 21 April 1950.

Reforms in the conservation campaign, 1948–1951

tackled in a comprehensive manner.[41] To this effect, the Board proposed making amendments to the Natural Resources Ordinance and the Natural Resources Rules so that they could take into account these issues, including the prevailing conditions on the estates. One of the proposed changes concerned section 11 of the Natural Resources Ordinance concerning the eviction of Africans on private estates. Although the government had intimated that it was going to revise the Africans on Private Estates Ordinance, the Board also felt that this matter should be clarified in the NRO by adding a clause to the effect that 'when any native resident is convicted of an offence against the provisions of this section, the court may, in addition to any other penalty, order such native resident to quit the estate on or before a date to be specified in the order, and such native resident shall not be entitled to any compensation by reason of such order.'[42]

The second amendment concerned the need to clarify the division of responsibilities between landlords and tenants in carrying out soil conservation measures. As pointed out earlier, there was a need to determine whether this should be clearly laid out in the Natural Resources Ordinance or whether to leave the *status quo* as it was under section 11. In the final analysis, the Board recommended an amendment of the clause, which, it was hoped, would help in the enforcement of Natural Resources Rules.

The third proposal sought to amend the Natural Resources Rules regarding ridging. In particular, rule 4(i) stated that 'all cultivated land shall be cultivated in ridges of not less than one foot in height and, if the land is on a slope, such ridges shall run across the slope'.[43] However, reports from various parts of the territory had shown that this rule was being violated on a large scale. A common practice among both planters and peasants in many districts was to make short planting ridges that did not provide any measure of soil conservation. Instead, the frequent breaks allowed water to run freely and tended to add loose soil from the ends of each short ridge, which could be washed away. Thus, the Board introduced an amendment that would make it an offence for anyone to put up ridges that did not run the full length of a garden on the contour and decreed that such ridges should be continuous across adjacent gardens without any break.

Initially, estate owners were immune from taking responsibility for failing to implement proper conservation methods. Recognising this problem, the 1946 Ordinance had made a specific provision requiring estate owners, for example, to undertake conservation measures on land that had been damaged by storm water. However, the 1949 Ordinance reversed this policy and the result was chaos. As we shall demonstrate in Chapter Seven, it was no longer easy to tell who was responsible

---

41. MNA NSG 2/1/2: Minutes of the Meeting of the Southern Province Natural Resources Board held in Blantyre on 13 November 1953.
42. MNA NSG 2/1/2: Minutes of the Meeting of the Southern Province Natural Resources Board held in Blantyre on 25 February 1955.
43. Nyasaland Government, *Natural Resources Rules*, April 1951.

The Natural Resources Board and the soil conservation campaign

for taking conservation measures on privately owned land. Consequently, the government assumed that responsibility, even though soil erosion may well have been caused by individual estate owners. A case in point is that of Mrs Wilmot-Smith of Namitete Estate in central Malawi. On many occasions, she had experienced problems with storm water from a section of the main road adjoining her estate. She did not want to undertake any conservation works herself, even though heavy damage had been inflicted on her estate. She argued that the government had to maintain both the estate and the adjoining road at their own expense. When this matter was reported to the Board in 1947, it was decided that government, through the Director of Public Works, should undertake the necessary conservation measures on her estate.

On occasion, the courts also intervened to frustrate the Board. For instance, the Provincial Commissioner, North, complained that many Africans had opposed the implementation of orders made under this section and when they were prosecuted and convicted by the courts, the Chief Justice unprecedentedly dismissed the convictions on the basis that no proper proof had been presented of the accused persons' actions. The Chief Justice advised that Native Authorities should have given directions to African users of the land to adopt measures ordered by the Provincial Boards.[44] The Board's agents, however, wanted simpler and more direct rules that would not require Native Authorities to give such directions and would ensure that the orders were actually carried out. Thus, subsequent to this and with the help of the Attorney-General, the Board proposed to prescribe standard rules and methods of cultivation to be applied over a much wider area. This was later effected through the rules made by the Governor in Council and subsequently published as the Natural Resources Rules of 1951.[45]

The preceding experiences demonstrate the limits of colonial power and the fact that state agents did not always speak with one voice. In the first place, colonial officials differed on the substance of policy and the legal implications of implementing soil conservation campaigns on both African and European privately-owned land. It suggests a certain degree of independence of the judicial system, even where the central interests of the state were threatened or risked being ridiculed. Secondly, the lack of a united voice or homogenous approach provided peasants with an opportunity to evade the effects of coercive state intervention programmes. Some but not all peasants realised weaknesses in the system and found ways of avoiding the demands of the anti-erosion measures, as discussed in Chapter Eight.

---

44. MNA S38/2/3/1: Legal Report by W.J. Lockhart-Smith, Attorney General on 'The Natural Resources (Amendment) Ordinance, 1950', dated 27 July 1950.
45. Nyasaland Government, *Natural Resources Rules, 1951*.

'No cultivation without conservation': 1951–1964

Figure 5.3. Training of agricultural field staff at Colby in 1956

'No cultivation without conservation': 1951–1964

Frustrated by the lack of progress in implementing conservation measures, the state decided, in 1951, to introduce harsher rules to supplement the Natural Resources Ordinance. The enactment of the Natural Resources Rules of 1951 and the Natural Resources (Amendment) Ordinance of 1952 further consolidated the conservation drive in the sense that the Provincial Boards immediately applied the rules to all parts of the country's three provinces.[46] Prior to this period, the Board's conservation campaign had been limited to a few sections – usually areas where the Board had its representatives to assess the local situation and effect the measures. In addition, one of the slogans used in the new conservation campaign was that there would to be 'no cultivation without conservation'. This became a major issue and, not surprisingly, the basis of peasant resistance right up to the end of the colonial period.

Moreover, for the first time in the country's history, the issue of protection and control of water resources was addressed in the new Ordinance. Reports by the departments of Geological Survey and Hydrology had brought to the attention of government the problem of dwindling surface water supplies and the reckless sinking of wells and boreholes. The Governor in Council had made it clear that the issue of comprehensive legislation for water policy would be tackled in the future but the immediate need for the state was to control borehole sinking. In order not to disappoint private entrepreneurs, the Chief Geologist began with a disclaimer

---

46. Nyasaland Government, *Natural Resources (Amendment) Ordinance, 1952*.

that the designed object of the legislation was not 'to curtail or discourage private enterprise but to obtain records and statistics for the future protection of both personal and national interests'.[47] Conservation of surface water resources was only partially mentioned and no specific policy intervention was put in place at this time. Meanwhile, detailed information continued to accumulate about water resources in the territory, with the most up-to-date being Frank Debenham's report on the survey of water resources in the country. While acknowledging the abundance of the resource in the territory generally, he bemoaned the lack of expertise for sound management of water and consequently recommended the need to establish training courses for Africans in the simpler constructions required for water development.[48]

An area of particular concern was the conservation of water level in the aquifer and in the catchment areas. For peasant farmers in the Shire Highlands, this aspect was important because, due to increasing population pressure, some of them had opened gardens in catchment areas. In addition, there was an increase in the number of wells being sunk in the region which, so the state believed, affected the underground water supply. In fact, section 6 of the 1952 Ordinance provided a schedule that required both Africans and Europeans to apply for a license or permission to carry out any work such as digging a well, drilling a borehole or doing other work for the extraction of underground water. When an individual sunk a well or borehole exceeding thirty feet in depth, s/he was required to report its exact location to the Provincial Board. The same section gave powers to the Governor in Council to declare any area in the Protectorate banned for the sinking of boreholes where underground water supplies were in danger of being exhausted. For implementation purposes, the Provincial Boards were given powers to ensure that the Governor's declaration was complied with, as well as to ensure that enough information was provided by the owner or occupier of the land within the concerned area.

It should be noted here that state action on water resources was reactionary rather than an outcome of any profound interest in water conservation. Apparently, the state responded to concerns of agricultural staff that European settlers and some Africans were disturbing the underground water supplies by sinking boreholes and wells in inappropriate areas. Until this time, there had been no comprehensive policy on water resource management. The state had only been interested in the protection of catchment areas, which were critical to the supply of rainwater. Water

---

47. MNA S38/2/3/1: Precis for Executive Council prepared by the Chief Geologist to amend the Natural Resources Ordinance to control borehole sinking and to provide for application piecemeal of rules made under section 20; and in the same file a Memorandum on Natural Resources: Water by D. Cooper, Director of Geological Services, dated 14 March 1951.

48. Frank Debenham, *Report on the Water Resources of the Bechuanaland Protectorate, Northern Rhodesia, The Nyasaland Protectorate, Tanganyika Territory, Kenya and the Uganda Protectorate*, (London: His Majesty's Stationery Office, 1948). See also Nyasaland Protectorate, Geological Survey Department, *Water Supply Investigation, Progress Report No.3 for the Year 1933* (Zomba: Govt Printer, 1934).

'No cultivation without conservation': 1951–1964

Figure 5.4. Controlling gully erosion with stone check dams, 1953

Figure 5.5. Strip rotation on a village land improvement scheme in Central Province, 1956

The Natural Resources Board and the soil conservation campaign

was viewed as part of the hydrological cycle affecting trees and the soil. Beyond that, water resources could be used by individuals and communities as they wished.

Finally, another important amendment of the 1949 Ordinance was the inclusion of section 5, which introduced more specific rules for the prevention and control of bush fires – something that had previously received relatively little attention in the activities of the NRB generally.[49] Nonetheless, in a number of districts, forestry officers complained about the relationship between bush fires, which were associated with the practice of shifting cultivation, and the destruction of vegetation. African peasants were prohibited from burning bushes as part of land preparation and any contravention of such rules was criminalised.

Accompanying new policies was a shift in strategy from propaganda and persuasion to an indiscriminate use of coercion. The Provincial Boards were given wide powers to make additional rules where necessary for the implementation of conservation policies and harsh penalties were imposed on those Africans who contravened such rules. In this regard, Mr and Mrs. H. Ching'anda of Mbalame Village in Chiradzulu district reminisced that the Agricultural staff 'intimidated those who stayed away [from conservation work] by using fines and imprisonment. Mr Thomas and Mr Don are the only white men we can still remember in this area ... They were very tough so that whenever one failed to follow what they taught, they would destroy the ridges and then asked peasants to remake them.'[50] In most cases, this campaign was seriously complicated by the coercive approach and operated in a highly volatile environment of nationalist struggle for independence. The methods for enforcing soil conservation laws and the resistance that such intervention generated are discussed in Chapter Eight.

It is difficult to gauge the performance and success of all the Provincial or District Boards. But since the bunding campaign became the most dominant issue in the 1950s, this could illuminate our understanding of the performance of the Boards. The available statistics for the period, from 1951 to 1957, show that a large area was marked out for bunding in all the three provinces of the country. The Director of Agriculture boasted that 'it would be no exaggeration to say that the Protectorate is now conservation conscious and much progress in this direction achieved in the past three years may be credited to the Provincial and District Natural Resources Boards'.[51] From the point of view of government, the success of the campaign was assessed by the number of yards that had been marked or bunded. As shown in Table 5.1 below, the bunding campaign reached its climax

---

49. A few District Natural Resources Boards discussed this matter of bush fires but rarely brought it to the Provincial Boards or the national level. At the end of his colonial service in Nyasaland, Richard Kettlewell wrote a small booklet; see Kettlewell, *The Importance of Controlling Fires* (Zomba: Government Printer, 1960).

50. Interview: Mr and Mrs H. Ching'anda, Mbalame Village, TA Mpama, Chiradzulu district, dated 4 June 1997.

51. *Nyasaland Annual Report*, (Zomba: Government Printer, 1952), p.50.

'No cultivation without conservation': 1951–1964

in 1953, the very year of intense peasant resistance in the country. It was assumed, usually wrongly, that those Africans who had carried out these activities had accepted or become conscious of the significance of the conservation programme. But, as subsequent chapters show, African peasants had different understandings of why the state was acting and these determined their responses.

Table 5.1. Impact of the Bunding Campaign, 1951–1955

Year	Area Marked	Area Bunded	Total Area Protected
1951	9788 miles	-	-
1952	31 million yards	23 million yards	>165 sq. miles
1953	16,126 million yards	12,512 million yards	146,303 sq. miles
1954	-	1.7 million yards	4712 sq. miles
1955	>8,000 miles	>6,000 million yards	>7,000 sq. miles

The intensification of the conservation campaign in 1952/3 was also indicative of the extent of coercion used by the colonial state to transform African production on Trust Land. In most cases, peasants spent a lot time making bunds and other conservation measures. This took away their valuable time from producing their own food crops and other household work. The demand on peasants' time and labour and the use of coercion made many of them resist the conservation drive. Mr Maganga Seyani of Nzundo Village in Thyolo pointed out that

> the introduction of milambala came with lots of tensions and conflicts. In 1953, at Chalunda Village, there was nkhondo-ya-milambala during which people were being woken up at night to go and work ... I tell you these were difficult times. There was nobody who was at peace. Everyone in the village was shaken. Some people ran away and hid in places like graveyards and forests.[52]

Village land improvement schemes were introduced, through which villages were reorganised into large population units for better implementation of soil and water conservation and land use practices. In 1955, the state established the Mechanical Soil Conservation Unit as the lead agency responsible for planning, designing and constructing physical soil and water conservation structures. Great emphasis was placed on mechanical conservation because agricultural officials thought that erosion was caused mainly by physical factors such as surface runoff. Yet, as recent studies have shown, erosion was caused not just by physical factors but by raindrop impact, which resulted into soil detachment.[53] In addition, most

---

52. Interview: Mr Maganga Seyani, Nzundo Village, TA Nsabwe, Thyolo district, dated 28 May 1997.
53. E.J. Mwendera, 'A Short History and Annotated Bibliography on Soil and Water Conservation in Malawi', *SADCC Report* No. 20 (September 1989).

of the soil conservation measures used at that time tended to be more applicable to estate farms where mechanisation had taken place than to smallholder farms.

By 1960, the Department of Natural Resources reported that over one million acres of land had been protected from gross erosion by conservation works.[54] However, the bunding drives of the 1953 agricultural season raised a considerable amount of consciousness among the peasants in the country. Because of the aggressive approach adopted, many peasants began to engage in hidden forms of resistance, such as simply neglecting or destroying the bunds that had been made. Also, in the 1950s, the tide of nationalism increased so much that government was compelled to loosen its stricter policies and consequently the conservation drive began to lose its direction.

One clear indication came about in 1957, when there was a shift in emphasis from the requirement of applying physical conservation measures (such as bunding, ridging and terracing) to land usage as a way of conserving natural resources. When Malawi attained self-government in 1961, Dr Hastings K. Banda, in his capacity as Minister of Natural Resources and Surveys, repealed the Natural Resources Ordinance and replaced it with the Land Use and Protection Ordinance No.10 of 1962. This new law tended to be more responsive to the needs of the peasants, in that it placed more emphasis on the provision of advisory services as opposed to propaganda. And, in place of the Provincial Natural Resources Boards, the new government established a Land Use Advisory Council. Its purpose was to help Africans with the use and protection of land resources. The specific functions were to advise the Minister on matters connected with the use and protection of the land of the Protectorate; to recommend to the Minister any special or general directions to be given to Area Committees; to advise Area Committees on their work and matters connected therewith; to obtain information on which to base advice to the Minister or to the Area Committees; and finally to stimulate by such means as deemed expedient public interest in the protection and sound use of land. At a lower level, Area Land Use and Protection Committees were also established to supervise the use and protection of land resources in local areas. The strategy adopted involved mainly persuasion and education and, if that failed, a penalty of £50 would be charged or six months imprisonment be imposed as a last resort measure. But the practice of uprooting crops was completely discontinued. As events led to the attainment of independence in 1964, the drive for soil conservation declined substantially. New issues and challenges quickly superseded conservation, even though it had helped foment rural peasant opposition to colonial rule.

Conclusion

One of the dominant historical narratives on African landscapes has been that of environmental degradation. Travel accounts and other contemporaneous writings

---

54. Nyasaland Government, *The Natural Resources of Nyasaland* (1960).

Conclusion

almost invariably depicted Africans as destroyers of the environment and further observed that if the situation continued, more damage would be done. That image appears to have been strong in the 1930s and contributed to the promotion of state intervention. When the Dust Bowl occurred, an opportune time had come for action to be taken. Ideologically, state intervention became defensible and there was a continuous flow of information from the community of scientists in all parts of the world to justify the formulation of policies and strategies in African societies. State intervention shaped colonial relations and altered meanings over environmental control and rural ecological change right up to the end of the colonial era. Conservation became an important tool of colonial state intervention and control of people and scarce resources. The view that conservation was a reflection of a progressive attempt by the colonial state to re-organise and protect resources from destruction needs to be read against the multiple forms of evidence that gave rise to the decisions made. Moreover, the official mind itself was not homogeneous even though by the 1930s the majority appeared to have shared the same narrative. Local knowledge systems which sustained African production systems further complicate matters of the narrative of conservation. We therefore need to view the notion of conservation as a contested terrain and one deeply embedded in colonial power relations and scientific ethos. This approach allows valuable insights into the contradictions, negotiations, tensions and struggles in rural society which must necessarily be at the centre of any discussion of improved use of natural resources. Scientific ideas and practices were considered to be the answer to the perceived problems of ecological degradation in Malawi. The state paid little attention to the labour required of peasants and the systems of land use that they were supposed to abandon in favour of western ones. Not unexpectedly, the conservationist drive met with much resistance, particularly when the state resorted to the use of coercion in the implementation of its policies.

The chapter has examined the history of natural resource conservation in Malawi. This analysis has shown that, through the agency of the Natural Resources Board, one of Nyasaland's most influential bodies in the crusade for the conservation, the state intervened in the peasant sector as part of the larger colonial scheme to conserve the country's natural resources. The peasants were not always enthused by such intrusive activities on the part of the Board and this only helped to prepare the ground for resistance in varying forms.

6

Colonial Intervention into African Trust Lands, 1939–1964

Introduction

This chapter examines the origins of colonial policies on environmental issues that formed part of the soil conservation campaign in the postwar period; here emphasis is placed mainly on wildlife and forestry services. The attention that has so far been paid to soil erosion should not in any way suggest that the state was only concerned about soil degradation. Other areas were equally important and indeed formed part of an integrated approach to natural resources management.

Wildlife resources

After the declaration of Protectorate rule in Malawi in 1891, a series of restrictive measures were introduced in an effort to put into practice some of Johnston's ideas about conservation. Wildlife resources were critical to both Africans and Europeans. Animals were used as a source of food and skin as well as for sport and, with time, different groups began to compete for access to animals. The late nineteenth century had seen a substantial increase in hunting activities, especially of elephants for ivory, as the slave trade came to an end. By the time of establishment of colonial rule, fears were expressed that the territory's animal population was declining. It was in this context that the new protectorate government began to develop measures of regulating the use of wildlife resources.

Starting from about 1897, several game ordinances were promulgated in order to control African game hunting. All of them required Africans to pay a much higher fee for possession of a gun. Later, the selling of guns and gunpowder to Africans was made illegal, unless one had obtained a permit. At £25 per year, the cost of the game license was prohibitive for the large majority of Africans. Ironically, while Africans were restricted in their hunting expeditions for food, many Europeans took to hunting for sport. At this time, the conflict was not just about the preservation of game for its own sake but about rights and opportunities to use the available resources. The 1911 Ordinance provided for the creation of game reserves in a number of places in the territory, even though most of the reserves that had been established were insufficiently supervised. Although in 1897 the Elephant Marsh and the Lake Chilwa were declared protected areas for the specific purpose of restricting game hunting, the first game reserve in the territory was declared in the Dzalanyama Range of the Central Angoniland in 1911. Great emphasis was placed on scheduling of animals that could not be killed or hunted, particularly ungulates such as elephant, zebra, buffalo and antelopes.

The establishment of game reserves followed the example of similar developments in South Africa and Kenya where, for instance, the Cape Act for the Preservation of Game was passed in 1886 and later extended to British South African territories in 1891. Subsequent to this, the Sabie Game Reserve, whose name changed to Kruger National Park in 1926, was established in the Transvaal. Brian Morris has observed that game regulations were not really meant to conserve wildlife from depletion but rather to restrict the hunting of game by Africans. He has further argued that such restrictions conferred special privileges on the European elite, especially the planters and missionaries, who could easily hunt different types of animals.[1] In addition, as David Njaidi has argued, up to 1926 the effect of these regulations was a disproportionate increase in the number of animals in some parts of the country. For example, in the lakeshore district of Mangochi, game tended to be found in abundance in areas closest to African settlements while there was wildlife depletion in areas inhabited by Europeans. The game became a menace and a constant source of insecurity to many Africans and their livestock and crops.[2]

However, the 1926 ordinance may be viewed as the most far-reaching game regulation, embracing, for the first time, the idea of game conservation in colonial Malawi. Under this law, both Europeans and Africans were forbidden from hunting game without the permission of District Residents. Anyone contravening these rules could be penalised by a fine of £100 or face imprisonment. The number of animals scheduled to require special state permission before any hunting could take place increased from four to eighty. In addition, new game reserves were gazetted, such as Lengwe and Tangadzi in 1928, Chidyampira and Kasungu in 1930, Nkhotakota reserve in 1938, Ngara/Nantundu in 1940, Viphya in 1938, Kazuni Lake Reserve in 1941. African traditional hunting techniques such as traps, snares, poison, pitfalls and fire were proscribed. This legislation was part of a much broader colonial initiative of natural resource conservation, which also encompassed soil, water and animal resources. Morris suggests that Rodney Wood, formerly a game warden and planter in Thyolo and Chiromo, was instrumental in pushing for this legislation, which was meant to transform the attitude of people towards conservation of animals.

The Game Ordinance of 1926 was received with mixed reactions by the African and European settler communities. The Africans never registered their complaints formally but the settler community prepared a petition. About two

---

1. Brian Morris, 'Conservation Mania in Colonial Malawi: Another View', *Nyala* 19 (1996): 17–36.
2. See David Njaidi, 'Towards an Exploration of Game Control and Land Conservation in Colonial Mangochi, 1891–1964', *Society of Malawi Journal* 48/2 (1995): 1–25.

hundred Europeans signed a petition sent to the Hon. Leopold S. Amery, Secretary of State for Colonies, arguing that the Ordinance contained too many prohibitions on hunting of game by Europeans and Africans and risked turning the whole Protectorate into a 'game reserve'. They complained that 'the licence fees, the penalties, the confiscatory clauses and the inquisitorial methods of the new Ordinance are widely resented as totally unsuited to the conditions of this Protectorate with its large native population'.[3] It is interesting that, although there was no African signatory, the petitioners claimed to speak for the Africans in opposing the Ordinance. They observed that African resentment came from the fact that the Ordinance '[withdrew] from them their old established and ancestral rights of killing game for food... also [prohibited] their own methods'.[4] In spite of these protestations, the Ordinance came into effect in April 1927. In subsequent years, and with strong lobbying from the Nyasaland Fauna Preservation Society, the state continued to establish game reserves in various parts of the country, such as the Mwabvi and Majete game reserves which came into existence in the early 1950s.[5] An important development took place in 1946, namely the setting up of the Game and Forest Commission to report on the value and suitability of all game and forest reserves in the territory. One of the key recommendations of this Commission was the establishment of the Department of Game, which came into being in 1949 as the Department of Game, Fish and Tsetse Control. In 1962, the department was reconstituted and renamed as the Department of Forestry and Game. After independence in 1964, more game reserves continued to be established but by now the notion of national parks had been adopted. For instance, Nyika was established in 1966 while Lengwe and Kasungu were gazetted in 1970 and Liwonde was proclaimed a national park in 1972.

Forestry resources

Besides game control, the other area where the state intervened at an early stage was forestry. Forest resources had to be protected against man, animals, fires and fungal diseases. As should now have become clear, several factors were advanced to account for the decline of forest resources in Malawi, such as deforestation and slash-and-burn, and the initial response of the state was to deploy forest staff in selected areas and also to introduce new legislation. The state used a two-phased approach: creation of forest reserves and then village forest areas. Forest reserves were areas demarcated by the state and designated as protected from any human

---

3. MNA S1/558/27: 'Petition against the Game Ordinance, 1926' to the Hon. Leopold S. Amery, Secretary of State for Colonies.
4. *Ibid.*
5. Brian Morris, 'G.D. Hayes and the Nyasaland Fauna Preservation Society', *Society of Malawi Journal* 50/1 (1997): 1–12. G.D. Hayes, 'Wildlife Conservation in Malawi', *Society of Malawi Journal* 25/2 (1972): 22–31.

Forestry resources

interference. Village forest areas, on the other hand, were communally managed forests on African Trust Lands.

The first legislation was introduced in 1911 and made three main provisions. First, it provided for the surveying and demarcation of forests throughout the country. By the time the legislation had been revised in 1926, nearly 3,000 square miles had been demarcated and designated as protected forests, which represented about nine per cent of the entire land of the Protectorate. Nearly 39 forest reserves had been constituted. The aim was to maintain water supply, as well as safeguarding against serious erosion. Most of these forests were located in main watershed and catchment areas on land that was free from use-rights of any kind. The areas protected were often those on hill slopes because colonial staff believed that there was a close relationship between forests and water retention. Such demarcated forests were restricted from African use. Secondly, the 1911 Ordinance also identified and reserved over thirty species of trees that could not be cut down by Africans without government permission. This created problems for many Africans who used hardwoods for various household tools. Third, it prohibited Africans from cutting down any trees within a distance of thirty yards of a stream or river and from cultivating near streams. Yet, these areas were good for *dimba* cultivation in the dry season.[6] These contradictions in the implementation of forest legislation laid the foundation for subsequent peasant opposition in the postwar period.

In 1926, the government came up with new legislation on forest management. In the first place, it provided for the establishment of the Department of Forestry – hitherto forest matters were under the Department of Agriculture. It also gave wide powers for the control of tree cutting and for the general preservation of forests. Very tough rules and penalties were introduced for offenders. There was to be no squatting, grazing of cattle or cultivating of land within thirty yards of a river or stream on any unalienated Crown land. More trees were added to the list of protected or reserved trees in undemarcated forests; for the demarcated forests, the prohibitions remained the same as those provided in the Ordinance of 1911. However, owing to shortage of staff and financial resources, implementation of these rules was difficult. Thus, one of the greatest problems experienced in regard to protection of forest reserves was encroachment. The offences ranged from cutting and cultivating on riverbanks to cutting of protected trees within forest reserves and or on Crown lands to burning of forested areas. For instance, in 1931, there were 559 convicted offenders while the figure of those convicted rose to 1,169 in 1935.[7]

Another important aspect of the legislation was the introduction of village forest areas (VFAs) and the prohibition of bush fires within a quarter of a mile of forests. The cumulative effect of these measures was that they reduced the amount of land available for peasant cultivation; peasants also complained that the plant-

---

6. Interview: Mai Mbebua and Mr S. Likome, Chalunda Village, TA Nsabwe, Thyolo district, dated 11 June 1997.
7. Nyasaland Government, Annual Forestry Report for 1935.

ing of exotic trees like bluegum did not help to create good firewood or bring about soil fertility.[8] The village forest areas scheme was one of the major colonial initiatives aimed at promoting the conservation of forest resources in the territory by using local communities. In many ways, it predated the community based management approaches now in vogue in many parts of Africa.[9] The scheme came into operation in 1926 at the recommendation of J.B. Clements, the Chief Forest Officer. The primary objective of the scheme was to plant trees in areas that had a serious scarcity of poles and firewood and also to reforest areas that had fallen under tobacco production in the central region, particularly Lilongwe and Dowa districts. Only those lands that were under native control or African Trust could be portioned out for village forest areas and the principle behind such allocations was to set aside two acres per hut. In modern terminology, that would be two acres of forest land per household.

The process of demarcating forest areas was to be done by two groups of people: first the Forestry Department through the divisional forest officers, who at that time were usually Europeans, and secondly the native administration through village headmen assisted by district native foresters. But the latter had to be approved by the District Commissioners before they could undertake their tasks. The first pilot exercise on VFA was conducted in Lilongwe and Dowa districts where 356 acres and 975 acres of land, respectively, were reforested in 1926. The scheme was extended in 1927 to other parts of the territory such as Kasungu and Thyolo districts. As in the case of anti-soil erosion campaigns later, propaganda was used to persuade headmen and villagers to implement the VFAs as well as to undertake proper fire-protection of the areas after demarcation.

From the beginning, the VFAs scheme experienced some challenges. The first concerned the question of land security. Some chiefs expressed fears that this initiative was a step in the direction of land alienation by the state. Since the Department of Forestry went about identifying and demarcating land for the VFAs, Africans felt this was a pretext for a larger scheme in land dispossession whereby such forests would be converted into state forest reserves. The second challenge concerned the lack of capacity to implement the scheme across the country. The Department of Forestry was very small – initially four European officers assisted by native foresters. It was practically very difficult to visit all the villages where the schemes had been established. In addition, the process of ratifying areas that had been demarcated was costly and cumbersome.

In an attempt to assuage fears, the Department of Forestry organised a tour in September 1930 for District Commissioner of Lilongwe and Dowa to visit some

---

8. Interview: Mr and Mrs Ching'anda, Mbalame Village, TA Mpama, Chiradzulu district, dated 4 June 1997.

9. See Leo C. Zulu, 'Community Forest Management in Southern Malawi: Solution or Part of the Problem', *Society and Natural Resources* 21 (2008): 687–703; and 'Politics of Scale and Community-based Forest Management in Southern Malawi', *Geoforum* 40 (2009): 686–699.

Forestry resources

VFAs that had been demarcated in previous years. According to Clements this project helped to gain on-the-spot experience with the scheme: 'This initial work on the part of the District Commissioners of Lilongwe and Dowa proved to be of enormous value, for apart from the settlement of land disputes and the definite allocation of areas, what the headmen most needed was authoritative assurances as to the future of the areas allocated.'[10]

When the Forestry Department reviewed the scheme towards the end of 1930, three procedures were recommended to improve the creation of VFAs. In the first place, village headmen had to select and demarcate their areas with the assistance of native foresters. Second, the areas thus selected had to be examined by the divisional forest officers and, where necessary, a recommendation be sought from the tobacco board supervisors. Third, once the above requirements had been fulfilled, the District Commissioner would allocate and register the areas. But this procedure was found to be equally difficult to use since the administrative officer in the office of the District Commissioner was usually busy with other matters and paid little attention to forestry matters. Thus, it became the responsibility of the forest officers to allocate and approve areas. In effect, this was a reversion to the old procedure that was used at the inception of the scheme in 1926.

Despite initial optimism, work proceeded very slowly, largely due to shortage of staff. In order to give more powers to village headmen to promote the establishment of VFAs, the state enacted, in February 1931, the Village Forest Area Rules. These rules empowered village headmen so that they could protect the areas allocated to them. The slow pace of the establishment of VFAs can be seen from the table below, which summarises the situation in 1931.

Table 6.1. Status of Village Forest Areas in 1931

District	No of VFAs	Total Acreage	Ratification Status
Lilongwe	539	23,041	Ratified
Dowa	90	3,725	Ratified
Ncheu	51	6,478	Ratified
Dedza	20	987	Ratified
Ft Manning	21	1028	Not yet ratified
Kasungu	28	3310	Ratified
Kota Kota	6	280	Ratified
Blantyre	75	2,795	Ratified
Chikwawa	6	Areas not given	Not yet ratified
Mlanje	19	Areas not given	Not yet ratified
Zomba	16	571	Not yet ratified

10. J.B. Clements, 'A Communal Forest Scheme in Nyasaland', *Fourth British Empire Forestry Conference* (South Africa: 1935).

Colonial intervention into African Trust Lands, 1939–1964

Barely three years after registering slow progress, the state began to boast of the success of the scheme. In 1934, the state reported that education and persuasion had effectively been used to get the support of the village headmen and their subjects. In particular, the following reasons were advanced for the presumed success of the scheme. First, that there was strong political will from the leadership of the territory; the Governor and the provincial and District Commissioners had given strong support for the scheme. Second, the approach whereby allocation of areas was made directly to village headmen and not to chiefs entailed basing the scheme on the cooperation, rather than the subordination, of the individual village head. From the point of view of the state, this gave people direct interest in the scheme and facilitated control. More importantly, this approach was compatible with Protectorate laws relating to Crown lands, which were under the jurisdiction of the Traditional Authorities. The third factor was that, by getting the District Commissioners to promulgate the allocations, village headmen and their subjects were assured of the future security of their areas. Fourth, all registered VFAs were exempted from the operation of general forest laws relating to reserved trees growing on Crown lands. It was the village heads and not the state that had control over such forest resources. The final factor had to do with the simplicity of the VFAs scheme and the rules regulating it. Since the idea was to protect natural forests or woodlands rather than to make elaborate planting schemes, even a small measure of protection would produce results.

The introduction of the VFAs scheme had certainly opened a new chapter in the management of natural resources in African Trust Lands. Careful as they were not to alienate the African peoples or create fear, the state authorities gradually began to exert their influence in areas controlled by Africans themselves. Since chiefs and village headmen were usually agents of the state, their roles became controversial. In subsequent years, the VFAs continued to be implemented amidst several challenges in the changing socio-political environment of the territory. For instance, the presence of income-earning opportunities, particularly in the southern region where towns and estates tended to attract many young people, reduced interest in village communal life. Such people did not pay much attention to the activities of the scheme. In addition, the disillusionment of some people, especially during times of drought, resulted in the loss of trees. Some people disregarded the rules of the scheme and cut down trees. On a related issue, the protection of plantations from fires and livestock grazing required continuous and arduous effort. This was particularly serious when forest conservation conflicted with other labour-demanding activities such as land preparation, planting and weeding.

The case of an integrated land use scheme

In the remote northern district of North Nyasa (later known as Karonga) the state experimented with an integrated approach to the management of natural resources

The case of an integrated land use scheme

in the Misuku Hills. This project came in the wake of an assessment conducted in 1937 by the Department of Forestry, which revealed that the area had been seriously degraded.[11] The study showed that the Misuku area had been mismanaged by the indigenous people and that their continued occupation of the area would only lead to a further deterioration of the land. Among the aspects of land mismanagement were intensive deforestation, severe soil erosion and bad husbandry of animals and land. As a possible remedy to the problem, the government at first decided to evacuate all residents from the worst affected areas. Misuku at that time had about 42 villages. This meant resettling them and the administration soon realised that the policy would not be accepted by the inhabitants of the area. Thus, after discounting the evacuation alternative, the DC and other government officials in Karonga suggested a multi-departmental agronomic policy to regenerate the land that had deteriorated. This was the genesis of the Misuku Land Usage Scheme, which was essentially a five-year development programme designed to work on soil conservation, cattle and crop management, reforestation, stream bank protection and other aspects concerned with proper land use.[12] Major D.N. Smalley, Agricultural Supervisor, assisted by James Mwamlima, was charged with the responsibility of coordinating the practical implementation of the scheme. At the beginning, the DC for Karonga applied for a grant of £355 to finance the development of the scheme but by 1942 he had received only £180.[13] In spite of limited financial assistance, the scheme nevertheless went ahead, relying mostly on local resources.

Agricultural production constituted another aspect of the land usage scheme where coffee farming had a special position. Realising its economic importance to the area, the scheme's technocrats attempted to improve coffee production by assisting mostly at the level of land husbandry. For example, coffee farmers were advised to use alluvial bottoms for planting coffee. Furthermore, it was also recommended that hilly areas be made useful by digging terraces. Beyond this, the scheme offered virtually no other kinds of instructions with respect to the development of the coffee industry. The onus of managing the plants until harvest was on the farmers themselves. As part of the reforestation programme, the forests of Mughese, Wilindi and Matipa, were, under the Forestry Ordinance of 1939, declared government forest reserves.[14] Although mixed farming was discouraged in Misuku, the government apparently took no measures to try to curb this practice.

---

11. NAM, NN 1/15/15: Letter from DC Karonga to DC, Northern Province, Lilongwe, dated 5 September 1941.

12. NAM, NN 1/5/15: Letter from Department of Agriculture, Lilongwe, to Provincial Commissioner, Northern Province, Lilongwe, dated 21 April 1942.

13. NAM NN 1/15/15: Letter from DC Karonga to DC, Northern Province, Lilongwe, dated 5 September 1941. The application was made on behalf of N. A. Kyungu for the grant from the Natives Welfare Fund to finance development schemes in the Misuku Area.

14. NAM, NN 1/10/2: Letter from District Commissioner, Karonga, to Provincial Commissioner, Northern Province, Lilongwe, dated 10 January 1939, about the implementation of Government's Land Policy on plans and boundary descriptions of proposed forest reserves.

Colonial intervention into African Trust Lands, 1939–1964

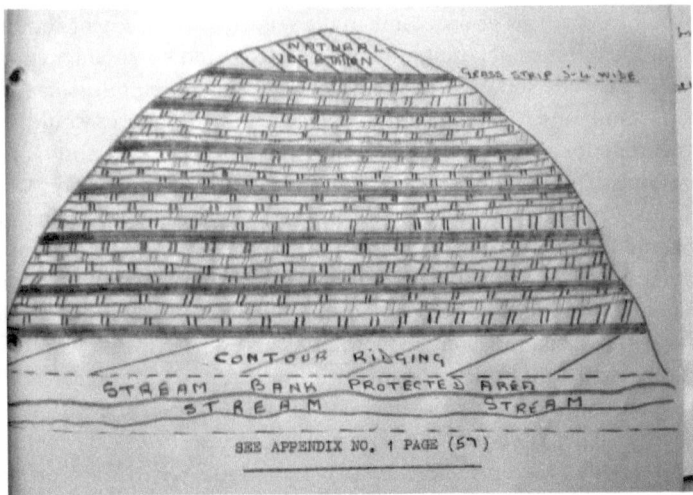

*Figure 6.1. Vingonyeka Traditional Method of Soil Conservation
(Source: Report of the Misuku Land Usage Scheme)*

By the end of 1943, the scheme was reported to have been successfully implemented and this was confirmed by all the heads of department concerned. These included Forestry, Agriculture and Veterinary Services. Major Smalley, the main architect of the scheme, was also greatly applauded for his zeal and enthusiasm, with the highest commendation coming from the Governor. In a letter to the Director of Agriculture the Chief Secretary said 'His Excellency (the Governor) read Major Smalley's report with great interest and considers that much assistance be given in taking selected chiefs to see the results in Misuku'.[15] In this respect, it is undoubtedly clear that the colonial government wanted the success of the Misuku Scheme to be carried across to other parts of the Protectorate. The Governor's suggestion was actually put into practice the following year. From 26 April to 8 May 1994 a party of 24 people, comprising chiefs and supporters from the districts of Dedza, Dowa, Mzimba and Nkhotakota, visited Misuku. Guided by Smalley and R.W. Kettlewell, the Provincial Agricultural Officer, North, they toured the scheme. At the end of the visit, the scheme was generally described in affirmative diplomatic language as an 'unqualified success'.[16] It seems almost certain that the visit was also a way of using people in strategic positions of leadership to implement government policies. In this case, the chiefs were essentially being reoriented in a way that would

---

15. NAM, NN 1/5/15: Letter from Chief Secretary, Zomba to Director of Agriculture, Zomba, dated 29 July 1943.
16. NN 1/15/15: Letter from District Commissioner, Karonga, to Provincial Commissioner, Northern Province, dated 19 May 1944.

The case of an integrated land use scheme

Figure 6.2. An improved Vingonyeka traditional method of soil conservation

Figure 6.3. Garden showing how Vingonyeka technique is used

Figure 6.4. Another garden showing Vingonyeka technique in the making

Figure 6.5. Gully erosion in Misuku hills

"......... and very often eroded gullies are opened up which increase in length depth and width with each successive rainy season."

A large gully at Misuku, the result of over-grazing. The size may be judged by comparison with the man standing on the near edge of the gully, near the top end, who appears as a minute white dot.

assist them when explaining to their people the necessity of introducing similar schemes in their respective areas. The idea was clearly explained by the Department of Agriculture in a circular letter sent to all Agriculture Officers and DCs in the districts from which the Chiefs had come advising that:

> as a follow-up of the visit would they please contact the above (chiefs) and make the most use possible of their tour of the Misuku in furthering their communications with the people in the areas on what they saw and learnt, with particular emphasis on getting the measures applied in their districts as and where possible.[17]

An example that clearly illustrates this kind of situation is that of Mzimba. A few months after the Misuku visit, the government unveiled plans to launch a similar land usage scheme in the distressed areas of that district.[18] The role of Inkosi ya Makosi M'Mbelwa and other Jere chiefs who had gone to Misuku was seen as indispensable to the success of the scheme.

The argument that the outcome of the scheme really satisfied the policy planners cannot be denied but the impact of the scheme on the local people, particularly coffee farmers, is more doubtful. It has already been noted that the scheme, probably as a way of living up to its primary goal, laid much more emphasis on land utilisation and conservation than on coffee production. However, the prevalence of court cases concerning offenders against conservation rules is testimony to the fact that the scheme was not totally acceptable to every Sukwa-Ndali. Indeed, in any innovative undertaking, laggards or slow adopters are bound to exist but in the case of the Misuku scheme, the rate at which the conservation rules were being contravened was alarming.[19]

Indemela or slash-and-burn, the traditional method of cutting down trees in preparation for millet growing, continued even after the scheme had been implemented. There were several reports by government officials complaining of the indiscriminate burning and cutting down of trees so as to prepare millet fields. As late as 1948, for example, the District Administration reported that there was still great opposition to agricultural policy in the area which, 'considering that this area had intensive propaganda and assistance for about ten years, is rather disappointing ... The opposition is not against contour ridging so much as against the rules which make millet cultivation from their point of view so difficult.'[20] *Indemela* was one of the greatest problems the government had to contend with for a long time. The main reason for this is that, apart from beans, millet had been the principal

---

17. NAM, NN 1/15/15: Letter from Department of Agriculture, Lilongwe, to Agriculture Officers and DCs of Dedza, Dowa, Mzimba and Nkhotakota, dated 14 June 1944.

18. NAM, NN 1/15/15: Letter from District Commissioner, Mzimba, to Provisional Commissioner, Northern Province, Lilongwe, dated 16 September 1943, on proposed visits to Misuku.

19. NAM, NN 4/2/11: Intelligence Reports, Monthly Karonga District, November 1944. Many cases were reported especially between Misuku centre and the Songwe River.

20. NAM, NN 4/2/11: Intelligence Reports, Monthly Karonga District, November 1944.

crop grown for food as well as for sale. In fact, the government used to accept millet and beans in payment for hut tax. In addition, millet was an important raw material for production of local beer. But millet was not grown on contour ridges which were being advocated by agricultural officials. It was the traditional method of slash-and-burn by which millet was grown that worked against the colonial conservationist project.

Another shortcoming of the Misuku Land Usage Scheme was that there is no indication whatsoever that it led to increased agricultural production. Smalley's teachings appear to have not been received seriously by the Africans. Like many other colonial projects of the time, much propaganda was issued in order to legitimate the state's actions. The people for whom these interventions were intended had different perspectives and this in part explains the rather hostile manner with which they greeted soil conservation policies. That is the subject of the next three chapters.

Conclusion

This chapter has shown that the notion of environmental conservation in colonial Malawi changed with the passage of time. In the pre-colonial period, conservation was closely tied to matters of food production and survival. Management of environmental resources almost invariably involved the continued supply of food in order to ensure human survival. Thereafter, the idea continued to be seen in those terms, but with emphasis increasingly shifting to new policies of the colonial state like game hunting and forest protection. It was only in the 1930s that a slightly more focused and fully-fledged policy of conservation was adopted and implemented. A widely accepted idea was that good knowledge for assessment of soils and their value for agricultural and forest purposes was critical for staff working in the Departments of Forestry and Agriculture. The colonial state came up with some specific pieces of legislation to operationalise its ideas of conservation. Whether in forestry or wildlife management, implementation of these policies entailed restricting African access to and use of natural resources. Here we had initial experiments in state regulation of natural resources at a local level, a process that marked the beginning of tensions and conflicts with Africans. Several pilot schemes were instituted in selected parts of the country with a view to testing the effect of the newly formulated policies.

7

State Intervention into Private Estate Production in the Shire Highlands

Introduction

This chapter examines the history of soil erosion on private estates in the Shire Highlands region of Malawi and the limits of the colonial state's coercive capacity to intervene. It shows that the problem of soil erosion on Shire Highlands estates was serious and widespread. In contrast to the intense, harsh conservation campaigns imposed on African Trust Land, the colonial state virtually ignored the environmental degradation taking place on these estates. The introduction of soil conservation measures on private estates exacerbated conflicts over many issues that had characterised the relationship between the state, the plantation and the peasant sectors. It generated controversy over such issues as labour, land, crop production and the state's powers to intervene in privately owned lands. After a description of the process of creating a plantation economy and European land use practices, this chapter argues that, until the 1950s, the state conservation policy toward private estates was one of benign neglect. After 1951, state officials finally began to focus on the massive environmental degradation on settler estates but the actual intervention was weak. Various factors are shown to have inhibited an effective state conservation programme on private estates and it is demonstrated that state policies in this period were met with either indifference or opposition by both estate owners and labour tenants

The question of the conservation of natural resources in colonial Malawi was, for a long time, confined to Africans on Trust Land. Although land degradation also took place on European-owned estates, state planners assumed that estate owners knew how to manage the land and that they were capable of dealing with any problems that would be encountered. This policy of benign neglect continued throughout much of the colonial period and only changed in the early 1950s. However, state intervention was weak and met with resistance, both by estate owners and the labour tenants who resided on the plantations. Through this uneven intervention and enforcement, the colonial state racialised the environmental issue and made it an African problem.

Throughout the 1950s, numerous cases were reported and discussed by the various District and Provincial Boards. But the response of the Provincial Natural Resources Board (PNRB) for the South was essentially weak: there was much talk

Introduction

but little action. In stark contrast to Africans on Trust Land, few estate owners were subjected to the vagaries of eviction, fines, imprisonment or uprooting of crops. Where the Board intervened with a modicum of force, it was often on estates that had been occupied by tenants but even then the wrath of the Board was largely moderate. Another complicating factor for the private estates was the question of African tenants, whose position remained highly ambiguous throughout the colonial period.

These developments in colonial Malawi resonate with many of the conservation policies and practices pursued in other parts of the southern African region. In South Africa and Zimbabwe, the state took a particularly sympathetic stance towards large-scale commercial farms as opposed to small-scale peasant production. Wherever possible, efforts were made to avoid competition between white commercial farming and African production. While political and economic concerns shaped the manner and extent of state intervention in these colonies, political and ecological factors were at the centre of state intervention in colonial Malawi.[1] Economic factors seem to have played a much less significant role in influencing conservation policies at that time.

This chapter focuses on three main issues. The first section describes the process of creating a plantation economy and European land use practices. Until the 1950s, the state effectively turned a blind eye toward the settlers and, even when there was evidence of substantial erosion, did not use its powers to enforce policy. For their part, the planters essentially ignored any orders to carry out conservation work. The second section examines the shift in state policy from benign neglect to reluctant intervention. It demonstrates that, in the period after 1951, some efforts were made to deal with the problem of soil erosion taking place on the estates. The state intervened through the Natural Resources Board (NRB), which was heavily understaffed, underfunded and lacked the will to use force on private estates. The third section examines the factors that inhibited an effective state conservation programme on private estates. The estate owners opposed such programmes because the conservation measures were costly, time consuming and cumbersome. Land tenants were reluctant to adopt these betterment schemes because their tenure on the estates was short-term and insecure and the burden of building ridges and contour bunds literally fell on their backs.

---

1. See P. Delius and S. Schirmer, 'Soil Conservation in a Racially Ordered Society: South Africa, 1930–1970', *Journal of Southern African Studies* 26/4 (2000): 719–742; D. Potts, 'Environmental Myths and Narratives: Case Studies from Zimbabwe', in P. Stott and S. Sullivan (eds.) *Political Ecology: Science, Myth and Power* (London, Edward Arnold; New York, Oxford University Press: 2000) pp. 45–65; and K. Wilson, '"Water Used to be Scattered in the Landscape": Local Understandings of Soil Erosion and Land Use Planning in Southern Zimbabwe', *Environment and History* 1/3 (1995): 281–96.

State intervention into private estate production in the Shire Highlands

Creation of the estate sector and early cases of soil erosion, 1870s–1950

Between the 1870s and 1891, European missionaries and settlers began to alienate large amounts of land in freehold in the southern region of Malawi. Some concluded negotiations with African chiefs, even though the concept of freehold rights was never fully understood by the Africans who ceded such rights. Others bought land with payments as low as £1 an acre.[2] As a result of these actions, some Europeans and African chiefs lodged complaints with Harry Johnston, the country's first Commissioner, as soon as Protectorate rule was established. Johnston immediately launched an investigation into the matter and his first step was to collect all land claims for consideration. In order to ensure that the problem never happened again, Johnston began, in 1892, to issue certificates of claim to both European settlers and aspiring African farmers. These certificates effectively gave settlers the legal freehold rights to land. By 1894, 66 certificates of claim had been issued and out of this number only one was to an African, for 38,000 acres. The total area alienated in freehold stood at 3,705,255 acres, representing about 14 per cent of the total land-holding potential in Malawi, estimated at 25,161,924 acres.[3] Although the European settler population in Malawi remained comparatively small throughout the colonial period, the amount of alienated land in their possession was exceedingly large.[4]

Johnston's second step in solving the land problems in the territory was to establish a classification system. This stipulated three broad categories. First, there was public land, formerly known as Crown Land, which fell under the control of the government. It could be used for such activities as building government offices or establishing forest reserves. A second category consisted of freehold and leasehold land. This was land that could be bought, leased or even given to individuals and companies for their private use. Individuals and companies could use this type of land for establishing schools, churches, plantations and other commercial concerns. The third category consisted of Trust Land, initially known as customary or traditional land, which was designated for the majority of Africans. Under the aegis of traditional chiefs, who controlled usufructory rights, customary land could be used by Africans as and when need arose.[5] These changes in land tenure

---

2. See B. Pachai, *Land and Politics in Malawi, 1875–1975* (Kingston, Ont: Limestone Press, 1978), pp. 3–36.

3. B. Pachai, *Land and Politics in Malawi*, p. 37.

4. There were only 51 Europeans in 1891 and 300 in 1896. See C. A. Baker, 'Malawi's Exports: an Economic History', in G. W. Smith, B. Pachai and R. K. Tangri (eds.) *Malawi: Past and Present* (Blantyre: CLAIM, 1971), pp. 89–90. In 1913 the number of Europeans stood at 750, which included about 100 government officials, 200 missionaries, 107 planters and the rest were females and children. See R. Tangri, 'The Development of Modem African Politics and the Emergence of a Nationalist Movement in Colonial Malawi, 1891–1958' (Ph.D. Thesis, Edinburgh University, 1970), p. 107.

5. For details on land politics, see B. Pachai, *Land and Politics in Malawi*, pp. 30–47; and B. S. Krishnamurthy, 'Economic Policy, Land and Labour in Nyasaland, 1890–1914', in B. Pachai (ed.) *The Early History of Malawi* (London, 1972), pp. 384–404.

Creation of the estate sector and early cases of soil erosion, 1870s–1950

had far-reaching implications for gender relations and resistance to state-sponsored conservation campaigns.

Most of the estates were established within Johnston's second category, under freehold and leasehold rights. The planters generally produced cash crops such as tea, tobacco and cotton, which were vital to the export-oriented colonial agricultural economy. The actual plantation work was done by labour tenants. From the beginning of Protectorate rule in Malawi, the state had encouraged estate owners to use wage labour on their plantations. Coerced labour was never entertained. The Native Labour Ordinance of 1903, which was in force until 1928, stipulated minimum conditions that every planter had theoretically to fulfil when employing African workers. These conditions concerned, among other things, remuneration, sanitation, food, working hours and transportation.[6] But this Ordinance was only good on paper. The implementation of these regulations was left in the hands of the planters themselves who, driven by the need to get cheap labour, flouted the provisions of the Ordinance in many ways.[7]

Africans became labour tenants in several ways. The first was through land dispossession. Many Africans who had been dispossessed of land ended up either moving to other areas or remaining on the land as tenants. Others moved from African Trust Land and settled on private estates to seek wage employment. The introduction of hut tax in 1893, at six shillings per head, increased peasant demand for wage employment. Since the means of raising money were extremely limited for the peasants, seeking work on the estates became an attractive alternative. Another group of Africans who became labour tenants were Lomwe migrants from Mozambique. With the passage of time, labour tenancy turned into *thangata*, a coerced labour system.[8] The planters began to require Africans to work for them under very strict conditions. Work became the defining factor in the relationship between planters and workers. Tenants did not make direct cash payments either to the planters for rent or to the state for taxation. These obligations were met by the planters themselves, who deducted the costs from the labour input of the tenants. The long working hours, the poor wages and the lack of security on the land[9]

---

6. MNA, *Native Labour Ordinance of 1903* published in the Government Gazette of 31 March 1903.

7. For details on the planters' views about African labour, see L. White, *Magomero*; and Simon S. Myambo, 'The Shire Highlands Plantations: a Socio-Economic History of the Plantation System of Production in Malawi, 1891–1938' (MA Thesis, University of Malawi, 1973).

8. For details on Lomwe immigration and contribution to the labour force on the Shire Highlands plantations, see A. Chilivumbo, 'On Labour and Alomwe Immigration', *Rural Africana*, 24 (1974): 49–57; T. Galligan, 'The Nguru Penetration into Nyasaland, 1892–1914', in R. Macdonald (ed.) *From Nyasaland to Malawi* (Nairobi, 1975) pp. 108–123; and W. C. Chirwa, 'Alomwe and Mozambican Immigrant Labour in Colonial Malawi, 1890s–1945', *International Journal of African Historical Studies* 27/3 (1994): 525–550.

9. R. Palmer, 'Working Conditions and Worker Responses on the Nyasaland Tea Estates, 1930–1955', *Journal of African History* 27/1 (1986): 105–126; and 'White Farmers in

became critical factors in understanding the reluctance of tenants to undertake soil conservation measures to prevent erosion on land that was not theirs.

One of the earliest studies to acknowledge the existence of soil erosion on private estates took place in the early 1920s when A.J.W. Hornby, the Agricultural Chemist and Assistant Director of Agriculture, published his survey's report in the Bulletin of Agriculture.[10] According to Hornby, 'the enormous loss in soil fertility on the cultivated and cleared slopes of the Shire Highlands of Nyasaland, due to the washing away of top-soil, [was] apparent to every observant person'.[11] Although he argued that a considerable amount of soil erosion had been taking place in the territory, he did not give details as to the areas affected and the extent of the problem. Nevertheless, he outlined the various methods that had been used by both the planters and some sections of the African community to control erosion on cultivated lands. These methods consisted basically of mechanical conservation works and included contour ridging, ridge terracing and drains.

It was not until 1930 that a much clearer picture emerged of the extent of the problem, when P.H. Haviland, the Irrigation Engineer for Matabeleland in Southern Rhodesia, undertook a survey of soil erosion in Nyasaland. Following his visits to nearly twenty estates in Thyolo, Zomba, Mulanje and Ntcheu districts, Haviland presented a rather gloomy picture of soil erosion on private estates. He observed that both sheet and gully erosion had been taking place to an alarming degree. 'Erosion has taken [a] heavy toll of the soil fertility of these lands where, in the majority of cases, no steps in any direction have been taken to prevent its occurrence'.[12] For uncultivated lands in the region, he also noted 'from observations made by me it is very evident that erosion is occurring on the uncultivated lands of Nyasaland and that the matter of its prevention is one of immediate concern'.[13] Like Hornby, he found that the only methods that planters had been using to control erosion were ridges, terraces and drains. For example, in Thyolo district, a predominantly tea-growing area, he found that 'where measures have been taken to reduce soil erosion, the method adopted has been similar to the Mlanje method as far as drains are concerned but there has been a greater tendency towards graded ridge terracing than at Mlanje'.[14] For this particular method, ridges were usually set out on the contours of the slope and drains were excavated immediately below

---

Malawi: Before and After the Depression', *African Affairs* 84/335 (1985): 211–245; and L. White, *Magomero*.

10. A. J. W. Hornby, 'The Erosion of Arable Soil in Nyasaland and Methods of Prevention', in F. Dixey *et al. The Destruction of Vegetation and its Relation to Climate, Water Supply, and Soil Fertility*, pp. 10-16.

11. A.J.W. Hornby, 'The Erosion of Arable Soil in Nyasaland', p. 10.

12. P. H. Haviland, Report on Soil Erosion Prevention and Reclamation of Eroded Arable Land in Nyasaland, 1930, p. 4.

13. *Ibid.* p. 12.

14. *Ibid.* p. 3.

Creation of the estate sector and early cases of soil erosion, 1870s–1950

each ridge. This method helped to draw off the water collected above each ridge, the water percolating through the ridge into the drain.

Haviland also described the antipathy of estate owners toward erosion control. A few estate owners thought that ridge terracing served no useful purpose and, in fact, encouraged soil erosion. In consequence, they did not make the effort to apply it correctly. He observed that 'there appeared to be a mistaken idea that part of the silt collected in the drains was wash from the soil above the ridge. It is difficult to know how such an erroneous conception found place.'[15] In fact, the purpose of the drains was to collect the silt off the downstream slope of the ridges. However, studies in other parts of the southern African region show that terracing was not always the most appropriate measure for controlling erosion. In her study of soil erosion in colonial Lesotho, Showers demonstrates that, far from arresting the process, poorly constructed and maintained terracing together with ploughing were largely responsible for the acceleration of soil erosion.[16]

The situation on the tobacco- and cotton-growing estates of Zomba, Ntcheu and some parts of Thyolo districts was even worse. Sheet erosion had taken place on a large scale. In fact, it was found on one piece of land 'that an average depth of six inches of topsoil had been removed in the course of a few years of cultivation'.[17] This erosion was attributed to the nature of the soil in the region, which tended to be of a sandy-loam type and very liable to sheet washing, which later developed into gully erosion. In this connection, Haviland advised that 'special attention should be given to combating soil washing in these areas as its occurrence is more difficult to observe initially than on steeper slopes'.[18]

On the whole, estate owners did not use many methods to control soil erosion. Those who did often lacked knowledge of how to make ridge terraces, graded ridges and drains so that 'mistakes in construction' were quite common and resulted in faulty and ineffective control of erosion. On one estate, located a few miles from Zomba, 'heavy erosion had occurred and it appeared doubtful whether reclamation could be effected in any comparatively short period. In fact it seemed useless to do anything with the land except to allow it to revert to its original grass covered condition.'[19] Both gully and sheet erosion had taken place on this estate and virtually no erosion control measures had been used. Haviland went on to argue that 'this highly eroded state appeared to be very common all over the tobacco and

---

15. *Ibid.* p. 4.
16. For a detailed understanding of the different causes of soil erosion, see K. Showers, 'Soil Conservation in the Kingdom of Lesotho: Origins and Colonial Response'; and K. Showers and G. Malahlela, 'Oral Evidence in Historical Environmental Impact Assessment: Soil Conservation in Lesotho', *Journal of Southern African Studies* 18/2 (1992): 277–95.
17. P.H. Haviland, Report on Soil Erosion Prevention, p. 4. Hornby felt that the loss of more than 6 inches of topsoil posed a serious threat to soil fertility and the erosion of arable land. See A.J.W. Hornby, 'The Erosion of Arable Soil in Nyasaland'.
18. P.H. Haviland, Report on Soil Erosion Prevention, pp. 4–5.
19. *Ibid.* p. 5.

cotton areas where cropping had been carried out for many years and no provision made for the control of storm water'.[20]

Having studied the erosion situation in the Shire Highlands region, Haviland proposed several recommendations for its control and for the reclamation of such eroded lands. He also elaborated on the requirements and usefulness of these measures in order to minimise errors in their construction. First, storm drains had to be used to prevent the entry of outside storm water into the cultivated lands. These needed to be constructed around land boundaries, in conjunction with ridge terracing. This method helped to control run-off water.

The second method of controlling erosion he suggested was ridge terracing, which was described as the most economical means of combating erosion on cultivated lands and also as one that was adaptable to varying slopes, rainfall conditions and soil textures. The method consisted of a series of low ridges of earth running across the slope of the land at intervals. Ridge terracing theoretically helped to control the removal of water in small, slow moving volumes; to prevent soil removal by deposition behind each ridge; to prevent waterlogging; and to maintain an efficient moisture content.

The Haviland report also recommended that ridge terracing should always be on a slope and never a level field.[21] In fact, the maximum length of a ridge had also to be the maximum length on a grade in one direction. All ridge terraces had to discharge into storm drains or onto uncultivated land that was sufficiently protected by natural vegetation to prevent erosion. Where ridges discharged into drains, some form of protection was required at the discharge points. This could consist of a grassed patch or a step down into the drain protected from potholing by the falling water. No definite ditch was to be formed on the top side of the ridge, as this could lead to an increase in velocity and the consequent transportation of the silt that should be collected. The initial cost of ridge terracing was estimated at 8 shillings per acre on very steeply sloping land and 5 shillings per acre on moderately sloping land. Many planters considered this to be a lot of money and refused to engage in these activities.[22]

Other measures for controlling soil erosion that Haviland proposed included silting up the areas where gullies had already formed, planting vegetation in the gullies to help reclaim the eroded areas, planting the lands with a cover crop immediately after the main crop had been harvested in order to reduce evaporation from the soil and consequent aeolian erosion, and prohibiting the cultivation of stream banks to prevent lateral erosion.

Finally, the report recommended a broad extension programme to educate the European settlers in matters of conservation. It was noted that the absence of

---

20. *Ibid*. p. 5.
21. This recommendation was made because making terraces on a level field resulted in waterlogging.
22. A.J.W. Hornby, 'The Erosion of Arable Soil in Nyasaland', p. 10.

Creation of the estate sector and early cases of soil erosion, 1870s–1950

this education allowed planters to make several unnecessary mistakes. 'One of the strongest impressions I gained during the course of my visit was the almost complete lack of general knowledge of the causes and effects of soil erosion in the minds of the majority of planters. This undoubtedly is due to the paucity of propaganda on the subject.'[23] One example of the recommended extension service included the provision of periodic publications on various aspects of conservation, such as the requirements for undertaking the measures and the costs involved.

When the Haviland report appeared, the colonial state advised the Department of Agriculture and the Native Tobacco Board to provide extension work on soil conservation to private estates. However, the settlers ignored the recommendations of the report. Faced with settler indifference, a senior agricultural officer raised the prospect of state intervention: 'The adoption of a wise agricultural and forest policy is necessary to minimise harm to the soil on which the country depends'.[24]

In the previous year, a meeting of the Board of Agriculture, convened to consider native agricultural production and the settlement of immigrants, decided that conservation measures that had initially been applied to African lands should also be extended to private estates. For example, the Board of Agriculture mentioned that the 'policy on hill slopes be brought to the notice of owners or holders of estates with a plea urging them to do everything possible to apply similar policy to their lands'.[25] But as an example of the racialising of the environmental issue, the state had no appropriate mechanism for enforcing the implementation of these policies. Throughout the 1930s and 1940s, the state had no legal framework to back up its concerns about the increasing rate of soil erosion on private estates. Estate owners were largely left to themselves and used the land in any way they wanted. For Africans on Trust Land, however, the state had very specific legal mechanisms to enforce conservation works, which it applied vigorously. Initially, these legal powers were spelt out in the Land Conservation Policy of 1939 and, later, in the Natural Resources Ordinance of 1946.

When the state attempted to intervene in the estate sector, however, its approach and actions were weak and superficial. For instance, in February 1938, the Director of Agriculture wrote to the Agricultural Officer for Mulanje district urging him to exercise caution in providing an extension service to estate owners. The Director explained that his department felt it undesirable to run the risk of antagonising estate owners or managers. He stressed that conservation work should be carried out only on those estates where the owner or manager was willing to accept such measures.[26] Even when the government issued a circular on Land

---

23. *Ibid.* p. 11.
24. A. J. W. Hornby, *Denudation and Soil Erosion in Nyasaland*, (Zomba, Government Printer, Department of Agriculture, Bulletin No. 11, February 1934), p. 6.
25. A.J.W. Hornby, *Denudation and Soil Erosion in Nyasaland*, pp. 20–21.
26. MNA A3/2/227: Letter by the Director of Agriculture, Zomba, to the Agricultural Officer, Mulanje, 7 September 1938.

State intervention into private estate production in the Shire Highlands

Conservation Policy in 1939, there was little mention of conservation on private estates.[27] It did, on the other hand, spell out the requirements for peasants and tenants to undertake such measures on the lands they occupied.

Following the settlers' disregard for the recommendations of the Haviland report and subsequent proposals by the Department of Agriculture, the state continued to close its eyes and pursue its policy of benign neglect with regard to environmental degradation on estates. Meanwhile, in the 1940s, the state introduced a new postwar agricultural policy, placing much emphasis on erosion control and proper land use practices. These policies were again not applied to soil conservation on private estates. Instead, most of the state's resources were directed at implementing the schemes on African Trust Land. The subsequent promulgation of the Natural Resources Ordinance in 1946 and the formation of the Natural Resources Board in the same year equally ignored degradation on the estates. This situation continued until 1951, when the Natural Resources Board raised concerns about the lack of a clear policy on the conservation of natural resources. In spite of overwhelming evidence of the occurrence of soil erosion, the Board failed to compel planters to undertake conservation measures on their estates.

State intervention into estate production, 1951–1958

In the period after 1951, state intervention into private estates was prompted by a combination of several factors. First, the evidence of degradation on the estates became increasingly glaring and appeared to be threatening long-term production. Secondly, the postwar agricultural policy placed much emphasis on increasing production of food and cash crops and the proper use of the land. This inevitably affected both the estate and peasant sectors of the economy. The colonial state established various bodies to implement these policies, such as the Postwar Development Committee and the Natural Resources Board.

However, the precipitating factor was a meeting of the Provincial Natural Resources Board (PNRB), which complained to government in October 1951 that, although the state encouraged conservation in all areas of the country, no provision had been made in the laws for the implementation of conservation measures on private estates. William Rangeley, the Provincial Commissioner for the South, and Chairman of the PNRB, conceded that 'the Natural Resources Rules appeared to have been designed almost exclusively for African Trust Land and private estates had been largely ignored'.[28] This reflected a racialised environmental policy and consequently created many problems for the Board, which strove to see measures for the conservation of natural resources implemented across the Protectorate.

---

27. Nyasaland Government, *Land Conservation Policy of 1939*, Circular No.1.
28. MNA NSG 2/1/2: Minutes of the Meeting of the Southern Province Natural Resources Board held in Blantyre on 24 October 1951.

State intervention into estate production, 1951–1958

Another problem confronting the Board was the position of the tenants on private estates. The Board acknowledged that 'one of the difficulties of applying orders to private estates was that it was desired to apply them principally to the tenants on private estates'.[29] This exempted the estate owners and, as we shall see later, created an inextricably difficult situation for the colonial conservationists. Furthermore, there was a belief within the planter community that some crops, such as tung and tea, did not require any conservation measures to be undertaken because they were perennial. On the other hand, crops such as tobacco, cotton and maize needed to be protected with conservation measures. The Board had to decide whether perennial crops did indeed adequately protect the soil and could therefore be exempted from conservation practices.

The Board's discussion came about as a result of environmental degradation taking place on several private estates. These included the Mambala Estate, owned by Muljibhai Chaturadas Parekh and located about fifteen miles from Limbe on the Midima Road. The condition of this estate was so bad that, on 10 October 1951, the Chairman called an extraordinary meeting to discuss the application of section 13 of the Natural Resources Ordinance. Even though the Board did not have the mandate to intervene in private estates, the meeting decided to carry out all the necessary works on the estate and to recover the cost from Mr Parekh. This decision was taken on an ad hoc basis because the government had not yet authorised the Board to deal with conservation on private estates. It may also have been relevant that this unusually interventionist approach occurred on private land where the estate owner was Asian, for at the time there was no representation of Asians (or Africans) on the Board.

Environmental degradation had been taking place on other estates as well. At the Blantyre and East Africa Ltd in Domasi district, the Board had raised great concern over the lack of maintenance of bunds on the lands occupied by tenants, which had resulted in serious soil erosion. Moreover, there was confusion between the tenants and the estate owners as to who should do the maintenance work. The tenants argued that since they paid rent, it was not their responsibility to make the bunds.[30] On the other hand, the owners of the estate argued that the tenants should do this work and that the government had to enforce this measure in the same way it did with Africans on Trust Land. After a thorough discussion, the Board decided that the Company should do the work.

The third example of environmental degradation concerned the Nabomba and Nchima Estates, property of the Thyolo and Michiru Tea and Tobacco Company, in Thyolo district. At the beginning of 1951, the manager of these estates wrote to the Chairman of the Thyolo District Natural Resources Board (DNRB) to request that it required the tenants to undertake conservation measures on the

---

29. *Ibid.* 30
30. Interview: Mr Subiya Anusa, Kapichi Village, T. A. Malemia, Zomba district, dated 15 May 1997.

land they occupied. He indicated that he had tried before but felt powerless to get Africans do the work. In turn, the PNRB issued an order under section 10 of the Ordinance to compel native residents on these estates to maintain the bunds already constructed.[31]

The deteriorating ecological situation presented serious challenges to the Board, which was in the process of sorting out the technicalities pertaining to policy and implementation of conservation measures on private estates. The Board had to justify not only its existence but also its intervention in privately owned lands. From its inception in 1946, the Board had been primarily concerned with the conservation of natural resources on African Trust Land and its mandate on private estates was very murky. Moreover, the Board did not have proper mechanisms for intervening in private estates.

The remaining part of this section examines specific examples of the state's ineffectual policies on private estates. First, however, there is a brief discussion of some concessions that the Board made to the demands and interests of the planters concerning conservation. These should be seen as part of the failed policy of state intervention in private estates owned by non-Africans.

The Board suggested that, in order to gain the support of the estate owners, some incentives should be given to them to implement conservation measures on their estates. The Board took the viewpoint that state support had been provided for Africans via the Native Development and Welfare Fund (NDWF) and similar support should be provided on European estates. But this argument was essentially misconceived because the NDWF did not subsidise conservation work on Trust Land. The majority of its support went to the promotion of food and cash crops in the postwar period. Nevertheless, there were historical precedents for the colonial state providing incentives to estate owners. For example, in Southern Rhodesia, the government had provided loans and subsidies to estate owners in the interests of soil and water conservation.[32] But in order to apply a similar scheme to Nyasaland, the Board noted that certain conditions should be borne in mind. First, such a scheme had to be part of an integrated agricultural production policy, including food and cash crops; and second, it would be necessary to provide some mechanical equipment to landowners since large-scale conservation work used an excessive amount of money and labour.[33]

The proposal to establish a special soil conservation unit attracted great interest among Board members and the planter community generally. The conser-

---

31. MNA NSG 2/1/2: Minutes of the Meeting of the Southern Province Natural Resources Board held in Blantyre on 24 October 1951.

32. *Ibid.* See also, I. Phimister, 'Discourse and the Discipline of Historical Context: Conservationism and Ideas about Development in Southern Rhodesia, 1930–1950', *Journal of Southern African Studies* 12/2 (1986): 263–75.

33. However, the greatest problem for Nyasaland was lack of money. MNA NSG 2/1/2: Minutes of the Meeting of the Southern Province Natural Resources Board held in Blantyre on 7 February 1952.

State intervention into estate production, 1951–1958

vation unit was designed to help private estate owners undertake soil conservation measures using tractors and auxiliary equipment. The major duties of the unit were, first, to mark out the land for bunding, at an estimated cost of ½d per yard marked; second, to make dams and storm drains; and third, to offer free advice to estate owners on the costs and sites of making dams.[34] In terms of personnel and equipment, the proposed unit would consist of one European supervisor, six African kapitaos, one truck and a variety of other kinds of equipment and incidentals. The Board strongly supported this idea, arguing that previous experience had shown that there were many people, especially Indian and Greek estate owners, who were prepared to undertake conservation measures but had insufficient knowledge to do the work on their own. In addition, it was hoped that the unit would meet and overcome the main difficulty confronting the private estate owner in the execution of soil conservation works, namely labour.[35] The estate owners had expressed willingness to pay for the services rendered.

In order to overcome the problem of shortage of skilled manpower, the Board suggested that the Agricultural Department should run training courses for estate kapitaos and labour supervisors in conservation methods and that the estate owners should pay for such courses.[36] That happened two years later when the Board organised a Soil Conservation Instructional Course at Masambanjati from 26 to 30 May 1954 for agricultural instructors and for the private estates community in Thyolo district. The training involved a series of technical lectures on conservation matters and a film on soil conservation and general farming.

Meanwhile, whilst waiting for the government's decision on these proposals and the general policy regarding conservation on private estates, the Chairman of the Board circulated the proposals to various farmers and planters' associations for comments. He also implored them to consider two additional proposals. First, that all stream banks (dimbas) on the estates be protected from cultivation for a distance of ten to twenty yards from the banks on either side and, secondly, that the protection of all natural and evergreen forests should be applied throughout the province and on all kinds of land, with the proviso that a permit be obtained from a European Forest Officer before cutting any timber from such forests.[37]

Regulations for prohibiting stream bank cultivation were common in other parts of southern Africa but for very different reasons. In Zimbabwe, studies have shown that the prohibition of *dambo* [pan field] cultivation was not driven only by concerns about ecological degradation but rather by the economic and politi-

---

34. MNA NSG 2/1/2: Minutes of the Meeting of the Southern Province Natural Resources Board held in Blantyre on 2 May 1952.
35. MNA NSG 2/1/2: Half Yearly Report of the Southern Province Natural Resources Board, 30 June 1954.
36. MNA NSG 2/1/2: Minutes of the Meeting of the Southern Province Natural Resources Board held in Blantyre on 7 February 1952.
37. *Ibid.*

cal concerns of the white commercial farmers.[38] In Malawi, such restrictions were instituted in order to contain the rate of soil erosion, even though the extent of the problem may have been exaggerated due to lack of reliable evidence on the subject.

The prohibition of stream bank cultivation raised great concern within the planter community. C.E. Snell, a representative of the Planters Association on the Board and one of the most prominent European farmers in the Shire Highlands, strongly argued in favour of allowing perennial crops, such as tea, to be grown along river banks. He felt no stream bank restriction was necessary since tea was a perennial crop and stressed that stream banks tended to be very fertile zones. Conceding to pressures from the planters, the Board decided to add other crops to this list of perennial plants, such as tung, yellow bamboos and bananas which, the Board hoped, would also serve to demarcate the reserved strip along streams. In any case, it was anticipated that these plants would be grown only with the permission of a European forest officer.[39]

It was not until April 1952 that Rangeley reported to the Board that the government had decided that the Natural Resources Rules, which had hitherto applied only to Trust Land, should be extended to private estates.[40] However, although the government authorised the Board to enforce the undertaking of conservation measures on private estates, it did not approve the proposal to form a soil conservation unit. This proposal was rejected on the grounds that it entailed a subsidisation of plantation production. On the role of the Board generally, Rangeley explained that:

> the policy of the Board had been to try and get people to fall in line by peaceful persuasion but if that was not possible, then to enforce orders up to the hilt, using the law, as orders were, in fact, only served in cases of non-cooperation. If these orders were not likely to meet with success in court, then they would have to be redrafted and fresh orders issued.[41]

After its role was clarified, the Board began to effect its orders on private estates with varying degrees of success. It decided that the same operational guidelines that the government had been using for Africans on Trust Land would have to be used on private estates. Although the rationale was not clearly explained, the

---

38. See D. Potts, 'Environmental Myths and Narratives: Case Studies'; K. Wilson, '"Water Used to be Scattered in the Landscape"' and 'Aspects of the History of Vlei Cultivation in Southern Zimbabwe' (Paper presented to the Dambo Research Project 'Use of Dambos' Workshop, University of Zimbabwe, August 1986); and R. Owen et al. (eds.) *Dambo Farming in Zimbabwe: Water Management, Cropping and Soil Potentials for Smallholder Farming in the Wetlands* (Harare: University of Zimbabwe Publications, 1995).

39. MNA NSG 2/1/2: Minutes of the Meeting of the Southern Province Natural Resources Board held in Blantyre on 2 May 1952.

40. MNA NSG 2/1/2: Minutes of the Meeting of the Southern Province Natural Resources Board held in Blantyre on 23 April 1954.

41. MNA NSG 2/1/2: Minutes of the Meeting of the Southern Province Natural Resources Board held in Blantyre on 13 November 1953.

State intervention into estate production, 1951–1958

Board aimed to conserve each year about 12.5 per cent of the land occupied by estates.[42] Three examples will be cited here to illustrate the way in which the Board intervened between 1951 and 1958 to implement soil conservation measures on private estates, the limits of its power and the opposition of settlers.

The first example is that of the Chilambe Estate, owned by Mr and Mrs S.J. Bell of Thyolo district. In May 1953, the Thyolo DNRB requested the PNRB to issue an order under section 10 of the NRO to be applied to tenants on the estate because of the poor condition of the land. Mr Bell had acquired this land from the British Central Africa Company and, at the time of purchase, the estate was in a very degraded condition. He noted that the 'tenants had been left to their own devices for many years and were consequently undisciplined in regard to the conservation of natural resources'.[43] Mr Bell argued that, although he had inherited the problem of land degradation from the previous owner, he was anxious to apply soil conservation measures on the estate. However, his previous attempts to get tenants to undertake conservation measures had failed. The tenants refused because, as discussed above, they felt that, since they paid rent to the owner of the estate, it was not their responsibility to carry out the measures. Mr Bell threatened that if the tenants continued to resist he would move a large proportion of them to a new site on the estate.

The threat to move the tenants out created a degree of consternation among the Board members because they feared that the Chilambe case would set a bad precedent for tenants on other private estates. Evacuation of tenants would mean the removal also of the labour necessary for carrying out conservation measures. But after examining this matter again, the Thyolo DNRB agreed to apply section 10 of the NRO, which provided for the Board to enforce the taking of conservation measures on a designated piece of land. It also recommended that Mr Bell should arrange for the training of kapitaos who should be responsible for the issuing of instructions and ensuring that the orders were complied with.[44] These decisions were, however, not acted upon. Mr Bell simply ignored the Board's orders as he did not want to pay the labour costs for conservation work.

In 1954, the Thyolo DNRB again requested the PNRB to serve an order under section 10 of the NRO to stop the cultivation by tenants of boundary areas of the Chilambe Estate, which threatened the destruction of a stream. This order was applied in conjunction with Rule 5 of the Natural Resources Rules (NRR), which required an occupier of land to construct bunds within six weeks of being served with a notice. Mrs Bell, who had taken over the management of the estate, expressed her willingness to cooperate with the Board but noted that the problem

---

42. MNA NSG 2/1/2: Minutes of the Meeting of the Southern Province Natural Resources Board held in Blantyre on 7 February 1952.
43. MNA NSG 2/1/2: Minutes of the Meeting of the Southern Province Natural Resources Board held in Blantyre on 2 May 1952.
44. *Ibid.*

State intervention into private estate production in the Shire Highlands

lay mainly with the tenants. As in 1953, she planned to move the tenants to another piece of land more suitable for their settlement and cultivation. At this point, she also complained that some tenants were not paying their rent for the use of the land. To give effect to her threats, Mrs Bell submitted an order to the Arbitration Board for the eviction of five tenants on grounds of non-payment of rent.

The uneasy relationship between Mrs Bell and her tenants on the Chilambe estate aroused much interest in both the District and Provincial Boards. It served as a litmus test of the efficacy of the Board on private estates. In view of this situation, the Board responded by making three far-reaching decisions. First, the tenants who were required to move from one part of the estate to another were to be given one year's notice that they would have to vacate their gardens by 31 May 1955. Secondly, no stream bank cultivation should be permitted during the present season and bunds should be constructed by communal labour in the area the tenants to be be served with eviction orders were at present cultivating. Thirdly, these instructions should be communicated to the tenants immediately by an Administrative Officer and, two days after this warning, the Soil Conservation Teams should move in to begin the implementation of conservation measures.[45] The Board planned that all these decisions would be carried out before the start of the rains in November or December of 1954.

The Provincial Natural Resources Board took a particularly strong position on this matter and warned that the tenants should be informed that they had the alternative of being moved off either to another part of the estate or to Trust Land or Public Land as desired by the owner. As for Mrs Bell, the Board warned that, if she did not intend to cultivate the land, Rule 16 of the Natural Resources Rules of 1951 would be applied to obviate the question of compensation.[46] This rule compelled her to undertake conservation measures on any land that she owned or occupied, whether she cultivated it or not.

Even when the eviction order had been effected at the end of 1954, the Chilambe Estate continued to be a problem to the Board. Mrs Bell had intimated that she would remove the tenants from the land so that she could use it for grazing purposes. This would have meant destroying the bunds made by the tenants that year. The Thyolo DNRB rejected that proposal and strongly warned her about her obligation to maintain the bunds under the NRO. By mid-1955, however, the Thyolo DNRB reported that the tenants had not been moved.[47] From a conservation point of view, no progress had been made on the estate despite the Board's instructions.

The second example of recalcitrant private estates is that of the Nswadzi Estate at Sandama in Thyolo district, which was a property of the Nyasaland Railways.

---

45. MNA NSG 2/1/2: Minutes of the Meeting of the Southern Province Natural Resources Board held in Blantyre on 5 November 1954.

46. *Ibid.*

47. MNA NSG 2/1/2: Minutes of the Meeting of the Southern Province Natural Resources Board held in Blantyre on 22 July 1955.

State intervention into estate production, 1951–1958

Sometime in 1952, Mr Stevens of Nyasaland Railways told the Thyolo DNRB that his company was not interested in developing the estate and had already put it up for sale. The Railways felt it unnecessary to undertake any conservation measures when no development was taking place. In response to this, the Thyolo DNRB decided, on 27 September 1952, that the estate must be protected in order to prevent erosion and preserve the fertility of the soil. To this effect, the Board made four recommendations. First, all existing gardens should be bunded. Secondly, no new land should be opened for cultivation except under very strict conditions. Thirdly, certain gardens situated on the steepest slopes to the south and east of the estate should be closed and the owners offered new gardens in more suitable areas. Finally, the area comprising steep slopes to the Nswadzi River and the railway should be closed to cultivation and tree cover be restored.[48] These recommendations were then communicated to the owners of Nswadzi estate for action. But the Railways procrastinated and the Board did nothing about it even though it had the powers to use force to implement conservation measures.

In February 1955, the Thyolo DNRB reported that the owners of Nswadzi estate were still not cooperating: 'the Railways had hinted that they were only prepared to carry out such soil conservation work as they were compelled to do'.[49] The Board's response was simply to say that no action would be taken at that time but that the estate should be targeted for inclusion in the following year's conservation drive. Yet the Board knew very well that the Nswadzi estate required serious ecological rehabilitation: it had become ever more severely eroded and there was urgent need to protect at least sixty yards either side of the Nswadzi River, which was described at that time as 'possibly one of the dirtiest streams in the Province'[50] because of the soil being washed away from the cultivated but unprotected sections of the estate.

In July 1955, the PNRB intervened again with the aim of controlling cultivation along the banks of the Nswadzi River. It invoked Rule 17 of the NRR to order people to move out of the area near the river and to turn it into a forest area. This rule also affected other adjacent estates, such as the Midimwe and Mirango estates, which covered an area of 5,700 acres. The owners of these estates complied only partially and reluctantly; as late as 1958, there were reports of some planters still violating the Board's orders.[51]

The third example of Board intervention is on some private estates in the Zomba district. Here, the PNRB had, at the recommendation of the DNRB in April 1953, served orders under section 10 of the NRO, for failure to take conserva-

---

48. MNA NSG 2/1/2: Minutes of the Meeting of the Southern Province Natural Resources Board held in Blantyre on 7 November 1952.
49. MNA NSG 2/1/2: Minutes of the Meeting of the Southern Province Natural Resources Board held in Blantyre on 25 February 1955.
50. MNA NSG 2/1/2: Minutes of the Meeting of the Southern Province Natural Resources Board held in Blantyre on 22 July 1955.
51. *Ibid.*

tion measures, on the following estates: Daud Tayub's estate at Chirunga, Jotham Chenyama's land at Thondwe, Osman Dada's Thondwe Estate, and the Yiannakis brothers' Namikhate Estate. Of these estates, Daud Tayub's at Chirunga sparked the most controversy within the Board. From a conservation point of view, it was divided into two sections. One section consisted of land occupied and cultivated by tenants. Although it had not been bunded it looked to be in a much better condition than the other section and no serious soil erosion had taken place in the agricultural year of 1952/3. According to Subiya Anusa of Kapichi Village in Zomba, Tayub allowed his tenants to produce crops the way they wanted: 'I never worked there myself but I knew some people who did. They built their own houses there and produced crops which they sold to the bwana. Then the bwana would pay the tenants after all the crops had been harvested and sold.'[52] The other section of the estate did not have any development on it except 'brickyards, holes and gullies with no grass cover whatsoever'.[53] It was this section that required more immediate attention. However, as with the other examples, the Board's directives were ignored. By 1954, no work had been done and the Board issued yet another order under section 10 to the Chirunga Estate. In the meantime, the Department of Agriculture began to apply conservation measures in accordance with Rule 5 of the NRR, which provided for the Board to compel the occupier of the land or any person authorised by him to undertake conservation measures. The Board also initiated a prosecution case in court to recover the money that had been spent on conservation measures on the estate. However, while waiting for the result of the prosecution, the Board changed its position and decided that 'some leniency could be allowed on Mr Tayub'.[54] While it was not really clear why this leniency should have been extended to Tayub, conflict between him and a village headman played some part in eliciting sympathy from the Board who remarked on 'the unpleasantness, antagonism and inefficiency displayed on the part of Village Headman Jailus'. Nevertheless, it was acknowledged that Tayub had failed to implement its conservation policies on the estate and it was clear that he had failed to maintain bunds. Moreover, other estate owners in similar conditions did not receive such leniency from the Board. In this particular case, the Board appeared to be demonstrating a lack of seriousness about enforcing conservation on private estates.

The decision to pardon Tayub and blame Village Headman Jailus was probably related to the highly ambiguous position of village headmen and chiefs in the soil conservation campaigns. Under section 12 of the NRO of 1949, Native Authorities had powers to order users of Native Trust Land to undertake conserva-

---

52. Interview: Mr Subiya Anusa, Kapichi Village, T. A. Malemia, Zomba district, dated 15 May 1997.
53. MNA NSG 2/1/2: Minutes of the Meeting of the Southern Province Natural Resources Board held in Blantyre on 27 April 1953.
54. MNA NSG 2/1/2: Minutes of the Meeting of the Southern Province Natural Resources Board held in Blantyre on 29 January 1954.

Factors inhibiting an effective state conservation programme

tion measures. However, on private estates, the government had made it clear in 1952 that landlords, and not Native Authorities, were responsible for issuing orders to their tenants. Thus, any decision to get chiefs to enforce conservation measures on private estates can be interpreted as an attempt at scapegoating. Private estates, established under freehold or leasehold rights, did not fall within the jurisdiction of the chiefs.

Factors inhibiting an effective state conservation programme

Although the state had enormous powers to implement conservation on private estates, it generally lacked the will to act and simply pursued a policy of benign neglect. The Provincial Natural Resources Board, which was the state's main body for intervention, was also bedevilled with many problems. First, it lacked a clear mandate. It attempted to use the Natural Resources Ordinance and Rules, which were primarily intended for Africans on Trust Land. Secondly, the Board was underfunded and understaffed. On many occasions, it was unable to enforce orders that had been served on estate owners. The Thondwe estate of Jotham Chenyama in Zomba was a case in point. The Board's meeting of 20 August 1954 reported that 'the Zomba DNRB ... [had failed] ... to give effect to the Order due to lack of funds and suggested that no further Orders be made on such estates unless adequate funds and staff were available for their enforcement'.[55] In fact, the Executive Officer of the Board complained at the same meeting that there had not been a single successful prosecution for non-compliance with such orders.[56] Funding for the Board was extremely limited and often came from the resources of the Departments of Agriculture and Forestry. The Department of Agriculture had contributed technical staff to construct conservation works, for example, while the special vote of the Board catered only for meetings, special schemes and other operational costs.

The Board's reliance on members of staff from the Agriculture Department who visited the environmentally degraded areas and marked bunds proved to be inadequate. There was a need for 'follow-up' work, which also required a certain amount of 'policing'. The Board noted that the Native Authorities could not do that policing work because it was not within their jurisdiction and previous attempts to get them involved had already proved ineffective. Given the circumstances, the Board broached the idea of employing Soil Rangers. These became 'the Board's Policemen ... [they] were given a degree of basic training in the rudiments of soil conservation, provided with a distinctive uniform, and sent to work with individual

---

55. MNA NSG 2/1/2: Minutes of the Meeting of the Southern Province Natural Resources Board held in Blantyre on 20 August 1954.
56. *Ibid.*

soil teams. It was further necessary for these Rangers to be given powers of arrest similar to those exercised by Boma messengers.'[57]

The third problem the Board had to deal with was the thorny issue of tenants on private estates. This related to the larger issue of land tenure policy. For a long time, it was not clear whether the individual tenants or the estate owners had to undertake conservation measures on the land. However, since tenants paid rent to the estate owners, it was assumed that the latter would be responsible for undertaking any conservation works. It was not until November 1953 that the Board received clarification on the subject from the government. William Rangeley, the Chairman of the Board, told members that the government had approved the following procedure for dealing with tenants on private estates. To begin with, the DNRB had to issue an order to an estate owner. The owner would, in turn, issue the order to the tenants and, if the tenants as a group refused to carry out the instructions of the owner, then the owner could apply for another order to be served on each individual tenant. In such a case, the orders on tenants had to be signed individually, delivered to each respective tenant and a receipt obtained and, until this procedure had been carried out, no prosecution could be made. If a tenant still resisted, he risked prosecution and eventual eviction from the estate.[58]

This procedure came under heavy criticism from some Board members who argued that it was too complicated and time-consuming. They particularly complained about the requirement for each individual tenant to be served with a notice; it was just too laborious and involved too much paperwork. The alternative suggested was to bypass the landlords and instead serve the notices on Village Headmen using section 11 of the NRO. Had this approach been adopted, it would have made the village headmen legally responsible for the implementation of conservation measures, as they were on African Trust Land. However, the procedure was not changed and the requirement to serve each tenant remained. Nevertheless, in practice, village headmen were drawn into the system. As noted earlier, one example was that of village headman Jailus of Zomba who was blamed for obstructing conservation measures on Tayub's Chirunga estate in 1954.[59]

The tenants often resisted these interventionist moves by the colonial state. In some cases, they refused to obey the orders requiring them to undertake conservation measures. In 1955, for example, it was noted that on the Sambankhanga Estate in Thyolo district, about ten tenant families had simply ignored the Board's orders and continued to cultivate the land the way they wanted.[60] Like their peas-

---

57. MNA NSG 2/1/2: Minutes of the Meeting of the Southern Province Natural Resources Board held in Blantyre on 13 November 1953.
58. *Ibid.*
59. MNA NSG 2/1/2: Minutes of the Meeting of the Southern Province Natural Resources Board held in Blantyre on 29 January 1954.
60. MNA NSG 2/1/2: Minutes of the Meeting of the Southern Province Natural Resources Board held in Blantyre on 22 July 1955.

Factors inhibiting an effective state conservation programme

ant counterparts on African Trust Land, the tenants were resisting conservation in ways that seriously undermined the image of the state's policies. For example, the Board's annual report for 1953 pointed out that:

> during the disturbances, especially in the Cholo, Blantyre and Chiradzulu districts, a great deal of completed and consolidated soil conservation work was destroyed and damaged by agitators. Bunds were hoed up, pegs uprooted and destroyed, storm drains damaged, and many new gardens indiscriminately opened up in previously closed areas.[61]

This resistance was a rational response by workers who disliked doing work on land that did not belong to them and where their security was short-term and insecure. Tenants had a long tradition of resistance to the structures of power and coercion. In the 1930s and 1940s, cases of tenants defaulting or refusing to pay rent were not unusual in the Shire Highlands estates.[62]

The struggles over conservation work on the estates are still remembered today in Malawi. Mai Abine Odireki of Luka Village in Chief Nsabwe's area, whose husband had worked as an agricultural kapitao in various parts of Thyolo district, stressed that working with tenants had been one of the most difficult aspects of her husband's career. Many tenants had hated conservation work because it was time-consuming and cumbersome. Some had two homes, one on the estate and the other on African Trust Land and would move from one to another to avoid such work. Others simply deserted to other places where the enforcement of conservation measures was less rigorous. As a member of the soil conservation teams implementing 'bunding drives', her husband had not been popular with peasants and tenants. 'When my husband visited the gardens of farmers he was often seen as a representative of the harsh boma. Some people insulted and called him all sorts of bad names but he was never assaulted physically as others experienced.'[63]

The fourth problem for the Board was that its approach tended to focus on short-term measures only. There was much emphasis on using conservation drives for particular areas identified as being environmentally degraded. Furthermore,

---

61. Annual Report of the Southern Province Natural Resources Board for 1953. The disturbances referred to took place on both private estates and Trust Land. Although the disturbances mirrored a political outlook, largely due to the rise of African nationalism, the enforcement of *malimidwe* (anti-erosion measures) became one of the major grievances in the postwar period. For details, see R. Rotberg, *The Rise of Nationalism in Central Africa: the Making of Malawi and Zambia, 1873–1964* (Cambridge, Mass: Harvard University Press, 1965); Roger Tangri, 'The Rise of Nationalism in Colonial Africa: the Case of Colonial Malawi', *Comparative Studies in Society and History* 10/2 (1968): 141–68; L. White, *Magomero*; J. Power, *Political Culture and Nationalism in Malawi*.

62. Wiseman Chirwa makes this point clearly in his article, '"The Garden of Eden": Share-Cropping on the Shire Highlands Estates, 1920–1945', in A. H. Jeeves and J. S. Crush (eds.) *White Farms, Black Labour: the State and Agrarian Change in Southern Africa, 1910–1950* (Portsmouth: James Currey, 1997), pp. 265–280.

63. Interview: Mai Abine Odireki, Luka Village, T. A. Nsabwe, Thyolo district, dated 12 June 1997.

State intervention into private estate production in the Shire Highlands

Figure 7.1. Mulanje tea experimental station during opening ceremony in 1954

even when the measures were being implemented by Board employees, they were often not as rigorous as they should have been. Estate owners often took advantage of the laxity of implementers. In 1954, for instance, the Board noted that 'one of the difficulties with soil conservation on private estates was that no complete conservation plan was produced prior to the implementation of physical measures of protection and therefore much of the work done was ineffective and the money spent wasted'.[64] The Board also focused mainly on mechanical conservation measures such as bunds and drains. This was undoubtedly effective in dealing with gully erosion but not sheet erosion, which was the most common and insidious form of erosion on the estates. Although the Board had long realised the severity of sheet erosion, the issue was often skirted and, as the Annual report for 1953 stressed, the failure to use any control measures was one of the Board's major weaknesses.[65]

Related to the problem of approach was a growing sense of disillusionment on the part of estate owners and some members of the Board about farming practices and the methods used to control erosion. The Board's meeting of January 1954 noted that the practice of mono-cropping, so common on the estates, was not as helpful as had originally been believed to be. Describing the difficulties of implementing conservation measures on mono-cropped fields, the Board observed that,

64. MNA NSG 2/1/2: Minutes of the Meeting of the Southern Province Natural Resources Board held in Blantyre on 29 January 1954.
65. Annual Report of the Southern Province Natural Resources Board for 1953.

Factors inhibiting an effective state conservation programme

through years of tobacco monoculture, the structure of the soil on these appreciably sloping fields had completely deteriorated and mechanical measures of conservation in themselves were inadequate to afford complete protection without the assistance of biological aids. Bunds four feet in height would, over a succession of heavy rains, breach after filling with silt and the only effective control of soil movement would be through a combination of graded bunds and grass leys incorporated into a strip-crop lay out.[66]

In order to deal with these problems, the Board made three proposals. One was that there was a need to make plans for the protection of an entire estate before conservation work commenced. The second proposal concerned the adoption of long-term plans. In its annual report for 1953 the Board argued that,

[it] felt that some longer term planning and greater concentration of effort was necessary if lasting benefit was to result from the efforts of the Department of Agriculture in the field. Piece-meal application of physical soil conservation measures cannot greatly contribute to the betterment of any particular area, unless the entire region is so treated. Undoubtedly, these measures arrest more serious soil erosion within each small locality so treated, but lasting benefit cannot accrue unless whole catchment areas are so conserved.[67]

The final proposal concerned the need to enlarge the representation of estate-owners on the District Natural Resources Boards. The Board explained that this would facilitate the dissemination of information to planters about any matters requiring the Board's attention. In addition, the Board took a very crucial step in the organisation of conservation campaigns, introducing in 1954 the idea of roving Soil Conservation Teams that would visit all areas in a region that had experienced environmental degradation, and would only move out once conservation work had been completed.[68] The previous policy had been to deploy soil conservation teams in selected localities throughout the whole protectorate. In establishing these teams, the Board hoped that it could concentrate its limited resources on the areas that were most susceptible to degradation.

The fifth problem the Board faced involved the implementation of conservation measures on leased estates. Lease periods were very variable, ranging from one year to 99 years. According to the Board's Executive Officer, 'one of the biggest contributing factors to the non-conservation of natural resources on estates was the short-term leases which Government was prepared to grant to prospective farmers'.[69] Problems related to leases were identified as holding up conservation work

---

66. MNA NSG 2/1/2: Minutes of the Meeting of the Southern Province Natural Resources Board held in Blantyre on 29 January 1954.
67. Annual Report of the Southern Province Natural Resources Board for 1953.
68. MNA NSG 2/1/2: Minutes of the Meeting of the Southern Province Natural Resources Board held in Blantyre on 13 November 1953.
69. MNA NSG 2/1/2: Minutes of the Meeting of the Southern Province Natural Resources Board held in Blantyre on 20 August 1954.

State intervention into private estate production in the Shire Highlands

on estates belonging to the Nyasaland Railways in Thyolo and on the Namweras estates in Mangochi district. Estate owners were reluctant to invest their resources into the land when they knew that they had only a short jurisdiction over it, and the Board suggested increasing the period of all leases to 99 years.

Finally, the Board faced the problem of resettling the surplus population that was putting heavy pressure on the land. The influx of Lomwe immigrants from Mozambique into Malawi, which had started at the turn of the century, continued well into the 1950s. The resultant overcrowding adversely affected agricultural production and soil conservation activities in the region. The Board felt that, unless the problem of immigration was controlled and the system of agriculture was stabilised, it would be difficult to get any positive and lasting results on its conservation campaigns.[70] At one point, the Executive Officer complained that,

> no development and no hard and fast improvement could be made in Nyasaland until the task of sorting out land tenure difficulties and resettlement problems had been tackled, and provision made for economic holdings to individual Africans and also for the creation of a landless class of Africans accommodated in secondary industries and residential areas.[71]

In expressing this idea, the Board came close to adopting the rather technocratic approach that had been used in both South Africa and Zimbabwe to enforce betterment schemes – the fencing and land consolidation policies of the 1940s and 1950s.[72] It was commonly assumed that the African land tenurial systems had to be transformed as it was generally perceived to be obstructive of colonial development programmes.

The Board also wanted to control the influx and settlement of other immigrants from Mozambique who were felt to be adding a disproportionate amount of pressure to the land. Although this problem was well known, the influx had brought many benefits to the planters because it fulfilled their needs for cheap labour and they often did not pay much attention to any environmental problems created by immigrants. Most immigrants settled on the estates as tenants and entered into ambiguous relationships with planters whereby the latter rented out land in return for labour and produce.[73] For tenants under such terms, there was no incentive to undertake conservation measures on land that was not theirs.

---

70. Annual Report of the Southern Province Natural Resources Board for 1953.
71. MNA NSG 2/1/2: Minutes of the Meeting of the Southern Province Natural Resources Board held in Blantyre on 13 November 1953.
72. W. Beinart, 'Soil Erosion, Conservationism and Ideas about Development: a Southern African Exploration; A. Mager, '"The People Get Fenced"'; J. McGregor, 'Conservation, Control and Ecological Change'.
73. Interview: Mai Iness Kaphesi and Mai Esther Kaphesi, Ndaona Village, T. A. Nsabwe, Thyolo district, dated 13 June 1997. Wiseman Chirwa also argues that these conditions, coupled with the financial difficulties experienced by the planters, led to the shift from reliance on labour tenancy to share cropping on the estates. See W. Chirwa, '"The Garden of Eden"'.

Conclusion

According to Mai Estery Nankhwele of Thekerani in Thyolo district, this arrangement was particularly attractive to newly arrived immigrants who needed land but, at the same time, were expected to pay taxes to the state. The estate owners provided for both of these needs, even though this practice encouraged the *thangata* system. However, after residing on the estate for a few years, some immigrants would move onto African Trust Land.[74] This strategy worked for many Lomwe-speaking people who settled in the Shire Highlands districts of Thyolo, Mulanje, Blantyre, Chiradzulu and Zomba.[75]

By 1955, it became clear that the Board had made little progress in implementing conservation on private estates. The position of tenants remained very complex and tenuous and there was generally a lack of cooperation from many planters in implementing conservation measures. In view of all these problems, the Board had lost direction and the will to act.

Conclusion

This chapter has discussed the problem of environmental degradation on private estates and the colonial state's partial intervention into this sector of the economy. It has shown that soil erosion was not just an African problem, as the colonial state tended to project it. On the contrary, soil erosion was a serious environmental problem that took place on European-owned estates as well as on African Trust Land. Yet, though the Natural Resources Board frequently discussed the problem of soil erosion at the highest levels of government, little was accomplished by way of enforcing conservation rules and policies on such estates. As was the case in other countries in the southern African region, where most of these ideas came from, state intervention was influenced by political and ecological concerns that tended to favour conservation. On the other hand, the Board itself was weak and lacked both the capacity and the political will to enforce conservation on private estates because it had racialised the issue of soil conservation. Soil erosion was essentially perceived to be an African problem that European estate owners had very little to do with. Moreover, the Board had no African or Asian representatives; all the members were drawn from a cross-section of the European community and included some of the most prominent farmers from the Shire Highlands region. One may safely argue that the racial composition of the Board and the tendency to racialise the is-

---

74. Interview: Mai Estery Nankhwele of Mussa Village, T. A. Nsabwe, Thyolo district, dated 12 June 1997.
75. Oral interviews conducted in Zomba and Chiradzulu districts show a similar pattern. Because of the great need for labour, private estates were used as initial points of settlement for many immigrants. Interviews with Mr Michael Sandaramu Kholopete of Mkanda Village, T. A. Mlumbe, Zomba, dated 21 May 1997; Mai Margaret Gulani of Joliji Village, T. A. Mpama, Chiradzulu, dated 5 June 1997; Mai Agnes Nyambi and Mai Emma Juliyo, Nchocholo Village, T. A. Likoswe, Chiradzulu, dated 17 August 1997.

State intervention into private estate production in the Shire Highlands

sue of soil erosion as an African problem help to explain the limited and ineffectual nature of the colonial state's intervention into private estates.

8

Conservation and Politics, 1952–1964

Introduction

Until fairly recently, scholarship on African resistance to colonialism in Malawi has tended to ignore the role played by *malimidwe* [conservation] policies.[1] Where *malimidwe* is considered, conventional historiography has almost invariably interpreted this kind of resistance in political terms – that is, as an expression of rising mass nationalism.[2] What has not been sufficiently addressed is the nature of *malimidwe* policies themselves and what they meant to the ordinary peasants. This chapter suggests that, while nationalist feelings certainly played an important role in peasant reactions, much of their opposition arose from the unbearably heavy amount of labour demanded by the state in implementing the conservation policies.[3] Moreover, such policies interfered with household relations and economies and restricted their much-valued local autonomy. Often beyond the gaze of the state, these local concerns were important. They both shaped initial community responses to the colonial state's effort to implement experimental conservation measures in the late 1930s and 1940s and influenced peasant support of nationalist leaders in the 1950s. State-orchestrated, labour-intensive conservation measures constituted unprecedented interference with local autonomy and control over scarce resources – both land and labour.

Through an examination of *malimidwe* policies, this chapter explores peasant responses to an increasingly intrusive colonial state. It focuses on the impact of important conservation laws and schemes developed in the country in the postwar

---

1. Some of the studies that have been done include J. Power, *Political Culture and Nationalism in Malawi*; J. McCracken, 'Conservation and Resistance in Colonial Malawi'; E. Mandala, *Work and Control in a Peasant Economy*; and Colin Baker, *State of Emergency: Crisis in Central Africa, Nyasaland 1959–1960* (London: Tauris Academic Studies, 1997).

2. See R. Tangri, 'The Development of Modern African Politics and the Emergence of a Nationalist Movement in Colonial Malawi'; R. Rotberg, *The Rise of Nationalism in Central Africa*, pp. 258–321; and Owen Kalinga, 'Resistance, Politics of Protest, and Mass Nationalism in Colonial Malawi, 1950–1960: a Reconsideration', *Cahiers d'Études Africaines* 36/143 (1996): 443–454.

3. Interview: Mr Katchenga, Chalunda Village, TA Nsabwe, Thyolo district, dated 11 June 1997. Ironically, in Zomba, Mr T.D. Thomson also expressed the same idea after having supervised the implementation of a tough soil conservation campaign in the Domasi area. See his article, 'Soil Conservation – Some Implications', *Journal of African Administration* 5/2 (1953).

period. What is striking about these episodes is the nuanced and varied ways in which peasants expressed their resistance to conservation measures. While some areas witnessed open resistance to *malimidwe*, others did not. Some peasants found more covert ways of resisting the structures of state power; they used ways other than open defiance to cope with or evade the effects of *malimidwe*. It also shows the limits of state power as reflected in the actions of some officials who showed a degree of sensitivity to local traditions and practices, which may help to explain why some areas experienced less open resistance than did their counterparts elsewhere.

The chapter also discusses the complex and intricate relationship that developed between nationalism and *malimidwe* and the *thangata* or forced labour system. It will suggest that, inasmuch as nationalist leaders capitalised on the grievances of the agrarian communities, peasants also found the nationalist movement an appropriate medium through which to express their dissatisfaction with the colonial state. By examining both violent and non-violent forms of resistance, the discussion will show that peasants maintained a long tradition of social protest against the colonial state.

The interface of Federation and Malimidwe

Although the nationalist movement stood for many issues, it was the British colonial government's proposal to form the Federation of Northern Rhodesia, Southern Rhodesia and Nyasaland that came to dominate and symbolise the larger anti-colonial struggle in the postwar period. Many issues that had been articulated by different constituencies of the nationalist movement were now conflated into the anti-Federation campaign. Opposition to the Federation became so intimately linked with resistance to conservation that these disparate issues have sometimes been treated as one and the same.[4]

The imposition of the white settler-backed Federation of Rhodesia and Nyasaland on 1 August 1953, sparked a great deal of controversy among Africans and liberal Europeans in Nyasaland, Northern Rhodesia, Southern Rhodesia and Britain. Proponents of the Federation argued that it would provide 'the only practical means by which the three Central African Territories can achieve security for the future and ensure the well-being and contentment of all the people'.[5] The idea had long fascinated the minds of many European settlers in all three territories, with support and inspiration from South Africa.[6] On the other hand, nationalist lead-

---

4. I discuss this in greater detail in Ch. 9 with the examples of Chief Phillip Gomani and Rev. Michael Scott.
5. *The Federal Scheme for Southern Rhodesia, Northern Rhodesia and Nyasaland*, Prepared by a Conference held in London, January 1953.
6. Although the debate on the Federation picked up in the early 1950s, the proposal goes as far back as the 1930s when behind the scenes talks on closer association took place among white settlers. The idea was expressed in different words, such as amalgamation, partnership, mutual cooperation and federation.

The interface of Federation and Malimidwe

ers in Nyasaland, and in the other two territories, maintained that the Federation would undermine their political aspirations for self-determination and ultimate independence from Great Britain. The Federation, which became the central focus of nationalist agitation, provided a unique opportunity for peasants to express their resistance to the colonial state's conservation policies and practices. While nationalist agitators, traditional leaders and peasants all opposed the Federation, they had very different reasons for doing so. For peasants, resistance against the Federation served essentially as an important vehicle through which to express their agrarian grievances as well as their aspirations for the future.

Opposition to the Federation was premised on several factors, the most important of which included land and labour policies, abrogation of the longstanding British policy of trusteeship and the fear of racial domination. In general, Africans in Nyasaland harboured fears that the adoption of a new and unknown federal arrangement would lead to a situation in which their influence would be significantly minimised. They had experienced Colonial Office rule for more than fifty years and, under this dispensation, they had begun to build hopes of attaining self-rule. But the proposed Federation appeared to reverse this trend and thus fomented a coalition of resistance from people across the spectrum of the society. We will first examine the general factors in opposition to the Federation before turning to the specific forms of resistance to *malimidwe*.

From the inception of the debate on Federation with the Rhodesias, Africans feared that closer union would diminish all their hopes and aspirations for self-determination and eventual independence. In 1944, the Nyasaland African Congress (NAC), the first nationalist movement to be formed in the country, maintained that the British government had established Protectorate rule essentially on principles of humanitarian considerations and trusteeship. Since that time, therefore, the British government had used this argument to justify colonisation of the territory and indeed a paternalistic view had developed that Africans would only attain self-rule when the colonisers deemed them ready. Thus, for the British government to allow the Nyasaland Protectorate to join the Federation in the name of promoting partnership was tantamount to a betrayal of their professed trusteeship role. The Africans thought the British government was deferring to the interests of the white minority settlers; they questioned its commitment to its historic promise of eventual transfer of power to the Africans. The Africans feared that the federal scheme would lead to the domination of Africans by whites – a proposal many Africans resoundingly rejected. In expressing their disapproval of the Federation, nationalist leaders contended that 'the cardinal principle in [Colonial Office] administration is guidance and guardianship. But under the Government provided by Southern Rhodesia, the relationship between us and the authorities will be one of slaves and masters, and the cardinal principle ... domination.'[7]

---

7. H. Kamuzu Banda and H.M. Nkumbula, *Federation in Central Africa* (London, 1 May, 1949), p. 13.

Conservation and politics, 1952–1964

Related to the above argument was the chiefs' concern about the loss of their traditional powers. They feared that the Federation would usurp their traditional powers over land and their subject people. They complained that the relationship that had existed between them and the Crown, through the indirect rule system, would be abrogated to the Federalists and whites in Southern Rhodesia. The chiefs were so disappointed with the federal proposal that a Commission of Enquiry appointed by the Nyasaland Government later reported that 'even among the chiefs, many of whom are loyal to the Government and dislike Congress methods, we have not heard of a single one who is in favour of federation.'[8]

Many Africans also expressed concern that the racial policies of South Africa and Southern Rhodesia would be replicated in the territories north of the Zambezi River. These countries in the south were regarded as 'white man's country' and Africans were considered their servants. Large numbers of Africans there had lost their traditional rights to land. They had also experienced different forms of discrimination, such as job segregation and restrictions on movement. Indeed, migrant workers from Malawi, who had worked in Southern Rhodesia and South Africa, gave testimony to the plight of Africans in these countries; they had seen for themselves the nature of the relations that existed between Europeans and Africans. So the proposal for closer association with the Rhodesias was viewed as one that would lead to extension of those conditions into Nyasaland. Articulating the fears expressed by many Africans, Dr H. Kamuzu Banda observed: 'If we accept the proposed Federation, we shall cut ourselves away from the United Kingdom, because under Federation Nyasaland and Northern Rhodesia will cease to be administered by the U.K. and will become part of Southern Rhodesia ... and our political and cultural clock will be put back.'[9] These were conditions they did not want to experience in Malawi.

Finally, Africans opposed some of the colonial policies on land and labour that were being practised in colonial Malawi and assumed that the Federation would exacerbate them. Although land shortage had been a serious problem for a long time in the Shire Highlands region, and the government had been well aware of this problem, little effort had been made to ameliorate the situation. Many Africans feared that the Federation would facilitate the immigration of more whites and thus accentuate the land shortage problem. Land problems were not new in the Shire Highlands; they had begun to develop in the late nineteenth century when large tracts of land were occupied by both European settlers and Lomwe immigrants from Mozambique. At about the turn of the twentieth century, *thangata*, a system of coerced labour, had also developed in the region in an attempt to address the

---

8. A.J. Hanna, *The Story of the Rhodesias and Nyasaland* (London, 1960), p. 260, quoting from the *Report of the Commission of Enquiry of 1959*.

9. H. Kamuzu Banda and H.M. Nkumbula, *Federation in Central Africa*, p. 10.

The nature of malimidwe

problem of labour shortage on European estates.[10] Although in theory the colonial state never encouraged the use of coerced labour and through the Native Labour Ordinance of 1903 provided a list of minimum working conditions for African employees, in practice the government never enforced these regulations. The implementation of these regulations was left to the individual planters themselves. Planters obtained labour from those Africans who had been dispossessed of their land. *Thangata* involved the provision of unpaid labour to European-owned estates for a period of three months in a year.[11] In many cases, Africans had to work for *thangata* in lieu of hut tax. Although by the 1950s *thangata* was in decline, the fact that the Federation would bring in more European settlers resuscitated African apprehensions about the oppressive labour system.[12]

The nature of malimidwe

Although peasants participated in opposing the Federation, they had other vested interests that they wanted to safeguard. They had taken part in other forms of resistance before and *malimidwe* and the Federation were only a continuation of that tradition. Opposition to Federation need not necessarily be conflated with resistance to *malimidwe*. Even though resistance to *malimidwe* reached a climax in the early 1950s, there had been smouldering forms of resistance since the promulgation of the first Natural Resources Ordinance in 1946. The new regulations sought to restructure African production in ways that had never been done before. Africans were called upon to undertake a series of conservation measures in their gardens and the implementation of these measures was accompanied by harsh penalties such as fines, imprisonment and uprooting of crops meted out to defaulters. Recalcitrant Africans who persistently refused to undertake conservation measures risked having their gardens closed to cultivation and/or declared protected hill slopes under the Natural Resources Rules of 1951 and the Natural Resources (Amendment) Ordinance of 1952.

The labour demanded by *malimidwe* was extreme, for the regulations required that all cultivable land in a designated conservation area had to be bunded. Bunds were a physical conservation measure for preventing erosion of the soil and according to Mr and Mrs. Ching'anda of Mbalame Village in Chiradzulu district,

---

10. *Thangata* literally means to assist. J.A. Kamchitete Kandawire argues that *thangata*, as a traditional social institution of reciprocal labour underwent a transformation during the colonial period into an economic institution of production. *Thangata: Forced Labour or Reciprocal Assistance?* (Zomba: Research and Publications Committee of the University of Malawi, 1979). See also 'Thangata in Pre-colonial and Colonial Systems of Land Tenure in Southern Malawi with Special Reference to Chingale', *Africa* 47/2 (1977): 185–190.

11. For details on the operations of *thangata* see J.A. Kamchitete Kandawire, *Thangata*; B. Pachai, *Land and Politics in Malawi*.

12. Throughout the colonial period, *thangata* persisted in different areas with different degrees of intensity. It was formally abolished in 1962 when new agricultural legislation came into force.

'the work of making *milambala* [bunds] usually began soon after harvest. A large channel was dug, leaving a big ridge or heap of soil beside the furrow which controlled the splash of water into the ridges in the garden.'[13] These conservation measures were aimed at protecting land, and particularly watershed areas, from erosion. This would also improve the fertility of the lands. On normal slopes, contour bunds had to be constructed at horizontal intervals of approximately thirty yards, so that, if the average land holding for peasants was six acres, a total of 1,000 yards of bunds had to be constructed. Calculated in terms of time, peasants could construct thirty yards a day and to complete the whole garden of six acres would require thirty days of work. A normal sized bund had to be two feet in height with a base of four feet. T.D. Thomson, a colonial administrator who had been at the forefront of implementing *malimidwe* at Domasi, later conceded that the conservation project was overly ambitious. It exacted too much labour from the peasants and he observed that 'a fit adult putting in a full day's work may be able to raise anything up to 50 yards of bunding daily, but a fair average is probably 30 yards, so that to raise the necessary bunds on an average holding may require about a month's work'.[14] Village Headman Mtwiche, whose village neighbours the Domasi station in Zomba and had been subjected to these measures, pointed out that,

> *milambala* were introduced here by Mr Thomson ... It was hard work which required us to work for many hours. Initially, we worked as individuals. But it became much easier when we started working in groups, say four or five people. We would start to work the land in turns... until we finished all the gardens. We did this because we wanted to finish all the gardens, otherwise failure to do so meant that some people in the village would be taken to prison.[15]

Farmers were also required to own a measuring device called a 'level', which was supposed to help them make ridges in a straight manner so that running water did not break them. A farmers' manual published by the office of Soil Erosion Officer described a level as 'a machine that will show you how to make each ridge so that the water will neither run away too fast nor will it collect in one place and break the ridge.'[16] The level, as shown in the diagram below, was made of bamboos and nails and was particularly ideal for measuring planting ridges but not contour

---

13. Interview: Mr and Mrs. Ching'anda, Mbalame Village, TA Mpama, Thyolo district, dated 4 June 1997.
14. T. D. Thomson, 'Soil Conservation – Some Implications', p. 66.
15. In most cases, Chiefs and Village Headmen were exempt from undertaking the work of conservation. In the 1950s, the current Village Headman Mtwiche had not yet acceded to the royal seat but, as a young man, worked on *milambala*, with his parents. Furthermore, chieftaincy in this society follows the matrilineal side of the family.
16. MNA S12/2/1/1: *How to Make a Level to Measure Mizera (mapangidwe a Levulo Yoyesela Mizera)* by Paul Topham, Soil Erosion Officer (Zomba: Government Printer, 1939) Agronomic Series No.1, p.2; see also Ian Scoones, 'Landscapes, Fields and Soils: Understanding the History of Soil Fertility Management in Southern Zimbabwe', *Journal of Southern African Studies* 23/4 (1997): 615–634.

The nature of malimidwe

drains. The basic assumption for using the level was that if one part of ridge was lower than the other parts the water would run to that part and the ridge would be broken, so the ridge had to be of the same height throughout its length.

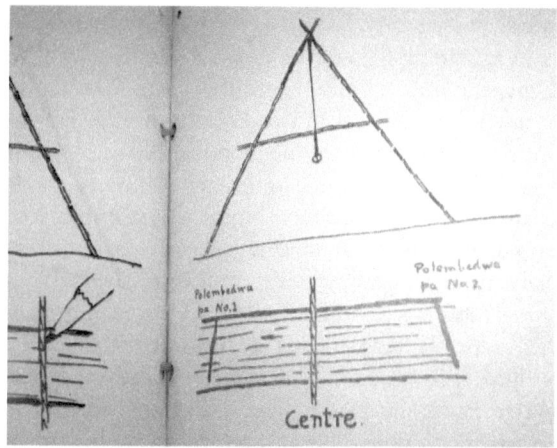

Figure 8.1. Level used for making ridges

One of the most egregious aspects of the conservation scheme was the 'bunding drives' that were carried out on a village or group village basis during the dry season, once the crops had been harvested. Following the agreement of the chief concerned, a number of meetings would be held with the headmen and villagers to explain the purpose of and procedures for the construction of conservation measures. The gardens would be visited and the layouts demonstrated. Dates for pegging out the contour lines would be decided upon. Contour lines were marked by a team of soil erosion rangers using simple instruments called road tracers. Once that had been done, occupiers of land had to hoe traces between pegs put in by the bunding team within one week of pegging. Some people were employed on a temporary basis and trained in their use, the average length of the training course being one week. The agricultural staff and road tracer operators would set up a camp in the area and commence pegging. The villagers would turn out very early in the morning and work in communal groups covering the village gardens. Mai Gemu Kapalamula in Chiradzulu district said that no one was spared for the bunding drives: 'Both men and women had to do *milambala*. We were usually starting at 6:00 a.m. and each person was given a portion of land to work on.'[17] According to one of the former Soil Conservation Officers, 'Peasants sang bunding

---

17. Interview: Mai Gemu Kapalamula, Kapalamula Village, TA Mpama, Chiradzulu district dated 3 June 1997.

songs which were not always complimentary to the Department of Agriculture!'[18] For the farmers, the day's work would stop at 11.00 a.m. and, on average, it took about five days to complete the gardens of a particular village. Bunding drives became so generally unpopular because they involved intimidation and compulsion of peasants, as we shall see below.

The task of realigning the crop ridges between the bunds was done at the time of garden preparation – ideally before the start of the rains in November. Peasants had to use a farmer's level in this exercise as well. Following the initial bunding and once the realignment of the crop ridges was complete, the villagers were not involved in any further work on physical conservation measures. They were, however, expected to maintain their bunds. For example, if bunds had been damaged by heavy downpours of rain, peasants had to repair them by adding more soil. They also had to undertake supplementary measures such as planting of grass on normally bare areas, those surrounding dwellings, schools, mosques and churches. Stream banks had to be planted with sugar canes and bananas. All planting areas had to be box-ridged. This meant adding soil across the ridges so as to block the movement of water. Paths and garden boundaries too had to be bunded to the same height as the planting ridges. Locally, these came to be known as *milambala*

Figure 8.2. Example of a well managed garden

Understandably, this was too much work for the peasants who already had a myriad of other work activities to attend to. According to Mr Lamuzi Milanzi of the Malemia area in Zomba district, '*milambala* were especially made by those people who carried out their farming activities in hilly areas. It was difficult to make them

---

18. Personal Communication with Mr Robert I. Green, former Soil Conservation Officer, dated 28 June 1997.

The nature of malimidwe

and a lot of energy was spent on them. Worse still, no crops could be planted on *milambala* thus made.'[19] When the grievances of the peasants had accumulated, it was easy for the nationalist leaders to appropriate these ideas and articulate them as one of their key factors for rejecting the Federation. Peter Brown, a former Director of Agriculture said, 'The bunding drives were, in retrospect, a mistake, especially as they provided an excellent stick with which the politicians could beat the colonial government, but they did show the farmers over a wide area which way the contours lay so as to ensure the ridge planting in future was more or less parallel thereto.'[20] This confession suggests that, while the idea of conservation may have been good, its implementation strategy left a lot to be desired.

Another unpopular aspect of the colonial conservation policy concerned restrictions placed on the opening of new land for cultivation and the protection of vulnerable areas such as stream courses. Land with more than a twelve per cent slope was considered unsuitable for cultivation. If people wished to establish gardens on slopes, they had to have the land inspected by a member of the Agricultural Department who, if he considered the area suitable, would issue a *mphanje* permit.[21] This policy was mainly applicable to new land since and which already under cultivation was subjected to conservation measures such as bunding. But the measure became unpopular because peasants were already experiencing problems of land shortage for settlement and cultivation. The increase in population in the Shire Highlands region forced many of the peasants to open gardens in areas declared by the state unsuitable for cultivation and to be left for forest growth.

Peasants resisted *malimidwe* for reasons that had to do primarily with the way anti-erosion measures were introduced and the kind of work they were expected to perform. Many complained that the work was overly demanding and difficult. Mai Maggie Dinafodi of Thyolo observed that '*milambala* were too demanding and tiresome work; they took up most of the farming land and people worked hard without payment. Hence, resistance took place.'[22] Another informant similarly noted that 'opposition to *milambala* was due to the problem of time; they were just too demanding'.[23] Concurring with these observations, Robert Green, a former Soil Conservation Officer, retrospectively noted: 'Few peasants saw the necessity of using soil conservation measures in their gardens. In fact, they found their construction an intrusion into their leisure time during the dry season. When

---

19. Interview: Mr Lamuzi Milanzi, Malemia Village, TA Malemia, Zomba district, dated 8 May 1997.
20. Personal communication with Mr Peter Brown, dated 17 June 1997.
21. The term *mphanje* means a piece of land that has not been cultivated before. Peasants talked of *kuswa mphanje* or to break a new ground when clearing a new piece of land for cultivation.
22. Interview: Mai Maggie Dinafodi of Mussa Village, TA Nsabwe, Thyolo district, dated 12 June 1997.
23. Interview: Mr Billiot Mlaliki of Nzundo Village, TA Nsabwe, Thyolo district, dated 29 May 1997.

they did the work, it was largely to keep Government happy.'[24] State intrusion into the private spaces of the peasants, particularly during the dry season when it is very hot and the temperature averages 25 degrees Celsius, predictably attracted resentment and rural social protest.

The second reason that made the peasants resist *malimidwe* was the coercion that accompanied anti-erosion measures. The heavy-handed behaviour of many agricultural advisors contributed to the souring of relations between peasants and the colonial state. Mai Estery Edward Phiri of Thyolo remarked, 'This work disrupted peace at Kalingalira and Chalunda villages. At Kalingalira, two places were chosen where everybody, whether man or woman, was intimidated and coerced to go and work. But that work was opposed to the people who were doing it.'[25] Katchenga likened *malimidwe* to slavery, noting, 'Many people were not interested in this work of making *milambala* because it was tough and its future was not clearly known. It was seen as something akin to slavery and had it not been stopped quickly, it would have turned into slavery.'[26] He offered a particularly revealing account of the impact of *malimidwe* on the lives of the peasants:

> [T]his was generally tough work and without beating about the bush, I once deserted in 1953. Just after experiencing the intimidation and the practice of working without receiving any payment, I found that I did not have any freedom at all. Therefore, I left at night with my friend for Sankhulani where there was total freedom. I started making timber there. We found one of the agricultural members of staff, Mr. Malemia, to be a very calm man. He gave us freedom and advised us that whoever wished to make *milambala* was free to do so and contact him for some advice and measurements. But he never forced or intimidated people.[27]

Few people in this area or indeed in many other areas could afford the opportunity that Mr Katchenga had, to move out as he had done. For a variety of reasons many remained in their local areas throughout the period of implementing *malimidwe*. Chiefs and local agricultural staff were under pressure to keep track of the work being undertaken by peasants in their gardens. Such a level of surveillance went a long way towards souring relations in the communities. In some cases, state-employed agricultural staff were harassed by the peasants. Some had their equipment damaged or stolen while others simply deserted from the work. In one incident, a ranger

---

24. Personal communication with Mr Robert Green, dated 28 June 1997.
25. Interview: Mai Estery Edward Phiri of Ndaona Village, TA Nsabwe, Thyolo district, dated 13 June 1997.
26. Interview: Mr Katchenga of Chalunda Village, TA Nsabwe, Thyolo district, dated 11 June 1997.
27. Interview: Mr Katchenga of Chalunda Village, TA Nsabwe, Thyolo district, dated 11 June 1997.

The nature of malimidwe

named Petro Namange was killed for uprooting the crops belonging to a farmer in Chief Nsabwe's area in Thyolo district.[28]

The third reason for resistance was that peasants were concerned about the practical benefits they would derive from undertaking such physical conservation works. Given the amount of time and labour spent on making *milambala*, peasants also complained that conservation works reduced their land for cultivation in an area already experiencing land shortages. While acknowledging the fact that *milambala* helped to control erosion, the magnitude of the work they were required to do offered them few practical benefits. Peasants had to make *milambala* anywhere, even on hill-slopes that had been closed and reserved for forest growth. Except for grasses, peasants were not allowed to plant any crops on *milambala* that had been made in gardens.

The fourth reason for resistance was that peasants were prohibited from cutting down certain types of trees without the permission of the DC; in most cases they actually had to buy them from the Forestry Department. Peasants opposed this measure because it restricted their ability to use forest resources for their own needs such as building houses, mortars for pounding cereals and beehives. Reacting to these conditions, George Simeon Mwase, a civil servant and political activist in the colonial period, complained that '[the] native is of one form of opinion, that the prohibition of cutting trees for use by the whiteman's law does not apply to our children's benefit at all, but it is applying to their own benefit, and for the benefit of their [white men's] own offspring'.[29] Like many Africans at the time, Mwase thought that the government was placing restrictions on the use of trees for the benefit of Europeans. However, some peasants ignored these restrictions and cut trees either discreetly or after corrupting forest guards.

Finally, peasants opposed *malimidwe* because of struggles over the meaning of resources. The land and other natural resources were seen as theirs, over which they had unbridled control. But the introduction of new conservation laws appeared to have taken away their traditional rights of ownership and control. Accusations of mismanagement of resources that had frequently been leveled against the Africans were rejected, as Mwase noted: 'Is it not clear that white man is the person who cuts a lot of trees in the country? He owns [a] big acreage of land and hoe[s] [a] very big area of land. Cut all the trees, dig out the shrubs, and make the land impossible to grow more trees on it.'[30] Mwase's ideas were widely shared by peasants who thought the state did not have to interfere in the use of their land and other natural resources. While the colonial state was committed to the campaign against the practice of shifting cultivation, peasants also complained about the rapid spread of commercial farming in the territory. Commercial farming involved

---

28. Interview: Mr Billiot Mlaliki of Nzundo Village, TA Nsabwe, Thyolo district, dated 29 May 1997.
29. G. S. Mwase, *Strike a Blow and Die*, p. 124.
30. *Ibid.* p. 125.

the use of large tracts of land that had been taken away from the Africans. Mwase challenged the colonial state by arguing that the practice of shifting cultivation was in fact a form of rotation. He maintained that what a native does to his garden is, 'cut a small patch [and] leave the stubs to grow more trees. And when he sees that the soil is washed out in that garden, he leaves it alone for trees to grow again from the stubs, and cuts another small patch for his new garden, leaving the other one to grow trees for future use.'[31] He further observed that it was not unusual for African chiefs to set aside *mizimu* forests that could not be used by the local people for harvesting trees or grass. While these forests existed in almost every village and were meant to be used by the ancestral spirits, they also promoted the conservation of forest resources.[32]

Conflict over land and labour: the case of Chiradzulu and Thyolo districts

Peasant resistance to the colonial state's policies and practices on conservation was particularly evident in conflicts over land and labour. Since the 1930s, the state had introduced various land usage schemes to enable Africans to protect forests and use the land resources properly so that soil erosion could be reduced and the fertility of the land under cultivation restored. These measures were not always favourable to the African peasants. Resistance centred on countering the colonial state's restrictions on the cultivation of prohibited areas such as hill-slopes, stream banks and forest reserves and ridge cultivation. In this section, discussion will centre on non-violent forms of peasant resistance in the Shire Highlands districts of Chiradzulu and Thyolo.

In Thyolo district, conservation work began in 1938 when Paul Topham, the first Soil Erosion Officer, experimented with various anti-erosion activities in the highland areas of Chiefs Nsabwe and Changata. The major objective of Topham's campaign was to control erosion from hill-slopes and stream banks, to protect forest reserves and to introduce ridge cultivation and bunding. In accordance with the provisions of the Native Authorities Ordinance of 1933, he asked chiefs to issue orders for the implementation of anti-erosion measures in their respective areas.[33] But the implementation of these measures encountered several problems. For example, Topham found that the area was too stony for the making of contour ridges and concluded that, 'The area is *sub-marginal* for native settlement; not only is agriculture poor but the whole standard of life is wretched and with little hope of future betterment'.[34]

---

31. *Ibid.* p. 125.
32. *Ibid.* pp. 121–22.
33. MNA NS 1/2/4: Agriculture: Soil Erosion. Letter by Paul Topham, dated 2 April 1938.
34. MNA NSE 1/3/2: Letter by Topham, Assistant Conservator of Forests, to the DC, Thyolo, dated 11 November 1940.

Conflict over land and labour: the case of Chiradzulu and Thyolo districts

The second problem that Topham faced was the general lack of support from the chiefs who only reluctantly enforced orders on their subjects. Meanwhile, in response to this recalcitrance, the state sent another team consisting of Pegler, the DC for Thyolo, Forbes, the Agricultural Officer for Mulanje district, and Topham himself, with instructions to be more assertive and uncompromising on the role of chiefs and their subjects. But peasants still ignored government restrictions on settling on or cultivating areas that had been declared protected lands. In 1938, for instance, Mphande Hills in Chief Nsabwe's area, which was considered an important watershed area, was closed off and declared a protected forest reserve. Human cultivation of any form was prohibited since it only encouraged the loss of soil through erosion. In one of the government reports, it was noted, 'The Mphande area has already reached such a stage of erosion and soil-deterioration that maize can no longer be grown ... the only remedy will be almost complete closure ... for fifteen or twenty years'.[35] This area was also an important source of the river systems in the Thekerani area and had to be protected if the water supply was to be assured. However, by the end of 1940, Topham decided to discontinue the whole experimental project because of continued lack of local support.[36]

In some ways, the blame for the destruction of these land and water resources lay with the immigration of Lomwe-speaking people. For example, J.B. Clements, the Conservator of Forests, noted, 'It is generally conceded that much of the over-crowding is due to the uncontrolled settlement in the Protectorate of immigrant Angulu [Alomwe] during the last 20 years, and it is often these people with their shifting cultivation, who are demanding steep hillslopes at a rapid pace'.[37] For example, in Thyolo district, the African population doubled within a period of ten years; it increased from 44,000 in 1930 to 96,000 in 1941. For the entire Shire Highlands region, the trend was basically the same. By 1945, the population of Lomwe immigrants accounted for a third of the total population of the whole Southern Region. About 375,000 Lomwe immigrants had settled in the region whose total population stood at 916,000.[38] Given that about two thirds of the land in this region comprised privately owned European estates, the immigration of these large numbers of Lomwe people accentuated the land crisis. Some settled on the estates as tenants while others moved on to the already over-crowded Native Trust Land. The land crisis in the Shire Highlands was so serious that, in 1935, Chief Nsabwe of Thyolo district told the Governor that 'my people find difficulty

---

35. MNA VET 1/9/1: *Soil Conservation: The Present Situation* by J.M. Howlett, Soil Conservation Officer.
36. MNA NSE 1/3/2: Thyolo District: Soil Conservation, April 1940–December 1949.
37. MNA S1/66/36: *Memorandum on Protection of Steep Hillslopes*, 1937.
38. Robert Boeder, *The Silent Majority: A History of the Lomwe in Malawi* (Pretoria: African Institute of South Africa, 1984); L. White, *Magomero*. For earlier population statistics, see Frank Dixey 'The Distribution of Population in Nyasaland', *Geographical Review* 18/2 (1928): 274–290.

in getting room for their gardens. My land is hilly and all the soil is washed down to the riverbanks, where we are not allowed to cultivate.'[39]

The most realistic way to solve the problem of overcrowding would have been to control the immigration of Lomwe-speaking people.[40] But the government was reluctant to do so because of lack of cooperation from both estate-owners and chiefs. Estate-owners benefited in terms of cheap labour. Chiefs also benefited in the sense that they got paid for taxes collected: a village headman got four pence from each tax paid.[41] The larger the number of tax-paying subjects the more the income of the chief.

In 1938, the colonial state warned that Chinyenyedi Valley in Chief Changata's area faced an ecological disaster because peasants were cultivating along the stream banks as well as on the surrounding hill slopes. The state decided to divide and reallocate land to the peasants. Cultivation was controlled and some areas were closed off. The state began to give out titles to individual land holders. The gardens of the villagers were marked out for permanent contour ridging and bunding. Peasants were also required to dig drains in the gardens.[42] But they often ignored these restrictions: they did not make contour ridges, bunding or drains. In addition, settlement in prohibited areas continued. By the early 1940s, the Department of Agriculture began to report on numerous cases of defaulters in Thyolo district. One agricultural official reported: 'I went along yesterday to see the garden of Muloya for which he had been reported to the Native Authority. He had planted groundnuts in this garden without either ridges or bunds and is therefore liable to punishment.'[43] Mr Muloya was but one example of offenders who tried to subvert state rules in the district. In October 1944, W.V. Rose, the same Agricultural Officer based at Masambanjati, listed over fifty names of offenders whom he recommended to the DC for tougher punishment, considering that his department had been teaching them ridging for more than five years.

The success of these conservation schemes depended to a large extent on the support of the Native Authorities. They were the ones who issued the orders on the areas or aspects that needed to be conserved. It was chiefs who, in collaboration with agricultural or forestry staff, enforced the implementation of conservation measures. But, in Thyolo, Chiefs Nsabwe and Ntondeza were, from the beginning, described as uncooperative and not very useful to the state. For instance, in December 1938, Pegler, DC for Thyolo, said: 'I have always found these two Native Authorities

---

39. MNA NSE 1/11/7: Cholo District: Land Usage, February 1941–January 1944.
40. Lomwe immigrants were running away from harsh Portuguese rule in Mozambique. For details, see R.B. Boeder, *The Silent Majority*; W.C. Chirwa, 'Alomwe and Mozambican Immigrant Labour in Colonial Malawi, 1890s–1945', *The International Journal of African Historical Studies* 27/3 (1994): 525–550.
41. MNA NSE 1/11/7: Cholo District: Land Usage, February 1941–January 1944.
42. MNA NSE 1/3/1: Chinyenyedi Soil Conservation and Resettlement Scheme, 1940–1946.
43. MNA NSE 1/3/2: Letter by Mr Rose to DC, Thyolo, dated 13 May 1945.

Conflict over land and labour: the case of Chiradzulu and Thyolo districts

outstandingly useless and it is only with the greatest difficulty that I can even get anything done in these areas'.[44]

Reacting to the problems encountered by the Soil Erosion Officer, the DC wrote to the Provincial Commissioner, Southern Province: 'I have received a complaint from Mr Topham about the lack of assistance being given to him by Native Authorities Ntondeza and Nsabwe in the measures he is taking against Soil Erosion in their respective areas ... Both these Native Authorities have issued their respective orders on Soil Erosion, but they ceased to be interested after issuing orders and they are definitely doing nothing to enforce those orders.'[45]

Chiefs were often placed in a very awkward position and found themselves issuing orders to their subjects on matters they did not always completely support. The Chinyenyedi case is just one example of such peasant resistance against state-induced conservation measures. Resistance was rampant and often took many forms. Even within the Thyolo district, where we shall later see the exploits of Pastor Gudu and his followers, peasants developed a variety of ways of frustrating the implementation of state conservation policies.

By the mid-1940s, the government had realised that removal of some Africans from the congested areas of the Shire Highlands had become not only necessary but inevitable. Consequently, in 1945, the government began to evacuate Africans in Thyolo for resettlement in Chikwawa district. The colonial authorities estimated that Chikwawa had enough space to absorb up to 20,000 Africans and perhaps even more if water supply was made available in most areas. A large number of the evacuees came from the Mphande, Chinyenyedi and Thyolo-Chikwawa escarpment areas. This figure was far too small to ease pressure on the land in Thyolo, which continued to receive a net inflow of immigrants from Mozambique.

Conflicts over land and labour were also experienced in the Chiradzulu district, which remained a tinderbox of African discontent throughout the colonial period. This was the place where Africans, led by the Rev. John Chilembwe, staged an uprising in January 1915 and the hysteria of that event never dissipated. Since that time, there had been smouldering tensions in various parts of the district. This section will demonstrate the various ways in which peasants resisted the colonial state's attempts to control their land and labour.

In Chiradzulu district, peasant resistance occurred both on African Trust Land and on private estates. Three major developments contributed to the emergence of tensions and conflicts over land and labour in the district. First, the government's revision of the Africans on Private Estates Ordinance in 1928 presented serious problems for many estate-owners. With the exception of labourers and domestic servants, the Ordinance required all Africans on private estates to pay rent at a figure ranging between two and three months of their annual wages. For their part, landlords were now expected to pay their tenants for the work done on the estates in

---

44. MNA NS 1/2/4: Agriculture: Soil Erosion, 1937–1939.
45. MNA NS 1/2/4: Agriculture: Soil Erosion, 1937–1939.

lieu of *thangata*.⁴⁶ However, landlords could evict not only those tenants who failed to pay rent but also, once in every five years, up to one tenth of the total number on their estates. In either case, the landlords had to give six months notice. Both Africans on private estates and on Trust Land felt a sense of insecurity. Those on the estates were subjected to a heavy burden of rent and also to threats of eviction. They had little security regarding their houses or gardens. Africans on Trust Land did not have to pay rent but they experienced overcrowding and were constantly subjected to rigorous conservation campaigning. Over and above all this, peasants had to pay taxes to the government.⁴⁷

The second development creating tensions was the souring of planter–peasant relations in the 1930s. There was a widespread belief among the planter community that cassava contributed to soil exhaustion. But they also hated the crop because it was not an annual crop. Cassava and *nandolo* were the two principal crops that had been promoted by the immigrant Lomwe-speaking people. The Lomwe grew cassava because it was a good insurance against drought, particularly as they migrated to different places with different ecological characteristics. At one point, in 1931, Captain Kincaid-Smith, General Manager of the A.L. Bruce Estates, sent out his rangers to uproot all cassava planted in the Africans' gardens. He argued that cassava drained the soil of nutrients and rendered it unsuitable for tobacco growing. The planters' disdain for African production of food crops had also to do with the competition for scarce labour supply.

As a third cause of growing tension, in the 1940s, the Department of Agriculture undertook significant steps to protect natural resources on Chiradzulu Mountain and its environs. Even though Chiradzulu Mountain had been declared a forest reserve in 1924, Africans had been cultivating on the mountain slopes and that caused soil erosion. So the government decided to close the gardens and evacuate the Africans from these areas. A demarcation line was established, beyond which no African could cultivate the land.⁴⁸ Many Africans left these closed areas and settled on the estates as tenants or on already overcrowded Trust Land.

These three factors created tensions among Africans on Trust Land and tenants on private estates. Changes in *thangata* meant that tenants could pay hut taxes directly to *boma*. Landlords, too, had to pay the tenants for their produce. For many estates that were heavily indebted, this Ordinance of 1928 came as a big blow. They lacked the cash to pay their tenants and other employees. The A.L. Bruce Estate at Magomero was one such estate in financial trouble. Consequently, in 1933, Captain Kincaid-Smith, General Manager of the Bruce Estates, introduced a deferred credit system whereby tenants were given a signed *chit* when they handed over their tobacco on the understanding that they would be paid when the tobacco had been graded and sold and Kincaid-Smith had the cash in hand to pay

---

46. Nyasaland Government, *Africans on Private Estates Ordinance, 1928*
47. See A.J. Hannah, *The Story of the Rhodesias and Nyasaland* (London, 1960), pp. 210–12.
48. See MNA PCS 1/2/24: Soil Conservation: Blantyre District, November 1944–June 1955.

Conflict over land and labour: the case of Chiradzulu and Thyolo districts

his debts. When the government got to know about this practice, K. Barnes, DC for Thyolo, described Kincaid-Smith as an 'autocratic manager' and 'a menace to the district owing to his intense hatred of his African tenants'.[49]

Then, in 1939, tension developed at Magomero estate. There were strong rumours that, during the Second World War, Africans would be forced by the military and *boma* to grow tobacco without payment. There were also rumours of an impending uprising in January 1940. The problem was that Kincaid-Smith was heavily indebted and had too many bills to clear, such as the unpaid wages for his employees, the unhonoured *chits* and also the mixed up accounts records of the estate. In December 1939, Kincaid-Smith called for a meeting of all tenants at Magomero factory, at which Capt. Parker, DC for Zomba, was the guest speaker. They told the natives of their obligations to the landlords. They also discouraged Africans from producing too much maize at the expense of tobacco produced with *thangata* labour. Meanwhile, tenants complained to the DC that they were not being paid for their labour and that Kincaid-Smith was not honouring the *chits*. As a result of this meeting, tension increased so much that the estate almost reached a point of crisis. This situation was reminiscent of that concerning William Jervis Livingstone, a former Manager of the same estate, who was killed in the Chilembwe Uprising of 1915.[50] When Governor Mackenzie-Kennedy learned of the 'Kincaid affair' in 1940, he immediately deported Kincaid-Smith from the country.

Meanwhile, the problem of land shortage among the African community worsened in the 1940s and 1950s. In order to ameliorate the situation, the government expressed its intention in 1952 to buy about 75,000 acres of land from the Magomero estate. Of this total, 46,000 acres were located in the eastern part, which was badly drained and sparsely inhabited. These were designated as Public Land for the establishment of a resettlement scheme. The remainder in the West became Trust Land but with no settlement to be allowed. This was a poor deal for the government because it bought land that was generally of poor quality as it tended to be water-logged or overpopulated.

In 1953, the government sent J.E.R. Emtage, the Resettlement Officer, to Magomero to help Africans make better use of their resources. The plan was to resettle some 3,000 families from the heavily congested Trust Lands in Chiradzulu and Thyolo on eight-acre plots, each measuring 100 by 400 yards. In a reversal of traditional Nyanja practice, land tenure was to be vested in the men and inheritance was to be by the nearest male heir. As in Zomba, this created problems in a society that followed a matrilineal system of marriage and inheritance. I discuss the implication of such policies in greater detail in Chapter Ten.

---

49. L. White, *Magomero*, p. 172.
50. The most comprehensive study on the Chilembwe Uprising remains George Shepperson and Thomas Price, *Independent African: John Chilembwe and the Origins, Setting, and Significance of the Nyasaland Native Rising of 1915* (Edinburgh: University of Edinburgh Press, 1958).

Conservation and politics, 1952–1964

Emtage's campaign focused on introducing bunding, contour ridging and hut concentration. The idea was basically to prevent Africans from building huts all over the place and in the middle of gardens.[51] But hut concentration was very difficult because Africans valued their access to different kinds of soils. The colonial officials overlooked an important aspect of peasant science here. Even when the agricultural staff began to encourage cash crop production, this went against the traditional practices of the Africans. According to Landeg White, Africans in this region had for a long time been growing well yielding crops like sorghum and pigeon peas and other emergency crops like cassava and sweet potatoes. Crops like pigeon peas grow very well in the area and also help in nitrogen fixing. But the encouragement of tobacco and maize reversed this tradition and undermined the survival strategies of the Africans. Landeg White further argues that, since the peasants had been producing enough crops for themselves, they also understood the problems of production on the soils available to them. Unfortunately, Trust Land was increasingly becoming overcrowded and less productive.[52] In 1954, the Chiradzulu District Natural Resources Board intervened by applying Rule No. 17 of the Natural Resources Rules to the Magomero estates. This order required Africans to undertake proper agricultural practices in the area under the Land Settlement Block.[53]

But the peasants resisted this government intervention. Emtage, the man on the spot, faced many difficulties as he attempted to implement conservation measures. Opposition to his campaign centred on the linkage of Federation and conservation issues. In particular, Africans opposed the adoption of contour ridging, hut concentration and the introduction of new crops, which was driven by price incentives, as was that of fertiliser. Peasants expressed their opposition in various ways. Landeg White found that women protested *malimidwe* even through pounding songs, such as the one below:

Federation kapitaos
e-e-e
Sooner or later you will die
e-e-e
Contour ridging kapitaos
e-e-e
Sooner or later you will die
e-e-e
e-e
You will die but you don't know it
a-i-a

---

51. L. White, *Magomero*, p. 214.
52. *Ibid.* p.260.
53. See MNA NSG 2/1/2: Minutes of the meeting of the Natural Resources Board, Southern Province, dated 20 August 1954.

Conflict over land and labour: the case of Chiradzulu and Thyolo districts

You will die but you do not know it![54]

After the riots of 1953, tension never ceased among the peasant communities in Chiradzulu district. Both the Federation and *malimidwe* contributed to the heightening of discontent in the district. While the Federation was associated with fears of more land alienation by European immigrants, *malimidwe* policies involved the resettlement of Africans, the use of coercion in implementing conservation measures and the uprooting of crops grown by Africans.

State policies about *malimidwe* also precipitated a number of rumours that heightened the level of anxiety in the countryside. One such rumour concerned the forced resettlement of Africans from Chiradzulu to Chingale in Zomba district. The story maintained that their land would be taken away and given to Europeans and Indians. Reacting to these rumours, the Native Authorities and the Village Headmen in Chiradzulu wrote, on 3 November 1954, a strongly worded letter to the DC protesting against government plans to resettle them to Chingale in Zomba. They stated that:

> We, the people of Chiradzulu District are very, very worried of being removed from our own mother District ... we are creatures of God as well as white people, no difference; the same blood, eyes, mouth, legs and arms too. Why should we be oppressed while you our DC are still alive? We don't want to leave Chiradzulu ... we were born and grown up here. Our parents died in this area and were buried here, why is it that we are alleged to leave from here to Chingale without our wishes?[55]

Although the chiefs dissociated themselves from Congress politics, they nevertheless shared the general fear that the Federation would bring in more Europeans, something to which they were very much opposed. Some indicated that their opposition was mainly based on peasant resentment to *malimidwe* policies of resettlement and land consolidation. A petition authored by Chiradzulu chiefs clearly distanced itself from the nationalist movement and argued that, 'We don't want Congress men to spoil our complaints before you, but we write directly to you, as you are one who works on behalf of our His Excellency the Governor or the Queen in England. We can't see the Queen, but we see her through you; without you, the DC there is no Government.'[56] Mindful of their ambiguous and sometimes contradictory position within the whole colonial set-up, the chiefs sought redress for their grievances through non-violent means, while their young and educated subjects were agitating for more radical approaches.

---

54. L. White, *Magomero*, p. 217.
55. MNA PCS 1/2/24: Letter by Native Authorities and Village Headmen in Chiradzulu to the Provincial Commissioner, Southern Province, dated 3 November 1954. Translation from original source.
56. MNA PCS 1/2/24: Letter by Native Authorities and Village Headmen in Chiradzulu to the Provincial Commissioner, Southern Province, dated 3 November 1954.

Conservation and politics, 1952–1964

The DC for Blantyre, who was also in charge of Chiradzulu, dismissed the rumours described above as stupid and baseless. The Provincial Commissioner for the South further emphasised that all the government was trying to do was to protect the natural resources of the district – to protect the headwaters of important streams and control soil erosion on steep slopes and stream banks. To achieve this, many gardens had to be closed and some Africans removed from areas considered susceptible to degradation. As for the proposed resettlement of Africans, the DC noted, 'The number of gardens which will have to be closed and the number of people who have to be removed are only small proportions of all the land and all the people in Chiradzulu. People to be moved will be given new places by the Boma if they wish to have them.'[57]

Although peasant resistance reached a climax in the 1950s, conservation rules began to be enforced in 1928 and, as in Thyolo district, these concerned the protection of stream banks, such as the area along the Chisombezi valley, and the protection of forest reserves, such as the Chiradzulu and Malabvi mountains. Cultivation of steep slopes was also prohibited and this affected several small hills in the district. Despite these restrictions, peasants still cultivated in the prohibited areas. There were frequent reports by colonial authorities that Africans reopened areas that had been closed to cultivation. In one instance, the DC complained that Africans reopened gardens whenever they noticed that there had been a change in personnel. Peasants' defiance of government regulations continued unabated up to the 1950s. But, at this stage, defiance attracted tougher action from the government. Through the application of Rule No. 16 of the Natural Resources Rules of 1951, the following areas were closed from any human settlement or cultivation: the southern slopes of Mambala hill in Chief Nkalo's territory, the eastern slopes of Chiradzulu Mountain in Chief Kadewere's and the slopes of Malabvi Mountain in Chief Likoswe's.

Then, in 1954, the state launched the Chiradzulu Mountain afforestation scheme with the main purpose of protecting the forest reserve. Funded by the Native Development and Welfare Fund, the scheme sought to protect forest reserves and improve land use practices in an area that had increasingly been ravaged by landless Africans. In his annual report, the agricultural officer for Chiradzulu sympathised with the Africans and noted that 'the District is so thickly populated that the native has been driven up the mountain slopes for lack of other land and not as seems to be the accepted idea in search of better soil'.[58] Under this afforestation scheme, a large area of excessive steepness had been closed to cultivation and several Africans were evacuated from the foot of the mountain. But the DC for Blantyre, who was also in charge of Chiradzulu sub-district, complained shortly afterwards that the scheme had put too much emphasis on forestry matters and ignored the situation

---

57. See MNA PCS 1/2/24: Soil Conservation: Blantyre District, November 1944–June 1955.
58. MNA S1/1567/23 folio 4, Annual Report for Chiradzulu District.

Non-violent forms of resistance to Federation and malimidwe

of Africans on Trust Land, which he described as not only serious but dangerous.[59] While acknowledging the need to reforest Chiradzulu Mountain, he argued that it was also necessary to deal with the problem of overcrowding on African Trust Land. 'It is certainly not practical politics to close steep cultivated land, in areas overloaded with population and largely dependent on maize stalks and garden trash for its fuel, and then to make no economic use (or no use at all) of the land thus freed of its economic burden'.[60]

The foregoing discussion points to some very important issues in understanding resistance to the Federation and *malimidwe*. It shows that resistance need not necessarily be expressed in the conventional ways of open revolts and violence. At times, peasant resistance might be seen from afar as being ephemeral or unimportant. Yet it was very significant in the minds of the peasants themselves. Peasant voices collected from interviews in the Shire Highlands demonstrate that we need to examine critically the notion of rural resistance.[61] Peasants stated that, in most cases, their resistance to *malimidwe* was deeply embedded in the fight against Federation. This resistance did not involve physical fighting and yet it was metaphorically described as war, the *nkhondo-ya-milambala* or war-of-bunding.

Non-violent forms of resistance to Federation and malimidwe

Nationalist leaders also opposed *malimidwe* but for reasons that had much to do with the advancement of their own political agendas. In the 1950s, they capitalised on the issue of *malimidwe* in order to marshal the support of the peasants. Initially, Africans, including spokesmen from the Shire Highlands, decided to oppose the Federation and *malimidwe* through constitutional means. They wrote letters, pleas, petitions and propositions, which were usually sent to Her Majesty's Government in London. Even before 1953, there had been several attempts to fight the proposal for Federation. For example, in September 1951, a delegation of African nationalists led by Chief Mwase of Kasungu went to Victoria Falls to dissuade participants from proceeding with the Federation. But when they returned home, people accused them of treachery because of their presence at the conference, which it was thought had compromised their opposition. In London, Dr Banda had similarly begun to organise resistance through constitutional means.[62] Soon after the Victoria Falls Conference of 1949, Dr Banda, who was at the time practicing medicine in London, organised

---

59. MNA PCS 1/1/17: Letter by DC, Blantyre, to Provincial Commissioner, Southern Province, dated 15 December 1954.
60. MNA PCS 1/1/17: Letter by DC, Blantyre, to Provincial Commissioner, Southern Province, dated 15 December 1954.
61. Similar studies have been done elsewhere: see, for instance, Ranger, *Voices from the Rocks: Nature, Culture, and History in the Matopos Hills of Zimbabwe* (Oxford: James Currey, 1999).
62. For details on the arguments against the Federation, see H.K. Banda and H.M. Nkumbula, *Federation in Central Africa*.

a meeting of African students in the UK at his London residence. They rejected the federal proposal and Dr Banda was actually asked to draft a memorandum of rebuttal to the Colonial Office. Although by 1952 it was a *fait accompli* that the Federation scheme would become a reality, largely because of the recommendation of the Lancaster Conference to draw up a draft federal scheme, Africans continued to oppose the federation through constitutional means.[63]

When, in January 1953, another delegation of three Chiefs and two senior members of the Nyasaland African Congress travelled to London to present their petition to the Queen, the delegation met Dr Banda and, with his help, presented the petition only to the Colonial Secretary. The effort to meet the Queen failed. This trip coincided with the final meeting of the Intergovernmental Conference on Federation, which was taking place in London at the time. At that point, Dr Banda advised Congress leaders and the chiefs to boycott all future conferences.[64]

Frustrated by the attitude of the British government and with the advice of Dr Banda, Congress and the Council of Chiefs decided, in early April 1953, to form the Supreme Council of Action, headed by Chief Mwase, with Lawrence Mapemba as Secretary. This body was charged with the responsibility of coordinating the policy of non-violent resistance to Federation. At its April 1953 meeting, the Supreme Council of Action came up with two main demands: first, the need to have an immediate African majority in the Legislative Council and, second, the need for government to cease promoting the idea of Federation, which was described as a 'threat to peace and good order of the country'.[65] The Council resolved that the time had come for Africans to publicly oppose the federation through the policy of non-violent resistance. This included strikes, boycott of European-owned stores, non-payment of taxes, defiance of government regulations and appeals to the United Nations and the International Court of Justice. The Supreme Council of Action also made calls for the eventual granting of self-government to Africans.

As the Supreme Council of Action was planning the launch of non-violent resistance, the Reverend Michael Scott, Director of the Africa Bureau in London, arrived in Blantyre on 5 April 1953.[66] He carried a message from Dr Banda encouraging Africans to use non-violent resistance to Federation as the only available option to them. In May 1953, the Supreme Council of Action sent another

---

63. When the Labour Party lost in the general election of October 1951, it became very difficult for the anti-federation group to have any influence in British politics. In fact, the Conservative Party, which won the election, indicated its intention to approve the federal proposal and thus organised another conference in April 1952.

64. Except for one, Congress boycotted all the conferences on Federation, that is, the Second Victoria Falls Conference held on 16 and 17 February 1949, the Third Victoria Falls Conference held in September 1951, the Lancaster Conference on the Federation proposal held in London in April/May 1952 and the Final Intergovernmental Conference held at the Carlton House Terrace in London in January 1953.

65. Philip Short, *Banda* (London, 1974), p. 71.

66. Details about the activities of the Rev. Scott are given in Ch. 9.

Conclusion

delegation of six senior African chiefs to London, this time to present a petition to the Queen. But the delegation was again refused an audience with the Queen; they were not even allowed to see the speaker of the House of Commons. The failure of this petition angered many Africans in Nyasaland who felt that the British Government was being insensitive to their plight. This delegation also suggested that the British Parliament could follow the precedent of 1931 to appoint a select committee that would establish the true feelings of the people of Nyasaland. They persistently argued that the Federation was being imposed on Africans against their wishes and aspirations.

After the delegation returned home, the Supreme Action of Council ordered Africans to stay away from all official functions. In addition, it sanctioned the boycott of the upcoming celebrations for the coronation of Queen Elizabeth in June 1953. Meanwhile, the Federal proposal had been passed in the British Parliament and only awaited the approval of the Queen. Chief Mwase made a last minute attempt to dissuade the Queen from assenting to the Federal Bill. In a strongly worded letter, he wrote:

> I am sorry many officials and some of the Lords feel it is an easy thing to oppress us in this way, forgetting that we are no [longer] slaves [having been] ... completely saved from all slavery ... by the Bible where a human being has equal rights [and] by the protection of ... Queen Victoria who ... granted to our Grandparents, a full protection from any power outside to attack us. Even today we trust ... Queen Elizabeth II will carry such protection ... [and will] not hand us over to a Government which ... aims to use Africans [as] labourers, and not as partners.[67]

Towards the end of the year, only one of the demands of the Supreme Council of Action had been met and only in part. This was the colonial government's decision to allow African representation in the Legislative Council, a process which saw, in December 1953, Messrs Manoah Chirwa and Clement Kumbikano being elected to the Federal Parliament. The rest of the demands remained unaddressed when the Federation became a reality on 1 August 1953.

Conclusion

This chapter has discussed the impact of state-sponsored conservation campaigns on peasants in the Shire Highlands. It has demonstrated that although peasants responded differently to different aspects of the conservation policies and practices, resistance was central to their daily encounters with the colonial state. In some cases, peasant resistance was violent and in others it was non-violent. The chapter has also shown that peasant participation in the anti-Federation opposition was driven by their fears about further state intrusion into their lives.

---

67. Letter to the Editor, *Nyasaland Times*, 13 July 1953; quoted in R.I. Rotberg, *The Rise of Nationalism*, p. 252.

9

The Religious Dimension to the Campaign against Soil Erosion in Colonial Malawi

> Look here, Government, I and my Christian followers, starting from today we shall never pay tax for the British Kingdom. I thought you were servants of God as the Bible says; that is why I was paying taxes, but now I realise that you are not the servants of God. (Wilfrid Gudu, 1938).

Introduction

Other than the Federation of Rhodesia and Nyasaland and the concomitant demands for self-government, soil conservation was probably one of the most heavily contested policy issues in the twilight years of British colonialism in Malawi. While existing scholarship has clearly documented the relationship between conservation and politics as well as the reaction of the peasants for whom these policies were initially intended, relatively little has been written about its religious dimension. Yet, conservation entailed transformation of the traditional practices, religious beliefs and experiences to which African production systems were integrally linked. For mainstream Christian churches, converts had to farm using agricultural methods that were in tandem with Christian values and practices and, crucially, these did not contradict state intervention efforts to transform African production systems. It is in this context that we explore the ideas and actions of the leaders of some religious groups whose fierce opposition to soil conservation policies in the 1940s and 1950s was part of their religious convictions and yet, on close examination, had little to do with the fundamental elements of conservation.

  We concentrate on Pastor Wilfrid Gudu of the Sons of God sect and the Rev. Michael Scott of the Anglican church, both of whom were conscientious objectors to the mainstream state and church systems; they charged that the two systems were not doing enough to address the oppression and suffering of the poor. One focused locally while another had a much broader international outlook. Gudu worked through a total religious institution, the *Zion za Yehovah* in Thyolo district, while Scott headed the Africa Bureau in London. Both were forced into a state of reclusiveness because of injustices earlier in their lives. Scott had been abused as a young boy by an ostensibly religious schoolmaster, while Gudu suffered perpetual injustice at the hands of the Traditional Authorities, the church and the state. In the end, both had experienced imprisonment, forced confinement, deportation and public embarrassment. Against this background, they both became convinced

Introduction

that the fundamental Christian principles of justice had been betrayed and they took it upon themselves to fight. As a way of staving off the interference of what he described as the corrupt and evil forces of the church in his attempts to realise his Christian ideals, Gudu decided to withdraw into a closed community, while Scott travelled widely and made public denunciations at every forum he could gain access to, such as the United Nations Assembly and political rallies. However, the actions of both men were invariably misunderstood by state authorities, who preferred to view them in political terms as trouble makers or malcontents or simply dismissed them as schizophrenics. That labeling made it all the more difficult for the state to understand who exactly they were and what ideas they held and perhaps more difficult still to know how to appropriately respond to their concerns. This chapter argues that although Pastors Gudu and Scott fought against soil conservation, their involvement was merely coincidental and not a reflection of any clearly articulated critique of the science and practice of conservation. Both were drawn to the centre of the controversy by extraneous factors. Until recently, neither Scott nor Gudu was accorded his rightful place in the history of Malawi and this chapter attempts to do that. Their experiences are murky and defy any conventional categories; the stories are convoluted and deeply embroiled in issues of politics, religion, petty jealousies, personal vendetta and social tensions.

Religious dissent and schisms have a long history in Africa. In the early part of the twentieth century, many independent churches emerged out of frustration with mainstream churches and also as a way of offering new hope to oppressed peoples. The sects often had an apocalyptic view of the world and preached millennial messages of the joys of New Jerusalem. For instance, in Belgian Congo, Simon Kimbangu set up his Kimbanguist preaching and healing ministry while Isaiah Shembe established the Ekuphakameni Nazarene church in the Natal region of South Africa. Similarly, Elliot Kamwana is best known for his Watch Tower movement in Malawi while Loti Nyirenda, a product of the Livingstonia mission, went on to establish the Mwana Lesa movement in Zambia. What all these sects attempted to do was to re-enact and ritualise the New Jerusalem or Zion on earth. In the process, they often came onto a collision course with colonial authorities as some of their actions translated into open defiance of state rules and structures. Determining the extent to which such ideas represented the aspirations of the larger African population remains difficult but, at the time of their appearance in their respective localities, they served as vital alternative avenues for people who did not agree with the church and state establishments.[1]

In the process of implementing the soil conservation campaign, the state came into direct conflict with many sections of the African community: the peas-

---

1. J.C. Chakanza, *Preachers in Protest*; J. McCracken, *Politics and Christianity in Malawi*; Terence Ranger and John Weller (eds.) *Themes in the Christian History of Central Africa* (London, 1975); Ian Linden and Jane Linden 'John Chilembwe and the New Jerusalem', *Journal of African History* 12/4 (1971): 629–651.

The religious dimension to the campaign against soil erosion

ants, chiefs, nationalist politicians and some sects of the Christian community.[2] While religious opposition illustrated the progressive feelings of the 'new men', that is the missionary-educated Africans, and religious independence from conservation, it also complicated the role of Christianity in colonial society. It has been argued elsewhere that the attitude of Christians towards conservation was not very clear and certainly was not the same throughout the colonial period.[3] Christian conservation attitudes varied not only according to time but also between different Christian groups. Some tacitly supported conservation measures while others opposed them. Among the churches that opposed conservation were the Sons of God and the Jehovah's Witnesses. In this connection, it is important to mention that John Chilembwe, a radical Baptist Minister and proto-nationalist leader, also opposed the agricultural practices of the colonial state in a violent manner. Although his resistance did not focus primarily on conservation, his grievances underscored some of the basic issues that were to become controversial later on.[4] However, like most people trained in mission schools, these new men increasingly began to develop consciousness and to be associated with the plight of the peasants in the face of heightened state conservation campaigns being imposed on African farming practices and labour processes.

Members of both the Jehovah's Witnesses and the Sons of God churches resisted the implementation of conservation measures principally on the grounds that these efforts emanated from laws made by man. They did not recognise any earthly authority because human beings were sinners. In the 1950s, adherents of the Jehovah's Witnesses in the Central and Southern regions of the territory put up spirited opposition to the introduction of soil conservation measures.[5] Their general argument was that the Bible did not disallow men from using the land as they wanted. The new rules about bunding or ridging were prescriptions of man, who had fallen from the glory of God. In their view, the old ways of farming represented the original state of nature where man cultivated without any disturbance. But Europeans changed all this and, further, introduced more injustices in the form of land alienation. This chapter will, however, focus on the experiences of Wilfred Gudu and his Sons of God church in Thyolo district, as well as the adventurous mission of Michael Scott in Ntcheu district.

---

2. See Roger Tangri, 'The Rise of Nationalism in Colonial Africa: The Case of Colonial Malawi', *Comparative Studies in Society and History* 10/2 (1968): 142–161; and J.C. Chakanza, *Preachers in Protest*.

3. W.O. Mulwafu, 'The Interface of Christianity and Conservation in Colonial Malawi'.

4. For more information on the Chilembwe Uprising, see George Shepperson and Thomas Price, *Independent African: John Chilembwe and the Origins, Setting and Significance of the Nyasaland Rising of 1915* (Edinburgh, 1958).

5. Personal communication with Robert I. Green, former Soil Conservation Officer, dated 28 June 1997. See also J.R. Hooker, 'Witnesses and Watchtower in the Rhodesias and Nyasaland', *Journal of African History* 6/1 (1965): 91–106; R.L. Wishlade, *Sectarianism in Southern Nyasaland* (London, 1965).

Wilfrid Gudu and resistance to conservation

Wilfrid Gudu and resistance to conservation

One of the most fascinating examples of religious opposition to conservation comes from Thyolo district, where members of the Sons of God Church tenaciously fought the state between 1938 and the mid-1950s. The founder and leader of the church was Wilfrid Gudu, whose last name was often transcribed as 'Good' in colonial documents. A former schoolteacher and evangelist, he virtually became the living symbol of religious resistance to conservation in the country.[6] Born of Nyanja parentage in Machiringa Village, near Malamulo Mission in TA Ntondeza,[7] Thyolo district, Wilfrid Gudu experienced many conflicts with the Traditional Authorities, the missions and the colonial state. He had initially worked for the Seventh Day Adventist Church in various capacities from 1911 to 1935 before breaking away to establish his own sect, *Ana a Mulungu* or The Sons of God Church, at Molere in Kaponda Village, TA Ntondeza. Between 1922 and 1935, he caused much furore in the Seventh Day Adventist Church by attempting to oust the leadership, which he claimed to be dominated by the Ngoni people. He was accused of wanting to replace the Ngoni with his own Nyanja people.[8]

In 1935, Gudu claimed to have been inspired by a vision in which God gave him the authority to look after his children, quoting Matthew 5:9 which states that 'Blessed are the peacemakers, for they shall be called children of God.'[9] It was this revelation that prompted Gudu to establish his own church station at Molere which he named *Zion ya Jehovah*. One of the guiding principles of this church was self-reliance. In view of this, Gudu opened a garden for the communal production of maize, which members of his Church had hoped to sell to the surrounding tea estates. He also introduced the teaching of various vocational skills to church members, such as carpentry, tailoring, pottery, weaving, bricklaying and shoe-making.[10]

---

6. Except for quoted information, I use the version 'Gudu' throughout this chapter, which is the form that Gudu himself and many of my informants used. More detailed information on him can be found in archival files ref. MNA S43/1/18/1. Other useful papers include, Robert B. Boeder, 'Wilfrid Good and the Ana a Mulungu Church' (Chancellor College, History Seminar Paper, 1981/82), Evans P.P. Murowa, 'Reverend Albert Kambuwa: A Critical Analysis of His Writings' (Chancellor College, History Seminar Paper, 1976/77).
7. T.A (Traditional Authority) is the modern usage of N.A. (Native Authority), referring to a chief whose jurisdiction encompasses several villages presided over by village headmen.
8. However, some of Gudu's acquaintances cast doubts on the sincerity of his actions. They argued that Gudu was a mentally deranged person who had gone mad while teaching at Msomela school in Malabvi, Chiradzulu district in the 1920s. He had disappeared into the bush and appeared again after four days without clothes. Since that time, he was a changed person with strange ideas. See, for example, the paper by James Ngaiyaye, 'The Sketch of Wilfred Good', 1938.
9. Parker, DC for Zomba, *Report on Wilfred Good*, dated 29 September 1941.
10. MNA S43/1/18/1: Wilfred Good to Superintendent of Police dated 18 March 1938. See also J.C. Chakanza, *Preachers in Protest*.

The religious dimension to the campaign against soil erosion

Gudu introduced a number of rules governing the community that settled at Molere. Church members were not allowed to wear shoes in the *kachisi*, a prayer house, in resonance with the belief that Jesus himself never allowed anyone to do so before him. Gudu also rejected the Western notion of time; he replaced the Gregorian calendar with his own which was based on the Bible. In addition, he changed the number of hours in the day from 24 to twelve. Gudu believed that he was the only man who had the true Gospel from God and that all the other churches failed to perform God's will correctly. While they preached about the second coming of Jesus Christ and told people to repent, the leaders themselves were sinners. But Gudu considered himself to be the true preacher because he had been called by God to preach His word. To this effect, he noted that God the Lord had sent him to save the people from their sins; he was, therefore, Jesus Christ No. 2, because the term 'Jesus' meant one who saves people from sins.[11]

Because of his radical ideas and rather truculent behaviour, Gudu frequently ran into conflicts with his own church, the colonial state and the Traditional Authorities. As early as the 1930s, Gudu had opposed state taxation policies and soil conservation measures on the grounds that it was against God's will for him and his church to obey any imposed political authority. He upheld a protracted resistance against the colonial state for nearly twenty years, during which time he was arrested on several occasions and sent to detention in the colonial capital of Zomba. Like the Watch Tower movement and other charismatic churches, Gudu's Sons of God was opposed to the payment of any form of taxation to the state and thus became a symbol of rural social protest against colonial policies and practices throughout Gudu's lifetime. Mr Maganga Seyani of Chief Nsabwe's area in Thyolo district pointed out that Gudu and Chief Mwase of Kasungu were two of the most prominent anti-conservation leaders in the country. He went on to say that 'if Gudu and Mwase had worked together we would have won the war against *malimidwe*'.[12]

When Gudu began his missionary work at Molere in 1935, he brought in many people from different villages. He gave them land to settle, even though he did not ask for permission from the relevant Traditional Authorities. Within a few months of the establishment of the church and the community, serious conflicts erupted between Gudu and the Traditional Authorities over the question of land. The conflict basically centred on the meaning and ownership of land. It was also a conflict about power relations and the perversity of local petty jealousies. Gudu claimed that in 1925 he had been given a piece of land at Kaponda Village, some 25 miles from Thyolo *boma*, by the previous chief, Village Headman Khwethemule, who was also his uncle. TA Chiputula had equally approved of the allocation of this piece of land, which was to be used for cattle grazing. The land deal was conducted

---

11. Albert Kambuwa, 'Malawi: Ancient and Modern History' (Unpublished Paper, University of Malawi Library, Zomba).

12. Interview: Mr Maganga Seyani, Nzundu Village, TA Nsabwe, Thyolo district, dated 28 May 1997.

Wilfrid Gudu and resistance to conservation

in a complicated web of family relationships. VH Kaponda was the son-in-law of VH Khwethemule and their villages were, at that time, about one mile apart. Since land shortage was a serious problem in Thyolo district, it is no wonder that Gudu had to ask for land from another village. In about 1929, Joseph, Ned, Taulo and a few other villagers from Kaponda began to cultivate part of the land that had been given to Gudu. Joseph, in particular, claimed the land belonged to him. To complicate matters further, Gudu's cattle at one point strayed and destroyed crops in the gardens of two of the villagers he had quarreled with. These individuals warned Gudu that they would kill his cattle. When the matter was reported to VH Kaponda, Gudu was told to be more careful with his cattle. By 1935, Gudu had lost both his cattle. Then within a short time, Gudu's sister had allegedly been assaulted and badly injured by Taulo, one of the people he was at loggerheads with over the question of land. When this matter was reported to the DC, it was referred back to the chief for trial by a Native Court. After the hearing, the case about the assault of his sister was dismissed for lack of evidence. Meanwhile, the social tensions had not dissipated.

Gudu's conflict with the local chiefs was not just due to the land he had given out to his church members. There were other longstanding tensions that conspired to blow this matter out of proportion. First, Gudu was reportedly a bitter enemy of Chief Ntondeza. At one point, the latter claimed that Gudu had attempted to take over his chieftainship. But Eric Smith, the DC at the time, intervened and settled the matter peacefully. Although the colonial state dismissed his claim to the chieftaincy, it is important nonetheless to stress that Gudu was no ordinary person; he came from a royal family. Two of his uncles were village headmen: Khwethemule and Petani. It is also possible that, because of his education and career as a teacher and evangelist, Gudu might have posed a threat to the local leadership. Governor Kennedy came closer to understanding the situation and consequently wrote to the Secretary of State for Colonies in 1939 that he thought the chiefs might have been envious of Gudu. He noted the 'natural jealousy of village headmen whose young men became no longer available after joining Good at Kaponda and of Kaponda himself who found his authority usurped in his own village'.[13]

The second source of tension between Gudu and the chiefs concerned the complaints lodged by several village headmen that many of the people who joined Gudu's church at Molere were individuals who had been avoiding the payment of taxes to the state. In late 1938, TA Ntondeza, village headmen Kaponda, Petani and others, all presented to S.J. Pegler, the DC for Thyolo, some of the names of the people who had moved out of their villages to join Gudu's church. TA Ntondeza also stated that Gudu had been preaching the non-payment of taxes, arguing that the word of God was not for sale. Gudu further said that he did not recognise

---

13. MNA S43/1/18/1: Governor D.M. Kennedy to The Right Honourable Malcolm Macdonald, Secretary of State for Colonies on 4 August 1939.

any earthly authority that imposed restrictions on human beings' desire to get to know God.[14]

When the land dispute matter had been settled against him, Gudu immediately issued a letter to the Government in 1938 stating that he had decided to stop paying taxes. 'Look here, Government, I and my Christian followers, starting from today we shall never pay tax for the British Kingdom. I thought you were servants of God as the Bible says; that is why I was paying taxes, but now I realise that you are not the servants of God.'[15] This decision came about as a result of his frustration with Government over the handling of a series of his cases between 1935 and 1937. Gudu cited three serious cases in which he felt the government had failed to mete out justice: the lack of impartiality in handling his cases involving the chieftaincy, grazing land, and settlement at Kaponda village. He questioned, 'Is it lawful to decide a case privately without hearing one's evidence? Is there a law to quit a person from his own home without judging his case? Is there a law to seize a person's food or to kill him before his case is settled?'[16] Setting aside legal opinion as to whether Gudu was right or wrong, these questions show the calibre of a man who was clearly aware of his own rights and wanted to see the due process of justice followed. At the same time, these questions also reveal contradictions in Pastor Gudu's behaviour. At one level, he tried to challenge earthly laws as not binding to him, a religious person seeking God's eternal kingdom. But when confronted with a court case here, he changed and tried to use the very same state laws to in order to exonerate himself. He argued that he was simply invoking the rules of natural justice. If anything, these contradictory episodes point not just to the character of the person but also to the complex environment in which he worked. Having alienated himself from his family, the mainstream Adventist church in his home area and the state, it may be possible to understand why Gudu decided to use different strategies when confronted in different circumstances.

As a result of his protest, Gudu was arrested in February 1938 and sentenced to three months imprisonment for non-payment of taxes for the year 1937. When Gudu had been taken to the *boma* at Thyolo, a large crowd of his followers followed him and presented themselves to the authorities, arguing that they too had evaded taxes and needed to be arrested. On close scrutiny, however, it was found that some of them had already paid taxes but simply wanted to show solidarity with their leader. Ultimately, 29 members of his church were arrested and sentenced with him to three months imprisonment with hard labour. While in prison, Gudu and his followers continued to be defiant of the authorities and insisted that they would obey no orders from human beings but only from God. For instance, they refused to work or wear uniforms.[17]

---

14. See S43/1/18/1: Wilfrid Good – Political Offender, March 1938–April 1942.
15. S43/1/18/1: Letter by Wilfred Good to Government, Thyolo, February 1938.
16. S43/1/18/1: Letter by Wilfred Good to Government, Thyolo, February 1938.
17. They were released at the end of their prison term on 23 March 1938.

Wilfrid Gudu and resistance to conservation

When Gudu and his followers returned to Molere in March 1938, they continued defying state authorities. In November 1938, Gudu was arrested again and this time sentenced to six months imprisonment with hard labour for non-payment of taxes for the year 1938. When his prison term ended in May 1939, Governor D.M. Kennedy issued an order to the DC for Zomba authorising the continued detention of Gudu for a further period of five years because he had conducted himself in a manner that was 'dangerous to peace, order and good government in the Protectorate'.[18] He invoked the provision on the Political Removal and Detention of Natives Ordinance, Cap. 23 of the Laws of Nyasaland, to extend Gudu's detention. It is also worth noting that, by that time, the Second World War had broken out and the state may have thought it necessary to keep him away from his trouble spot. After May 1939, Gudu was moved from Zomba Central Prison to the Police Camp where he lived under close supervision of William Barry Bithrey, the Commissioner of Police, and Parker, the DC for Zomba.

Meanwhile, Gudu's family was still at Molere in Kaponda Village. Phillips, the DC for Thyolo, visited the family in August 1939 and reported that Gudu's wife, Maggie, and their seven children were in good health. Of these children, aged between three and eighteen, the first born son was epileptic and the second born girl was disabled. When asked by the DC to move out of the village to go and live with her uncle, Village Headman Maonga, Gudu's wife refused.[19] In Zomba, however, Parker, the DC, observed Gudu on a weekly basis for three months and noted that, although he appeared to have behaved very well at the Police Camp, it was doubtful whether he had completely changed his mentality. Parker remarked that Gudu considered himself 'a martyr ... and a religious fanatic'.[20] He further wrote that, like many other African preachers, Gudu took the view that 'the Word of God is of greater practical importance than the laws of the Government and, if God tells him to take a certain action he is bound to do it, even if that involves breaking the law. It is difficult to reason logically or argue with a man of this mentality.'[21]

By 1941, police reports indicated that Gudu had changed substantially in his behaviour. Thus, on 25 May 1941, he was granted an audience with Governor Kennedy who reviewed his case and, on 20 March 1942, issued an order for the release of Wilfred Gudu on the understanding that he behave well and stop his proselytising activities. However, ten days later, Governor Kennedy retracted his decision on preventing Gudu from proselytising, saying that 'no man born of woman can prevent Good from preaching the "Word" as he understands it'.[22] Governor Kennedy confessed that, in retrospect, he had made a mistake in placing

---

18. See S43/1/18/1: Wilfrid Good – Political Offender, March 1938–April 1942.
19. *Ibid.* District Commissioner, Thyolo, to the Chief Secretary, Zomba, dated 19 March 1940.
20. MNA S43/1/18/1: Parker, DC for Zomba *Report on Wilfred Good*, dated 29 September 1941.
21. *Ibid.*
22. MNA S43/1/18/1: Minute by Governor D.M. Kennedy to Chief Secretary, titled Wilfred Good, dated 30 March 1942.

The religious dimension to the campaign against soil erosion

restrictions on Gudu. During the audience, it became clear to the Governor that Gudu's main complaint centred on the injustice wrought on the people who reaped his maize crop and yet got no compensation for it. He also mentioned that he did not appreciate the way in which Gudu's case had been dealt with, stating that 'all through this business I have been a little unhappy as to the manner in which Good was handled in the first instance. With the utmost appreciation of his many good qualities I must express the opinion that Mr Pegler has very little practical instinct: what he has is derived from the technique which obtains to the south of us.'[23] The Governor apparently put the blame on Pegler because his oppressive attitude was taken to have been influenced by his South African background.

But it was the issue of soil conservation concerning which Gudu posed his most serious challenge to the state. He frequently defied orders to undertake conservation measures like constructing bunds in his gardens. In fact, prior to this, the Thyolo District Natural Resources Board had requested the Provincial Board to make an order under section 10 of the Natural Resources Ordinance to compel Gudu to carry out conservation measures in his garden. Accordingly, Gudu was given two weeks to do the work. It was also expected that Gudu would maintain the bunds once they had been made. The Board further warned that failure to carry out the conservation measures would result in the government doing the work on his behalf and recovering the costs from him.

By November 1952, more than a year after the warning had been issued, Gudu had not yet done the work. The Board authorised the Department of Agriculture to carry out the conservation work, which cost £11. The Board also initiated legal action to recover the money from Gudu. Meanwhile, he and his followers started to break down the bunds and other conservation measures that had been constructed in his garden. This action infuriated many Board members because some of them feared that Gudu's action would set a bad precedent for other Africans in the district. E.J. Rumsey, a prominent planter in Thyolo district, mentioned that 'Gudu's defiance of the Board's order was having a very bad effect upon neighbouring Africans'.[24] At the next meeting of the Southern Province NRB, held on 23 January 1953, William Rangeley, the Chairman, reported that Gudu had already been prosecuted by the Thyolo NRB. He was sentenced to three months' imprisonment for breaking down the bunds made by the Agricultural Department. On the question of recovering the money, the Chief Secretary intervened and decided, much to the consternation of his staff, that Gudu should not be charged on the grounds that he had not been given sufficient time to construct the bunds. The Chief Secretary's decision centred on a technicality, based on the principle that the amount of time stipulated in the NRO should have been followed accurately. He went on to explain that, since Gudu was a religious 'maniac' and had already

---

23. *Ibid.*
24. MNA NSG 2/12: Minutes of the Meeting of the Provincial Natural Resources Board, Southern Province, held in Blantyre on 7 November 1952.

Wilfrid Gudu and resistance to conservation

served his prison sentence, the government found it no longer necessary to pursue the matter. Echoing the Chief Secretary's remarks, Rangeley emphasised that the government had thought it necessary to give some licence to religious maniacs. That was a strange decision, coming as it did from colonial authorities who were very concerned with the question of social control. It had been just under forty years earlier that the Chilembwe Uprising had shaken the already uneasy relationship between the church and state in colonial Malawi.

But the Thyolo DNRB was not satisfied with the decision of the Chief Secretary. In July 1953, it recommended to the Provincial Board that Gudu be removed from the area and deprived of any garden land. Moreover, E.J. Rumsey insistently complained that Gudu's actions were having a bad influence in the Thyolo district. At one of the Board's meetings, he emphasised that he wished to place on record that he would like to see 'stronger action taken as he considered the present system was not satisfactory and Government should take firm and definite action to stop an extremely bad example'.[25] But this was not the first time that a proposal had been made to evict Gudu from his home area. On 2 April 1938, the Chief Inspector of Prisons wrote to the Chief Secretary that 'Gudu is an egotistical type of native and in my opinion will always be a nuisance unless removed far from the Cholo area'.[26] Indeed, Gudu's ideas had spread to other areas in Thyolo district and this was confirmed by oral testimonies. For instance, Katchenga of Chalunda Village in Chief Nsabwe's area mentioned that 'we had heard about Gudu's protests at Molere. His activities gave us the encouragement to continue resisting *malimidwe*'.[27]

In November 1953, the Provincial Board succumbed to pressure from the Thyolo DNRB and invoked section 16 of the NRO, forbidding Gudu from further cultivating his land. However, this order carried the proviso that it could be rescinded as soon as Gudu had bunded his garden. A fundamental issue of concern for the Board was that Gudu had been prosecuted, imprisoned and fined before and so it was not necessary to prosecute him again. But his defiant actions had made the Agricultural Department in Thyolo 'a laughing stock'.[28] The other problem was the position of Gudu's garden. It lay above the Thyolo–Thekerani road and, when it rained heavily, the storm water running from his unbunded garden damaged the road, thereby making the movement of motor vehicles very difficult. Tired of this long history of defiance and resistance, the Board decided, in 1954, to permanently close Gudu's garden to further cultivation. Deprived of the means of production, Gudu left the Molere area and went to settle at Bvumbwe near Limbe in Blantyre district. At the meeting of the Provincial Natural Resources Board held in Blantyre

---

25. MNA NSG 2/1/2: Minutes of the Southern Province Natural Resources Board held in Blantyre on 31 July 1953.
26. MNA S43/1/18/1: Wilfrid Good – Political Offender, 1938 March–April 1942.
27. Interview: Mr Katchenga, Chalunda Village, TA Nsabwe, Thyolo district, dated 11 June 1997.
28. See MNA NSG 2/1/2: Minutes of the Southern Province Natural Resources Board.

The religious dimension to the campaign against soil erosion

on 24 October 1954, the Chairman reported that Gudu was still refusing to obey all orders because he said he 'received his orders direct from God'.[29]

Wilfrid Gudu's case is also significant in many other respects. It shows that the role of Christian missionaries in Malawi cannot be homogenised. Certainly, it would be unfair to consider all Christian missionaries as acting in unison towards African agricultural production and conservation activities. Some tacitly supported state conservation measures and others opposed them in numerous hidden ways. Initially, the missionaries exerted a great deal of influence on the evolution of colonial conservation policies and practices through their on-the-spot observations and writings.[30] For much of the colonial period, however, Christian missionaries generally had a low-key attitude toward the issue of conservation.

Although Gudu was initially trained within the tradition of the Seventh Day Adventist Church, many of his radical religious ideas appear to have been derived from his strong personality as well as from Zionism and Ethiopianism.[31] The state described him as a religious maniac but, in fact, he was a conscientious priest, protesting against what he perceived as unjust laws imposed on him and his fellow Africans. Early on, J.C. Abraham, the Senior Provincial Commissioner in the South, described him as a malcontent, not dissimilar to George Simeon Mwase of Lilongwe.[32] Governor Harold Kittermaster described him as 'an individual of fanatical temperament and antagonistic mentality'.[33] Colonial state officials did not speak with the same voice.

Several scholars have attempted to explain the actions and beliefs of Wilfred Gudu within the framework of Malawi's political and religious history. Robert Rotberg argues that Gudu's church was a means through which the aggrieved Africans sought to express their rejection of foreign domination. It was a religious expression of the rise of nationalism within a rural context. Not unlike many other breakaway churches, Gudu's sect emphasised 'the control by Africans of the religious present and offered their adherents an avenue of advancement that rivaled that of European mission churches'.[34] Rotberg considers Gudu's actions to correspond to those of John Chilembwe in the sense that they both were proto-nationalists. On the other hand, Joseph Chakanza views Gudu as a conscientious objector who resisted different forms of injustice wrought by different sections of the colonial society. For Chakanza, Gudu was a liberator of 'his people from the injustices and hypocrisy

---

29. See MNA NSG 2/1/2: Minutes of the Provincial Natural Resources Board, Southern Province.
30. Details are discussed in Ch. 3.
31. Robert Boeder argues that Wilfrid Gudu's anti-government and anti-mission tendencies were drawn from diverse sources including Ethiopianism, Zionism and Watch Tower Theology.
32. MNA S43/1/18/1: Letter by J.C. Abraham, Senior Provincial Commissioner, dated 16 December 1938.
33. MNA S43/1/18/1: Wilfrid Good – Political Offender, 1938 March–April 1942.
34. R. Rotberg, *The Rise of Nationalism*, p. 146.

of the missions, the colonial administrators and their collaborators'.[35] He objected to the handling of court cases, payment of taxes and many other instances because he perceived the process to be lacking in impartiality.

Although these two interpretations are both valid to some extent, they do not take into account the impact of state intervention in the lives of men and women in the region. Religious and political factors aside, Gudu opposed conservation campaigns because they entailed colonial intrusion into his space and the spaces of his church members. As a preacher, educator and, more importantly, a farmer, Gudu needed land on which he wanted to produce crops. When the state decided to take away his land, following a dispute, Gudu used a religious platform to express his opposition. Further attempts by the state to implement conservation measures on his garden and those of his church members were resisted because they constituted an imposition intended to restructure their production systems. Given the seriousness of the land shortage problem in the Thyolo district, men and women strongly guarded against any interference with their access to this scarce resource.

Until his death on 14 March 1963, Gudu sustained his resistance to the colonial authorities over various issues. For example, he objected to the manner in which the Malamulo Church had handled a case of adultery in 1935. He argued that the Church should have suspended the young man who had committed adultery and, when the Church refused to do that, he also refused to attend Holy Communion for six months. Later, the Church excommunicated him on the grounds that he had not paid church tax while on suspension. He was subsequently demoted from schoolteacher to carpenter. Then he protested to the colonial authorities over the way in which the DC for Thyolo had handled the maize garden issue in which he was also involved. While the cause may have been a controversy over the maize garden the result was eventually much wider and had more serious long-term consequences. This chapter takes the stand that the actual outcome of both the church decision and the maize garden case could be found in the actions and writings of Gudu.

Insofar as his defiance of colonial authority was concerned, he was a quintessential proto-nationalist. He did not necessarily crave general African self-determination but emphasised self-reliance in his followers. The *Zion of Jehovah* community was a model of what he would probably have wanted in other parts of the country. He considered the hut tax an important symbol of African submission to colonial authority. By refusing to pay taxes, Gudu should be seen as a resister who attempted to seriously undermine the colonial hegemony. Like Mahatma Gandhi in India, even if not directly influenced by him, Gudu refused to buy European manufactured goods such as shoes and clothes. He relied mainly on those goods that his community produced. Kambuwa wrote that, at one time, Gudu reported that God had spoken to him in a dream and instructed him that 'it was time to separate from the Europeans, that Wilfrid Gudu was now the government. Taxpayers were

---

35. J.C. Chakanza, *Preachers in Protest*.

The religious dimension to the campaign against soil erosion

the Sons of Evil; non-taxpayers the Sons of God. Since the government had stolen his means of paying taxes, Gudu decided not to pay them at all.'[36]

Even the introduction of soil conservation measures was rejected by Gudu on the basis that it signified the further extension of European hegemony. Pegler, the DC for Thyolo, persistently submitted reports that the activities of Gudu were posing a threat to the society and must be dealt with in a heavy-handed manner. 'The whole native population of the district was eagerly waiting to hear the result of this case of refusal to pay tax. It caused quite a stir in the district and several planters were asked by their labour what the District Commissioner would do.'[37] Pegler also mentioned in one of his reports that the actions of Gudu had created a certain degree of suspicion among his own people. For example, he reported an incident in which the Head Clerk at Thyolo *boma*, a certain Stephen, had told him that Gudu was a dangerous person and he did not want to be associated with him because of the fear of being suspected by the colonial authorities. Stephen is further reportedly to have cited the case of the Chilembwe uprising when some innocent people were interrogated or imprisoned. Against the background of Gudu's growing influence and popularity, Pegler described him as 'a fanatic – not by any means harmless – I do not think that any Medical man would certify him as insane – He has formed this mission, and it has taken on with astonishing success, in fact so much so that [Gudu] has lost his mind.'[38] Most of my informants in Thyolo district told me that they believed Gudu was a person of great courage and conviction. He had tenaciously stood up against the soil conservation campaign, one of the most coercive aspects of the postwar agricultural policy.[39] At that time, the government utterly failed to understand the motive of Gudu's actions, preferring to view him in political terms only as a malcontent. It was not long after, however, that the Governor lamented that Gudu had been mishandled and that he was actually a sincere and above average person. It is possible that the state, concerned as it was with social control, may have initially viewed Gudu as a political threat and have wanted to contain his influence from spreading widely. Accordingly, the Chief Inspector of Prisons advised the Chief Secretary that 'I would prefer to keep Good at the Central Prison because it is a good thing to let his friends see that really he is a very ordinary person and has to obey orders the same way as anyone else'.[40]

---

36. See A. Kambuwa, 'Malawi: Ancient and Modern History'.
37. MNA S43/1/18/1: Wilfred Good – Political Offender, March 1938–April 1942. Pegler, *Report on Wilfred Good*.
38. MNA S43/1/18/1: Pegler, DC for Thyolo, *Report on Wilfred Good*, 1938.
39. The following people interviewed expressed the same point: Mr Maganga Seyani of Nzundu Village, TA Nsabwe, Thyolo district, dated 28 May 1997; Mr Katchenga, Chalunda Village, TA Nsabwe, Thyolo district, dated 11 June 1997; Messrs Dexter Jobo, Handson Mzengeza and Frank Likome, Chalunda Village, TA Nsabwe, Thyolo district, dated 11 June 1997.
40. MNA S43/1/18/1: Letter from the Chief Inspector of Prisons to the Chief Secretary.

Wilfrid Gudu and resistance to conservation

Throughout the period Gudu was in prison, his followers continued to meet and pray under the leadership of Gideon, Zalimba and Binnet.

Although Gudu's behaviour was so eccentric, he was by no means an unintelligent person. Even more so, he was not a schizophrenic; he was a well-informed person who knew pretty well the operations of the church and state. He knew his own limits in terms of speech and actions. Unlike Chilembwe, he never resorted to violence as a means to address his grievances. Instead, he used passive action which, it is surmised here, he may have heard about or read about in books. There is little doubt that he was well read in religious matters. When the police searched his house in 1938, they found that he was in possession of several books of the Watch Tower movement, such as *Vindication*, *The Kingdom* and *Who Shall Rule the World*. All these books were on the government's banned list. Gudu had been reading these books along with the Bible. He was a person who used religion to fight all forms of injustice in society. For him, soil conservation represented one of the injustices of the colonial system, which he had to resist at all costs. Like Scott, he identified himself with the oppressed and powerless people in the wake of the tyranny of the colonial system. This explains why he opposed various aspects of social injustice such as the uncaring attitude of the church to the suffering masses in the cases of land shortage and the segregation of African staff; the obligations placed on Africans to wear shoes and hats in public places; the unfair handling of the adultery case; and the unfair judgement over his maize garden.

Gudu cannot be seen as simply a victim of circumstances. He was a historical agent who sought to shape the course of events in the world in which he lived. As a highly principled person, whose life was deeply embroiled in local politics, he viewed religion as a panacea for all the problems in society. The creation of *Zion ya Jehovah*, as an ideal society in which the demands of soil conservation, state taxation or local petty politics were non-existent, offered Gudu and his followers a ray of hope for a fulfilling Christian life. To that extent, Gudu may have attempted to bring about a new world order for his followers. As Chakanza has pointed out, he sought to recreate a world where God-given resources like land would be used without any interference from Europeans. Gudu argued that there was no biblical justification for soil conservation measures as propagated by the state. This is why he decided, after the initial conflicts, to set up a private space for himself and his adherents, to move away from polluted worldly systems. Gudu has been described as a visionary and courageous prophet who considered himself as having had 'a mandate from God to liberate his people from the injustices and hypocrisy of the missions, the colonial administrators and their collaborations'.[41] Although his message was not always very clear, he expressed himself eloquently in words and symbols that earned him the admiration of his followers.

---

41. J.C. Chakanza, *Preachers in Protest*.

The religious dimension to the campaign against soil erosion

Michael Scott and resistance to conservation

Michael Scott's association with conservation in colonial Malawi is by all accounts accidental. As his biographers have cogently argued, he is perhaps better known for his struggles against social injustice in different parts of the British Empire, including issues of colonialism, federation and human rights. He was a mysterious and paradoxical figure who embarked on a series of one-man missions to fight against injustice in southern Africa. Described as a great admirer of Gandhi, his activities saw him work in many parts of Africa including Botswana, South West Africa, South Africa and Nyasaland. In Uganda, he facilitated the return of the Kabaka who had been exiled to England. In Botswana, he reconciled the regent Tshekedi Khama with Prince Seretse Khama who had been forced into exile for marrying an Englishwoman. In South Africa, he supported defiance campaigns against the introduction of apartheid laws. In other countries, such as Kenya and Southern Rhodesia, he was simply declared a *persona non grata* for fear that he might incite violence in the settler dominated colonies even though he had not set foot there. Scott was once imprisoned in South Africa and later banned from visiting that country again. At one point, he was also deported from India and in his own country, Britain, he served three prison terms.

Scott was born in Sussex on 30 July 1907 of Scottish parents, the Rev. Perceval Caleb and Ethel Scott. As a young man, growing up in Northam, one of the slum parts of London, he was generally perceived to be a privileged child in a largely poor and unprivileged world. Although Scott was ordained as an Anglican priest, he became alienated from his church and the white community. He was a priest without a parish and is believed to have lived on handouts for some years. Early on, he was greatly influenced by the Quaker movement in their pursuit of the restoration of the true Christian church after apostasy – emphasising Christ as the light to the world. Subsequently, he became a peace campaigner and travelled widely in different parts of the world speaking on issues of human rights and social justice. He worked solely to champion these ideals and his campaign was driven by Christian ideals and beliefs, although he often strayed to pursue his own ideas. He had a 'question' for which he relentlessly sought an answer in his life and the world at large – a search for justice and the truth. By 1952, he had become a kind of celebrity and began to work with a number of well known liberal personalities in the UK, such as Lord Hemingford, Arthur Creech Jones, prominent journalists like David Astor and Colin Legum, and leading scholars such as Margery Perham. In April 1952, they established the Africa Bureau with the following aims:

> To inform people in Britain and elsewhere about African problems and African opinion thereon, and to convey to Africa accurate reports on events and attitudes in Britain that concern them;

> To help peoples in Africa in opposing unfair discrimination and inequality of opportunity and to foster cooperation between races;

Michael Scott and resistance to conservation

To promote polices for furthering economic, social and political development of all communities in Africa and especially the establishment of responsible self-government in countries where this does not exist.[42]

The Bureau was committed to working with Africans to advance the process of decolonisation in fourteen territories. With the passage of time, however, other issues were added to the agenda, such as the disarmament campaign. When he was appointed the first Director of the Bureau, he was charged with the major responsibility of advancing its mission. At the time of the establishment of the Bureau, the proposal to set up the Federation of Rhodesia and Nyasaland was already a highly controversial issue. Many liberals did not support it, as it was perceived to be a step in the direction of promoting white supremacy against the interests and aspirations of Africans. Although by 1952 it was almost a *fait accompli*, the Bureau thought that last minute efforts should be made to encourage chiefs to challenge the decision. It was also believed that such a move would help avoid the Kenyan scenario, where the African delegation to negotiations in London had not received good advice, with the undesirable consequence of violence by Mau Mau protesters.

Scott immediately took it upon himself to intervene and, on 5 April 1953, left London for Nyasaland without informing the Bureau's advisers. His aim was to provide advice to the African chiefs against the Federation, using the civil disobedience approach. In Nyasaland, he met nationalist leaders and chiefs and spoke at political rallies in different parts of the country. But instead of restricting his advice to the issue of the Federation, he stumbled into the issue of soil conservation whose implementation had already stirred up tensions in various parts of the country. Through the Natural Resources Board, the government had issued stringent rules for implementation by peasants across the country. Chiefs were instructed to enforce rules among their subjects. Chief Phillip Gomani of Ntcheu, one of the staunch opponents of the Federation, was caught up in this quagmire.

Although Gomani's story has been discussed elsewhere, it has not been subjected to critical analysis supported by both oral sources and colonial records. Moreover, the drama surrounding the actions and subsequent death of Gomani is intriguing and merits more detailed discussion here. The standard narrative holds that on 12 May 1953 Chief Gomani issued a duly signed notice directing his people to disregard agriculture, forestry and veterinary laws in all areas of his jurisdiction. In addition, he urged his subjects not to pay the legal native tax until such a time as the leaders of the Nyasaland Chiefs Council had decided otherwise. He also warned his people not to follow state instructions, stating derogatorily that 'his stomach will be his Capitao'.[43] At that time, Gomani also served as Secretary of the

---

42. Anne Yates and Lewis Chester, *The Troublemaker: Michael Scott and His Lonely Struggle Against Injustice* (London: Aurum Press, 2006), p. 129.
43. See *Nyasaland Times* of 25 May 1953; and MSS.Afr.S.864: R.H. Keppel Compton, A Factual Account of Events Leading to Deposing Phillip Gomani.

The religious dimension to the campaign against soil erosion

Nyasaland Chiefs Council and may also have been influenced by the Nyasaland African Congress.

Gomani had probably reacted in such a manner partly because of his experience with previous state intervention in his area. In 1948, destocking laws had been widely applied in the Livulezi valley, resulting in the loss of nearly 1,000 herds of cattle in four villages. The state had done this in order to reduce the problem of overstocking. But, considering that cattle were and still are so central to the culture and lives of the Ngoni-speaking people, they felt that state action was calculated to deprive them of an opportunity for livelihood. Such a reaction was not unique to the Ntcheu area in Malawi; a similar kind of resistance took place in South Africa and other parts of Africa.[44]

Government orders had been aimed at curtailing a number of practices being undertaken by Africans, such as stopping the indiscriminate cutting of trees in forest reserves and protected areas and reducing the number of livestock kept, while at the same time encouraging their dipping. Gomani's reaction was considered subversive and the government wasted no time in immediately pouncing on him. He was accused of issuing unlawful orders meant to defy government instructions on soil conservation. As part of the initial diplomatic effort, the Governor sent Keppel-Compton, the Provincial Commissioner for the Centre, to try and persuade him to withdraw the orders and avoid shame and dethronement. During this visit, Compton was accompanied by the DC for Ntcheu and an African interpreter. When asked to revoke the order, Gomani is reported to have initially hesitated, showing signs that he would acquiesce, but he later refused to sign a document that would have served as evidence of his decision to cancel the orders. Without showing any trace of remorse, Gomani admitted full responsibility for the illegal instructions he had issued to his people but still refused to revoke them. Just as Compton was preparing to issue an order of deposition, Rev. Scott who had been hiding and listening to all the discussions from another room appeared suddenly. Scott had apparently travelled to Ntcheu district to advise the chief not to relent in his resolve to resist the proposed introduction of a Federation, as well as to challenge government on the implementation of soil conservation regulations.

When the Provincial Commissioner realised the complexity of the situation, he decided to serve the Governor's order on the Chief, requiring him to vacate office within 24 hours. But he also told the chief that, since he was sick, he would return to Malamulo hospital where he had previously been admitted, for further treatment. At this point, interesting developments began to take place in the uneasy relations between Chief Gomani and the Rev. Scott on the one hand and the state on the other. Chief Gomani was deposed for ordering his people to disobey government laws. In fact, when he was initially suspended from duty by the Governor on 19 May, the DC for Ntcheu was appointed in his place as the

---

44. A.Mager, "'The People Get Fenced'"; W. Beinart and C. Bundy, *Hidden Struggles in Rural South Africa*.

Michael Scott and resistance to conservation

acting Native Authority for area. On the same day, however, the Chief's son, Willard, attempted to seek permission from the DC's office to hold a meeting on 22 May at the headquarters of sub Native Authority Kwataine. Among key people invited to this meeting were Chief Mwase of Kasungu and some members of the Nyasaland African Congress like Ralph Chinyama, A.J.M. Banda, B.W. Mathews and Lawrence Mapemba. The Rev. Michael Scott also planned to attend the meeting. Permission to hold the meeting was refused by the Magistrate of Ntcheu on the grounds that it would promote public disaffection. Meanwhile, most of the invited persons came to Ntcheu and a crowd of nearly 800 people gathered. But, in a surprising twist of events, Chief Kawinga of Kasupe, who had also been invited, left the territory on Saturday 23 May by air from Blantyre to represent the people of Nyasaland at her Majesty's coronation in London! This news confirmed what people like the Rev. Scott had long believed – that the government was practising divide and rule by appeasing moderate African rulers.

On 26 May, the government sent a vehicle, purportedly to transport the chief to the hospital, but he refused and instead went to his court at Lizulu. As tension began to rise, the government sent the police to forcibly get him into the car so that he could be taken to Malamulo hospital. The police had no kind words for the Chief; they said he was 'obdurate and refused to leave quietly'.[45] In the end, they forced him into the car but, just before driving off, the car's way was blocked by a large crowd that had gathered when news spread about the chief being taken away under suspicious circumstances. In the ensuing pandemonium, the crowd helped Chief Gomani to exit the car and he disappeared soon thereafter. He apparently fled with his son, Willard, and the Rev. Scott to Mozambique where they stayed under cover for some days. Before long, they were discovered by Mozambican authorities and later sent back to Malawi. Chief Gomani was taken to Malamulo hospital right away while the Rev. Scott was deported. The government found a house close to the hospital in Blantyre in which it hoped that chief Gomani would stay with his family but he refused the offer. Unfortunately, he did not live long – he died a few months later under circumstances that have been the subject of great controversy.

Two days later, on 28 May 1953, the Executive Council endorsed the Governor's decision to deport the Rev. Scott and to depose Chief Gomani. In the case of Gomani's deposition, the government invoked section 3(5) and (6) of Native Authority Ordinance, cap.74. Official correspondence and intelligence reports show that the state feared that the Chief's continued disobedience of government regulations would result in the breakdown of law and order. His refusal to withdraw the orders meant that the political consequences of keeping Gomani in the position would have been chaos and lawlessness. Again, using the policy of divide and rule, the government took advantage of divisions in the royal family to denounce and isolate Gomani. In this regard, Sub-Chief Chakhumbira was reported to have

---

45. MSS.Afr.S.864: R.H. Keppel Compton: A Factual Account of Events Leading to Deposing Phillip Gomani.

The religious dimension to the campaign against soil erosion

opposed Gomani's actions and given support to the government. When the time came for the prosecution of all known offenders against both the forest and cattle dipping rules, as a result of the chief's illegal orders, Chakhumbira and sub-NA George were praised for assisting the government. Thus, a record number of 1,000 offenders were prosecuted and eventually convicted by the magistrate's court and the majority of them quickly paid their fines. Later, when peace had returned to the area, several loyal sub-Chiefs, excluding all those under the jurisdiction of Gomani, were promoted to the rank of Native Authority.

Several issues can be raised from this incident and the general role of religious leaders like Rev. Scott. First, is the validity of reasons for state action against both Gomani and the Rev. Scott. Nationalist leaders like Kanyama Chiume argued that both Gomani and the Rev. Scott had been victimised by the state for speaking the truth and in this case opposing policies deemed repressive. In his book, *Nyasaland Demands Secession and Self Government*, Chiume is quoted as having alleged that Gomani had been ruthlessly forced out of his home, deposed and manhandled and died later in hospital. He further complained that Michael Scott, who had accompanied him, was unceremoniously deported.[46]

Second, is the question of the death of Chief Gomani. While he was sickly and hence his death may not have been totally unexpected, the timing of and explanation for the cause of his death raise questions. The official colonial view at the time, as reflected in many government correspondences, was that Gomani had died of a strange disease called St. Vitus Dance; Compton described it as a chronic disease of syphilitic origin. But the government blamed Congress leaders for exerting pressure on a sickly person, which only exacerbated his condition. One report noted that Gomani's actions and, by implication, his death were 'a result of pressure from Congress, his innate obstinacy, pathetic trust in Scott because he was a clergy man'.[47] In retrospect, Keppel-Compton further alleged that Congress had taken advantage of the sickness of Phillip Gomani to encourage the young and unsuspecting acting chief, Willard, to agitate for and meddle in the nationalist movement.[48]

The third issue concerns the deportation of the Rev. Scott. As indicated above, Governor Colby approved Rev. Scott's deportation order on 28 May 1953, citing his continued presence as a threat to security in a disturbed area. There was fear that, even though he had not committed any specific criminal act, he would nonetheless have exploited the situation to his advantage. In fact, prior to this inci-

---

46. Rhodes House Library, University of Oxford: Letter from L.B. Greaves to Keppel-Compton, then in Higher Leigh, Kingsbridge, to clarify the matter, dated 11 November 1959. MSS. Afr.S.864: R.H. Keppel Compton: A Factual Account of Events Leading to Deposing Phillip Gomani.
47. MSS.Afr.S.864: R.H. Keppel Compton: A Factual Account of Events Leading to Deposing Phillip Gomani.
48. Rhodes House Library, University of Oxford: Letter by Keppel-Compton to L.B. Greaves, dated 18 November 1959. MSS.Afr.S.864: R.H. Keppel Compton: A Factual Account of Events Leading to Deposing Phillip Gomani.

Michael Scott and resistance to conservation

dent, the government reported that they had extended his visitor's pass when it had expired on the grounds that they had no choice but to renew it because refusing him would have been worse. In order to justify his deportation, the government cited section 9 of the Immigration Ordinance No.20 of 1949 in which Scott was accused of being an accessory to Gomani's escape from unlawful custody. To this effect, the Governor wrote, 'I might add that had it not been for Scott, Gomani would have probably gone quietly and might have repented'.[49] Thus, as soon as the government had declared Scott a prohibited immigrant, the police took him into custody, initially in Dedza and then later to Chileka whence he was flown back to London, via Dar-es-Salaam and Nairobi. The main bone of contention was that Scott had encouraged Gomani and members of the Nyasaland African Congress to boycott government rules and public functions. While he had all along played an instrumental role in encouraging Africans to adopt a policy of non-violent civil disobedience in their opposition to the Federation, Scott decided this time around to take advantage of the contentious soil conservation issue to advise them to challenge the newly imposed government rules. Although he spent barely six weeks in the territory, his stay was long enough to stir up trouble with the authorities. In fact, just a few days after his arrival in Blantyre, the media had already complained about his mission and character; they probably did this on the basis of his confrontations with authorities in other parts of the world. For instance, *The Nyasaland Times* of 16 April described him as 'the peripatetic Don Quixote … a most unreliable guide, philosopher and friend'.[50] Since he had been pre-judged, there can be little wonder that the authorities were looking for an opportunity in which to implicate him and deport him.

The Nyasaland trip not only stirred up controversy in the territory but also got Scott into trouble with his advisers back in England. Apart from the embarrassment of not being informed about his mission, some members opposed the approach he used, which appeared to have been supporting violence. The Bureau argued that, while civil disobedience was compatible with Christianity, they did not accept Scott's view that it was necessary to Christianity. Some members even went to the extent of accusing Scott of being a communist, although he vehemently rejected such accusations. With the benefit of hindsight, Scott should be seen as a fearless leader but one prone to courting trouble with the authorities with which he came into contact. Yet, for all his shortcomings, he goes down in the annals of history as someone who contributed enormously to internationalisation of the issue of the Federation of Rhodesia and Nyasaland. Perhaps much less well known is his undaunted effort to establish several trusts, such as the African Development Trust

---

49. Rhodes House Library, University of Oxford: Letter by Governor G. Colby to Secretary of State for Colonies dated 28 May 1953.
50. The *Nyasaland Times* of 16 April 1953, quoted in A. Yates and L. Chester, *The Troublemaker*, p.131.

and the Africa Educational Trust, whose purpose was to further his grand vision of the liberation and education of Africans.

Conclusion

Obviously, it would be grossly unfair to compare in any meaningful manner the Rev. Michael Scott with Pastor Wilfred Gudu. The two came from different racial and cultural backgrounds and operated in different social and political spaces. But one striking thing is that, driven by strong religious convictions, they both came to symbolise the spirit of resistance to social injustice. As it happened, Nyasaland had become a battlefield for their crusade. They had their own specific grievances against state authorities – Federation in the case of Scott and land dispute for Gudu – but it was the introduction of soil conservation rules and the authoritarian manner in which this was done that provided a unique opportunity for the two religious leaders to come into direct confrontation with the authorities. It mattered less whether they agreed or not with the merits of conservation as a scientifically proven idea for the better management of natural resources.

Both believed that the world in which they lived was so corrupt and unjust that the state and the church had become complicit in the injustice. They both had personal experiences of injustice, with Scott having been abused by the principal of his school while a teenager. Gudu underwent a spiritual rebirth whereby he spent several days wandering in the bush. These very different events had transformational effects on the two. Gudu believed himself to have been caught by the Holy Spirit and declared himself 'Jesus Christ No. 2'. Scott's abuse did permanent damage to his life, forcing him to become introverted and independent-minded; he was described as a 'mixture of Gandhi and Jesus, a lion, a great man more than a dozen Bishops and Popes'.[51] In order to get rid of injustice, the spiritually pure had to delink and create a holy city of adherents in the case of Gudu while, for Scott, a fight using civil disobedience was called for.

State authorities never liked to see the two religious leaders going about their business freely, preferring to label them troublemakers or malcontents. At a time when nationalist agitation was rising in the territory, the state virtually decided that the best option available to them was to keep such people at bay either through imprisonment or deportation. That was easily effected – Gudu was arrested on three different occasions and spent a total of six years in prison before eventually being deported from his home village of Kaponda to Bvumbwe. For his part, Scott was a celebrated jailbird, having been arrested and detained in South Africa four times and then deported from or declared a prohibited immigrant in India, Kenya and Southern Rhodesia – all former British territories experiencing serious debates on the future of the colonised inhabitants.

---

51.   A. Yates and L. Chester, *The Troublemaker*.

10

Ecological Change, Gender Relations and Peasant Resistance in Zomba District

Introduction

On 3 October 1953, three African demonstrators were killed in the fight that broke out between peasants and colonial state officials at the Domasi subdistrict, some sixteen kilometres from the former colonial capital of Zomba, Malawi. Several other demonstrators and colonial state employees were wounded in the ensuing scuffle.[1] Although the colonial state attempted to play down the significance of this event by dismissing it as simply an expression of agitation by a few misguided individuals, the peasants in and around the Domasi area remembered it as an important phase of their resistance against the policies and practices of the colonial state in the context of changing ecological relations. At the heart of this conflict was the issue of *malimidwe* [conservation] which, through its coercive implementation strategy, opened the Pandora's box of tensions that had been building up in the area for many decades before. They described it derisively as *nkhondo-ya-thomusoni*.[2] Although this event has not been thoroughly investigated by scholars, it is nevertheless an important one in the modern history of Malawi and peasants vividly remember the violent incident as a climax of their resistance to the colonial state's policies and practices on conservation. It was an event that underscored the changing nature of the relationship between British colonial rulers and their African subjects in the dying years of colonialism.

Scholarly literature on resistance to conservation in Africa is copious. We now know a great deal about the policies that precipitated resistance, about peasant production systems and the ways in which such resistance was gendered.[3] But one missing point in the literature is the way in which peasants viewed state actions in

---

1. See *The Nyasaland Times*, 5 October 1953; R. Tangri, 'The Development of Modern African Politics and the Emergence of a Nationalist Movement in Colonial Malawi'.

2. In the Chichewa vernacular, this expression literally means the 'War of Thomson' and almost every informant I interviewed in Chief Malemia's area remembered something or mentioned the name of Mr Thomson. His administration, running from 1952 to 1957, was marked by a heavy-handed approach in dealing with the local people of Domasi at the height of mass nationalism in the country.

3. For studies on these issues, see W. Beinart, 'Introduction: The Politics of Conservation', *JSAS* 15/2 (1989): 143–62 and 'Soil Erosion, Conservationism and Ideas about Development in Southern Africa'; A. Mager, '"The People Get Fenced"'; F. Mackenzie, 'Political Economy of

Ecological change, gender relations and peasant resistance

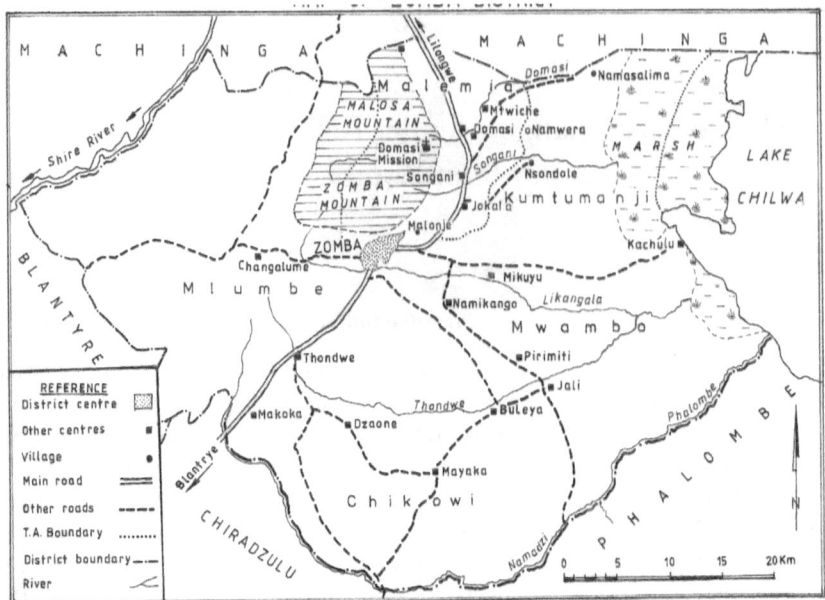

Figure 10.1. Map of Zomba district

light of the changing ecological and social relations. This chapter argues that state intervention in the peasant agricultural economy in the immediate postwar period was uneven and yielded different results. In the Domasi area of Zomba district in southern Malawi, state attempts to restructure social and economic relations were compromised by ecological and political nationalist activities. This chapter shows that ecological changes and social engineering activities not only altered gender relations but also precipitated widespread rural social protest against state-sponsored soil conservation campaigns. The women, who under the new arrangements were required to surrender their traditional rights to land and to change their marriage and inheritance systems, resisted state intervention. Furthermore, the success of conservation work itself was compromised by its demands on the time and labour of peasants.

The chapter is an attempt to place the Malawian experience within the growing body of literature and accordingly explores three main issues. First, it discusses the memories and lived experiences of the peasants, many of whom participated in the Domasi riot itself. It shows that such memories and accounts offer an illuminating perspective on the history of this area, one that is glaringly absent

the Environment, Gender and Resistance under Colonialism'; P. Maack, "'We Don't Want Terraces!"'.

The 1946 floods and emergence of the napolo legend

in the existing literature on Malawi. Virtually all scholars tend to treat the Domasi uprising simply as an example of African discontent against colonial rule and fail to show how peasant activities and experiences also shaped the colonial system. The chapter argues that, in order to treat peasants as historical actors, it is necessary not to rely on written sources only, as most scholars have hitherto done, but also to use the peasants' own testimonies and listen to their voices. A lot of literature now exists about the legitimacy of oral testimony as a credible source for writing African history.[4] Valuable insights can be gained from such sources.

The second issue concerns the place of the myth of *napolo* in the historical context. It is a phenomenon that has shaped and continues to shape the lives of the peasants in and around Zomba. It explains and provides meaning to history and the future of the environment and its people. The third issue concerns the argument that gender relations played a significant role not only in determining peasant response to the introduction of soil conservation schemes in Zomba but also in shaping the structure of the new emergent economy. Given the fact that the people of Zomba followed a matrilineal system that empowered women's access to land, the colonial state's approach, emphasising men's responsibility for the use of land, stirred up gender conflicts at both generational and household levels.[5] Before going into the actual discussion of the uprising of 1953, it is necessary to explore a series of developments that took place in the area, had a profound impact on the daily lives of its peasants and in some ways precipitated widespread rural protest. These included the activities of the Domasi Community Development Scheme, the floods of 1946 and the famine of 1949.

The 1946 floods and emergence of the napolo legend

It is difficult to talk about the social and environmental history of Zomba without making reference to the floods of 1946 or the famine of 1949. Both disasters had a significant impact on the lives of the people in this area and particularly reconfigured the relationship between human beings and nature. The floods, locally known as *napolo*, have bequeathed a complex mythical legend to Zomba and neighbouring districts. They are highly venerated and their remembrance has produced songs,

---

4. See Louise White, *et.al.* (eds.) *African Words, African Voices: Critical Practices in Oral History* (Bloomington: Indiana University Press, 2001); Susan Geiger *et.al. Women in African Colonial Histories* (Bloomington: Indiana University Press, 2002); and Jan Vansina, *Oral Tradition as History* (London and Nairobi: James Currey and Heinemann, 1985).

5. See D. Hirschmann and M. Vaughan, *Women Farmers of Malawi: Food Production in Zomba District* (University of California: Institute of Development Studies, 1984); P. Peters, 'Revisiting the Puzzle of Matriliny in South-Central Africa'; Jean Davison, *Agriculture, Land and Women: The African Experience* (Boulder: Westview Press, 1988) and 'Challenging Relations of Production in Southern Malawi's Households: Implications for Innovating Rural Women in Development', *Journal of Contemporary African Studies* (1992): 72–84.

Ecological change, gender relations and peasant resistance

folktales, books and names of people and beverages.[6] For example, Steve Chimombo, a renowned Malawian writer, captured the impact of this cataclysmic event in poetry that is as illuminating as any historical account. This work will quote his writings in greater detail in order to highlight the social and literary meaning of *napolo*.

> *Yes it rained*
> *Oh, how it rained that time!*
> *The parched throat of the earth drank it up,*
> *swelled its stomach in pregnancy;*
> *but it came so late,*
> *and with it came Napolo.*
> *Napolo gnawed the womb of the earth,*
> *the earth groaned and aborted, showing its teeth,*
> *its teeth uprooted the trees on the banks,*
> *the banks where birds sang around the python's flanks.*[7]

The devastating impact of the landslide imaged above was profound and it was felt far and wide. One contemporary observer chronicled that,

> Throughout the afternoon of Saturday a number of serious landslides occurred on Zomba Mountain and torrents of water, carrying boulders and large trees with them, swept down the side of the mountain. European officials and their servants whose houses were situated on the edge of the gullies had some terrifying experiences and, in some cases, considerable damage was done to their belongings as the water tore through their houses leaving heavy deposits of silt.[8]

An estimated 21 Africans and one European lost their lives in these floods of 1946.[9] Much property was also damaged, including the disruption of piped water supply, electric power, telegraph and telephone services. Two villages in the Ntiya area were literally decimated and 21 bridges were swept away. Houses, roads and bridges in the township were destroyed.[10] Heavy boulders rolled down the slopes of Zomba Mountain and blocked rivers. The total cost of repairing the damage caused by the floods was estimated at £10,000 but the social and psychological impact was far greater. In fact, the impact of the floods was so great that the colonial authorities even thought of moving the seat of government to Blantyre since Zomba had proved unsafe. The Governor immediately set up a Committee whose assignment

---

6. For example, there is a song by the Paseli brothers, an epic by Steve Chimombo and a locally brewed beer called *Napolo*. See also an article by Talbot Edwards, 'Zomba Flood, December 1946', *The Nyasaland Journal* 1/2 (1948).
7. Steve Chimombo, *Napolo and the Python* (Oxford and Portsmouth NH: Heinemann, African Writers Series, 1994), p.c3
8. T. Edwards, 'Zomba Flood, December 1946', p.c53.
9. Most of the victims came from Ntiya village in TA Mlumbe's area. A white man, simply identified as Mr Ingram of the Prisons Department, was also swept away by the floods on Mponda river.
10. Interview: Mr Kayesa Ntuluko, Kapichi Village, TA Malemia, Zomba district, dated 15 May 1997; see also T. Edwards, 'Zomba Flood, December 1946'.

The 1946 floods and emergence of the napolo legend

was 'to examine the advisability of removing the capital from its present site with particular regard to the financial implications'.[11] After a thorough investigation, the Committee recommended removal of the capital but for quite different reasons. It argued that Zomba was generally unhealthy due to the prevalence of malaria and also noted the high costs involved in moving to and from the commercial and railway town of Blantyre. Even with the high cost of moving, estimated at £500,000, the government seems to have been decidedly interested in moving the capital out of Zomba. However, this proposal was later dropped, only after assurance was received from the Government Geologist on the general safety of the area from disasters. The Government Geologist argued that,

> There is no reason to regard Zomba as doomed to destruction, but the extraordinarily heavy rainfall has caused considerable damage, the repairing of which must be faced. It should be remembered that the wearing down of the mountain is a normal natural phenomenon. Sometimes, as recently, the process is accelerated, sometimes retarded, but it is always progressing. The earth is no dead thing, but one of endless change. The Master Architect is ever pulling down here and building there.[12]

There are many conflicting explanations for the occurrence of this cataclysm. The popular explanation holds that the floods were caused by incessant rains that had been falling in the area for three consecutive days. Rains started on Friday, 13 December 1946, and, by the end of that day, about 202mm of rain were recorded. The following day the rainfall was a record high of 509mm. Thus, by Sunday morning, Zomba had recorded more than 711mm within a period of forty hours. Serious landslides developed on Zomba Mountain and torrents of water carried boulders and large trees with them. According to meteorologists at the time, the floods were caused by a tropical cyclone in the Indian Ocean. The cyclone crossed the Mozambican coast and followed a trough of low pressure to Zomba in Malawi.[13]

Africans had their own interpretations of the floods. It was widely believed that they were caused by the wrath of ancestral spirits. According to oral traditions, the spirits were angry with the activities of both Europeans and Africans in opening up the mountain for farming and settlement. As a result the spirits sent *napolo* [a big snake], based in the subterranean lake at the heart of the plateau, which came down on different sides of the mountain, through the Likangala, Mulunguzi and Domasi rivers all the way to Lake Chilwa. The water came down with *napolo* to Lake Chilwa, where he would stay as long as there was enough water in the lake. When the water level in the lake fell, he would go up to the plateau again.[14] The loss

---

11. This was a high-powered three-member committee chaired by Mr F.L. Brown, the Chief Secretary, with Mr M.P. Barrow and Mr J.M. Marshall as members.
12. Quoted in B. Pachai, *Malawi: A History of the Nation*, pp. 297–8.
13. T. Edwards, 'Zomba Flood, December 1946'; and C.M. Chikusa, 'The Phenomenon of "Napolo" in Zomba with reference to the 1985 Ntonya–Ulumba Events' (Unpublished Paper, Geological Survey of Malawi, Report No. CMC/2, Zomba: 1985).
14. Steve Chimombo, 'An Integrated Theory of Napolo' (Unpublished Paper, Zomba).

Ecological change, gender relations and peasant resistance

of life and property was viewed as a punishment visited by supernatural powers on humans for their transgressions. A slightly different version of this interpretation is that the snake changed its position within the subterranean lake and the act of shifting from its sleeping position on its back with ears up caused the mountainside to burst. A popular song composed by the late Black Paseli is often sung on the national radio in remembrance of this disaster:

Napoloo! Wachabe 2x	Napolo is treacherous 2x
watenga anthu/mudzi ku Ntiya	It has taken people/village at Ntiya
kukataya ku nyanja/Chilwa	And thrown them in the Lake/Chilwa
nasiya anthu nalila	And left many people crying
mayo! wachabe	Mother! It is treacherous
Napoloo! Wachabe 3x	Napolo is treacherous 3x.
Watenga Ingiramu	It has taken Mr Ingram
Kukataya ku mchenga	And dumped him in the sandy valleys
Akaidi kukatola	Where prisoners had to pick him up
Napoloo! Wachabe 3x	Napolo is treacherous 3x.

One of the most interesting aspects of *napolo* is its powerful imagery that is often associated with natural disasters in Zomba today. Oral traditions maintain that *napolo* is still alive in the subterranean world and can come out at any time if he so wishes. All heavy and unusually incessant downpours, cyclones and floods are interpreted as manifestations of *napolo*. Following the incessant rains of March 1985, local people's interpretation was that *napolo* had passed through. A study undertaken by the Department of Geological Survey concluded that the flooding and landslides were a result of heavy rainfall between 18–22 March. During that period, 234mm of rains were recorded on 18 March while 124mm fell on 22 March. Strong winds from the south-west, under the Congo Inter-Tropical Convergence Zone, brought persistent rains. Although many rivers in Zomba, such as the Likangala, Mulunguzi, Satema, and Mponda, were flooded, the greatest impact was felt in the Ulumba and Ntonya hills and on Zomba Mountain. There, pebbles and boulders were seen rolling down the hills in a manner characteristic of the image of *napolo*. In 1997 another wave of floods swept through the northern part of Zomba mountain, along the Domasi river in the Namasalima area. The floods affected the villages close to Lake Chilwa and the areas of Traditional Authorities Malemia and Kuntumanji and the people in the environs interpreted them as the result of Napolo. Chimombo has expressed the same point is his poetry, arguing that *napolo's* legendary itinerary is an ongoing process that means people must refrain from lapsing into complacency.

> *I was lured to the shade of the rock*
> *by Chiluwe's arts and lullabies*
> *Chiluwe, performing frenetic dances on the rock,*
> *waiting for Napolo to surface from the womb of the earth.*

The 1946 floods and emergence of the napolo legend

... And when Napolo, eternal, bloodied,
ancient chaosis
after the complicity and the complacency,
emerges from the oblivious waters,
what revisitation? What devastation?[15]

Although *napolo* has been translated as deluge or floods, it is much more than that; it is a complex myth, intricately woven into the history and environment of the area. As Chimombo has pointed out, the word itself is indeterminate and ambiguous and can mean *chirombo* [a monster] and *mzimu* [a spirit] and is indeterminate in sex. In addition, *napolo* is not a divine entity and consequently 'no offerings or sacrifices are given to him as is done with ancestral spirits since no one is certain in what shape he appears, when he is going to appear next, and even whether his appearance is due to anger or pleasure. Furthermore, unlike other deities, the destructive effects of appearance are manifest in landslides, earthquakes, or cyclones which only indicate after the event, his previous residence.'[16] As a theory, therefore, *napolo* explains the traditional mythological relations between man and the supernatural world. It has different meanings to different groups of people: for instance, scientists hold that *napolo* is due to geomorphological processes. It is argued that the Zomba area receives a lot of rainfall and yet the mountain has fractures in the base rock which act as water feeders into the base soil cover. In addition, the soil cover is less stable and this weakness is further exacerbated by the slope and absence of vegetation, which would ideally help to strengthen the soil cover. This situation makes Zomba highly susceptible to landslides.[17] But the *napolo* phenomenon cannot easily be explained by geomorphological factors alone. According to Chimombo, any sensible explanation must view 'Napolo as a multifaceted phenomenon in which a meteorologist sees it as a cyclone, a geologist as a landslide or meteor, a reporter as literacy, a believer as a subterranean serpent or spirit'.[18] An all-embracing theory must conceive of 'Napolo as a metaphor that exists in an analogous relationship to its representations at all levels'.[19] In other words, the explanation must be general and flexible enough to include diverse and unexpected phenomena. For instance, Chimombo emphatically argues that 'concluding that the events around Ulumba–Ntonya hills were caused by landslides does not prove that Napolo does not exist or that it was not his work at all!'[20]

Although *napolo* is often associated with the 1946 floods, it has a much longer history in Malawi. The Scottish missionary David Clement Scott first used

---

15. S. Chimombo, *Napolo and the Python*, p. 43.
16. S. Chimombo, 'An Integrated Theory of Napolo', p. 36.
17. C.M. Chikusa, 'The Phenomenon of Napolo in Zomba'.
18. S. Chimombo, 'An Integrated Theory of Napolo', p. 38.
19. *Ibid.*
20. *Ibid.*

Table 10.1. Relationship between Napolo and Geomorphological Changes

Geomorpho-logical Features	*Napolo* Myth	Effect of Landslides (Heavy Rains)	Conclusion
Topmost steep scarp with slip scarp	Point where the *napolo* creatures erupted	Scarp produced after the soil cover slid down induced by: Saturation of water in the soil. Lubrication of contact between soil and bedrock. Creep due to steep slope and gravity.	Produced in landslide event
Mud pool at the base of the steep scarp	*Napolo* creatures erupt at the top of the flow channel, leaving a mud pool at the base of the scarp.	Residual mud left after lands-liding	Produced in landslide event
Flow path gully and scratch marks on the bedrock	Gully formed by tramping of feet, while scratches are produced by teeth and claws of the *napolo* creatures.	Gully formed by erosion Scratch marks caused by erratic impacts into each other and dragging on the ground of the pebbles and boulders	Produced in landslide event
Pile of pebbles and boulders at the end of the flow channel	Cover point of entry into the ground of *napolo* creature(s)	Pebbles and boulders swept down slopes along flow path. Deposited due to: (a) blockage by *in situ* rocks and trees, and (b) increase of friction between the gully floor and the pebbles and boulders due to decrease of gradient.	Produced in landslide event
Sound and light reported	Sound is hand clapping, drum beating and jubilation by the *napolo* creature(s), while the light is not well explained	Lithic fragments carried by the water flow. These have high kinetic energy which transforms into sound and light energies when they knock into each other, i.e. Kinetic Energy Heat Energy + Sound Energy ± Light Energy.	Produced in landslide event

Source: adapted from C.M Chikusa, 'The Phenomenon of Napolo in Zomba with Reference to the 1985 Ntonya–Ulumba Events' (Unpublished Paper, Geological Survey of Malawi, Zomba, Report No. CMC/2, November 1985), p18–19.

The 1946 floods and emergence of the napolo legend

the word *napolo* in his dictionary of the Mang'anja in 1892 to mean 'a kind of fish, about three feet long, with a long sword-jaw wth many feet; attacks and kills the crocodile; red paddle-fin; red body like *nchengo*'.[21] This definition shares the basic characteristics of *napolo* then and now: it is aquatic, unusual in size and has enormous strength and multiple limbs. *Napolo* existed in the minds of local residents as an outlandish and powerful being with the capacity to cause damage to human beings. However, since 1946, the word has assumed even greater significance in explaining human–nature relations in the area. Local beliefs hold that *napolo* moves up and down the mountain in cycles of ten to fifteen years. But although scientists may differ from local communities in explaining the causes, the basic physical manifestations of *napolo* are the same. Indeed, even eyewitness accounts, whether official or not, concur that in his movements *napolo* tends to be accompanied by noise, wind, darkness and extensive damage to landscape. Accordingly, four common characteristics can be discerned from both meteorological and geomorphological explanations: 'first, Napolo's manifestations appear during the rainy season; second, the manifestations are always preceded by an extended period of heavy rains; third, the devastation of the environment is a common feature; and finally, Napolo is associated with cyclones and landslides'.[22]

In the next three years, the area was struck by yet another catastrophe – this time a drought that caused untold suffering. The drought was caused by rain failure in the farming season beginning in November 1948. Peasant farmers whose agricultural production was, and still is, solely dependent on rainfall, failed to harvest enough crops that year. There was a general shortage of food in the area. The government assisted with relief supplies but these were inadequate to meet needs of the large numbers of starving people. The consequences of this famine were severe. Many people died, while others migrated to places that had not been severely hit by the famine, such as Mulanje district to the south of Zomba. In some cases, marriages broke up as a result of this famine. Some men who had travelled to look for food in other areas never came back to their families.[23]

Both the floods of 1946 and the famine of 1949 had a significant impact on the lives of peasant farmers in Domasi and neighbouring areas in the Shire Highlands region. Peasants viewed these ecological disasters as the result of disruption of the

---

21. Quoted from *Ibid.* p. 34.
22. *Ibid.* p.31.
23. Peasants noted that catastrophes such as floods and drought were not necessarily new to them. There were famines in 1862 and in 1922, a locust infestation in 1935 and floods in 1939. But what was new about this period was the frequency and the magnitude of the disasters. Never before had Africans been required to take stock of their environment as frequently and intensely as they did after 1946. State intervention in the early 1950s was also seen as an intrusion into African interaction with an environment that was increasingly becoming unpredictable and uncontrollable. See, for example, M. Vaughan, *The Story of An African Famine*, pp. 119–147; L. White, *Magomero*, p. 209; David Livingstone, *Letters and Documents, 1841–1872*, p. 83, Livingstone's letter to James Young; H. Rowley, *The Story*.

relationship between supernatural forces in the world of the dead and people in the world of the living. Territorial cults had an influence on the ecological processes through sanctioning mechanisms. For example, rain cults played important social and political functions in society through beliefs and practices that governed people's use of environmental resources. In times of droughts, plagues and epidemics, chiefs worshipped at the shrines controlled by spirit mediums. In pre-colonial times, the most notable cults were the Chisumphi at Msinja for the northern Chewa and the Mbona for the southern Chewa of the Lower Shire valley.[24]

Given the significant role that agricultural production played in the lives of ordinary people, knowledge of the environment was very important to the society. Such knowledge often intersected with issues of age, power and gender relations. Generally, chiefs and other elders possessed and controlled this knowledge, which placed them in a privileged position in society. Knowledge of the environment was a mark of political and social accomplishment. Anyone who possessed knowledge about crop production, rainfall patterns, soils, vegetation, fish and animal science occupied a socially important position. Oral sources testify to this direct relationship between the environment, through the production of crops depending upon the climatic conditions of a particular region, and human agency. For instance, although rainfall was seen as a sacred gift from *Chisumphi* or *Mulungu* [God] above, human beings could affect its arrival through their actions and practices. Mr Anusa Nkupata of Kapichi Village argued that, while Sakata hill and Zomba mountain have been desecrated in recent years, they nevertheless used to serve as an important religious and cultural centre for the chiefs' family and other people in Zomba district. Whole sections of the hills were covered with indigenous trees such as *mphodza, tchonya, mombo, mphini* and *miwanga*. In addition, they were treated as a sacred place for performing rainmaking ceremonies. Whenever there was drought, the chief would organise his people to prepare beer and food to be given to their *mizimu* [ancestral spirits]. When the spirits had heard their petitions, the rains would suddenly start to fall.[25] Similar practices were followed at Malabvi hill in Chiradzulu district and Namvula hill in Thyolo district.[26] Any changes in the patterns of weather or the surrounding environment were closely tied to the

---

24. M. Schoffeleers, 'The Chisumphi and Mbona Cults in Malawi: a Comparative History' in J.M. Schoffeleers (ed.) *Guardians of the Land: Essays on Central African Territorial Cults* (Gwelo: Mambo Press, 1978) pp. 147–186; Ian Linden, 'Chisumphi Theology in the Religion of Central Malawi' in J.M. Schoffeleers (ed.) *Guardians of the Land*, pp. 187–208; Steve Feierman, *Peasant Intellectuals: Anthropology and History in Tanzania* ((Madison: University of Wisconsin Press, 1990); Terence Ranger, 'Territorial Cults in the History of Central Africa', *Journal of African History* 14/4 (1973): 581–597.

25. Interview: Chief Nsabwe's mother, Nzundo Village, TA Nsabwe, Thyolo district, dated 28 May 1997; Interview: Mr Maganga Seyani, Nzundo Village, TA Nsabwe, Thyolo district, dated 28 May 1997.

26. Interview: Mai Elina Sitima, Mkwanda Village, TA Likoswe, Chiradzulu district, dated 17 August 1997; Mr Ala Kachenjera, Magombo Village, TA Likoswe, Chiradzulu district, dated 19 August 1997.

The Domasi community development, 1949–1954

economic, social and religious life of the communities in question. When this rhythm of activities had been disturbed, as in the case of droughts, explanations were sought in the relations between humans and nature. Traditional authorities had the responsibility of organising their people to give offerings to their ancestral spirits.[27] Knowledge about the relationship between human beings and the landscape has increased vastly. In his recent paper on memoryscapes, Timothy Clack holds that landscape is the fusion of culture and nature and for that reason physical features shelter meanings associated with cultural aspects such as beliefs, myths and legends. Among the Chagga people of northern Tanzania, Kilimanjaro Mountain is not just an ordinary landscape feature but it is also part of the cultural milieu that expresses the past, the present and the future. It is a convergence zone of memories, emotions and beliefs practiced over time through rituals, sacrifices and offerings. Even when the Christian missionaries had established their churches in the area, the significance of the landscape did not change radically as seen in the performance of new rituals like prayer, communion and hymn-singing. Similarly the position of the altars was aligned with the mountain, which corresponded with traditional Ruwa deities.[28]

Residents close to Lake Chilwa and the Domasi River had a somewhat different relationship with their environment.

The Domasi community development, 1949–1954

Prior to the 1953 uprising, Domasi had gone through a period of sustained social engineering that put heavy pressure on men and women in the area. The peasants complained of fatigue and of being frequently harassed by ecological disasters and state intervention programs. In 1949, the colonial state established the Domasi Community Development Scheme with the main objective of fostering rural development and particular attention was paid to issues of local government, taxation and land usage. The Domasi Scheme, which began immediately after the completion of a feasibility study by J. Clyde Mitchell, a leading sociologist at the Rhodes-Livingstone Research Institute, was to be a model for the country's postwar policy on rural development. Funded with a grant of £63,000 from the Colonial Development and Welfare Fund, the Domasi Scheme became an important centre for training Africans from all parts of the country in matters of local government, hygiene and other vocational skills. Another important component of the Scheme was soil conservation and land reorganisation. Thomson, a lawyer by training but

---

27. J.M. Schoffeleers (ed.) *Guardians of the Land: Essays on Central African Territorial Cults* (Gwelo: Mambo Press, 1978); Steve Feierman, *Peasant Intellectuals: Anthropology and History in Tanzania* ((Madison: University of Wisconsin Press, 1990).

28. T. Clack, 'Thinking Through Memoryscapes: Symbolic Environmental Potency on Mount Kilimanjaro, Tanzania', in T. Myllyntaus (ed.) *Thinking Through the Environment: Green Approaches to Global History* (Cambridge: The White Horse Press, 2011), pp. 115–34.

at the time District Commissioner for Domasi, was appointed the Officer-in-Charge of the Scheme and was personally fully committed to the implementation of conservationist ideals. Prior to that he had been DC for Liwonde and had written extensively about the history and culture of the local Yao people. In relation to the Domasi scheme, he wrote subsequently that,

> There seems to be ample evidence that the mere introduction of elementary forms of soil conservation may have a marked effect on social life as well as on economic stability and progress. It is of great importance that when intensive soil conservation campaigns are being planned the matter should not be treated as one of agricultural improvement alone, but that very careful consideration should also be given to all political and social factors involved by varying local conditions. It is not merely a matter of saving soil from going down the drain causing a break-up of the existing social pattern; it may very probably be a case of taking steps which may lead to the emergence of a very different social pattern, and we must be sure that that pattern is one which we want to see.[29]

The choice of Domasi as an ideal place for this experimental project had mainly to do with its unique physical characteristics. The Domasi sub-district covered a total area of 93 square miles. Half of this was taken up by forest reserves, the two major ones being Zomba and Malosa. These forest reserves were established on mountains and steep slopes and served as a good experiment in forest conservation. The rest of the land area was under human settlement and cultivation. The actual Domasi centre consisted of an area of five square miles, portioned out as follows: two square miles of freehold land owned by a European company (although that had been occupied by tenants); one square mile of freehold/leasehold land in mission hands; one square mile for the Domasi station of the Government Teacher Training Centre; and one square mile that had formerly been an estate but was taken over by Government in 1928 and still remained unoccupied. The Domasi area had a population of 15,000 and, of this number, only 175 were Europeans, the rest being Africans. The African population was ethnically mixed. It included the Yao, who made up about 75 per cent, with the Nyanja and Lomwe accounting for the remaining 25 per cent.[30] The area also had a high population density. The most densely populated area was the southern zone, close to Zomba, a town with an average density of 600 people per square mile. In the middle part of the district, the density was 300 people per square mile. There was only a small area for farming. The northern zone had the lowest density, about 160 people per square mile, and, as such, had more land available for farming.[31] The government also wanted

---

29. T.D. Thomson, 'Soil Conservation – Some Implications', p. 69.
30. For details on the composition of the population see J. Clyde Mitchell, 'An Outline of the Social Structure of Malemia Area', *The Nyasaland Journal* 4/2 (1951): 15–48.
31. T.D. Thomson, *The Domasi Community Development Scheme, 1949–1954* (Zomba: Government Press, 1955).

The Domasi community development, 1949–1954

Figure 10.2. Peasants filling in one of the eroded gullies at Domasi in the early 1950s

Figure 10.3. Student accommodation and farm at the Jeanes training school, Domasi, 1936. Note the soil conservation lay-out of the fields with ridge and furrow cultivation along the contour.

to develop the Domasi valley, lying between the Zomba and Malosa mountains, which had long been viewed as a good place for crop production.

Even before the introduction of this Scheme, Domasi had played a vital role in the training of traditional rulers in the country. The Jeanes Training School, established in 1929, provided training opportunities for chiefs and their senior men.[32] The government believed that, in order for traditional leaders to function effectively, it was necessary to ensure that they possessed the requisite knowledge of the functions and structure of government and also leadership skills. However, some scholars have argued that the government set up the Jeanes Centre in order to counter the growing level of snobbish behaviour among young men educated in mission schools, who were politically active and lacking the discipline of their families and ethnic groups.[33]

Domasi was developing into an urban settlement. By the 1950s, it was already attracting large numbers of people from all walks of life. There was an influx of people from surrounding villages, particularly male migrants. The growth of Domasi urban centre offered waged employment opportunities for young and able-bodied men and women in clerical, technical, janitorial, domestic and agricultural work. In fact, the road between Zomba and Domasi was lined with developments such as shops and other amenities, which attracted people from rural areas. As many young men left their villages to work in urban centres, the already scarce labour force in the villages was reduced.[34] Subsequently, the introduction of conservation campaigns in the 1940s and 1950s put new strains on the labour demands of the peasants. Although many young men had gone away to seek wage employment, within or outside the country, they did not lose touch with their homes. In some cases, Africans claimed rights to/ownership of land even if they did not use it. In addition, their gardens continued to be worked by wives, children and relatives. This ran contrary to the objectives of the colonial state, which wanted to promote agricultural production through the agency of men and created a dilemma for the colonial state's bid to implement postwar agricultural policies. In fact, in 1953, the DC for Domasi complained about the negative impact of increased labour migration from Domasi. He criticised the practice of juggling farming and wage employment and hoped that the requirements of conservation would force Africans to remain on the land.

---

32. However, the Jeanes Centre was converted into a Teacher Training College just before the launch of the Domasi Scheme in 1949. T.D. Thomson, *The Domasi Community Development Scheme*; M. Vaughan, 'Better, Happier and Healthier Citizens'.

33. For details, see John G. Pike, *Malawi: A Political and Economic History* (London, 1968) and A.J. Hanna, *The Story of the Rhodesias and Nyasaland* (London, 1960); and also Martin Chanock, 'The New Men Revisited: an Essay on the Development of Political Consciousness in Colonial Malawi', in R.J. Macdonald (ed.) *From Nyasaland to Malawi: Studies in Colonial History* (Nairobi: E.A.P.H., 1975) pp. 235–53.

34. Interview: Mr Kayesa Ntuluko, Kapichi Village, TA Malemia, Zomba district, dated 15 May 1997.

Life histories and the Domasi uprising of 1953

Conservation may therefore be a means of bringing home to people in that position that it is not easy to be both a clerk or an artisan and a cultivator. If pressure is kept up it may result in some reducing their claims on the land to the acre or so which they can look after properly and which should provide them with what they want in the way of relishes, fruit and vegetables, while they buy most of their staple food. This in itself would lead to a considerable reduction in the pressure of population on the land.[35]

Labour migration was facilitated in this area by the presence of several pull factors such as Indian shops, missionary stations and government departments. Migration consisted of both temporary and seasonal forms and, although some women would also migrate, it was mainly the young men who tended to do so in large numbers. The seasonal migrants often sought waged employment during the dry season when there was little farming activity in the villages. This situation allowed migrants to stay in cities for a few months before returning to their villages. Others commuted on a daily basis using bicycles. Such villagers moved to urban areas for a specific job and, once that was completed, they would return to their villages. The income earned from waged employment was often invested in agricultural materials, such as livestock and hoes, and in non-agricultural activities like commodity trading, fishing and social festivities. Some enterprising women responded to urbanisation by participating in income-generating activities including beer brewing and selling of snacks like *zitumbuwa*, fried cakes made from mashed bananas mixed with flour. These products were sold at seasonal and roadside markets that had emerged in the area, at Domasi station and Songani, for example.

Life histories and the Domasi uprising of 1953

The Domasi uprising of 1953 provides a window on the social and environmental history of the area. It is an event so well known that almost every elderly person in Chief Malemia's area still recalls something about it. It is a story that made the head of Ng'ombe village shed tears as she narrated the course of events to the writer. Her tale and those of others in the village demonstrate the human drama associated with the Domasi Community Development Scheme and the ways in which the Scheme also precipitated the uprising. Working with life histories of three women, this chapter raises broader issues about ways in which conservation was gendered and how official discourses distort the meaning of conservation. The uprising was a complex event, mediated by various factors, such as ecological change and changing power relations between men and women. It has been necessary to include the life histories of the three women who were closely affected by the uprising, partly because they were relations of the late Ng'ombe and partly because they lived in the same village and inherited the position and history of the former village headman. Their life histories also provide another dimension to understanding the uprising

---

35. T.D. Thomson, 'Soil Conservation – Some Implications', p. 68.

itself since oral sources have not so far been used in analyses of the event. It is also clear from these life histories that, far from dismissing the uprising as an act of agitation, those involved saw it as a complex episode of rural resistance against the intrusive activities of the colonial state.[36]

The launch of the Domasi Community Development Scheme came on the heels of an ecologically changed society. Memories of the *napolo* of 1946 and the drought of 1949 were still very strong in the minds of the peasants. *Napolo* had taken away the crops, livestock and other property of the residents of Zomba. The drought had deprived many people of a good harvest so that starvation occurred. The state-sponsored Community Development Scheme and the conservation campaign sought to restructure society in ways that altered gender relations and the land tenure system. While the floods and the famine were seen as the responsibility of supernatural forces, the Scheme was interpreted as an intrusion by the colonial state into the private spaces of the peasants. Since some of the land had been alienated, what remained in their possession had to be used without any interference from the state. Some peasants resisted the implementation of the Domasi Scheme by not carrying out all the conservation works required by the state in their gardens and by refusing to build sanitation structures around their houses.[37]

In the summer of 1953, a group of nearly two hundred angry women and men from four villages surrounding Kapichi, Ng'ombe and Kumikochi marched towards the administrative headquarters of Domasi, carrying with them stones and sticks. As they made their way to Domasi, they danced and chanted anti-colonial protest songs. Mai Rexa Chilenga of Zomba mentioned this as one of the songs sung by the demonstrators:

Tikamenye nkhondo yee!	We should go and fight, yee!
Nkhondoyo idzabwera	That war will come
watibweretsera mazunzo Thomson	Thomson has brought us suffering

When they reached the office of the District Commissioner, they explained that they had come there to free Chief Malemia, their Traditional Authority, and the two village headmen who had been taken hostage by T.D. Thomson, the famous and forceful District Commissioner. Thomson had apparently summoned village headmen Kapichi and Ng'ombe for their negligence in enforcing the construction of conservation measures in their respective villages and had then detained them (and Malemia).[38]

As in many colonies, chiefs played an important but rather controversial role in colonial Malawi. Although they had been incorporated into the colonial

---

36. I conducted interviews with Village Headman Ng'ombe separately but Mai Gladys Nthyola, a sister to the village headman, and Mai Mbulaje were interviewed jointly.
37. Interview: Mr Kimu Mbatata, Malemia Village, TA Malemia, Zomba district, dated 19 May 1997.
38. Interview: Village Headman Nkuzang'ombe, Ng'ombe Village, TA Malemia, Zomba district, dated 14 May 1997.

Life histories and the Domasi uprising of 1953

structure through the Native Authorities Ordinance No. 13 of 1933, they did not always fulfil the duties required of them by the state. The Ordinance recognised native authorities as chiefs-in-council with powers to appoint subordinate native authorities in their areas of jurisdiction and to levy local rates and dues. Furthermore, under the Native Courts Ordinance of 1933, the state also established native courts with powers to apply customary laws for a wide range of offences where all parties were Africans. It is possible that the idea for establishing the courts may have been to destroy the power base of the native associations, which were becoming increasingly influential, especially among educated Africans. What is clear, though, is that, through these Ordinances, the colonial state had put in place a mechanism for implementing a policy of indirect rule to which chiefs became integral.[39]

The position of chiefs in the colonial system was highly ambiguous. Chiefs often oscillated in their political allegiance. Sometimes they took very radical positions in opposing colonial policies and practices. At other times, however, they acted as stooges of the colonial state and thus alienated their African subjects. Crises such as the Domasi riot of 1953 provided a unique opportunity for chiefs to express their ideas and true feelings about the workings of the colonial system.

Prior to that incident, Thomson had personally visited the villages in Chief Malemia's area to assess progress in the implementation of *malimidwe*. As chairman of the Domasi District Natural Resources Board, the main body supervising the Natural Resources Ordinance, Thomson worked tirelessly towards getting African compliance with the implementation of conservation schemes.[40] The committee consisted of some prominent African members, such as Mr Stapleton Mchoma of Ngalango Village in Chief Malemia's area, and Mr Snowden Muyere of Mtwiche Village. In 1952, Mr Muyere was replaced by Mr Lawrie Mmanga who was replaced by Mr Richard Mgwede of Malosa in 1955.[41] Disappointed with the quality of the work that had been done, Thomson is reported to have given specific deadlines for the completion of conservation measures and further warned that tougher measures would be taken against any defaulters. After a few months, he again visited several villages in Chief Malemia's area and found, much to his frustration, that only a few people had undertaken conservation measures in their gardens. At that point, Thomson sent for Chief Malemia, in whose jurisdiction the two villages were, to appear at the *boma*. Thomson believed that Chief Malemia had either covertly supported the activities of the rebellious village headmen or had simply not been tough enough to oversee the implementation of *malimidwe*. Hence, as a way of

---

39. Tony Woods, 'Capitaos and Chiefs: Oral Tradition and Colonial Society in Malawi', *International Journal of African Historical Studies* 23/2 (1990): 259–268; Joey Power, 'Individualism is the Antithesis of Indirect Rule: Cooperative Development and Indirect Rule in Colonial Malawi', *JSAS* (1992): 317–347.
40. MNA: NSG 1/2/2: Domasi District Natural Resources Board, July 1950 to October 1955.
41. The other members were the Provincial Forest Officer; the Livestock Officer, Zomba; the Agricultural Assistant, Zomba; and Mr T.W. Williamson, the Agent of BT and EA Ltd in Zomba.

getting the work done and to make the chief an example to other village headmen, Thomson decided to detain him at the *boma* for further interrogation.[42]

The news of the Chief's detention spread far and wide and angered some people in Malemia's area. Although they were not necessarily representatives of the other village headmen, Kapichi and Ng'ombe took the lead in following up the matter. They travelled to Domasi to check on the condition of their chief. Other sources say they were summoned by the DC himself. Upon arrival at Domasi, the village headmen found Chief Malemia, who had been detained there for some days, a deeply embittered person. The two intransigent village headmen were also detained. The summoning and detaining of these chiefs was no ordinary affair in the eyes of the local people. When much time had passed without the chief and his village headmen returning home, word went round that the DC was intending to take them to court for trial. The people in their villages became apprehensive and tension mounted. In the end, the villagers decided to pursue the matter by going directly to see the DC.[43]

As the days went by, things turned sour. There was complete loss of trust by both parties, and tension increased.[44] At that point, the DC sent out Clement Kumbikano, an administrative assistant at Domasi, to try and persuade the protesting Africans to calm down and put away their stones and sticks. The discussions proved fruitless. African peasants began to hurl stones and sticks at the offices of Thomson, breaking windows and injuring some members of staff. The DC immediately called for assistance from Zomba. The police arrived and tried to disperse the crowd, initially by firing in the air. But the peasants insisted that they would not go home until their chiefs were released. At that point, the police began to fire at the crowd. This incident marked the culmination of longstanding tension that had been developing in the area since the introduction of the conservation campaign in the 1940s.[45]

The fighting ended with three casualties, one of whom was village headman Ng'ombe, grandfather to the woman who was village headman during the time of the interviews for this book in 1997. He had been shot several times and died upon arrival at Zomba General Hospital. The second victim was a young man named

---

42. Interview: Mr Kimu Mbatata, Malemia Village, TA Malemia, Zomba district, dated 19 May 1997.
43. Interviews with the following informants: Village Headman Nkuzang'ombe, Nkuzang'ombe Village, TA Malemia, Zomba district, dated 14 May 1997; Mai Gladys Nthyola and Mai Emmie Mbulaje, Nkuzang'ombe Village, TA Malemia, Zomba district, dated 14 May 1997.
44. Interview: Mr Kimu Mbatata, Malemia Village, TA Malemia, Zomba district, dated 19 May 1997.
45. Interview: Village Headman Nkuzang'ombe, Ng'ombe Village, TA Malemia, Zomba district, dated 14 May 1997.

Life histories and the Domasi uprising of 1953

Raiti Kaulu from Kapichi village. Raiti died on the spot. A female relation of village headman Ng'ombe, known as Abiti Matuta, was also killed.[46]

The current holder of the village headship of Ng'ombe was born in 1947 in this village but her parents migrated from Liwonde through the Machinjiri area. As a child, Village Headman Ng'ombe was told the history of her own Yao-speaking people and she has, in turn, maintained the tradition of passing on historical accounts to younger generations. Village Headman Ng'ombe's area, which is about four kilometres from Domasi station, lies to the northeast of Zomba township. During the late colonial period, Ng'ombe's village fell under the administration of the Domasi sub-district. It was during her early childhood years that Village Headman Ng'ombe first heard of the tensions that had developed between the colonial state and her own people. But she also recalled that she saw:

> Thomson and other white men come to their home. My mother later told me the reasons why those white men came. From those conversations I was told that Thomson and his people came here to supervise the implementation of *malimidwe* in our village. At that time, everyone, including the chief, was required to make conservation works in their gardens. Failure to do so would result in fines by the *boma*.[47]

Her elder sister, Mai Mbulaje, although old enough to travel to Domasi station in 1953, did not participate in the riot. VH Ng'ombe and Mai Nthyola, another sister, heard the story of the Domasi riot from their mother and other people who had joined the demonstrators to the Domasi station. The village headman who died was their grandfather, their '*ambuya athu*', as they affectionately called him. After he had been shot, he was taken to Zomba General Hospital where he unfortunately died of his wounds the same day. His nephew, Che Nchoma of Nkhalango village, rushed to the hospital and found his uncle dead. He then pleaded with the DC to provide transport to take the body to his village for burial. The DC allowed a police vehicle to carry the body to Kapichi village.

When the body arrived in the village, the place was unusually quiet. The villagers only murmured to each other and those who talked did so with great fear about what had just happened and more about what would happen next. They were afraid the white men might come again with aeroplanes and guns to attack the rebellious villages and were even afrid about how they were going to bury the body.

The dead chief was succeeded by his nephew, who died recently. After him came the village headman who is currently working in Chikwawa district. His sister is acting on his behalf as a regent Village Headman. Ng'ombe noted that for

---

46. Interview: Mai Gladys Nthyola, Ng'ombe Village, TA Malemia, Zomba district, dated 14 May 1997; Mai Rexa Chilenga, Ngwale Village, TA Malemia, Zomba district, dated 12 May 1997; Mr Kimu Mbatata, Malemia Village, TA Malemia, Zomba district, dated 19 May 1997.
47. Interview: Village Headman Nkuzang'ombe, Nkuzang'ombe Village, TA Malemia, Zomba district, dated 14 May 1997.

a long time people lived in perpetual fear and it was not until mass nationalism had peaked in the late 1950s that they began to relax.

The personal testimonies of the three women, VH Ng'ombe, Mai Mbulaje and Mai Nthyola, point to the fact that there is a great deal of historical information that cannot be captured by written sources only. The attitudes and perceptions of peasants towards policies and practices of the colonial state and what they thought of state agents are some of the issues that come out clearly through life histories. In the case of the Domasi area, we are able to know the feelings and perceptions of the peasants towards Thomson, one of the main architects of the conservation campaign in the area. This information makes the narrative of the Domasi uprising richer and much more complex.

The Domasi riot of 1953 was not unique; there had been disturbances in other parts of the country during the same period. As previously noted, peasants rose up against *malimidwe* in the districts of Ntcheu, Nsanje, Chiradzulu, Nkhota Kota and Nkhata Bay.[48] In the districts of Thyolo, Nsanje and Chiradzulu, chiefs were molested by peasants for apparently collaborating with the state in enforcing conservation rules. In Ntcheu district, the Traditional Authority, Chief Gomani organised his Ngoni people to defy conservation rules pertaining to agriculture, grazing and forestry. As in Zomba, the state sent in the police and riots broke out. In the case of Ntcheu district, it is not clear how many people died or were injured in the pandemonium but, in the end, the chief was deposed by the government.[49] These episodes were discussed in greater in detail in Chapter Eight.

Perhaps nowhere else in the country did peasant opposition to *malimidwe* reach the magnitude it did in the Domasi area of Zomba district. The Domasi uprising is important for two reasons. First, it illuminates the larger issue of resistance: how and why peasants resisted the power of the state the way they did. Peasants in the Domasi area rebelled, not because they believed they could destroy the intrusive regime, but rather because they wanted to retain their autonomy to decide where to farm, how to organise their fields and what crops to grow. It was the state's penetration into the peasants' spaces and land in particular that encouraged the Domasi peasants to fight back when they felt the pressure had become unbearable. Secondly, the uprising demonstrates the clash between Western scientific ideas and approaches to conservation and the peasants' systems of knowledge. For example, bunding and terracing, which were emblematic soil conservation measures, were seen as incompatible with the beliefs and practices of the peasants in this area.

---

48. It is estimated that a total of eleven people died and several hundreds were injured during this wave of disturbances. See *The Nyasaland Times* of 5 October 1953, quoted in B. Pachai, *Land and Politics in Malawi*), pp. 139–141.

49. Roger Tangri has discussed the issue of nationalism extensively in his works. See, for example, 'The Rise of Nationalism in Colonial Africa: The Case of Colonial Malawi', *Comparative Studies in Society and History* 10/2 (1968): 142–161; 'From the Politics of Union to Mass Nationalism: the Nyasaland African Congress, 1944–1959', in R.J. Macdonald (ed.) *From Nyasaland to Malawi: Studies in Colonial History* (Nairobi: E.A.P.H. 1975) pp. 254–81.

Life histories and the Domasi uprising of 1953

The Domasi uprising was interpreted differently by different groups of people. For the peasants in Domasi, the riot was seen not only as a confrontation between the state and Traditional Authorities but also as resisting an attack on their autonomy and their livelihoods. The colonial state had totally different views on African resistance to *malimidwe*. This resistance was interpreted as further evidence of recalcitrant peasants, who were unwilling to accept modernisation ideas and insisted on sticking to their traditional ideas and beliefs. According to Thomson, the activities of Chief Malemia and Village Headmen Ng'ombe and Kapichi had nothing to do with politics. Instead, their agitation centred on agricultural matters and particularly on the implementation of bunding and other conservation measures.[50] The uprising was viewed as an isolated case, involving a few misguided agitators.

Another school of thought has explained the Domasi uprising in the context of the nationalist framework. Indeed, the orthodox explanation is that these disturbances were facilitated by mass nationalist politics. But, as this discussion will show later, this interpretation is true only up to a point. While nationalism provided an important rallying point for peasants and political activists to express their problems and grievances against the colonial state, it did not cause peasant protests. Peasants had deep-rooted grievances against the colonial state, which they expressed in the form of resistance as and when they saw fit to do so. Although, by the 1950s, the nationalist movement had begun to make significant inroads into the rural areas of the country, it still lacked a strong rural base. In many cases, the nationalists capitalised on the grievances of the peasants by telling them not to undertake conservation measures required by the colonial state. They told them these measures were new ways of oppression by the colonialists and that the Africans had a right to resist.[51] Thus the general conclusion to be drawn from this discussion is that nationalism only increased peasant discontent; it did not trigger the peasant uprising. We have to look elsewhere for explanations. Before considering these specific explanations, we will first examine the general factors relating to nationalism.

As in other parts of the country, peasant restlessness heightened in the early 1950s due to a combination of several factors. First, nationalism played a part. From the early 1940s, young and educated Africans began to express anti-colonial feelings and the Zomba–Domasi area became an important centre for people from different parts of the country to meet and organise. Clement Kumbikano worked as an administrator at Domasi while many teachers, civil servants and chiefs frequently attended short courses at Domasi or Zomba. J.F. Sangala, a founder member of the Nyasaland African Congress, settled at Songani too. From Zomba, the nationalist movement began to mobilise support from all over the country and its strongest base long remained in urban areas, at least before the return of Dr Kamuzu Banda in 1958. Rural areas were often neglected, even though the nationalist leaders used

---

50. T.D. Thomson, *The Domasi Community Development Scheme*, p. 44.
51. Interview: Mr A.W. Chitenje, Ngwale Village, TA Malemia, Zomba district, dated 12 May 1997.

Ecological change, gender relations and peasant resistance

peasant grievances as one of their main campaign issues in the fight against colonial rule. When the implementation of conservation measures began to assume political overtones, the colonial state was aware of the implications but probably did not consider them a major threat to colonial hegemony. Writing in 1953, Thomson, the DC for Domasi, advised, 'It is therefore of great importance that when intensive soil conservation campaigns are being planned, the matter should not be treated as one of agricultural improvement alone, but that very careful consideration should also be given to all the political and social factors involved by varying local conditions'.[52] That advice was not taken up by the colonial state immediately. Years of coercive implementation of *malimidwe* were repeatedly met by different forms of peasant resistance including desertion, slow-downs and destruction of gardens that had already been conserved.[53]

As a second factor contributing to peasant restlessness, nationalist leaders made a link between their opposition to the Federation of Rhodesia and Nyasaland and the issue of conservation in Domasi. Many nationalists argued that the Federation would encourage the immigration of more European settlers into Malawi who would alienate more land. If anything, what the nationalists wanted was not more European settlers but the surrender of those underdeveloped chunks of land to the ever-increasing group of landless Africans. Bunding itself was also detested because Africans believed it decreased valuable land by about five to fifteen per cent.[54] In an area already experiencing land shortages, the proposal to bring Nyasaland into the Federation was hard to accept or appreciate. In this area, land shortage had been accentuated by the alienation of land by estate owners and increasing urbanisation. Various groups of Europeans and Asians had settled in the vicinity of Domasi, among whom were R.S. Hynde and Jussab at Songani, and Mrs. A.A. Skinner with her 1,100 acre freehold estate along the Likwenu valley.

A third factor in the growth of restlessness concerned the intrusive nature of the colonial state itself. After the outbreak of the Second World War, the state intervened more frequently and forcefully in African production than ever before. Throughout the duration of the War, the state encouraged the production of food crops, which were supplied to different places engaged in the fighting. But after the War, the state came up with a broad development program, to be supervised and implemented by the Postwar Development Committee. In the Domasi area, a Community Development Scheme was launched in 1949 to promote crop production, land use practices and sanitation practices. To crown it all, the state promulgated very harsh rules on natural resources in 1951, which became an integral part of the

---

52. T.D. Thomson, 'Soil Conservation – Some Implications', p. 69.
53. Interview: Mr Kayesa Ntuluko, Kapichi Village, TA Malemia, Zomba district, dated 15 May 1997.
54. T.D. Thomson, *The Domasi Community Development Scheme*, pp. 43–4.

Life histories and the Domasi uprising of 1953

Domasi Scheme.[55] The peasants were also suspicious of the activities and intentions of the colonial state in forcing them to undertake conservation measures in their gardens. Close state supervision and control of African production were viewed as an unnecessary encroachment on Africans' land and their daily lives.

Peasants in the Domasi area opposed *malimidwe* for other practical reasons as well. First, the topography of the area did not render it easy to undertake conservation measures. Given the fact that Domasi is generally a flat area, peasants feared that conservation measures and particularly bunding allowed the land to become waterlogged. Because of the flat terrain and its low altitude, the ridges easily collected water, making the gardens waterlogged. This soil condition caused tubers of plants such as cassava to rot.[56] In addition, peasants argued that conservation practices encouraged white ants in the gardens.[57] Others maintained that bunds blocked paths for cyclists.

Second, the work itself was very hard, especially in view of the fact that it was done during the dry season, the traditional period of rest. In the dry season, the area was very hot, with a mean maximum temperature of 28 degrees Celsius, and the land dry and hard. Making contour bunds with simple hand tools like an iron hoe was extremely hard and often took a long time.[58] The Yao people also held various traditional ceremonies such as *chinamwali* and *jando* at this time of the year when they had harvested their crops.[59]

Third, peasants tended to establish their gardens in different areas to take advantage of different micro-ecological zones. Farming in these different micro-zones was a fundamental part of the indigenous agronomic system. The fragmentation of gardens enabled peasants to plant different crops at different times of the year. For example, rice was grown in fields close to Lake Chilwa or the Domasi River. Maize, cassava and sorghum were grown in the upland gardens. Some crops like groundnuts required *mtsilo-wa-mchenga* [sandy loamy] soils, found in the intermediate zones between the uplands and the lakeshore areas. Peasants ensured that particular crops were grown in particular areas where suitable soils existed.[60] Thus, the introduction of *malimidwe* changed not only the peasants' farming techniques but also their view and sense of the meaning of gardens. For example, *malimidwe*

---

55. Nyasaland Government, *Natural Resources Ordinance, 1946*; *Natural Resources Ordinance, 1949*; *Natural Resources Rules, 1951*; *Natural Resources (Amendment) Ordinance, 1952*.
56. Interview: Mr Marko Kanjedza and Mai Irina Wilson, Nkuzang'ombe Village, TA Malemia, Zomba district, dated 16 May 1997.
57. R.W. Kettlewell, *Agricultural Change in Nyasaland*, Vol. 5, No. 3, p. 256; J. Clyde Mitchell, 'The Political Organisation of the Yao': 159.
58. This point was expressed by my informants during oral interviews and by Mr Thomson. See his report, *The Domasi Community Development Scheme*.
59. Both *chinamwali* and *jando* are initiation ceremonies for boys and girls practised in some parts of southern and central Malawi.
60. Details about different farming regimes are given in Ch. 2. See also E. Mandala, *Work and Control*; and H. Moore and M. Vaughan, *Cutting Down Trees*.

required that peasants pursue conservation measures in all the gardens that they cultivated. In some cases, soil erosion rangers instructed Africans to consolidate their use of gardens by cultivating only one piece of land.[61]

Malimidwe also struck at another important aspect of rural societies. Since a lot of labour was required to undertake the conservation measures, communities that had been exporting migrant labourers for markets within Malawi were particularly vulnerable. In many cases, the work burden befell women as most men had migrated for wage employment as far as South Africa, although most worked in the adjacent towns and plantations. As Roger Tangri observed, this situation was clearly noticeable in the Shire Highlands region from the early years of colonialism. He noted that 'the concentration of the administration, commercial and planting aspects of European enterprise made the Shire Highlands the largest centre of employment for Africans in Malawi'.[62]

Gender relations

Although peasant resistance to *malimidwe* was organised around common dislike for the way in which conservation laws were introduced, peasants also fought over issues like space, time and work processes. In the Zomba district, peasant resistance also had a gendered dimension, since the Domasi Development Scheme tended to subvert the economic and social power of women. The gender factor featured prominently, particularly because of the roles that women played in society. Given that gender is a socially constructed category, deeply embedded in power relations, it is important that we consider the different gender roles played by peasants in Zomba. In this particular case, it will also be necessary to realise that gender intersected with class to shape the lives of both men and women.

When a senior African clerk at Domasi was warned by the colonial administrators in 1953 that he would get into trouble unless he took proper conservation measures in his garden, he replied unequivocally that 'I am not a farmer. I am a clerk who gets a little food from small gardens hoed by my wife'.[63] The answer tells us much about the complexities of peasant lives in colonial societies, as it also raises questions about the definition of the peasantry, class and gender relations, production and the whole meaning of work. In many ways, it represents a situation that many Africans found themselves in as a result of their encounter with the forces of colonialism, for colonialism restructured rural societies in ways that even altered gender roles and production processes. New forms of social differentiation

---

61. These measures were covered in the various laws and policies: see, for instance, Nyasaland Government, *Natural Resources (Amendment) Ordinance, 1952*; Nyasaland Government, *Natural Resources Rules, 1951*; and Nyasaland Government, *Natural Resources Ordinance, 1949*.
62. R. Tangri, 'The Development of Modern African Politics', p. 22.
63. T.D. Thomson, 'Soil Conservation', p. 68.

Gender relations

began to emerge that would have lasting consequences for society. The impact of colonialism was also demonstrated in the case of the Domasi uprising of 1953 when some peasant communities reacted to its restructuring influences.

Through the implementation of the Domasi Community Development Scheme, the state sought to restructure African society along the three main lines of land tenure, marriage system and the rights and duties of men. The colonial authorities believed that the African social structure worked against the effective development of a progressive agricultural economy. As Pike noted, it was repeatedly mentioned that 'the subdivision of holdings, the uxorilocal system, the deep-rooted conservatism have all inhibited the development of sound agricultural practices in Malawi'.[64] All these issues had a strong bearing on gender relations because it is the women who were the *eni dziko* [owners of the land] and controlled the rights to cultivate the land.[65]

Land tenure was based on a pattern of seniority of residence. The first conqueror or the earliest chief to settle in an area allocated land to his henchmen and from the henchmen to their followers. More recent arrivals in the village acquired land from the first-comers. At the family level, land was given out to daughters and their husbands. The pattern of land holding was closely related to the matrilineage and uxorilocal systems of social organisation. In an uxorilocal society a man marries and lives at the home of the woman. It is the women who stabilise society because they do not have to move away from their villages. On the other hand, a man is seen as a stranger in the village in which he marries and lives, and any children born into the family follow the woman's side, using the principle of matrilineal descent.[66] According to Clyde Mitchell, uxorilocal marriages were the norm in this area except for among chiefs and guardians of sorority groups. A husband was viewed as *fisi* [hyena] or as a 'visiting cock'.[67] Chiefs were regarded as custodians of the land who could delegate their power and responsibility to subordinate chiefs or village headmen. A village headman was always a matrilineal descendant of *likolo*, a founding ancestress of the Yao matrilineage. At the village level, it was the village headmen who had the powers to grant rights of land cultivation to members of the village.

Many observers viewed this arrangement as counter-productive to the process of development in the area. Colonial officials often argued that unless men fully committed themselves to long-term plans in the villages they married into,

---

64. See John Pike, *Malawi*, p.189.
65. *Ibid*. pp. 185–6.
66. Matrilineal descent was an important aspect of Yao social organisation. In a matrilineage, a group of kinsfolk are believed to have descended through females from one common ancestress. See Pauline Peters, 'Bewitching Land: the Role of Land Disputes in Converting Kin to Strangers and in Class Formation in Malawi', *JSAS* 28/1 (2002): 155–178; and P. Peters, 'Revisiting the Puzzle of Matriliny in South-Central Africa'.
67. Clyde Mitchell defines uxorilocal marriages as a situation where a man lives in his wife's home village, as contrasted with virilocal marriages where a woman goes to live in her husband's home village. For details, see his article, 'An Outline of the Social Structure of Malemia'.

Ecological change, gender relations and peasant resistance

agricultural development would be difficult to achieve. 'A man has no interest in long range agricultural plans in his wife's village. If he invests capital, it is in moveable goods; if he builds a substantial house it is in his matrilineage village.'[68] Clyde Mitchell gave an example of a case where he had given out avocado pear seedlings to some men for planting. He made it clear that the fruit took about seven years to grow and mature. But to his surprise none of the men planted the seedlings in the villages in which they were married, even though they lived there. Instead, they all planted the fruit in their matrilineage villages, that is, their mothers' homes.[69] Obviously, this scenario presented significant problems to development agents. It was argued that this idea was not just wasteful but also served as a deterrent to the emergence of a 'progressive man' who might leave his improvements on the land even if he fell out with the local 'landlord' or his wife's kin.[70] In the course of trying to restructure African societies and promote rural development, the state sought to empower men rather than women and expected more responsibilities from them as well.

The Domasi Scheme attempted to undermine the position of women in society. The architects of the Scheme sought to get African men to hold title deeds to land. The state concluded that a matrilineal marriage as such was not inimical to economic and political change but that the major problem was the high rate of divorce.[71] It really did not matter whether land was passed on to children through the mother. But because men did not stay in the homes of their wives for long, it was difficult for them to make long-term investments. The other reason is that the state needed men for tax registration and settlement of deceased's estates. This was a reflection of the Victorian ideas about gender roles that nineteenth century missionaries and settlers had introduced in many parts of Africa.[72]

As long as women controlled the rights to cultivation of land, men had very little security of land tenure under this system. But the men did not always conform to this standard social structure. As Mitchell points out, men made creative adaptations to advance their own interests as well. With the coming of colonialism, and especially the promotion of a cash economy, some men sought gardens of their own, especially by borrowing land in foreign villages.[73] In other cases, urbanisation

---

68. *Ibid*: 24.
69. *Ibid*: 40–48.
70. See R.W. Kettlewell, *Agricultural Change in Nyasaland*.
71. See J. Clyde Mitchell, *The Yao Village: A Study of the Social Structure of a Nyasaland Tribe* (Manchester: Manchester University Press, 1956).
72. Interview: Group Village Headman Mtwiche, Mtwiche Village, TA Malemia, Zomba district, dated 19 May 1997. See Jean Allman, 'Making Mothers: Missionaries, Medical Officers and Women's Work in Colonial Asante, 1924–1945', *History Workshop Journal* 38 (1994): 25–48; and Jean Allman and Derek Peterson, 'New Directions in the History of Missions in Africa: Introduction', *Journal of Religious History* 23/1 (1999): 1–7.
73. See for example, J.A.K. Kandawire, *Thangata*; and J. Clyde Mitchell, *The Yao Village*.

Conclusion

provided an opportunity for families to settle in a neutral place where they could establish new homes and command access to a family-owned piece of land.

The colonial state also attempted to redefine the gender relations surrounding marriage and inheritance of property by giving more power to men. Traditionally, the inheritance of property followed the matrilineal system whereby the wife's relatives had the right to inherit property. The children, too, belonged to the wife's relatives. But, from the standpoint of the colonial state, this system was viewed as retrogressive. The Department of Agriculture maintained that, for its conservation legislation to work, it was necessary for men to be more involved. They believed that African men needed to have a greater stake and security in land than the prevalent system allowed them. As a result of the integration of the traditional society into the colonial structure, it was deemed necessary to redefine the rights and duties of husbands in this area. Although women did not pay poll taxes, they controlled access to land and children, two important resources of production. Since payment of poll tax was the responsibility of adult males only, the state felt that it had to be men who had unfettered access to land and other means of wealth accumulation. The state began to give title deeds to the land to men rather than to women.

In this society, there was a gendered division of labour. The women did the bulk of the agricultural work and they were the main producers of agricultural goods.[74] People did not just cultivate one field; they had gardens located in different areas: near the household or far away, in the mountains or in the *dambos*. In this respect, the nature of agricultural production depended on a gender division of labour. From the point of view of the colonial state, women could not be used as agents of progressive farming. Women were seen as too traditional and an obstacle to progress and their work was relegated to the status of subsistence farming. There was a concerted effort by colonial authorities to undermine the matrilineal system through social engineering mechanisms.

Conclusion

This chapter has discussed the impact of state intervention on African peasants in the Domasi area in Zomba district, highlighting the particular ways in which that intervention, combined with ecological changes, transformed the lives of ordinary men and women. It has shown that ecological changes and social engineering activities by the colonial state created restlessness among the peasants, which later resulted in the uprising of 1953. In addition, state intervention had a gendered impact on the African communities in the area. The women, who were required to surrender their traditional rights to land, and to change their marriage and inherit-

---

74. See, for example, Jean Davison, 'Tenacious Women: Clinging to Banja Household Production in the Face of Changing Gender Relations in Malawi', *JSAS* 19/3 (1993): 405–21; and J. Clyde Mitchell, *The Yao Village*.

ance systems, resisted state intervention. Furthermore, the conservation work itself demanded too much time and labour from the peasants.

11

Post-colonial Environmental Discourses, 1964–2000

Introduction

This chapter takes up the story of soil conservation from the end of British colonial rule in 1964 and well into the post-colonial African-run government. In so doing, it outlines the legal and policy framework, the strategies used to implement policies and the response of African peasants to the same. It also looks at the challenges experienced in the course of addressing the insidious problem of soil erosion, which include population increase, the expansion of commercial crop production and introduction of new ideas about rights and responsibilities pertaining to natural resource management.

Significance of the conservation debate in the contemporary period

Today, the issue of sustainable natural resource management has become central in environmental discourses in Malawi, to the extent that it has produced a certain measure of environmentalism. This is a reflection not only of growing international concern about the environment but also of the challenges prevailing at the local level. The obsession with environmentalism has been demonstrated by the sprouting of numerous laws, policies and institutions dealing with a range of environmental issues. For instance, between 1994 and 2000, no fewer than ten pieces of legislation and policies related to environmental matters were promulgated in Malawi.[1] The conditionalities placed on aid were meant to synchronise policies with the new political and economic climate which emphasised reduced public spending, reduced state power over resources, promotion of decentralised management systems and introduction of market-based strategies. The discourse on environmentalism has also been noticable in the activities of numerous government departments and non-governmental organisations.[2] Sixty years ago, the colonial state similarly attempted

---

1. The following bills have been debated and passed in Parliament: *The Environmental Management Act of 1996*, *The Forestry Act of 1997*, *The Fisheries Management Act of 1998*, *The Wildlife Act, Water Policy, Parks and Wildlife Act, and the Irrigation Act*.

2. The Malawi Government created the National Environmental Action Plan (NEAP) and later the Department of Research and Environmental Affairs. At the same time, there have been several organisations working on environmental issues, such as the United Nations Development Programme, United States Agency for International Development, Coordinating Unit for the Rehabilitation of the Environment (CURE), Malawi Environmental Endowment

to grapple with similar issues. Thus, one would naturally expect that the increased current concern and consciousness would make heavy use of experiences from that period. However, it seems little effort is made to learn from or use historical experience. In part, this may be due to the negative legacy often associated with the coercive approach used to implement colonial conservation laws and programmes and the absence of in-depth historical analyses to link activities during the two periods.

Concern about environmental conservation in Malawi has deep historical roots, often neglected in contemporary debates. Many of the issues that were discussed half a century ago, for example, continue to appear in the post-dictatorship environmental discourses. What have changed are the kinds of questions that are asked, the terminology used and the form in which such ideas are expressed but the basic assumptions remain essentially the same. It is maintained that anthropogenic factors, population pressure and land use practices, among other factors, are generally the most destructive agents to the environment. Therefore some control mechanisms need to be put in place if further environmental destruction is to be averted. To achieve this, we need to know precisely what form earlier efforts at environmental conservation took, how they fared and what lessons we can learn from them.

Colonial soil conservation efforts tended to overlook the general understanding of issues of conservation among the indigenous communities in the same way efforts today overlook lessons and experiences from colonial soil conservation attempts. In Africa more generally, issues of the environment are no less important. Scholarship has shown that received wisdom projected the view that African land use practices were environmentally degrading and therefore in need of reform. Environmental degradation has generally been assumed to result in poverty, landlessness and social tension. While specific factors were identified and documented, little attention was paid to the larger processes underway such as land dispossession and the promotion of cash cropping. Yet the underlying structural inequalities in land distribution and access to scarce resources remain unchanged. In Namibia for instance, the case of Damaraland, an area that continues to be presented as experiencing desertification due to land use practices in common areas, shows quite contrary conclusions when empirical data is presented. Interestingly, the narrative of environmental collapse through human-induced desertification has remained a powerful explanatory framework in relation to land use in Damaraland. Sian Sullivan has suggested two factors responsible for the persistence of this narrative. The first issue concerns knowledge production, whereby environmentalist groups often require countries to adhere to green values and policies. Much aid was conditional on governments setting up environmentally friendly legislation, forming environmental bureaucracies and promoting these values. For Namibia, which is already classified as a desert country, any contrary knowledge on desertification

---

Trust (MEET) and Community Partnership for Sustainable Resource Management in Malawi (COMPASS).

Significance of the conservation debate in the contemporary period

would mean going against the grain. The second explanation has to do with power relations. The Namibian state has appropriated the narrative presented by international environmental groups to continue with policies and projects that regulate rural land use practices in the name of desertification.[3]

Numerous examples exist in other parts of Africa. In Kenya, for example, Homewood and Rodgers have demonstrated ways in which the conventional view of the tragedy of commons has been applied indiscriminately to explain the destruction of pastoralist regimes. Received wisdom holds that destruction of pasturelands in Kenya was the logical outcome of overstocking and overgrazing by herders due to their traditional practices. Providing compelling evidence and context, Homewood and Rodgers have shown that the process leading to overgrazing was not necessarily due to the practices of the herders but rather to economic and environmental factors.[4] Moore and Vaughan have equally discussed the production system among the Bemba in the Northern Province of Zambia. They have shown that the Bemba had developed one of the most diversified crop regimes in southern Africa, which enabled them to cope with extreme weather conditions. However, received wisdom had persistently presented their production system as being characterised by a *chitemene* [slash-and-burn] system that was primitive and wasteful. It was further projected that it would not survive the socio-economic transformations taking place, including the development of capitalism and wage labour. But contrary to the prevailing colonial mythology, Moore and Vaughan have argued that *chitemene* was a highly adaptive system that defied all conventional beliefs and survived well into the post-colonial period.[5] Another case comes from West Africa where Fairhead and Leach have pointed out that the African landscape has generally been misread or misrepresented as being deforested, degraded or dessicated while forest patches existing in some places are seen as evidence of the last relics of an original forest from the past. Human beings are often held responsible for the process of converting such forest areas into derived savannah through the practices of shifting cultivation and bush burning. In this regard, Fairhead and Leach have argued that what may be seen as destruction was in fact read in a very different way by the local people. Indeed, local narratives show that forests were actually formed by the people themselves or their ancestors. Rather than disappearing under human pressure, forests are associated with human settlement.

---

3. S. Sullivan, 'Getting the Science Right'.
4. Katherine Homewood and W.A. Rodgers, 'Pastoralism, Conservation and the Overgrazing Controversy', in D. Anderson and R. Grove (eds.) *Conservation in Africa* (Cambridge, 1987), pp. 111–128. Similar ideas have also been expressed in Pauline E. Peters, *Dividing the Commons: Politics, Policy, and Culture in Botswana* (Charlottesville: University of Virginia Press, 1994); and Pauline Peters, 'Embedded Systems and Rooted Models: the Grazing Lands of Botswana and the "Commons" Debate', in Bonnie J. McCay and James M. Acheson (eds.) *The Question of the Commons: the Culture and Ecology of Communal Resources* (Tucson: University of Arizona Press, 1987), pp. 171–194.
5. H. Moore and M. Vaughan, *Cutting Down Trees*.

Post-colonial environmental discourses, 1964–2000

Conservation policies and practices in the post-colonial period

The post-colonial Malawian state has experienced a particularly tough ride in its attempts to create sustainable societies. As stated earlier, the conservation momentum that developed during the colonial period tapered off in the run-up to independence in 1964. Since then, and until a few years ago, there had been relatively little serious discussion of environmental conservation and sustainability. The absence of any strong legislation or institutions concerned with the environment seriously weakened the state's capacity to achieve a sustainable use of the country's environmental resources. The fragile nature of the economy also exacerbated this problem. Consequently, the post-colonial state has repeated some of the mistakes committed during the colonial period, such as paying mere lip service to the problem of overcrowding on African Trust Land and continuing with the policy of benign neglect of environmental degradation wrought by commercial farming on private estates.

After independence, soil conservation was still viewed as a necessary approach to reducing land degradation although the strategies used to attain it had to change. The various colonial schemes designed in the 1950s to promote conservation, such as the master farmer schemes and the village land improvement schemes, were abandoned in favour of smallholder-based production systems. The Banda regime did not push for radical transformation of the agricultural economy, knowing full well that African memories of the harsh colonial conservation campaigns were still fresh. For some time, there was a lukewarm attitude, characterised by weak policy implementation, with little action taken against people responsible for degradation of the environment. In part, this was due to the fact that some members of the ruling elite were involved. In fact, Banda himself, together with his political henchmen, had opened up estates in various parts of the country. Degradation continued to take place both in the African Trust Lands and the privately owned estates. A policy of benign neglect largely characterised the early years of the post-colonial period.

Some scholars have argued that post-colonial conservationist policies were still heavily influenced by ideas imported from outside and were implemented in the African states with little success. Such ideas involved, as we have already noted, persuasion, demonstration and bulletin publicity.[6] Writing in the context of the Kingdom of Lesotho, Showers argues that, in fact, the intensification of anti-erosion measures such as terracing led to more erosion. Soil conservation techniques created paths and channels for the movement of water.[7] Another challenge is that soil conservation programme did not proffer any direct incentives to the African farmers and, as a result, the measures collapsed for lack of adequate maintenance. In Malawi, the uptake of these measures has generally been slow: for instance, between 1968 and 1977, the government terraced about 288,000 hectares under

---

6. J.N. Pretty and P. Shah, 'Making Soil and Water Conservation Sustainable: From Coercion and Control to Partnerships and Participation', *Land Degradation and Development* 8 (1997): 39–58.

7. K. Showers, 'Oral Evidence in Historical Environmental Impact Assessment'.

Conservation policies and practices in the post-colonial period

the Lilongwe Land Development Programme. But by the early 1980s, less than half of this had been maintained.

The newly independent state of Malawi had to come to terms with the fact that most of the land use problems were of a social nature and required social change rather than technical solutions.[8] Indeed, although physical factors like rainfall intensity and terrain played a part, social problems were largely responsible for degradation of the environment. As the population of the country increased, so did pressure on the land, which resulted in people farming marginal areas, a process that accelerated soil erosion. In a way, this created a dilemma for the state: the need to increase agricultural production to feed the growing population and promote exports against the declining quality of the land.

Concern for soil conservation was amplified by neo-Malthusian views about an impending ecological crisis. While the government had changed, many of the experts and civil servants, along with their ideas, remained essentially the same. It was widely believed that the writing was on the wall, as evidenced by, among other things, droughts, floods and water shortages. This was all the more reason for the state to avoid complacency and intervene in order to avert future disasters. What they saw at the time should not 'lull us into a belief that we have been granted exemption in perpetuity'.[9] In fact, the challenge of developing agriculture in Malawi went hand in hand with the degradation of susceptible areas due to 'the ever increasing pressure of population density and the limited available land; the steep slopes of much of the arable and grazing land and the heavy storms we experience'.[10] Quoting J.J. Devenage, the Chairman of the Natural Resources Board of Rhodesia, T.F. Shaxson, Malawi's soil conservation expert lamented:

> If we are to continue to enjoy the products of the soil we must ensure that we will not destroy it in the process of use. Once soil is lost, it can never be replaced. No man can live without soil, nor can he make it, only Nature can, and she takes her time – an inch in 500 years or longer, the scientists tell us. All man can do is to guard and cherish it as though it were his very life, which indeed it is. Man was blessed with all the wisdom and physical capabilities to perform his task and function to *develop* and *conserve* the natural resources of the earth with all its living creatures.[11]

To emphasise the point, agricultural experts were never short of florid language and entrancing examples to illustrate the deleterious effects of soil erosion. Shaxson strongly believed that soil erosion was man-made and further demonstrated

---

8. Malawi Government, *Land Husbandry Manual Vol. 1*, (Zomba: Land Husbandry Branch, 1971).
9. Malawi Government, Ministry of Natural Resources, Extension Circular No. 3/67 under the title 'Conservation for Survival'. This circular was later revised and presented as a talk to the Society of Malawi where it got published as T.F. Shaxson, 'Conservation for Survival', *Society of Malawi Journal* 23/1 (1970): 48—57.
10. Malawi Government, Ministry of Natural Resources, 'Conservation for Survival', p. 2.
11. *Ibid.* p. 5.

that human beings had historically (and still have) failed in their responsibility to perform the task of conservation in the process of using natural resources. This neglect was linked to the downfall of nations and the disappearance of civilisations such as those in the holy lands of the Middle East. In his view, the cause of all this was the lack of understanding and appreciation of the delicate balance between nature and human activity. When that balance is disturbed, the result is processes of erosion. Agricultural technical staff also made frequent references to the Dust Bowl, which was described as a most destructive enemy, to be defeated not by money and machines alone but through change of attitude. The American experience was still relevant to the Southern African region and, as one official noted, 'the Kalahari desert looms like a monster ready to engulf the rest of southern Africa, as man destroys the vegetation in the process of misuse'.[12] Such ideas were frequently used to express fears about the relentless effects of human intervention. Citing the example of central Malawi, 'one can still see dust stirred up by the *kamvulumvulu* dust devils in September, the dense haze of smoke from uncontrolled bush fires, the rivers dry, sandy rocky gullies in September and October and raging brown torrents during the rains robbing the country of uncountable thousands of tons of rich, irreplaceable topsoil and taking it to feed the fish – or smother them – in the Indian Ocean'.[13] To control the process of soil erosion, Shaxson proposed the idea of catchment management, whereby watershed and other ecologically vulnerable areas would be protected from any human interference.

The agricultural experts had identified gully erosion and the loss of topsoil as the most serious problems in the country.[14] These were caused mainly by rainfall, continuous cultivation of the land, the removal of vegetation cover, burning and overgrazing and cultivation on steep slopes. Faulting the farmers for these problems, the state used very graphic methods to illustrate the nature of erosion: the picture of village people having to go further each year to get their pots filled with water; the picture of having to work the soil harder each year to fill the maize granaries.

Having discussed the compelling factors for arresting soil erosion, as seen by Malawi's agricultural officers, we need to examine the policies and strategies that were put in place to deal with the problem. But two points should be mentioned here. First, it should be noted that agricultural officers had observed that conservation of natural resources was the responsibility of everyone – not just farmers – because everyone depends on those resources for life. Secondly, the concept of human beings as part of a total environment was underscored – and this environment must be conserved and used wisely. Human beings had the power to bring about great changes in their environment – the power to destroy or conserve.

---

12. *Ibid.* p. 7.
13. *Ibid.* p. 10.
14. Malawi Government, Ministry of Agriculture and Natural Resources, Circular No. 7/71, 'Water and Soil Conservation Measures for Customary Land', dated March 1971.

Conservation policies and practices in the post-colonial period

The state devised several strategies to deal with soil erosion in the immediate post-independence period. These included the use of physical conservation measures, land use planning and research. New institutional arrangements were set up to facilitate the implementation of soil conservation policies. In 1968, the state created the Land Husbandry Department of the Ministry of Agriculture and Natural Resources, which was responsible for designing and constructing anti-erosion works as well as providing services surrounding land use planning. It worked to ensure that land was managed in a way that would also sustain production. It further advised on the construction of physical conservation features such as bunds, terraces and waterways. Convinced that control of erosion was critical for profitable farming, the Department worked towards demonstrating to farmers that there was a close link between land husbandry and good crop production. Another important development was the establishment of the Land Husbandry Training Centre in Zomba to offer training and advice to extension staff, who would work with farmers. It was basically designed to provide in-service training to soil conservation staff in the Ministry of Agriculture. In the 1970s, the government also developed manuals and training materials for use by both professional and technical staff in the Ministry of Agriculture and Natural Resources.[15]

In relation to policy direction, two important changes took place. First, it was realised in hindsight that the old colonial strategy, bent on coercion and punishment, did not help solve the problem of erosion. It generated a lot of resistance and farmers had to abandon most of the soil conservation programmes. Hence, farmers had to be encouraged to adopt conservation practices through education and persuasion. The second change concerned a shift in emphasis from mechanical to agronomic conservation, whereby farmers had to be shown the relationship between conservation and production. In order to deliver better land husbandry services to smallholder farmers, the government established the National Rural Development Programme in the late 1970s. The country was subsequently divided into several Rural Development Programmes where various activities were undertaken to increase food production as well as rural incomes.

In the 1980s, the government adopted an integrated approach to soil conservation, which involved a much broader view of land use systems. Here anti-erosion measures had to consider the social, cultural and economic environmental conditions under which the land user operated. The approach was based on the premise that any farming practice is unique and that the needs of farmers must be taken

---

15. See for example, T.F. Shaxson, *A Manual of Land Use Planning and Conservation Techniques* (Zomba: Land Use and Conservation Branch, Ministry of Agriculture and Natural Resources, April 1971); T.F. Shaxson, *A Manual of Land Husbandry* in two volumes – Vol.1 on Land Use Planning, and Vol. 2 on Physical Conservation (Lilongwe: Land Husbandry Branch, Ministry of Agriculture and Natural Resources, April 1974); and T.F. Shaxson, N.D. Hunter, T.R. Jackson and R.J. Alder, *Land Husbandry Manual: Techniques of Land use Planning and Conservation* (Lilongwe: Land Husbandry Branch, Ministry of Agriculture and Natural Resources, April 1977).

into consideration for any effective measure to work. The second development was that the state began to link explicitly the issues of soil loss to yield reductions and conversely soil conservation to increased crop yields, so that the farmers could see for themselves the advantages of adopting such measures. Thirdly, the post-colonial state encouraged research into soil conservation, particularly as related to smallholder farmers. Previously, research was concentrated on production of estate-based cash crops such as tea and tobacco. In the 1970s and 1980s, for instance, research trials were set up in many places such as Hora in Mzimba, Zunde in Chikwawa, Nathenje and Chitedze in Lilongwe, Bvumbwe in Thyolo and Nkhande in Ntcheu. The crops on which research was undertaken include those produced by peasants such as cassava, maize, beans and groundnuts.

The guiding principle for post-colonial conservation policy rested on mass education and this involved two aspects. First, that conservation should transcend any local or national boundaries, since activities in one country can affect resources in another. To this effect, it was noted that, although efforts had been made at various levels of the education system to instill knowledge of conservation, there was still need to mobilise the general public so that they could quickly adopt the idea. Secondly, conservation should not be used in its narrower sense of physical measures but should be about understanding human interaction with the environment. This is the sense in which conservation education would be made relevant and taken as the responsibility of education institutions: schools, colleges and universities. Moreover, the philosophy of conservation had to be included in all educational materials so that citizens would be equipped with knowledge to appreciate not only the elements of agricultural practice but also conservation in its widest sense. Ultimately, that required a change in people's attitudes that went beyond the culture created by the existing educational systems. The need for universal education on conservation was clearly underscored when a government circular observed that,

> unless there is a universal appreciation and awareness in the minds of every man, woman, and child that conservation is a way of life to be observed every day of our lives in all spheres of occupation, then no laws, no money, no projects or anything else will save us from the same fate that has befallen many nations and civilizations throughout the ages.[16]

In addition, conservation had to be adopted by all people across time and space. It was not just a concern of rural communities – urban people had an equally important role to play. While previous efforts had targeted the rural population, the new policy viewed urban people as contributors to the destruction of natural resources. In fact, the approach based on mass education came in as one of the key recommendations of the Southern African Regional Commission for Conservation and Utilisation of the Soil (SARCCUS) symposium held in 1967 in Johannesburg, on the theme of 'Conservation and Education'. Prior to this, the first SARCCUS

---

16. Malawi Government, Ministry of Natural Resources, 'Conservation for Survival', p. 9.

Conservation policies and practices in the post-colonial period

meeting, held in Pretoria in 1952, had passed a resolution calling upon territorial governments to collect information on the status of conservation education as well as to create conservation consciousness in the minds of all people. What the Malawi government attempted to do at this time was very much in line with the trend prevailing in other countries in the region.

It is not surprising therefore that, between 1964 and 1969, the state focused very much on providing education to all farmers across the country through the extension services branch of the Ministry of Agriculture. It was hoped that, through that approach, farmers would respond and increase agricultural production. However, in a strange turn of events, the government shifted its focus from the mass of the farmers to individual progressive farmers in 1969. A government ministerial statement advised: 'No more time-wasting meetings and demonstrations! The mass approach must be left to the radio and mobile units.'[17] On the other hand, the individual progressive farmer, called *achikumbe*, would become the backbone of the agricultural development of Malawi. *Achikumbe* was defined as a progressive farmer, 'a man who makes a business of farming and leaves his land to his children in a better condition than he found it'.[18] Since the smallholder farmer had apparently not responded well to the need to increase agricultural production, this provided an opportunity for the state to begin to promote large-scale estate production.[19] Accordingly, the work of extension staff had to be concentrated upon the production of *achikumbe*. To this end, each of the three geographical regions of the country was given targets for raising and supporting *achikumbe*. For instance, in the year 1970 the total targeted number of *achikumbe* for the country was 3,000 farmers, distributed as follows: 500 for the northern region, 1,500 for the centre and 1,000 for the south. These targets were to be reviewed in subsequent years. Just as in Kettlewell's days in the colonial period, a *mchikumbe* was always assumed to be a male farmer. Women farmers were not accorded any special recognition despite their dominating the agricultural sector.

The procedure for identification and selection of *achikumbe* was quite elaborate. First, after identifying the names of farmers in particular areas, the field staff had to submit the same to the District Development Committee. The lists thus generated would be sent to Minister responsible for agriculture for approval and thereafter to the President for the award of *achikumbe* certificates. This marked the beginning of the growth of a new cadre of farmers who, with state support,

---

17. Gwanda Chakuamba, MP, Minister of Agriculture, addressed to all Field Staff Speech on Achikumbe in 1969.
18. *Ibid*.
19. F. Pryor and C. Chipeta, 'Economic Development through Estate Agriculture: the Case of Malawi', *Canadian Journal of Africa Studies* 24/1 (1990): 50–74; J. Kydd and R. Christiansen, 'Structural Change in Malawi since Independence: Consequences of a Development Strategy Based on Large Scale Agriculture', *World Development* 10/5 (1982): 355–385; D. Ghai and S. Radwan, 'Growth and Inequality: Rural Development in Malawi', in D. Ghai and S. Radwan (eds.) *Agrarian Policies and Rural Poverty in Africa* (Geneva: ILO, 1983).

would eventually dominate agricultural production in the 1970s and 1980s. This was, in many ways, similar to the progressive farmers' scheme set up in the 1950s by agricultural technocrat, Kettlewell.

Achikumbe farmers had to operate within rules and guidelines set by the Ministry of Agriculture. The basic rules for their operation were as follows:

> The farm should be planned and the farmer working within the framework of the plan;
> The soil and water conservation measures recommended in the plan should have been carried out to a high standard;
> The essential development of the farm should have been completed;
> The farmer must be farming profitably and to a high standard on all the land under his control.

In the course of assisting farmers to control erosion, extension staff recommended the following measures. First, building marker ridges and planting them with permanent crops. These ridges had to be built on a contour with the aid of hand levels. The making of permanent marker ridges was recommended and these had to be marked by planting either Napier grass for cattle feed or thatching grass. In a complete departure from the previous colonial approach, contour ridges had to be slightly larger than normal ridges but not as large as those used for contour bunds. Planting ridges spaced in horizontal lines twenty yards apart had to be realigned so that they ran parallel with the marker ridges. Second, farmers were encouraged to construct small boxes at about one-yard intervals in the planting ridges. Third, farmers had to build paths, to be raised and joined to the ridges. Unlike sunken paths, which were prone to erosion, raised paths had several advantages such as being easier for people to walk on and requiring little maintenance. Fourthly, drainage lines had to be left under vegetative cover. Realising that erosion is severe in drainage lines, the state recommended covering them with vegetation. Farmers were prohibited from cultivating across drainage lines and had to leave any natural vegetation as protection against the effects of flowing water. The state believed that successful completion of all these measures by farmers would lay a strong foundation for an effective system of soil conservation. It was further argued that these measures were critical to the future wellbeing of the farmers and the country as a whole. By the late 1970s, these measures were codified into a government publication that served as a key operational manual for agricultural field staff.[20]

The 1990s was a watershed period insofar as policy reform was concerned. Partly in response to international trends and the changing local political and economic situation, many environmentally-related policies and laws underwent revisions. With donor conditions attached to technical and financial support from donors, soil conservation and the environment more broadly became a hot subject of debate among academics, activists and policy-makers. Fears were expressed that

---

20. T.F. Shaxson, N.D. Hunter, T.R. Jackson and R.J. Alder, *Land Husbandry Manual: Techniques of Land-Use Planning and Conservation* (Lilongwe: Land Husbandry Branch, Ministry of Agriculture and Natural Resources, April 1977).

Conservation policies and practices in the post-colonial period

the environment was under threat of continued destruction and that the legal and policy framework was weak and outdated. This resulted in the creation of the National Environmental Action Plan (NEAP) in 1994 to provide a framework for integrating the environment in the overall socioeconomic development of the country through broad public participation. It also led to the establishment of the Department of Environmental Affairs and the promulgation of both the National Environmental Policy and the Environmental Management Act. Subsequently, the department came up with the National Strategy for Sustainable Development whose aim was 'to manage the environment responsibly, prevent degradation, provide a healthy life for all, protect the rights of future generations and conserve and enhance biological diversity'.[21] NEAP had identified soil erosion as the most serious of the nine environmental problems facing the country at the time. Deforestation and water resource degradation appeared as the second and third problems respectively. In July 2000, the Department of Land Resources developed its National Land Resources Management Policy and Strategy to facilitate the promotion of the efficient, diversified and sustainable use of land based resources, both for agriculture and other purposes, in order to avoid sectoral land use conflicts and ensure sustainable socio-economic development.

Table 11.1. Land Use and Vegetation

Land Use Category	Total (in Hectares)
Rain fed Cultivation	4,436,950
Dimba	39,550
Wetland Cultivation	78,200
Irrigation Agriculture	25,550
Grassland	893,850
Plantations	111,650
Natural Forests	3,514,850
Bare	47,800
Marshes	168,000
Open Water	152,850
Built up areas	26,700
TOTALS	9,495,950

(Source: Adapted from Department of Land Resources and Conservation, 1992.)[22]

These developments were critical to the emergence of a new strategy on soil conservation in the period after 1994, commonly referred to as the post-dictatorship period because of the end of President Banda's authoritarian regime.

---

21. Malawi Government, *Malawi National Strategy for Sustainable Development* (Lilongwe: Ministry of Mines, Natural Resources and Environment, 2004).

22. I was able to find more up-to-date information on land use and vegetation in the country but it is not available in a consolidated form as in the table above.

Post-colonial environmental discourses, 1964–2000

The Ministry of Agriculture had for some time been developing policies and strategies on soil conservation whose impact in terms of implementation left much to be desired. The subsequent restructuring of the Department of Land Husbandry and the Ministry of Agriculture affected the capacity of the agricultural technical staff to effectively deal with soil erosion. In addition, the changed environment where the farmers and the general citizenry were proffered freedoms and rights created new challenges to the approaches used for fighting soil erosion. Top-down approaches were generally decried in favour of more grassroots-oriented strategies. In 2007, the Agricultural Development Programme (ADP), which is essentially an operational tool of the Malawi Growth and Development Strategy (MGDS) in the area of agriculture, food security, irrigation and disaster risk reduction, noted that poor management of natural resources was a major contributing factor to land degradation, soil erosion, deforestation, diminishing water resources and declining biodiversity.[23] The government therefore came up with the following measures to promote sustainable land use management. First, the promotion of an integrated and synergistic resource management approach, embracing locally appropriate techniques such as rainwater harvesting, contour ridging, application of manure, preparation of compost, minimum tillage, agro-forestry and box ridging. Second, the adoption of people-centred, self-learning and investigating approaches. Third, the use of community-based participatory approaches to planning and technology development. The fourth measure concerns better land husbandry, offering farmers tangible economic, social and environmental benefits. It is clear that the new approach attempted to be sensitive to needs of the people and encouraged the participation of local farmers.

Challenges to conservation of natural resources

A number of challenges confront the post-colonial Malawian state in its efforts to conserve natural resources. Some of these challenges are due to the policies pursued after independence while others are rooted in the structures created during the colonial period. A systematic examination of conservation policies and programmes has allowed us to assess whether there have been any continuities or disjunctures with the colonial past. Our attention will now focus on the issues of deforestation, population growth and commercial crop production.

Deforestation

Notable among the challenges to sustainable natural resource management is deforestation, currently at an alarming rate across the country. Most mountains and hills have been denuded and it is an eyesore to see only few remaining patches of

---

23. GOM, *Agricultural Development Programme* (Lilongwe: Ministry of Agriculture and Food Security, December 2007).

Challenges to conservation of natural resources

forested areas in the country. Malawi has one of the highest rates of deforestation in southern Africa, currently standing at 2.4 per cent.[24] In this regard, Ezekiel Kalipeni argued in 1992 that, although forests provided ninety per cent of the country's fuel requirements and timber for various industries, only 38 per cent of the land was under forest cover.[25] More recent data shows a declining trend in the percentage of land under forest cover. Not unlike the colonial state, the post-colonial Malawian state's conservation efforts have been driven by the narrative of deforestation, which is deeply embedded within the idea of an impending energy crisis. In response, state energies have largely been directed at conserving or planting more trees. Peter Walker argues that, in spite of the general understanding of the importance of trees, local farmers, to whom most of the tree-planting exercises are directed, have not responded effectively. The farmers hold perceptions that are different from those of state officials. Again, as in the colonial period, the state has conveniently avoided engaging the estate sector, which is one of the greatest culprits in the deforestation of forested areas.[26] Charcoal production is another activity that contributes in no small measure to deforestation. Although its negative effects are clearly known by most forestry professional staff and policy-makers, political will is lacking to stamp out this malpractice. If anything, it has recently become a thriving business enterprise with the product finding a market in urban areas where persistent electricity failures have forced people to resort to charcoal as an alternative form of energy. In addition, media reports frequently cover stories of forest officials and politicians being among the major encroachers-upon and destroyers of forests in the country.

During the colonial period, the state was overzealously concerned with the regulation and protection of resources which, in its view, faced destruction by the Africans. Alarmist arguments were, as ever, powerfully raised, proclaiming that, unless some control measures were taken, the country faced an environmental crisis and the sustainable use of resources would be adversely affected. This prompted the state to intervene in the peasant rural economy at the point of production with an array of conservation policies and practices. But, because peasants are not irrational users of the land, state intervention to control their land and labour sparked various forms of peasant resistance. In the post-colonial period, state intervention has yielded a degree of indifference and slow adoption of forest conservation initiatives, as the farmers perceive the cause of and solution to the problem differently.

One classic example of deforestation and cultivation of the catchment area is that of the Shire River, which has had serious consequences for land and water resources. The Shire is the biggest river in the country and, after passing through the Shire Highlands region, empties its water from Lake Malawi into the Zambezi

---

24. Peter Walker, 'Roots of Crisis: Historical Narratives of Tree Planting in Malawi', *Historical Geography* 32 (2004): 89–109.
25. Ezekiel Kalipeni, 'Population Growth and Environmental Degradation in Malawi', *Africa Insight* 22/4 (1992): 273–282.
26. P. Walker, 'Roots of Crisis'.

Figure 11.1. Cultivation extending on the fringes of a forest reserve in the Misuku Hills

River. For many years, Africans have been steadily encroaching on the watershed area. Trees have been cut down and land cleared for cultivation. These activities have resulted in serious erosion of soil from the catchment area. The eroded soil has been taken down to the Shire River, silting it up. The siltation of the river has, in turn, slowed down the movement of the water to the waterfalls at Nkula, which produce hydro-electric power for many parts of the country. When the efficiency of the Nkula hydro-electric plant was reduced, the electrical output plummeted to such an extent that the plant could no longer supply power with the same regularity and effectiveness. This began to manifest itself in January 1997, when power outages and inadequate pumping of water became a daily occurrence in the country.[27]

The case of the destruction of the Shire River catchment area, as cited above, is not unique in Malawi. Several other mountainous areas have been deforested, accelerating the process of soil erosion with deleterious consequences. Yet protection of watershed areas had been an important component of colonial conservation

---

27. See Malawi Government, *Parliamentary Debates (Hansard)* for 1997 and especially the Fourth Sitting, Thirty First Session, held on Tuesday, 18 March 1997.

Challenges to conservation of natural resources

campaigns. For example, conservationists had worked relentlessly for the protection of such watershed areas as Chiradzulu, Zomba, Tangadzi, Ndirande, Michiru and Namvula mountains. Today, most of these mountains are heavily denuded and have become a source of concern to both environmentalists and local farmers. Mr Maganga Seyani of Nzundo Village in Thyolo, while making a comparison between the past and the present condition of the Namvula Mountain, observed that it had been

> a special forest where people used to pay homage to their *mizimu* (spirits) during times of problems. For example, in times of drought, the people would conduct a ceremony to pray for rains. Soon after this process the rains really came and the people therefore decided to name the place Namvula, meaning 'that which brings rain'. In recent times, however, this place has become desecrated so that people started cutting down trees in order to have land for their farming activities. This is because of the population increase. Now in view of [this desecration] ... the present Traditional Authority, Chief Nsabwe, ordered everybody to stop carrying out their farming activities around that place. He instead brought in seedlings of bluegum trees, which he gave to people and ordered them to plant there. Namvula is a protected area but it is not the same place we knew as children.[28]

Population growth

Another problem that continues to threaten the creation of sustainable societies in Malawi is population pressure. In colonial Malawi, Paul Topham, the country's first Soil Erosion Officer, eloquently argued that African settlement and cultivation of watershed areas had to be controlled at all costs if sound catchment management was to be achieved. He wrote that,

> in many areas, quick action had to be taken to protect important catchment areas and watersheds, because it was foreseen that a movement of natives would take place into them. The numbers of people moving towards the watersheds were continually being increased by native immigrants from Mozambique, Tete, and Northern Rhodesia, and vegetation was being destroyed by shifting methods of cultivation at an alarming rate.[29]

Although immigration has declined considerably in recent years, the country still continues to experience problems of overcrowding and environmental degradation. This is largely caused by the natural increase of population which has been growing at a rapid rate of 3.3 per cent per annum, which is higher than the 2.9 per cent growth rate for the African continent. Pressure on the land has also been intensified by the expansion of commercial farming. Droughts and floods have equally produced considerable stress in agricultural production so that the

---

28. Interview: Mr Maganga Seyani of Nzundo Village, T.A. Nsabwe, Thyolo district, dated 8 May 1997.
29. MNA A3/2/20: 'Memorandum: Coordination of Departmental Work in Soil Erosion Control' by P. Topham, dated 1 December 1937.

country finds it extremely difficult to maintain the sustainable use of environmental resources. The result of all these developments is that the peasants, who constitute the majority of land users in the country, experience phenomenal levels of poverty. As one of my informants remarked:

> nowadays problems have increased a lot. Poverty has increased and so has the population. We continue to cultivate the same pieces of land. Our children and their children too will be expected to work the same pieces of land. Yet the yields continue to decline. Some people are forced to open gardens in graveyards, forests and stony areas.[30]

The population of Malawi increased significantly between the 1960s and 2000, a period when the enforcement of conservation measures was relatively weak. Although we do not have precise evidence on the extent of environmental degradation, it would not be implausible to conclude that the effect on natural resources must have been great. From 4.4 million in 1966, the population increased to 5.5 million in 1977, then eight million in 1987 and ten million in 1998. The population and housing census conducted in 2008 showed that, despite the incidence of HIV/AIDS, the population had increased to thirteen million. This represents an increase of 32 per cent in the last decade alone, with a growth rate of 2.8 per cent.[31] The implication of all this is that the figure has trebled in the forty-year period of post-independence history. In addition, in 1987, Malawi had a population density of 85 persons per square km, which at the time was the fourth highest in Africa.[32] The size of each peasant land holding has been reducing over the years and now averages 1.2 hectares per household. Notwithstanding these pressures, Malawians have recently adopted some coping strategies, which may conceal the effects of high population growth. By analysing intercensal data, Deborah Potts argues that there is a growing pattern of intra-rural migration as a coping strategy, with the main direction being from the southern to the northern part of the country.[33] Growing opportunities in the north, and particularly the expansion of tobacco production, have certainly attracted such internal migration. But one thing is clear for the whole

---

30. Interview: Mai Rose Chisambula of Mbawa Village, TA Malemia, Zomba district, dated 13 May 1997.

31. Government of Malawi, *Population and Housing Census* (Zomba: National Statistical Office, 2008). For details on the relationship between population and the country's broader developmental challenges, see GOM, *Rapid: Population and Development in Malawi* (Lilongwe: Ministry of Development Planning and Cooperation, 2010).

32. E. Kalipeni, 'Population Growth and Environmental Degradation in Malawi': 277. The population density tends to be much higher in the southern part of the country with figures hovering around 200 persons per sq. km. For more details on landholding size, see Malawi Government, *Agricultural Development Programme* (Lilongwe: Ministry of Agriculture and Food Security, December 2007); and A. Dorward, 'Farm Size and Productivity in Malawian Smallholder Agriculture, *Journal of Development Studies* 35/5 (1999): 141–161.

33. Deborah Potts, 'Rural Mobility as a Response to Land Shortages: the Case of Malawi', *Population, Space and Place* 12 (2006): 291–311.

Challenges to conservation of natural resources

country – resources on which human survival depends, such as water, forests and land for agriculture, are declining. In contributing to the debate on the relationship between population and the environment in Africa, Stephen Carr has echoed the neo-Malthusian perspective by noting that the increase in Malawi's population has resulted in more soil degradation.[34] While challenging the argument posited by Tiffen, Mortimore and Gichuki in the context of the Machakos area in Kenya, he argues that population has resulted in soil nutrient loss and inter-seasonal changes in food production with the effects of child stunting and high mortality rates. These problems present additional pressures on a country that is almost completely dependent on the soil or agriculture for its economic survival.

Commercial crop production

The relationship between unfettered expansion of commercial crop production and environmental degradation is now clearly understood. In the USA, for instance, careless commercial agriculture resulted not only in poor yields but also in serious environmental degradation of the Great Plains in the early decades of the twentieth century. Such ideas have not disappeared: for instance, recent studies in the USA and other countries like Brazil have documented the severe ecological effects of the modes of production and scale of industrial agriculture.[35] Meanwhile, as early as the 1930s, Frank Stockdale, the agricultural advisor to the Secretary of State for Colonies, observed that cash crop production was responsible for much of the soil erosion in the colonies. Colonial authorities were certainly aware of these ideas but there does not seem to be much evidence that they attempted to restrict the production of cash crops. It would be too simplistic to argue that cash crop production alone would everywhere cause soil erosion, for there are exceptional cases. But the commercialisation and promotion of particularly maize and tobacco have had some negative effects on the land. The cultivation of these crops has not only reduced the amount of land available for agriculture but has also led to the opening up of ecologically vulnerable areas. Anthony Young, a renowned scholar who worked in Malawi for many years, realised through personal observations and aerial photographs made between 1962 and 1973 that maize cultivation had been widely adopted, to the extent of opening up gardens on steep slopes, the consequence of which was land degradation including shoestring gullies.[36] The history of maize

---

34. S. Carr, 'More People More Soil Degradation: the Malawian Experience', *African Crop Science Society* 6 (2003): 401–406.

35. Tony Weis, 'The Accelerating Biophysical Contradictions of Industrial Capitalist Agriculture', *Journal of Agrarian Change* 10/3 (2010): 315–341; Jason W. Moore, 'The End of the Road? Agricultural Revolutions in the Capitalist World-Ecology, 1450–2010, *Journal of Agrarian Change* 10/3 (2010): 389–413; Felix Mkanda, 'Contribution by Farmers' Survival Strategies to Soil Erosion in the Linthipe River Catchment: Implications for Biodiversity Conservation in Lake Malawi/Nyasa', *Biodiversity and Conservation* 11 (2002): 1327–1359.

36. B.H. Farmer, *et al.* 'Soil Survey and Land Evaluation in Developing Countries, a Case Study in Malawi: Discussion', *The Geographical Journal* 143/3 (1977): 431–438.

adoption in Africa is too well known[37] but what needs more attention is why peasants maintain its cultivation despite its low nutritional value and comparatively low returns. More importantly, empirically-based studies are required to show the effect of maize production on the soils of particular localities. Because of the close association between maize and food security, increased production of the crop has been viewed as an engine of Malawi's economic success and Green Revolution.[38]

Agriculture remains the backbone of Malawi's economy; in fact, the sector contributes about 35–40 per cent of the GDP, 85–90 per cent of the foreign exchange earnings and employs about 85 per cent of the workforce. The pattern of the economy was structured at the time of colonisation such that, until fairly recently, no major changes have taken place except perhaps in the order of importance of particular crops to the national economy. The principal crops have alternated over time between tea, tobacco and cotton as the main cash crops, while maize has been produced as both a food crop and cash crop.

The intensified production of maize and tobacco has also affected the environment in other ways. Many precious natural resources have also been destroyed due to production of these crops. Trees have been felled either to allow for the opening up of new gardens or as fuel. Dark fire-cured tobacco has been particularly conducive to environmental degradation, through the cutting down of trees used in processing the crop. As van Donge has shown, the process of curing tobacco by means of fire is technologically undemanding and can easily be done by ordinary farmers under sharecropping arrangements. So the more tobacco produced, the higher their income and the greater the impact on the environment. In aggregate terms, the contribution of tobacco to national export earnings has grown from 37 per cent in 1974 to 69 per cent in 1993 and its share remains high in the post-dictatorship period.[39]

The quality of the soil has also been declining and farmers must regularly use manure or fertilisers to improve it. Since independence, and particularly from the 1990s, there has been a substantial increase in the number of farmers, the hectarage under these crops and production levels. For tobacco alone, for instance, in 1990, Malawi had registered 4,355 tobacco estates covering nearly 759,000 hectares of land. The estate sector produced about 45,600 tonnes of burley of

---

37. James McCann, *Maize is Grace: Africa's Encounter with a New World Crop, 1500–2000* (Cambridge, Mass: Harvard University Press, 2005).

38. Melinda Smale, '"Maize is Life": Malawi's Delayed Green Revolution', *World Development* 23/5 (1995): 819–831. Similar views are expressed in a subsequent report by Melinda Smale and Thom Jayne, 'Maize in Eastern and Southern Africa: "Seeds" of Success in Retrospect', EPTD Discussion Paper No.97. Jan 2003, as well as by S.J. Carr, 'A Green Revolution Frustrated: Lessons from the Malawi Experience', *African Crop Science Journal* 5/1 (1997): 93–98.

39. J.K. van Donge 'Disordering the Market: the Liberalisation of Burley Tobacco in Malawi in the 1990s', *Journal of Southern African Studies* 28/1 (2002): 90.

Challenges to conservation of natural resources

the total 142,000 tonnes.[40] Martin Prowse has observed that smallholder burley production increased from 10,000 tonnes in 1994 to 97,000 tonnes in 2000. Of this figure, smallholder production accounted for sixty per cent of total national burley production between 1997 and 2003.[41]

As in colonial times, the expansion of the estate sector was not immune from the problems of soil erosion, although the general state position was to ignore this. There was a general disregard for anti-erosion measures and this time some of the culprits were people serving in senior government positions. Despite the establishment of the Estate Extension Service, charged with monitoring erosion and promoting better land use practices, soil erosion continues to take place in the estate sector.

In the post-dictatorship period, the state virtually lost its grip on the management of natural resources. Individuals, beneficiary communities, private companies and in some cases civil society organisations took over some of the responsibilities previously performed by the state. The period has also been marked by radical public policy reform, as evidenced in the reorganisation of the natural resources departments, the retrenchment of staff and in some cases privatisation of government institutions. By articulating universal environmental ideals, the conservationist movement has become quite amorphous and uncoordinated. This is reflected in delays experienced in policy implementation as well as the proliferation of organisations, which sometimes compete for influence and visibility.[42]

Since the dawn of the new millennium the issue of climate change has become a topical one among environmental scholars and activists. Whatever emphasis might have been laid on soil conservation, it appears that the debates have now shifed to climate change and adaptation. In fact, climate change has become such a strong buzzword that sometimes discussions about the environment are increasingly being equated to climate change. This is due to the fact that Malawi experiences the worst effects of both extremes of climate change. With its agriculture being predominantly rain-fed, droughts result in poor crop yields, leading to serious food shortages, hunger and malnutrition. On the other hand, flooding also tends to disrupt food production, especially among smallholder farmers. The effects of climate change are also noticed in other sectors, such as fisheries, where production has declined in tandem with drying of water bodies.

---

40. R.J. Tobin and W.I. Knausenberger, 'Dilemmas of Development: Burley Tobacco in Malawi', *Journal of Southern African Studies* 24/2 (1998): 405–24; J.K. van Donge 'Disordering the Market'; Martin Prowse, 'Becoming a Bwana and Burley Tobacco in the Central Region of Malawi', *Journal of Modern African Studies* 47/4 (2009): 575–602.
41. M. Prowse, 'Becoming a Bwana': 578.
42. Paul Mnyenyembe and Felix Kalowekamo, *Baseline Study: Country Assessment of the State of the Environment Movement in Malawi* Final Report (Lilongwe: 2008); W.M. Adams and J. Hutton, 'People, Parks and Poverty: Political Ecology and Biodiversity Conservation', *Conservation and Society* 5/2 (2007): 147–183.

Conclusion

We began this chapter by discussing the challenge of creating sustainable post-colonial societies in Malawi and the southern African region generally. That challenge is as critical to the question of environmental conservation today as it was half a century ago. Problems of population growth, declining land productivity and climate change figure prominently in current environmental discourses. The chapter has also demonstrated remarkable continuities in conservationist thinking about the environment. The new legislative measures promulgated since the mid 1990s are anything but adequate to the gravity of the environmental crisis, which calls for immediate attention. Environmental problems have not only increased in number but have also become more complicated.[43] Although soil erosion is no longer the central focus of the conservation controversy, its occurrence has far-reaching ramifications for the environment in general. The relative expansion of focus from erosion to wider ecological or environmental issues is certainly welcome, even though action is another question.

In the post-colonial period, the conservation tempo that reached a climax in the 1950s subsided remarkably, to the extent of the issue almost being neglected in the public discourse. It was to re-emerge only in the 1990s as a result of the liberalisation policies that introduced changes in the governance of both state and natural resources. Meanwhile, the state focused on persuasion and demonstration, tactics that were initially used in the 1930s and 1940s. Progressive farmers, now rebranded as *achikumbe*, were charged with the responsibility of demonstrating conservation measures to peasant farmers. But, unlike in the colonial period when European technical expertise dominated the managerial and supervisory roles, a cadre of African technical staff assumed responsibility for the implementation of soil conservation policies, which, not surprisingly, did not generate any overt resistance from the peasants. This period was also marked by the expansion of commercial production, particularly tobacco, which required not only the opening up of new fields but also the use of valuable natural resources such as trees for curing tobacco. Although this brought the ruling elite into complicity with key agents of increased environmental degradation, little action was taken, which reflects contradictions in the state's approach as well as in the nuanced understanding of the issue of soil conservation.

---

43. See the different 'environmental' laws that have been debated and passed in Parliament since 1994, such as *The Environmental Management Act of 1996*, *The Forestry Act of 1997* and *The Fisheries Management Act of 1997*.

12

Conclusion

This book has examined the impact of state intervention on the peasant economy in Malawi, with special emphasis on the Shire Highlands districts of Zomba, Chiradzulu and Thyolo. It has shown that, in the immediate pre-colonial period, Africans used various local conservation practices to sustain their production systems. The arrival of different African immigrant groups and European settlers in the last half of the nineteenth century significantly transformed these production systems and the use of natural resources. By focusing on the problem of soil erosion and on efforts to control it, the study has demonstrated that various social and power relations competed and negotiated for control of access to scarce resources in the country. The notion of conservation became a contested one in the social and environmental history of Malawi.

In the early colonial period, African production systems and local conservation practices increasingly came under attack from colonial state officials and some missionaries who sought to control access to land and labour resources. After the 1930s, the colonial state began to intervene with the aim of controlling environmental degradation. This degradation was not confined to African Trust Land; it also took place on private estates. However, from the beginning of this period, state intervention was bifurcated. The state intervened in peasant production at an early date, with intense and harsh conservation campaigns that sparked rural resistance throughout the country. On the other hand, state intervention on the mainly European-owned private estates came much later and, when it did come, it was weak and met with indifference and opposition by the estate owners and the labour tenants. Throughout much of the colonial period, the state racialised the environmental problem and pursued a policy of benign neglect towards degradation taking place on private estates.

I have also argued that the interpretation of peasant resistance to the colonial state needs to go beyond the nationalist paradigm that confines such debates to the rise of mass nationalism in the postwar period. That orthodoxy is inadequate in explaining peasant resistance, which, in fact, predated the Second World War. Peasants opposed state conservation policies and practices because the measures were in themselves difficult to undertake – they demanded much time and labour – and also because they constituted an interference with their autonomy. Although violence was used in some cases to resist state intervention, peasants often used non-violent means, such as refusing to do the work, destroying conservation measures that had already been put in place and opening gardens in prohibited areas. Peasants resorted to violence when the colonial state became too intrusive and used coercive means to implement conservation campaigns.

State intervention and ecological changes also had a profound impact on gender relations in the Shire Highlands region. The attempt to redefine the land tenure system by giving title deeds to men rather than the women who were the traditional land holders contributed to the disempowerment of women, a phenomenon that precipitated peasant resistance in various parts of the region. The case of the Domasi area of Zomba district demonstrates that women and men opposed conservation because it sought to restructure the matrilineal system that empowered women's access to the land.

My study has also debunked one of the myths surrounding African interaction with the environment. During the colonial period, Africans were viewed as irrational actors on the environment, as people who did not know how to use natural resources properly and whose farming practices were inherently destructive to the environment. These perspectives obscure much of the indigenous systems of knowledge that had been passed down to the peasants from generation to generation. Peasants developed various conservation techniques and strategies to cope with changing environmental conditions. These forms of knowledge must be appreciated in order to understand why degradation took place and what measures the peasants themselves used to conserve environmental resources. Finally, conservation was an important facet of the colonial policy of social control. The implementation of conservation measures required peasants not only to consolidate their land holdings but also to open up their spaces for state control of how they could use their land resources.

Although we talk about the colonial state in general terms, it was by no means a homogenous entity. Christian missionaries in general did not actively promote the campaign for conservation of resources but the actions and writings of some early missionaries frequently evoked biblical images and ideas that had a strong bearing on the perception and management of the environment. Later, some Christian beliefs were used in order to support or oppose state-sponsored conservation schemes in the colonial period. At the same time, African religious beliefs and customs played an equally critical role in creating a set of ideas about conservation and the environment as well as their engagements with the state.

One of the principal arguments of the book has been to show that the role of the Imperial Forestry Institute at Oxford University has been grossly under-played in studies of natural resource conservation in British colonial Africa. Predating even the occurrence of the American Dust Bowl, which caused a great sensation in the global community, the Institute had from the 1920s been central to the generation of scientific ideas about conservation. Through training of colonial technical staff, research and distribution of literature, the IFI became pivotal in producing key agents of change in the colonies. Strongly believing in the power and efficacy of scientific knowledge, many colonial experts sought to replace African ways of managing the

Conclusion

environment with western scientific methods. Many of colonial Malawi's forestry and agricultural experts who spearheaded the soil conservation campaign had strong connections with the Institute. Contemporary debates about conservation illustrate a certain degree of historical amnesia. The policy-makers have not seriously taken into account peasant needs and problems, such as poverty and landlessness. This has forced peasants to use resources in ways that not only engender environmental degradation but also threaten efforts towards realising conservation and sustainability. Moreover, recent trends which show the conservation ideology being captured by powerful interest groups, and in some cases promoting commercial conservation and commodification, have raised more questions as to whether the conservationist cause can still be realised. In his recent thought-provoking book, Dan Brockington, for example, has bemoaned developments in the new movement for conservation, which tends to be highly influenced by money, power and celebrities. These are critical issues to consider in conservation debates.[1]

This book has demonstrated that peasants are not irrational in their use of environmental resources. Neither should they be seen simply as victims of their own poor environmental practices. Rather, they are important historical actors who shape their own destinies in ways that are not easily perceptible by the state authorities. In the colonial period, peasants resisted state intervention in conservation because it reduced their autonomy and sought to control their labour and land resources. In more recent years, peasants have virtually ignored state restrictions on cultivation of watersheds in order to fulfill their own needs to obtain land for food gardens, cultivate stream banks for *dimbas* and use forest products for fuelwood and other domestic activities. Even the harshest of state policies has failed to stop peasants from doing what is central to their livelihoods and survival although it may not necessarily make sense to the scientific community.

This book suggests that the needs and interests of peasants must be central to discussions about environmental conservation and sustainability. Unless, and until, policy-makers begin to appreciate that problems such as landlessness, overcrowding and poverty are integrally related to environmental degradation, it will be difficult to achieve the sustainable use of resources in a peasant economy. These peasants' needs must necessarily be included in the post-colonial state's policy formulation plans and practices.

---

1. D. Brockington, *Celebrity and the Environment: Fame, Wealth and Power in Conservation* (London: Zed Books, 2009).

Bibliography

Unpublished sources

Oral Sources

Zomba district

Village Headman Namasalima (Mr Stewart G. Mabvumbe), 72 yrs old, Namasalima Village, TA Kuntumanji: interviewed 2 April 1997.

Group interview: (a) Village Headman Kumikochi (Jones Makungwa), b.1924; (b) Mr Bercher Malola, c.72 yrs old; (c) Mr Sabiston Peresi, c.81 yrs old; (d) Mai Linley Ching'oma, c.55 yrs old; (e) Mai Ngabane Ajusu, c.60 yrs old; Kumikochi Village, TA Malemia: interviewed 2 April 1997.

Mai Chipengule (nee Nete Chisale, sister to VH Nyani), Nyani Village, TA Malemia, Zomba: interviewed 2 April 1997.

Mr James Lupoka, Geography Department, Chancellor College, Zomba: interviewed 17 April 1997.

Mr William Maluwa, 80 yrs old, born at Nkwanda Village at Songani but interviewed at Malemia Village, TA Malemia on 8 May 1997.

Mr Lamuzi Milanzi, b.1913 at Mkanda Village, TA Chikowi but interviewed in TA Malemia on 8 May, 1997.

Mai Rosa Kunamano, (she is also Village Headman Berte Ngwale) b. 1920, Ngwale Village, TA Malemia: interviewed 8 May 1997.

Mai Ethel Ngwale, b. 7 July 1917 and Mai Betty Nyalapa, b. 9 July 1944, Ngwale Village, TA Malemia: interviewed 12 May 1997.

Mr A.W. Chitenje, 57 yrs old, born in Zimbabwe but came to Malawi in 1941. Ngwale Village, TA Malemia: interviewed 12 May 1997.

Mrs Rexa Chilenga, b. 1920 at Ngwale Village, TA Malemia: interviewed 12 May 1997. (She is a former teacher but her husband worked in the Accounts section at Domasi).

Mai Rose Chisambula, 75 yrs old, Mbawa Village, TA Malemia: interviewed 12 May 1997. (Her husband worked as a court clerk at Domasi).

Mai Kelise Chisambula, b. 1914 at Mbawa Village, TA Malemia: interviewed 13 May 1997.

Village Headman Nkusang'ombe, b. 1947 Nkusang'ombe Village, TA Malemia: interviewed 14 May 1997.

Mai Gladys Nthyola, b.1949 and Mai Emmie Mbulaje (nee Kumitawa), Nkusang'ombe Village, TA Malemia: interviewed 14 May 1997.

Mr Kayesa Ntuluko, c.70 yrs old, Kapichi Village, TA Malemia: interviewed 15 May 1997.

Bibliography

Mai Ayesi Nsalika, 75 yrs old, Kapichi Village, TA Malemia: interviewed 15 May 1997.

Mr Subiya Anusa c.70 yrs old, Kapichi Village, TA Malemia: interviewed 15 May 1997.

Mai Rexa Malidadi, 65 yrs old, born in Namadidi area in TA Mlumbe but interviewed at Nkusang'ombe Village, TA Malemia on 16 May 1997.

Mai Mercy Ntuwa, b.1942, Nkusang'ombe Village, TA Malemia: interviewed 16 May 1997.

Mai Esme Kimu, b. 1941 and originally came from Mozambique, Nkusang'ombe Village, TA Malemia: interviewed 16 May 1997.

Mr Marko Kanjedza, b. 1914 in Mulanje, and his wife Mai Irene Wilson, b. 1920, Nkusang'ombe Village, TA Malemia: interviewed 16 May 1997.

Mr James Anusa Nkupata, b. 1 June 1933 at Nkwela Village but settled in Nkusang'ombe Village, TA Malemia: interviewed 16 May 1997.

Mai Linley Kambwiri, c.97 yrs old, Ntogolo Village, TA Malemia: interviewed on 16 May 1997.

Group Village Headman Ntwiche, c.70 yrs old, Ntwiche Village, TA Malemia: interviewed 19 May 1997.

Village Headman Mjojo, c.60 yrs old, Mjojo Village, TA Mlumbe: interviewed 21 May 1997.

Mr Michael Sandaramu Kholopete, b. 1918, Mkanda Village, TA Mlumbe: interviewed 21 May 1997.

Mr Kimu Mbatata, b.1936, Malemia Village, TA Malemia: interviewed 19 May 1997.

Mr Elwin Massi, b.1932, Chilasanje Village, TA Malemia, interviewed 26 May 1997.

Mai Elvery Mponda, b. 29 April 1933, Mponda Village, TA Malemia: interviewed 10 August 1997.

Mai Jessie Kumtengula, b. 1922 and Mai Winnie Kazembe, b. 1933, Kalinde Village, TA Malemia: interviewed 10 August 1997.

Mai Dorothy Misoya, b. 1928, Mtenje Village, TA Malemia: interviewed 11 August 1997.

Mr Wilfred Mtenje, b. 1919, Kalinde Village, TA Malemia: interviewed 11 August 1997.

Mr McRey Kandulu, 70 yrs old, Kundecha Village, TA Malemia: interviewed 11 August 1997.

Chiradzulu district

Mai Gemu Kapalamula, b.1935, Kapalamula Village, TA Mpama: interviewed 3 June 1997.

Mai Patuma Pitala, c.80 yrs, Tuweni Makanani, c.75 yrs and Group Village Headman Mbalame, Mbalame Village, TA Mpama: interviewed 4 June 1997.

Mr H. Ching'anda, b.1911 and Mrs Ching'anda, b. 1918, Mbalame Village, TA Mpama: interviewed 4 June 1997.

Mr H.M. Selemani, b. 1 January 1922 and Mai Garaundi, b. 1938, Jekete Village, TA Mpama: interviewed 4 June 1997.

Bibliography

Mai Mpakati, c.90 yrs old and daughter, Mai Estere Mpakati, b. 1928, Joliji Village, TA Mpama: interviewed 5 June 1997.

Mr Yakobe, born c.1886 [by his own account], Joliji Village, TA Mpama: interviewed 5 June 1997 (started school in 1903).

Mai Margaret Gulani (nee Kawerawera), born 1919, Joliji Village, TA Mpama: interviewed 5 June 1997 (wife of former agricultural officer).

Mr Simon Benson Chimpeni, b. 1909, Joliji Village, TA Mpama: interviewed 5 June 1997 (born in Zomba but came to Chiradzulu in 1937).

Mai Agness Nyambi, b. 1897 and Mai Emma Juliyo, born 1934, Nchocholo Village, TA Likoswe: interviewed 17 August 1997.

Mai Elina Sitima, b. 1916, Mkwanda Village, TA Likoswe: interviewed 17 August 1997.

Mr Ulaliya Macheso, b. 1910, Mkwanda Village, TA Likoswe: interviewed 17 August 1997.

Mr Aloniya Joseph, 75 yrs old, Mkwanda Village, TA Likoswe: interviewed 18 August 1997.

Mr Alefa Billy, 70 yrs old, Nkwasenga Village, TA Likoswe: interviewed 18 August 1997.

Mai Enesi Mailoni, b. 1912 and Mr James Magareta, b. 1943, Nkwasenga Village, TA Likoswe: interviewed 19 August 1997.

Mr Ala Kachenjera, b. 1902, MagomboVillage, TA Likoswe: interviewed 19 August 1997.

Thyolo district

Chief Nsabwe's mother, c.90 yrs old, Nzundo Village, TA Nsabwe: interviewed 28 May 1997.

Mr Lekisemu, b. 1915, Nzundo Village, TA Nsabwe: interviewed 28 May 1997.

Mai Edna Kamoto, b. 1928, Khozombe Village, TA Nsabwe: interviewed 28 May 1997.

Mr Maganga Seyani, b. 1930, Nzundo Village, TA Nsabwe: interviewed 28 May 1997.

Mr Billiot Mlaliki, born 1918, Nzundo Village, TA Nsabwe: interviewed 29 May 1997.

Mai Gulaye, c.80 yrs old, Khozombe Village, TA Nsabwe: interviewed 29 May 1997.

Mai Mbebua, c.80 yrs old and Mr S. Likome, c.70 yrs old, Chalunda Village, TA Nsabwe: interviewed 11 June 1997.

Group Interview: Mr Dexter Jobo, c.70 yrs old, Mr Handson Mzengeza, c.90 yrs old and Mr Frank Likome, b. 1925, Chalunda Village, TA Nsabwe: interviewed 11 June 1997 (Mr Jobo was once arrested for defying soil conservation laws).

Mr Katchenga, c.80 yrs old, ChalundaVillage, TA Nsabwe: interviewed 11 June 1997.

Mai Nangozo, c.82 yrs old, Ndaona Village, TA Nsabwe, interviewed 11 June 1997.

Mai Abine Odireki, c.70 yrs old, Luka Village, TA Nsabwe: interviewed 12 June 1997.

Mai Maggie Dinalafodi, c.75 yrs old, Mussa Village, TA Nsabwe: interviewed 12 June 1997.

Bibliography

Mai Estery Nankhwele, c.75 yrs old, Mussa Village, TA Nsabwe: interviewed 12 June 1997 (she worked as a nanny for Webster, a priest at Thekerani Mission).

Group Interview: Mr James Misoya, b.1930; Mr Evanson Mateyu, b.1941; and Mrs Elizabeth Khozombe, c.90 yrs old – Khozombe Village, TA Nsabwe: interviewed 13 June 1997.

Mai Estery Edward Phiri, c.70 yrs old, Ndaona Village, TA Nsabwe: interviewed 13 June 1997.

Mai Iness Kaphesi, b.1934, and Mai Esther Kaphesi, b.1945, Ndaona Village, TA Nsabwe: interviewed 13 June 1997.

Village Headman Khozombe, b.1930, Khozombe Village, TA Nsabwe: interviewed 14 June 1997.

Personal Communication with Former Colonial Officials

Mr Peter Brown, former Director of Agriculture, now living in England: dated 17 June 1997.

Mr Robert Green, former Soil Conservation Officer in Malawi, now living in South Africa: dated 28 June 1997.

Mr John Killick, former Agricultural Officer at Thuchila and Makanga Agricultural Experimental Stations, now living at Bvumbwe, Malawi: dated 5 August 1997.

Unpublished Papers and Theses.

Boeder, Robert B. 'Wilfrid Good and the Ana a Mulungu Church' (Chancellor College, History Seminar Paper, 1981/82).

Chikusa, C.M. 'The Phenomenon of "Napolo" in Zomba with reference to the 1985 Ntonya–Ulumba Events' (Unpublished Paper, Geological Survey of Malawi, Zomba, Nov 1985).

Chimombo, S. 'An Integrated Theory of Napolo' (Unpublished Paper, Zomba).

Cooper, F. and R. Packard, 'Introduction: Development Knowledge and the Social Sciences' (Unpublished Paper, 1996).

Elliot, J. 'Soil Erosion and Conservation in Zimbabwe: Political Economy and the Environment' (Ph.D. Thesis, Loughborough University, 1989).

Johnson, S. 'Views in the South Seas: Nature, Culture and Landscape in Pacific Travel Accounts, 1700–1775', unpublished Ph.D. dissertation (University of Cambridge, 2005).

Kadzamira, Z.D. 'Agricultural Policy and Change During the Colonial Period in Malawi' (Chancellor College: History Seminar Paper, 1975/76).

Kambuwa, Albert, 'Malawi: Ancient and Modern History' (Unpublished Paper, University of Malawi Library, Zomba).

Mnyenyembe, P. and Felix Kalowekamo, *Baseline Study: Country Assessment of the State of the Environment Movement in Malawi*, Final Report (Lilongwe: 2008 - unpublished).

Bibliography

Murowa, Evans, P.P. 'Reverend Albert Kambuwa: A Critical Analysis of His Writings' (Chancellor College, History Seminar Paper, 1976/77).

Myambo, Simon, S. 'The Shire Highlands Plantations: A Socio-Economic History of the Plantation System of Production in Malawi, 1891–1938' (M.A. Thesis: University of Malawi, 1973).

Nzunda, M. 'Of Law on Soil Conservation' (Paper Presented at the Second Conference of the University of Malawi Research and Publications Committee, April 1993).

Potter, John R. '*Mizimu*: "Demarcated Forests" and Contour Ridges: Conservation in Malawi from 1800 to 1960' (B.A. Thesis: Williams College, Mass. 1987).

Smale M. and Thom Jayne, 'Maize in Eastern and Southern Africa: "Seeds" of Success in Retrospect' (EPTD Discussion Paper No.97. Jan 2003).

Tangri, R.K. 'The Development of Modern African Politics and the Emergence of a Nationalist Movement in Colonial Malawi, 1891-1958' (Ph.D. dissertation, Edinburgh University, 1970).

Vaughan, M.A. 'Uncontrolled Animals and Aliens: Colonial Conservation Mania in Malawi' (Chancellor College: History Seminar Paper, 1977/78).

Vaughan, M.A. 'Better, Happier and Healthier Citizens: the Domasi Community Development Scheme, 1949–1954' (Chancellor College: History Seminar Paper, 1982/83).

Vaughan, M.A. 'Social and Economic Change in Southern Malawi: a Study of Rural Communities in the Shire Highlands and Upper Shire Valley from Mid-Nineteenth Century to 1915' (Ph.D. dissertation, University of London, 1981).

Wilson, K. 'Aspects of the History of Vlei Cultivation in Southern Zimbabwe' (Paper presented to the Dambo Research Project 'Use of Dambos' Workshop, University of Zimbabwe, August 1986).

Archival Material

Government Reports and Laws

Haviland, P.H. *Report on Soil Erosion Prevention and Reclamation of Eroded Arable Land in Nyasaland*, 1930.

Malawi Government, *Rapid: Population and Development in Malawi* (Lilongwe: Ministry of Development Planning and Cooperation, 2010).

Malawi Government, *Parliamentary Debates (Hansard)* for 1997.

Malawi Government, *The Environmental Management Act of 1996*.

Malawi Government, *The Forestry Act of 1997*.

Malawi Government, *The Fisheries Management Act of 1997*.

Malawi Government, *Vision 2020: National Long-Term Perspective Study* Vol.1 (1998).

Malawi Government, *National Environmental Action Plan* (NEAP), 1994.

Malawi Government, *Malawi National Strategy for Sustainable Development* (Lilongwe: Ministry of Mines, Natural Resources and Environment, 2004).

Bibliography

Malawi Government, *Agricultural Development Programme* (Lilongwe: Ministry of Agriculture and Food Security, December 2007).

Malawi Government, *Population and Housing Census* (Zomba: National Statistical Office, 2008).

Nyasaland Government, *Report of the Postwar Development Committee* (Zomba: Government Printer, 1946).

Nyasaland Government, *Land Conservation Policy of 1939*, Circular No.1.

Nyasaland Government, *Native Labour Ordinance of 1903*, Government Gazette of 31 March 1903.

Shaxson, T.F. *A Manual of Land Husbandry Manual*, two vols. Vol.1 on Land Use Planning and Vol. 2 on Physical Conservation (Lilongwe: Land Husbandry Branch, Ministry of Agriculture and Natural Resources, April 1974);

Shaxson, T.F. *A Manual of Land Use Planning and Conservation Techniques* (Zomba: Land Use and Conservation Branch, Ministry of Agriculture and Natural Resources, April 1971).

Shaxson, T.F., N.D. Hunter, T.R. Jackson and R.J. Alder, *Land Husbandry Manual: Techniques of Land use Planning and Conservation* (Lilongwe: Land Husbandry Branch, Ministry of Agriculture and Natural Resources, April 1977).

Thomson, T.D. *The Domasi Community Development Scheme, 1949-1954* (Zomba: Government Press, 1955).

Topham, P. *How to Make a Level to Measure Mizera (Mapangidwe a Levulo Yoyesela Mizera* (Zomba: Government Printer, 1939).

Topham, P. 'Notes on Soil Erosion in the United States' Paper No.6 (Oxford: IFI, 1937).

(b) Files Containing Minutes and Correspondences

A3/2/11: Agricultural Survey – General, 1930 Feb–1935 April.

A3/2/12: Agricultural Survey – General, 1936 Nov–1938 June.

A3/2/20: Agronomic Sub-committee – General, 1937 Dec–1938 Dec.

A3/2/21: Agronomic Sub-committee – Minutes, 1937 July–1939 Dec.

A3/2/26: Board of Agriculture – General, 1932 Sept–1938 March.

A3/2/27: Board of Agriculture – Native Agriculture Committee, 1933 Jan–1934 Feb.

A3/2/155: Native Agriculture Development Board, 1929 Nov–1934 Aug.

A3/2/156: Native Agriculture – General, 1931 May–1939 Jan.

A3/2/157: Native Agriculture – Improvement, 1922 Jan–1925 Dec.

A3/2/162: Native Welfare Committee – Minutes, 1935–1938.

A3/2/191-192: Reports – monthly by Agricultural Supervisors, 1934–5 and 1936–7.

A3/2/203: Reports – District Agriculturalist, Zomba, 1934 May–1938 Aug.

A3/2/227: Soil erosion – prevention, 1930 Nov–1938 Dec.

A6/1/55: Soil Erosion – instructions for prevention, 1932 Feb–1938 Aug.

F1/3/1: Imperial Forestry Institute, 1921 May–1938 Aug.

Bibliography

FE 1/4/1: Appointment of Soil Erosion Officer.
FE 1/3/4: Legislation.
FE 1/3/1: Proposed Land Protection Ordinance.
NC 1/30/1-11: Soil Conservation and Land Usage Policy, 1940–1952.
NS 1/2/4: Agriculture, Soil Erosion, 1937 Sept–1939 Oct.
NSG 1/2/2: Domasi District Natural Resources Board, 1950 July–1955 Oct.
NSG 2/1/1: Domasi district team, 1951–1953.
NSG 2/1/2: Southern Province Natural Resources Board, 1951 Oct–1955 Oct.
NSZ 1/2/1: Zomba District, Natural Resources Board, 1949 Sept–1952 June.
NSZ 1/2/2: Zomba District, Natural Resources Board, 1952 Aug– 1953 May.
NSZ 1/2/3: Zomba District, Natural Resources Board, 1953 May–Dec.
NSZ 2/1/2: Southern Province Natural Resources Board, 1951 Oct–1953 Nov.
PCN 1/2/42: Soil Conservation, 1951 June–1953 Sept.
PCN 1/2/43: Soil Conservation, 1953 October–1958 Sept.
PCS 1/1/17: Re-afforestation scheme, Chiradzulu mountain, 1954 June–1955 Apr.
PCS 1/2/21: Mechanical Soil Conservation Unit scheme, 1954 Sept–1960 Feb.
PCS 1/2/24: Soil Conservation – Blantyre district, 1944 Nov–1955 June.
S1/66/36: The Control of Soil Erosion in Nyasaland, 1935–1939.
S1/148/35: Native Welfare Committee – appointment and minutes, 1935–1941.
S1/148.A/35: Native Welfare Committee – minutes, 1937–1939.
S1/523/31: Soil Conservation Reports, 1931–1935.
S1/526/25: Ordinance-1925, 1925–1935.
S1/558/27: Ordinance –Draft, petitions against, 1927.
S1/664/26: Ordinance –Draft, criticisms, 1926.
S1/566/23: Ordinance –Draft, 1923.
S1/583/26: Afforestation Memorandum, 1926–1930.
S11/1/13/1: General policy –postwar development, 1944 Oct–1946 May.
S11/1/13/2: Committee- appointment of members, 1943 Mar–May.
S12/1/6/3: Planning Committee report, implementation of, 1948 July–Sept.
S12/1/10/12: Soil erosion control, 1939 Mar–1947 Apr.
S12/2/3/1: Natural Resources Board, 1946 Feb–1949 Apr.
S12/1/6/4: Protection – Memorandum on legislation by Agronomic Subcommittee of the Native Welfare Committee, 1940 Jan–1941 Nov.
S12/2/1/1: Agronomic Subcommittee of the Native Welfare Committee, 1936 Feb–1941 Nov.
S38/2/3/1: Natural Resources – Preservation, 1949 May–1953 June.
S47/1/5/1: Forestry – Conservation of Natural Resources and Soil Erosion, 1944 Feb–1945 Apr.

Bibliography

VET 1/12/1: Postwar development – Veterinary considerations, 1943 Nov–1947 Jan.

Research Conducted in the United Kingdom

Documents from the Rhodes House Library, Oxford University

MSS.Afr.S.941: D.J. Turner on Intensive Village Survey, Ntcheu.

MSS.Afr.S.1811: R.W. Kettlewell: Memoirs of a Colonial Career.

MSS.Afr.S.864: R.H. Keppel Compton: A Factual Account of Events Leading to Deposing Phillip Gomani.

MSS.Afr.S.1158: T.D. Thomson Draft Annual Reports.

MSS.Afr.S.901: P. Topham, Correspondence, Reports.

MSS.Afr.S.918: Dennis Smalley, The Misuku Land Usage Scheme.

MSS.Afr.S.1742: Nyasaland.

MSS.Afr.S.1681: Africa Bureau.

757.14.S.5 1928: British Empire Forestry.

757.14.S.5 1935: Empire Forestry Conference.

757.14.r.1 1960: Natural Resources of Nyasaland.

Documents from the British National Archives at Kew

CO 525/176/15: Nyasaland Original Correspondence case of Rex vs. Wilfred Good and George Simeon Mwase, 1938 May 13–1938 October 25.

CO 1015/272: Banishment of Scott and Gomani from Nyasaland.

CO 525/192/1: Colonial Office – Nyasaland Original Correspondence.

CO 1015/652: Annual Report of the Domasi Community Development Scheme in Nyasaland, 1951–1954.

CO 927/33/3: F. Debenham, Report on the Water Resources of Bechuanaland Protectorate, Northern Rhodesia, the Nyasaland Protectorate, Tanganyika Territory, Kenya and the Uganda Protectorate London, 1948.

KV2/20/55: Rev Michael Scott, 1953–1956.

Published Books and Articles

Adams, W.M. *Green Development: Environment and Sustainability in the Third World* (London and New York: Routledge, 1990).

Adams, W.M. and J. Hutton, 'People, Parks and Poverty: Political Ecology and Biodiversity Conservation', *Conservation and Society* 5/2 (2007): 147–183.

Agnew, Swanzie, 'Environment and History: The Malawian Setting' in B. Pachai (ed.) *The Early History of Malawi* (London: Longman, 1972) pp. 28–48.

Allan, W. *The African Husbandman* (New York: Barnes & Noble, 1967).

Bibliography

Allman, J. 'Making Mothers: Missionaries, Medical Officers and Women's Work in Colonial Asante, 1924–1945', *History Workshop Journal* 38 (1994): 25–48.

Allman, J. and Derek Peterson, 'New Directions in the History of Missions in Africa: Introduction', *Journal of Religious History* 23/1 (1999): 1–7.

Amanor K. and S. Moyo (eds.) *Land and Sustainable Development in Africa* (London and New York: Zed Publications, 2008).

Ambler, C. *Kenyan Communities in the Age of Imperialism: the Central Region in the Late Nineteenth Century* (New Haven and London: Yale University Press, 1988).

Anderson, D. 'Depression, Dust Bowl, Demography, and Drought: the Colonial State and Soil Conservation in East Africa During the 1930s', *African Affairs* 83/332 (1984): 321–44.

Anderson, D. and R. Grove 'The Scramble for Eden: Past, Present and Future in African Conservation', in D. Anderson and R. Grove (eds.) *Conservation in Africa: People, Policies and Practice* (Cambridge, 1987) pp. 1–12.

Anker, P. 'The Politics of Ecology in South Africa on the Radical Left', *Journal of the History of Biology* 37, 2(2004): 303–331.

Atkins, K. *The Moon is Dead! Give Us Our Money! The Cultural Origins of an African Work Ethic, Natal, South Africa, 1843–1900* (Portsmouth, NH: Heinemann, 1993).

Attwell and Cotterell, 'Postmodernism and African Conservation Science' *Biodiversity and Conservation* 9 (2000): 559–577.

Baker, C.A. 'Depression and Development in Nyasaland, 1929–1939' *The Society of Malawi Journal* 27/1 (1974): 7–26.

Baker, C.A. 'Malawi's Exports: An Economic History' in G.W. Smith, B. Pachai and R.K. Tangri (eds.) *Malawi: Past and Present* (Blantyre: C.L.A.I.M. 1972).

Baker, C.A. *Development Governor: A Biography of Sir Geoffrey Colby* (London: British Academy Press, 1994).

Baker, C.A. *Seeds of Trouble: Government Policy and Land Rights in Nyasaland, 1946–1964* (London: British Academy Press, 1993).

Baker, C.A. *State of Emergency: Crisis in Central Africa, Nyasaland 1959–1960* (London: Tauris Academic Studies, 1997).

Banda, H.K. and H.M. Nkumbula *Federation in Central Africa* (London, 1949).

Bassett, T.J. 'Introduction: the Land Question and Agricultural Transformation in Sub-Saharan Africa', in T. J. Bassett and D.E. Crummey (eds.) *Land in African Agrarian Systems* (Madison: University of Wisconsin Press, 1993) pp. 3–34.

Beinart, W. 'Farmers' Strategies and Land Reform in the Orange Free State', *Review of African Political Economy* 21/61 (1994): 389–402.

Beinart, W. 'Introduction: the Politics of Conservation', *JSAS* 15/2 (1989): 143–62.

Beinart, W. 'Soil Erosion, Conservationism and Ideas about Development: a Southern African Exploration, 1900–1960', *JSAS* 11 (October, 1984): 52–83.

Beinart, W. and Colin Bundy, *Hidden Struggles in Rural South Africa: Politics and Popular Movements in the Transkei and Eastern Cape, 1890–1930* (London: James Currey and Berkeley: University of California Press, 1987).

Bibliography

Beinart, W. *The Rise of Conservation in South Africa: Settlers, Livestock, and the Environment 1770–1950* (Oxford: James Currey 2003).

Beinart, W., Karen Brown & Daniel Gilfoyle, 'Experts and Expertise in Colonial Africa Reconsidered: Science and the Interpenetration of Knowledge', *African Affairs* 108/432 (2009): 413–433.

Berkes, F. (ed.) *Common Property Resources: Ecology and Community-Based Sustainable Development* (London: Belhaven Press, 1989).

Berry, S. *No Condition is Permanent: the Social Dynamics of Agrarian Change in Sub-Saharan Africa* (Madison: University of Wisconsin Press, 1993).

Berry, Veronica and Celia Petty (eds.) *The Nyasaland Survey Papers, 1938–1943*, Agriculture, Food and Health (London: Academy Books, 1992).

Blaikie, P. 'Environment and Access to Resources in Africa', *Africa* 59/1(1989): 18–39.

Blaikie, P. and H. Brookfield (eds.) *Land Degradation and Society* (London and New York: Methuen, 1987).

Blaikie, P. *The Political Economy of Soil Erosion* (London and New York: Longman, 1985).

Boeder, R. *The Silent Majority: a History of the Lomwe in Malawi* (Pretoria: African Institute of South Africa, 1984).

Braudel, F. *On History* (London, 1980).

Brockington, D. *Celebrity and the Environment: Fame, Wealth and Power in Conservation* (London: Zed Books, 2009).

Brokensha, D., D.M. Warren, O. Werner (eds.) *Indigenous Knowledge Systems and Development* (Lanham, MD: University Press of America, 1980).

Bromley, D.W. and M.M. Cernea, 'The Management of Common Property Resources: Some Conceptual and Operational Fallacies', *World Bank Discussion Papers* 57 (Washington, DC: World Bank, 1989).

Buchanan, J. *The Shire Highlands (East Central Africa) as a Colony and Mission* (London, 1885).

Carney, J. 'Struggles over Land and Crops in an Irrigated Rice Scheme', in J. Davison (ed.) *Agriculture, Women and Land: The African Experience* (Boulder, CO: Westview Press, 1988) pp. 59–78.

Carr, S.J. 'A Green Revolution Frustrated: Lessons from the Malawi Experience', *African Crop Science Journal* 5/1 (1997): 93–98.

Carr, S.J. 'More People More Soil Degradation: the Malawian Experience', *African Crop Science Society* 6 (2003): 401–406.

Carswell, G. 'Soil Conservation Policies in Colonial Kigezi, Uganda: Successful Implementation and an Absence of Resistance', in W. Beinart and J. McGregor (eds.) *Social History and African Environments* (Oxford: James Currey, 2003), pp. 131–154.

Chakanza, J.C. *Preachers in Protest: the Ministry of Two Malawian Prophets: Elliot Kamwana and Wilfrid Gudu* (Blantyre: CLAIM, 1998) Kachere Monograph No.7.

Chambers, R. *Rural Development: Putting the Last First* (London: Longman Scientific and Technical, 1983).

Bibliography

Champion, H.G. 'The Silver Jubilee of the Imperial Forestry Institute', *Journal of Forestry* 49/7 (1951): 486.

Chilivumbo, A. 'On Labour and Alomwe Immigration', *Rural Africana* 24 (1974): 49–57.

Chimombo, Steve *Napolo and the Python* (Heinemann, African Writers Series, 1994).

Chirwa, W. '"The Garden of Eden": Share-Cropping on the Shire Highlands Estates, 1920–1945', in A. H. Jeeves and J. S. Crush (eds.) *White Farms, Black Labour: the State and Agrarian Change in Southern Africa, 1910–1950* (London: James Currey, 1997), pp. 265–280.

Chirwa, W. C. 'Alomwe and Mozambican Immigrant Labour in Colonial Malawi, 1890s–1945', *International Journal of African Historical Studies* 27/3 (1994): 525–550.

Clack, Timothy. 'Thinking Through Memoryscapes: Symbolic Environmental Potency on Mount Kilimanjaro, Tanzania', in T. Myllyntaus (ed.) *Thinking Through the Environment: Green Approaches to Global History* (Cambridge: The White Horse Press, 2011), pp.115–34.

Clements, F.E. 'Plant Succession: An Analysis of the Development of Vegetation', *Carnegie Institute Publications* 242 (1916): 1–512.

Clements, J.B. 'A Communal Forest Scheme in Nyasaland', *Fourth British Empire Forestry Conference* (South Africa, 1935).

Clements, J.B. 'Land Use in Nyasaland', Imperial Forestry Institute Paper No.9 (Oxford, 1935).

Clements, J.B. 'Protection of Forests in Nyasaland', *Empire Forestry Journal* 5 (1926): 211–217.

Clements, J.B. 'The Cultivation of Finger Millet (*Eleusine coracana*) and its Relation to Shifting Cultivation in Nyasaland', *Empire Forestry Journal* 12 (1933): 16–20.

Cline-Cole, R. 'Livelihood, Sustainable Development and Indigenous Forestry in Dryland Nigeria', in T. Binns (ed.) *People and Environment in Africa* (Chichester: Wiley, 1995) pp. 171–85.

Clutton-Brock, G. *Dawn in Nyasaland* (London: Hodder and Stoughton, 1959).

Colby, GFT, 'Recent Developments in Nyasaland', *African Affairs* 55/21 (1956): 273–282.

Davison, J. 'Challenging Relations of Production in Southern Malawi's Households: Implications for Innovating Rural Women in Development', *Journal of Contemporary African Studies* (1992): 72–84.

Davison, J. *Agriculture, Land and Women: The African Experience* (Boulder: Westview Press, 1988).

Davison, J. 'Tenacious Women: Clinging to Banja Household Production in the Face of Changing Gender Relations in Malawi', *JSAS* 19/3 (1993): 405–21.

Debenham, F. *Nyasaland: The Land of the Lake* (London, 1955).

Bibliography

Debenham, F. *Report on the Water Resources of the Bechuanaland Protectorate, Northern Rhodesia, The Nyasaland Protectorate, Tanganyika Territory, Kenya and the Uganda Protectorate*, (London: His Majesty's Stationery Office, 1948).

Delius, P. and S. Schirmer, 'Soil Conservation in a Racially Ordered Society: South Africa, 1930–1970', *Journal of Southern African Studies* 26/4 (2000): 719–742.

Dixey, F. 'The Distribution of Population in Nyasaland' *Geographical Review* 18/2 (1928): 274–290.

Dixey, F., J.B. Clements and A.J.W. Hornby, *The Destruction of Vegetation and its Relation to Climate, Water Supply, and Soil Fertility* (Zomba: Government Printer, 1924) Bulletin No.1.

Dodson, B. 'A Soil Conservation Safari: Hugh Bennett's 1944 Visit to South Africa', *Environment and History* 11/1 (2005): 35–53.

Dominick, R.H. 'The Nazis and the Nature Conservationists', *Historian* 49/4 (1987): 508–38.

Dorward, A. 'Farm Size and Productivity in Malawian Smallholder Agriculture', *Journal of Development Studies* 35/5 (1999): 141–161.

Drayton, R. *Nature's Government: Science, Imperial Britain, and the Improvement of the World* (New Haven: Yale University Press, 2000).

Duff, H.L. *Nyasaland Under the Foreign Office* (London, 1906).

Edwards, Talbot, 'Zomba Flood, December 1946', *The Nyasaland Journal* 1/2 (1948): 53–63.

Escobar, A. *Encounter Development: The Making and Unmaking of the Third World* (Princeton, NJ: Princeton University Press, 1995).

Fairhead J. and M. Leach *Misreading the African Landscape: Society and Ecology in a Forest-Savanna Mosaic* (Cambridge and New York: Cambridge University Press, 1996).

Fairhead J. and Melissa Leach, 'False Forest History, Complicit Social Analysis: Rethinking Some West African Environmental Narratives', *World Development* 23/6 (1995): 1023–1036.

Fairhead, J. 'Indigenous Technical Knowledge and Natural Resources Management in Sub-Saharan Africa: A Critical Review', *Paper Prepared for the Social Science Research Council Project on African Agriculture* (Dakar, January, 1992).

Fairhead, J. and M. Leach 'Contested Forests: Modern Conservation and Historical Land Use in Guinea's Ziama Reserve' *African Affairs* 93/373 (1994): 481–512.

Farmer, B.H. *et al.* 'Soil Survey and Land Evaluation in Developing Countries A Case Study in Malawi: Discussion', *The Geographical Journal* 143/3 (1977): 431–438.

Feeley-Harnik, G. *A Green Estate* (Washington: Smithsonian Institute Press, 1991).

Feierman, S. *Peasant Intellectuals: Anthropology and History in Tanzania* (Madison: University of Wisconsin Press, 1990).

Ford, J. *The Role of Trypanosomiasis in African Ecology: a Study of the Tsetse Fly Problem* (Oxford, 1971).

Fraser, Donald *Winning a Primitive People* (London, 1914).

Bibliography

Galligan, T. 'The Nguru Penetration into Nyasaland, 1892–1914', in R. Macdonald (ed.) *From Nyasaland to Malawi* (Nairobi, 1975) pp. 108–123.

Gamitto, A.C.P. *King Kazembe and the Marave, Cheva, Bisa, Bemba, Lunda and other Peoples of Southern, being the Diary of the Portuguese Expedition to that Potentate in the years 1831 and 1832*, Vol.1, Translated by I. Cunnison (Lisbon, 1960).

Gardiner Rolf 'Nyasaland: from Primeval Forest to Garden Landscape', *African Affairs* 57/226 (1958): 64–69.

Geiger, S. *et.al. Women in African Colonial Histories* (Bloomington: Indiana University Press, 2002).

Ghai, D. and S. Radwan, 'Growth and Inequality: Rural Development in Malawi', in D. Ghai and S. Radwan (eds.) *Agrarian Policies and Rural Poverty in Africa* (Geneva: ILO, 1983).

Giblin, J. *The Politics of Environmental Control in Northeastern Tanzania, 1840–1940* (Philadelphia, 1992).

Grove, R. 'Scottish Missionaries, Evangelical Discourses and the Origins of Conservation Thinking in Southern Africa, 1820–1900', *JSAS* 15/2 (1989): 163–187.

Grove, R. *Green Imperialism: Colonial Expansion, Tropical Island Edens and the Origins of Environmentalism, 1600–1860* (Cambridge: Cambridge University Press, 1995).

Hanna, A.J. *The Beginnings of Nyasaland and North-Eastern Rhodesia, 1859–95* (Oxford: Clarendon Press, 1956).

Hanna, A.J. *The Story of the Rhodesias and Nyasaland* (London, 1960).

Hayes, G.D. 'Wildlife Conservation in Malawi', *Society of Malawi Journal* 25/2 (1972): 22–31.

Hays, S.P. *Conservation and the Gospel of Efficiency: the Progressive Conservation Movement, 1890–1920* (Cambridge, Mass: Harvard University Press, 1959).

Henderson, J. 'Northern Nyasaland', *Scottish Geographical Magazine* 16 (1900): 82–89.

Hirschmann, D. and M. Vaughan, *Women Farmers of Malawi: Food Production in Zomba District* (University of California: Institute of Development Studies, 1984).

Homewood K. & W.A. Rodgers, 'Pastoralism, Conservation and the Overgrazing Controversy', in D. Anderson and R. Grove (eds.) *Conservation in Africa* (Cambridge, 1987), pp. 111–128.

Hooker, J.R. 'Witnesses and Watchtower in the Rhodesias and Nyasaland', *Journal of African History* 6/1 (1965): 91–106.

Hornby, A.J.W. 'The Erosion of Arable Soil in Nyasaland and Methods of Prevention' in F. Dixey, J.B. Clements and A.J.W. Hornby *The Destruction of Vegetation and its Relation to Climate, Water Supply, and Soil Fertility* (Zomba: Government Printer, 1924) Bulletin No.1.

Hornby, A.J.W. *Denudation and Soil Erosion in Nyasaland* (Zomba: Government Printer, 1934) Dept of Agriculture, Bulletin No.11.

Hornby, A.J.W. *Soil Survey of Nyasaland* (Zomba: Agriculture Department, Bulletins No. 2 of 1924 and 1 of 1925).

Bibliography

Hulme D. and Marshall Murphree (eds.) *African Wildlife and Livelihoods: the Promise and Performance of Community Conservation* (Portsmouth NH: Heinemann, 2001).

Hurt, R.D. *The Dust Bowl: an Agricultural and Social History* (Chicago: Nelson–Hall, 1981).

Huxley, J. *The Conservation of Wildlife and Natural Habitats in Central and East Africa* (Paris: UNESCO, 1960).

Isaacman, A. 'Historical Amnesia, or, the Logic of Capital Accumulation: Cotton Production in Colonial and Post-Colonial Mozambique', *Environment and Planning D: Society and Space* 15 (1997): 757–790.

Isaacman, A. 'Peasants and Rural Social Protest in Africa', in Frederick Cooper *et.al. Confronting Historical Paradigms: Peasants, Labor, and the Capitalist World System in Africa and Latin America* (Madison: University of Wisconsin Press, 1993) pp. 205–317.

Isaacman, A. and E. Mandala 'Rural Communities Under Siege: Cotton, Work, and Food Insecurity in Colonial Malawi and Mozambique, 1907–1960', in R.W. Harms *et al.* (eds.) *Paths Towards The Past* (Atlanta, GA: African Studies Association Press, 1994).

Isaacman, A. *Cotton is the Mother of Poverty: Peasants, Work, and Rural Struggle in Colonial Mozambique, 1938–1961* (Portsmouth, NH: Heinemann, 1996).

Jack, J.W. *Daybreak in Livingstonia* (Edinburgh: Anderson and Ferrier, 1901).

Jacobs, N.J. *Environment, Power and Injustice: a South African History* (Cambridge: 2003).

Jarosz, L. 'Defining and Explaining Tropical Deforestation: Shifting Cultivation and Population Growth in Madagascar (1896–1940)', *Economic Geography* 69/4 (1993): 366–79.

Johnston, Harry H. *British Central Africa* (London, 1897).

Jones, Griff, B. *Britain and Nyasaland: A Study of the Political Development of Nyasaland under British Control* (London, 1964).

Kalinga, O.J. 'Resistance, Politics of Protest, and Mass Nationalism in Colonial Malawi, 1950–1960: A Reconsideration', *Cahiers d'Études Africaines*, 36/143 (1996): 443–454.

Kalipeni, E. 'Population Growth and Environmental Degradation in Malawi', *Africa Insight* 22/4 (1992): 273–282.

Kandawire, J.A.K. 'Thangata in Pre-Colonial and Colonial Systems of Land Tenure in Southern Malawi with Special Reference to Chingale', *Africa* 47/2 (1977):185–190.

Kandawire, J.A.K. *Thangata: Forced Labor or Reciprocal Assistance?* (Zomba: Research and Publications Committee of the University of Malawi, 1979).

Kettlewell, R.W. *Agricultural Change in Nyasaland, 1945–1960* (Stanford: Food Research Institute, 1965), Vol.5, pp.229–285.

Kettlewell, R.W. *An Outline of Agrarian Problems and Policy in Nyasaland* (Zomba: Government Press, 1955).

Kettlewell, R.W. 'Nyasaland – Whence and Whither?' *African Affairs* 63/253 (1964): 258–265.

Kettlewell, RW. *The Importance of Controlling Bush Fires* (Zomba: Govt Press, 1960).

Bibliography

Kjekshus, H. *Ecology Control and Economic Development in East African History* (London: Heinemann, 1975).

Kreike, E. *Re-creating Eden: Land Use, Environment, and Society in Southern Angola and Northern Namibia.* (Portsmouth, NH: Heinemann, 2004).

Krishnamurthy, B.S. 'Economic Policy, Land and Labour in Nyasaland, 1890–1914' in B. Pachai (ed.) *The Early History of Malawi* (London 1972) pp. 384–404.

Leach, M. and R. Mearns (eds.) *The Lie of the Land: Challenging Received Wisdom on the African Environment* (Portsmouth, NH: Heinemann, 1996).

Lele, S. 'Sustainable Development: A Critical Review' *World Development* 19/6 (1991): 607–21.

Leopold, Aldo *A Sand County Almanac* (New York, 1949).

Linden, I. 'Chisumphi Theology in the Religion of Central Malawi', in J.M. Schoffeleers (ed.) *Guardians of the Land: Essays on Central African Territorial Cults* (Gwelo: Mambo Press, 1978) pp. 187–208.

Linden, I. and J. Linden, 'John Chilembwe and the New Jerusalem', *Journal of African History* 12/ 4 (1971): 629–651.

Livingstone, D. *Letter and Documents, 1841–1872*, edited by Timothy Holmes (London, James Currey, 1990).

Livingstone, D. and C. Livingstone *The Narrative of an Expedition to the Zambezi and its Tributaries and of the Discoveries of Lakes Shirwa and Nyassa, 1858–1864* (London, 1865).

Livingstone, D. *Last Travels*, edited by Horace Waller, Vol.1 [1874] (Connecticut, 1970)

Long, N. *Social Change and the Individual: a Study of the Social and Religious Responses to Innovation in a Zambian Rural Community* (Manchester: Manchester University Press, 1968).

Maack, Pamela '"We Don't Want Terraces!" Protest and Identity under the Ulugulu Land Usage Scheme', in G. Maddox *et.al.* (eds.) *Custodians of the Land: Ecology and Culture in the History of Tanzania* (Athens, OH: Ohio University Press, 1996) pp. 152–74.

MacDonald, Rev. Duff, *Africana or The Heart of Heathen Africa* (London, 1882).

Mackenzie, F. 'Political Economy of the Environment, Gender and Resistance under Colonialism: Murang'a District, 1910–1950', *Canadian Journal of African Studies* 25/2 (1991): 226–56.

Mackenzie, J.M. *Imperialism and the Natural World* (Manchester: Manchester University Press, 1990).

Mackenzie, J.M. *The Empire of Nature: Hunting, Conservation and British Imperialism* (Manchester, 1988).

Mager, Anne '"The People Get Fenced": Gender, Rehabilitation and African Nationalism in the Ciskei and Border Region, 1945–1955', *JSAS* 18/4 (1992): 761–782.

Mandala, E. *The End of Chidyerano: A History of Food and Everyday Life in Malawi, 1860–2004* (Portsmouth, NH: Heinemann, 2005).

Mandala, E.C. *Work and Control in a Peasant Economy: a History of the Lower Tchiri Valley in Malawi, 1860–1960* (Madison: University of Wisconsin Press, 1990).

Bibliography

Marks, S. *The Imperial Lion: Human Dimensions of Wildlife Management in Central Africa* (Boulder, CO: Westview Press, 1984).

McCann, J. *Maize is Grace: Africa's Encounter with a New World Crop, 1500–2000* (Cambridge, MA: Harvard University Press, 2005).

McCann, J. *People of the Plow: an Agricultural History of Ethiopia, 1800–1990* (Madison: University of Wisconsin Press, 1995).

McCracken, J.K. 'Colonialism, Capitalism and Ecological Crisis in Malawi: a Reassessment', in D. Anderson and R. Grove (eds.) *Conservation in Africa: People, Policies and Practice* (Cambridge, 1987) pp. 63–78.

McCracken, J.K. 'Experts and Expertise in Colonial Malawi', *African Affairs*, 81/322 (1982): 101–116.

McCracken, J. 'Conservation and Resistance in Colonial Malawi: the 'Dead North' Revisited', in W. Beinart and J. McGregor (eds.) *Social History and African Environments* (Oxford: James Currey, 2003) pp. 155–174.

McCracken, J. 'Share-cropping in Malawi: The Visiting Tenant System in the Central-Province, 1920–1968', in *Malawi: An Alternative Pattern of Development* (Edinburgh: Centre of African Studies, 1985) pp. 44–51.

McCracken, J. *Politics and Christianity in Malawi, 1875–1940: the Impact of the Livingstonia Mission in the Northern Province*, Kachere Monograph No. 8 (Blantyre: CLAIM, 2000).

McDean, Harry C. 'Dust Bowl Historiography', *Great Plains Quarterly* (Spring 1986): 117–126.

McGregor, Joan, 'Conservation, Control and Ecological Change: the Politics of Colonial Conservation in Shurugwi, Zimbabwe', *Environment and History* 1 (1995): 257–79.

McKay, Anthony 'Harry Johnston: Writer', *The Society of Malawi Journal* 23/2 (1970): 12–28.

Mitchell, J.C. 'An Outline of the Social Structure of Malemia Area', *The Nyasaland Journal* 4/2 (1951): 15–48.

Mitchell, J.C. 'The Political Organization of the Yao of Southern Nyasaland', *African Studies* 8/3 (1949): 141–59.

Mitchell, J.C. *The Yao Village: a Study in the Social Structure of a Nyasaland Tribe* (Manchester: Manchester University Press, 1956).

Mkanda, F. 'Contribution by Farmers' Survival Strategies to Soil Erosion in the Linthipe River Catchment: Implications for Biodiversity Conservation in Lake Malawi/Nyasa', *Biodiversity and Conservation* 11 (2002): 1327–1359.

Mlia, J.R.N. 'History of Soil Conservation in Malawi', in *History of Soil Conservation in the SADCC Region* (SADCC, March 1987).

Moore, Donald, S. 'Clear Waters and Muddied Histories: Environmental History and the Politics of Community in Zimbabwe's Eastern Highlands', *JSAS* 24/2 (1988): 377–402.

Bibliography

Moore H.L. and M. Vaughan, *Cutting Down Trees: Gender, Nutrition and Agricultural Change in the Northern Province of Zambia, 1890–1990* (Portsmouth, NH: Heinemann, 1994).

Moore, J.W. 'The End of the Road? Agricultural Revolutions in the Capitalist World-Ecology, 1450–2010', *Journal of Agrarian Change* 10/3 (2010): 389–413.

Morris, B. 'G.D. Hayes and the Nyasaland Fauna Preservation Society', *Society of Malawi Journal* 50/1 (1997): 1–12.

Morris, Brian 'Conservation Mania in Colonial Malawi: Another View', *Nyala* 19 (1996): 17–36.

Morris, B. *The History and Conservation of Mammals in Malawi* (Zomba: Kachere Book Series, 2006).

Mukamuri, B. 'Local Environmental Conservation Strategies: Karanga Religion, Politics and Environmental Control', *Environment and History* 1 (1995): 297–312.

Mulwafu, W.O. 'The State, Conservation and Peasant Response in Colonial Malawi: Some Preliminary Observations, 1920s–1964', in Alan H. Jeeves and Owen J.M. Kalinga (eds.) *Communities at the Margin: Studies in Rural Society and Migration in Southern Africa, 1890–1980* (Pretoria: University of South Africa Press, 2002), pp. 201–215.

Mulwafu, W.O. 'The Development of the Coffee Industry in the Misuku Hills of Northern Malawi, 1924–1964', *Malawi Journal of Social Science* 18 (2004): 1–16.

Mulwafu, W.O. 'The Interface of Christianity and Conservation in Colonial Malawi, 1891–1930', *Journal of Religion in Africa* 34/3 (2004): 298–319.

Murray, S.S. *A Handbook of Nyasaland* (London, 1922).

Mwase, G.S. *Strike a Blow and Die: a Narrative of Race Relations in Colonial Africa*, edited by Robert I. Rotberg (Cambridge, Mass: Harvard University Press, 1967).

Mwendera, E.J. 'A Short History and Annotated Bibliography on Soil and Water Conservation in Malawi', *SADCC Report* No.20 (September, 1989).

Njaidi, D. 'Towards an Exploration of Game Control and Land Conservation in Colonial Mangochi, 1891–1964', *The Society of Malawi Journal* 48/2 (1995): 1–25.

O'Riordan, T. 'The Politics of Sustainability', in R.K. Turner (ed.) *Sustainable Environmental Economics and Management: Principles and Practice* (London and New York: Belhaven Press, 1993) pp. 37–69.

Omari, C.K., 'Traditional African Land Ethics', in J.R. Engel and S.G. Engel (eds.) *Ethics of Environment and Development* (London, 1990), pp. 167–175.

Owen, R. et al. (eds.) *Dambo Farming in Zimbabwe: Water Management, Cropping and Soil Potentials for Smallholder Farming in the Wetlands* (Harare, University of Zimbabwe Publications, 1995).

Pachai, B. 'Christianity and Commerce in Malawi: Some Pre-Colonial and Colonial Aspects', in G.W. Smith, B. Pachai and R.K. Tangri (eds.) *Malawi: Past and Present* (Blantyre: C.L.A.I.M., 1972) pp. 37–68.

Pachai, B. *Land and Politics in Malawi, 1875–1975* (Kingston, Ont: Limestone Press, 1978).

Bibliography

Pachai, B. *Malawi: the History of the Nation* (London, 1973).

Palmer R. 'White Farmers in Malawi: Before and After the Depression', *African Affairs* 84/ 335 (1985): 211–245.

Palmer, R. 'Working Conditions and Worker Responses on the Nyasaland Tea Estates, 1930–1955', *Journal of African History* 27/1 (1986): 105–126.

Peters, P.E. 'Embedded Systems and Rooted Models: the Grazing Lands of Botswana and the "Commons" Debate', in Bonnie J. McCay and James M. Acheson (eds.) *The Question of the Commons: the Culture and Ecology of Communal Resources* (Tucson: University of Arizona Press, 1987), pp.171–194.

Peters, P.E. *Dividing the Commons: Politics, Policy, and Culture in Botswana* (Charlottesville: University of Virginia Press, 1994).

Peters, P.E. 'Revisiting the Puzzle of Matriliny in South-Central Africa', *Critique of Anthropology* 17/2 (1997): 125–145.

Peters, P.E. 'Bewitching Land: the Role of Land Disputes in Converting Kin to Strangers and in Class Formation in Malawi', *JSAS* 28/1 (2002): 155–178.

Phillips, S. 'Lessons from the Dust Bowl: Dryland Agriculture and Soil Erosion in the United States and South Africa, 1900–1950', *Environmental History* 4/2 (1999): 245–266.

Phimister, I. 'Discourse and the Discipline of Historical Context: Conservationism and Ideas about Development in Southern Rhodesia, 1930–1950', *JSAS* 12/2(1986): 263–275.

Phiri, Kings 'Production and Exchange in Pre-Colonial Malawi', in *Malawi: An Alternative Pattern of Development* (Edinburgh: Centre of African Studies, 1985): 3–32.

Pike, John G. *Malawi: A Political and Economic History* (London, 1968).

Potts, D. 'Environmental Myths and Narratives: Case Studies from Zimbabwe', in P. Stott and S. Sullivan (eds.) *Political Ecology: Science, Myth and Power* (London: Edward Arnold, 2000): 45–65.

Potts, D. 'Rural Mobility as a Response to Land Shortages: the Case of Malawi', *Population, Space and Place* 12 (2006): 291–311.

Powell, J.M. 'The Empire Meets the New Deal: Interwar Encounters in Conservation and Regional Planning', *Geographical Review* 43/4 (2005): 337–360.

Power, J. 'Individualism is the Antithesis of Indirect Rule: Cooperative Development and Indirect Rule in Colonial Malawi', *JSAS* (1992): 317–347.

Power, J. *Political Culture and Nationalism in Malawi: Building Kwacha* (Rochester, NY: University of Rochester Press, 2010).

Pretty, J.N. and P. Shah, 'Making Soil and Water Conservation Sustainable: From Coercion and Control to Partnerships and Participation', *Land Degradation and Development* 8 (1997): 39–58.

Prowse, M. 'Becoming a Bwana and Burley Tobacco in the Central Region of Malawi', *Journal of Modern African Studies* 47/4 (2009): 575–602.

Ranger, T. and John Weller (eds.) *Themes in the Christian History of Central Africa* (London, 1975).

Bibliography

Ranger, T. 'Territorial Cults in the History of Central Africa', *Journal of African History* 14/4 (1973): 581–597.

Ranger, T. *Voices from the Rocks: Nature, Culture, and History in the Matopos Hills of Zimbabwe* (Oxford: James Currey, 1999).

Ranger, T. 'Godly Medicine: The Ambiguities of Medical Mission in Southeastern Tanzania, 1900–1945', in S. Feierman and J. Janzen (eds.) *The Social Basis of Health and Healing in Africa* (London, 1992).

Rankin, D. *Zambezi Basin and Nyasaland* (Edinburgh, 1893).

Richards, P. 'Community Environmental Knowledge and African Rural Development', *IDS Bulletin*, 10/2(1979): 28–36.

Richards, P. 'Ecological Change and the Politics of African Land Use', *African Studies Review* 26 (1983): 1–72.

Richards, P. *Indigenous Agricultural Revolution: Ecology and Food Production in West Africa* (London: Hutchinson, 1985).

Richards, P. et al. 'Indigenous Knowledge Systems for Agriculture and Rural Development: the CIKARD Inaugural Lectures', *Studies in Technology and Social Change*, 13 (1989): 1–40.

Robbins, Paul *Political Ecology: A Critical Introduction* (Oxford: Blackwell Publishing, 2004).

Robinson, R.L. 'Forestry in the Empire', *Empire Forestry Journal* 1 (1922): 11–34.

Rollins, W.H. 'Whose Landscape? Technology, Fascism, and Environmentalism on the National Socialist Autobahn', *Annals of the Association of American Geographers* 85/3 (1995): 494–520.

Roosevelt, Theodore, 'Conservation', in T. Roosevelt, *The New Nationalism*, edited by W.E. Leuchtenburg (Englewood Cliffs, NJ: Prentice-Hall, 1961) pp. 49–76.

Rotberg, R.I. *The Rise of Nationalism in Central Africa: the Making of Malawi and Zambia, 1873-1964* (Cambridge, Mass: Harvard University Press, 1965).

Rowley, Henry H. *The Story of the Universities Mission to Central Africa* (London, 1867).

Schoffeleers, M. 'The Chisumphi and Mbona Cults in Malawi: a Comparative History', in J.M. Schoffeleers (ed.) *Guardians of the Land: Essays on Central African Territorial Cults* (Gwelo: Mambo Press, 1978) pp. 147–186.

Schoffeleers, M. (ed.) *Guardians of the Land: Essays on the Central African Territorial Cults* (Gwelo, Zimbabwe, 1978).

Schoffeleers, M., *Religion and the Dramatization of Life: Spirit Beliefs and Rituals in Central and Southern Malawi*, Kachere Monograph No. 5, (Zomba, 1977).

Scoones, I. 'Landscapes, Fields and Soils: Understanding the History of Soil Fertility Management in Southern Zimbabwe', *Journal of Southern African Studies* 23/4 (1997): 615–634.

Scott, J.C. *Weapons of the Weak: Everyday Forms of Peasant Resistance* (New Haven: Yale University Press, 1985).

Scott, Rev. Michael *A Time to Speak* (London, 1958).

Sears, P. *Deserts on the March* (Norman: Oklahoma University Press, 1959, 3rd edition).

Bibliography

Shaxson, T.F. 'Conservation for Survival', *Society of Malawi Journal* 23/1 (1970): 48–57.

Shepperson G. and T. Price, *Independent African: John Chilembwe and the Origins, Setting and Significance of the Nyasaland Rising of 1915* (Edinburgh, 1958).

Short, Philip, *Banda* (London, 1974).

Showers, K. and G. Malahlela, 'Oral Evidence in Historical Environmental Impact Assessment', *JSAS* 18 (1992): 277–95.

Showers, K.B. 'Soil Conservation in the Kingdom of Lesotho: Origins and Colonial Response, 1830s-1950s' *JSAS* 15/2 (1989): 263–286.

Showers, K.B. 'Soil Erosion in the Kingdom of Lesotho and Development of Historical Environmental Impact Assessment', *Ecological Applications* 6/2 (1996): 653–664.

Singini, Lincoln, W.S. 'Soil Erosion and its Control in Malawi', *Dziko: The Geographical Magazine* 8 (1980): 10–18.

Smale, M. 'Maize Research in Malawi Revisited: An Emerging Success Story?' *Journal of International Development* 6/6 (1994): 689–706.

Smale, M. '"Maize is Life": Malawi's Delayed Green Revolution', *World Development* 23/5 (1995): 819–831.

Stocking, M. 'Soil Conservation Policy in Colonial Africa', *Agricultural History* 59/2 (1985): 148–161.

Strayer, R., 'Mission History in Africa: New Perspectives on an Encounter', *African Studies Review* XIX/1 (1976): 3–15.

Sullivan, S. 'Getting the Science Right, or Introducing Science in the First Place? Local "Facts", Global Discourse – "Desertification" in North-west Namibia', in P. Stott and S. Sullivan (eds.) *Political Ecology: Science, Myth and Power* (London: Arnold, 2000).

Swain Donald C. 'Conservation in the 1920s', in Roderick Nash, *American Environmentalism* (New York: McGraw-Hill, 1990).

Tangri, R. 'From the Politics of Union to Mass Nationalism: the Nyasaland African Congress, 1944–1959', in R.J. Macdonald (ed.) *From Nyasaland to Malawi: Studies in Colonial History* (Nairobi: E.A.P.H. 1975) pp. 254–81.

Tangri, R. 'The Rise of Nationalism in Colonial Africa: the Case of Colonial Malawi' *Comparative Studies in Society and History* 10/2 (1968): 142–161.

Terry, PT, 'African Agriculture in Nyasaland, 1858–1894', *Nyasaland Journal* 15 (1962): 27–35.

Thomson, T.D. 'Soil Conservation – Some Implications', *Journal of African Administration* 5/2 (1953): 66–69.

Tiffen, M., M. Mortimore and F. Gichuki, *More People, Less Erosion: Environmental Recovery in Kenya* (London & New York: John Wiley, 1994).

Tilley, H. 'African Environments and Environmental Sciences: the African Research Survey, Ecological Paradigms and British Colonial Development, 1920–1940', in W. Beinart and J. McGregor (eds.) *Social History and African Environments* (Oxford: James Currey, 2003), pp. 109–130.

Tobin, R.J. and W.I. Knausenberger, 'Dilemmas of Development: Burley Tobacco in Malawi', *Journal of Southern African Studies* 24/2 (1998): 405–24.

Bibliography

Toman, M.A. 'The Difficulty of Defining Sustainability', *Resources* 106 (1992): 3–6.

Topham, P. 'Land Conservation in Nyasaland: an Attempt at Widespread Control, 1937 to 1940', in *Farm and Forest* (Ibadan, 1945), Vol.6, pp. 5–8.

Topham, P. 'Man and the Forest in Northern Nyasaland' *Empire Forest Journal* 9 (1930): 213–220.

Tropp, J. *Natures of Colonial Change: Environmental Relations in the Making of the Transkei* (Athens: Ohio University Press, 2006).

Troup, R.S. *Colonial Forest Administration* (Oxford, 1940).

Uekötter, Frank, 'The Nazis and the Environment – a Relevant Topic?' in T. Myllyntaus (ed.) *Thinking Through the Environment: Green Approaches to Global History* (Cambridge: The White Horse Press, 2011), pp.40–60.

Ukaga O. and A.G. Afoaku (eds.) *Sustainable Development in Africa: a Multifaceted Challenge* (Trenton, NJ: Africa World Press, 2005).

Vail, L. 'Ecology and History: the Case of Eastern Zambia', *JSAS* 3/2 (1977): 129–55.

Vail, L. 'The State and the Creation of Malawi's Colonial Economy', in R. Rotberg (ed.) *Imperialism, Colonialism and Hunger* (Lexington, 1983) pp. 39–86.

Vail, L. 'The Making of the "Dead North": A Study of the Ngoni Rule in Northern Malawi, c. 1855–1907', in J.B. Peires (ed.) *Before and After Shaka: Papers in Nguni History* (Grahamstown: Institute of Social and Economic Research, 1981) pp. 230–65.

Van Donge J.K. 'Disordering the Market: the Liberalisation of Burley Tobacco in Malawi in the 1990s', *Journal of Southern African Studies* 28/1 (2002): 89–115.

Vandergeeste, P. and Nancy Lee Peluso, 'Empires of Forestry: Professional Forestry and State Power in Southeast Asia', Part 2, *Environment and History* 12 (2006): 359–93.

Vansina, J. *Oral Tradition as History* (Madison: University of Wisconsin Press, 1985).

Vaughan, M. *The Story of an African Famine: Gender and Famine in Twentieth Century Malawi* (Cambridge: Cambridge University Press, 1987).

Walker, P. 'Roots of Crisis: Historical Narratives of Tree Planting in Malawi', *Historical Geography* 32 (2004): 89–109.

Walker, Peter, 'Democracy and Environment: Congruencies and Contradictions in Southern Africa', *Political Geography* 18 (1999): 257–284.

Watson, Elizabeth E. *Living Terraces in Ethiopia: Konso Landscape, Culture and Development* (London: James Currey, 2009).

Watts, M. '"Good Try, Mr Paul": Populism and the Politics of African Land Use', *African Studies Review* 26 (1983): 73–83.

Watts, M. 'Idioms of Land and Labor', in T. Bassett (ed.) *Land Tenure in Africa* (Madison: University of Wisconsin Press, 1992) pp. 159–196.

Watts, M. *Silent Violence: Food, Famine and Peasantry in Northern Nigeria* (Berkeley, 1983).

Webster, J.B. 'Drought, Migration and Chronology in the Lake Malawi Littoral', *Transafrican Journal of History* 9/1 & 2 (1988): 70–90.

Bibliography

Weis, T. 'The Accelerating Biophysical Contradictions of Industrial Capitalist Agriculture', *Journal of Agrarian Change* 10/3 (2010): 315–341.

Werner, A. *The Natives of British Central Africa* (London, 1906).

White, L. '"They Could Make Their Victims Dull": Gender and Genres, Fantasies and Cures in Colonial Southern Uganda', *American Historical Review* 100/5 (1995): 1379–1402.

White, L. *et.al.* (eds.) *African Words, African Voices: Critical Practices in Oral History* (Bloomington: Indiana University Press, 2001).

White, Landeg *Magomero: Portrait of an African Village* (Cambridge: Cambridge University Press, 1987).

Wilson, K. '"Water Used to be Scattered in the Landscape": Local Understandings of Soil Erosion and Land Use Planning in Southern Zimbabwe', *Environment and History* 1/3 (1995): 281–96.

Wilson, Ken 'Trees in Fields in Southern Zimbabwe', *JSAS* 15 (1989): 369–83.

Wishlade, R.L. *Sectarianism in Southern Nyasaland* (London, 1965).

Woods, T. 'Capitaos and Chiefs: Oral Tradition and Colonial Society in Malawi', *International Journal of African Historical Studies* 23/2 (1990): 259–268.

Woods, Tony, '"Why Not Persuade Them to Grow Tobacco": Planters, Tenants, and the Political Economy of Central Malawi, 1920–1940', *African Economic History*, 21 (1993): 131–150.

Worster, D. 'The Dirty Thirties: A Study in Agricultural Capitalism', *Great Plains Quarterly* (1986): 107–116.

Worthington, E.B. *The Ecological Century: A Personal Appraisal* (London: Oxford University Press, 1983).

Yates, A. and Lewis Chester, *The Troublemaker: Michael Scott and His Lonely Struggle Against Injustice* (London: Aurum Press, 2006).

Young, Anthony and Peter F. Goldsmith, 'Soil Survey and Land Evaluation in Developing Countries a Case Study in Malawi', *The Geographical Journal* 143/3 (1977): 407–431.

Zulu, L.C. 'Community Forest Management in Southern Malawi: Solution or Part of the Problem', *Society and Natural Resources* 21 (2008): 687–703.

Zulu, L.C. 'Politics of Scale and Community-based Forest Management in Southern Malawi', *Geoforum* 40 (2009): 686–699.

Index

A

Abraham, J.C. 176
achikumbe 4, 223, 224, 234
Africa Bureau 164, 166, 180–1, 185
Africa Educational Trust 186
African Development Trust 185
African farming practices 1, 4, 10, 12, 31, 34, 38, 40, 43, 44, 47, 54, 65, 66, 87, 138, 168, 209, 219, 221, 236
Agricultural Development Programme (ADP) 226
agricultural scientists 1, 219
Agriculture, Department of 37, 61, 62, 63, 72, 73, 75, 83, 92, 93, 94, 109, 114, 116, 117, 125, 126, 129, 134, 135, 150, 151, 156, 174, 175, 213, 221, 226
Amery, L.S. 108
Ana a Mulungu 169
ancestors/ancestral spirits 23, 32, 53, 56, 57, 95, 108, 154, 191, 193, 196, 211, 217
Anderson, David 37, 57, 68
animal husbandry 65, 87, 113
arable 20, 70, 219
Astor, David 180
Australia 77

B

bananas 7, 22, 23, 30, 34, 35, 41, 88, 130, 150, 201
Banda, A.J.M. 183
Banda, H.K. 104, 146, 163–4, 207, 218, 225
Barnes, K. 159
Beinart, William xi, 9, 59, 66, 68

Belgian Congo 167
Belgium 78
Bemba 217
benign neglect 118, 119, 126, 135, 218, 235
Bennett, H.H. 68, 70
Blantyre 22, 43, 58, 90, 111, 127, 137, 141, 162, 164, 175, 183, 185, 190, 191
Blixen, Karen 15, 41
boma 136, 137, 158, 159, 162, 170, 172, 178, 203, 204, 205
botanical gardens 48, 78
Botswana 180
box-ridging 54, 66, 87, 150
Brazil 231
Brockington, D. 237
Brown, J.C. 47
Brown, Peter 151
Buchanan, J. 22, 26, 29, 30, 43, 47, 49, 58
bunds/bunding 4, 38, 54, 56, 58, 66, 81, 87, 88, 92, 95, 96, 102–04, 119, 127–139, 147, 148–51, 154, 156, 160, 163, 168, 174, 175, 206, 207–09, 221, 224
burning 24, 25, 28, 29, 87, 102, 109, 116, 217, 220
Burrt Davy, J. 75, 77

C

Canada 77
Cape Town 78
capitalism 22, 49, 55, 65, 79, 217
Carr, Stephen 231
Carver, J.E.A. 73, 74, 75

Index

cash/commercial crop(s) 3, 4, 21, 22, 26, 38, 41, 54, 57, 58, 64, 65, 83, 87, 121, 126, 128, 160, 216, 222, 231, 232
cassava 22, 23, 24, 34, 35, 158, 160, 209, 222
cattle 22, 49, 87, 88, 89, 109, 113, 170, 171, 182, 184, 224
Ceylon 71, 78
Chagga (people) 197
Chakanza, Joseph 176, 179
Chakhumbira, Sub-Chief 183, 184
Champion, H.G. 75–8
charcoal 227
Chewa (people) 196
Chichewa (language) 34
Chikwawa (district) 111, 157, 202, 222
Chilambe Estate 131, 132
Chilembwe, John, Rev. 157, 168, 176, 179
Chilembwe Uprising 159, 175, 178
Chimombo, Steve 190–3
Chingale 161
Chinyama, J.R.N. (Ralph) 94, 183
Chinyenyedi 156–7
Chiputula, TA 170
chire 25, 37, 56
Chiromo 107
Chirunga Estate 134, 136
chitemene 8, 25, 38, 217
Chiume, Kanyama 184
civil disobedience 181, 185, 186
Clack, T. 197
class 94, 140, 210
Clements, Frederick 66
Clements, J.B. 63–5, 69, 73–5, 83, 84, 111, 155
climate change 233–4
coffee 4, 38, 47, 54, 57, 58, 87, 113, 116
colonial
  discourse 13, 16, 59–80
  economy 4, 21, 68, 118, 119, 121, 126, 141, 188, 189, 211, 212, 218, 227
  encounter 13, 15, 19, 23, 39, 40–2, 45, 46, 58, 67
  experts 4, 46, 64, 66, 68, 72, 75, 219

farming methods/systems 4, 38, 40, 41, 54, 58, 65, 221 224
forestry 64, 72–8, 85, 106, 108–12, 117, 162
officials 4, 28, 31, 40, 48, 50, 51, 53, 60, 61, 62, 64, 65, 67, 72, 83, 82, 83, 88, 89, 91, 98, 103, 116, 117, 118
period 3, 4, 6, 7, 12, 16, 17, 19, 31, 38, 54, 58, 59, 60, 77, 99, 118, 119, 120, 153, 157, 168, 176, 205, 218, 223, 226, 227, 234, 235, 236, 237
policies 1–4, 6, 7, 9, 13, 14, 16, 41, 42, 48, 58, 60, 71, 68, 70, 71, 78, 79, 81–165, 166, 170, 176, 187, 200, 203, 206, 218, 221, 227, 234
records 29, 181
rule 7, 12, 19, 23, 34, 37, 47, 48, 50, 51, 52, 55, 68, 71, 85, 104, 106, 121, 145, 187, 189, 208, 215
science 3, 16, 59, 74, 78
service 5, 21, 69, 71, 73, 74, 77, 83
state 3, 4, 6, 7, 9, 12, 13, 17–17, 37, 38, 40, 42, 44, 47–54, 56–8, 59–64, 66, 68, 81–99, 103, 105, 106–147, 151–7, 161, 162, 165, 166–71, 175–79, 187–89, 197, 200, 202, 203, 205–09, 211–13, 215, 227, 235, 236
Colonial (Native) Development and Welfare Fund 128, 162, 197
Colonial Office 68, 77, 82, 145, 164
contour ridging 4, 38, 56, 58, 81, 92, 97, 116, 117, 119, 122, 148–48, 151, 154, 156, 160, 209, 224, 226
cotton 4, 22, 23, 24, 36, 49, 57, 64, 65, 121, 123, 124, 127, 232
Creech Jones, A. 180
Crown lands 109, 112, 120
cults 55–6, 196

D

Damaraland 216
dambo 129, 213
Davison, J. 29

Index

Debenham, Frank 100
degradation of environment and land 1–4, 7, 10, 16, 18, 25, 31, 46, 49, 50, 56, 57, 61, 62, 65–7, 84, 87, 105, 106, 113, 118, 126–7, 129, 131, 135, 137, 139, 141, 162, 216, 217–19, 225, 226, 229, 230–2, 234, 235–7
Dehra Dun 76
Denmark 78
desertification 46, 216, 217
Devenage, J.J. 219
dimba 27, 32, 34, 88, 109, 129, 225, 237
Domasi 7, 81, 94, 127, 148, 187–9, 191, 192, 195, 197–213, 236
  Community Development Scheme 94, 189, 197–202, 208, 209, 211
Dominick, Raymond 79
Dowa 110, 111, 114
drains/drainage 56, 117, 122, 123–4, 129, 137, 138, 149, 156, 158, 159, 198, 224
Drayton, R. 48, 50
drought 2, 3, 20, 21, 27, 32, 35, 55, 112, 158, 195–7, 202, 219, 229, 233
dry season 26, 27, 32, 88, 109, 149, 151, 201, 209
Duff, H.L. 21, 51
Dust Bowl 5, 16, 54, 61, 65–8, 75, 76, 85, 92, 105, 220, 236

E

ecological
  holism 78
  mechanism 78–9
education (*see also* training) xii, 42, 44, 62, 73, 78, 104, 112, 125, 171, 186, 221–3
employment 121, 200, 201, 210
Enlightenment 58, 61
environmentalism 17, 72, 79, 215
erosion (*see also* soil erosion)
  gully 10, 122–3, 138, 194, 220
  sheet 10, 122–3, 138

F

Fairhead, J. xi, 217
famine 14, 20, 21, 27, 30, 35, 46, 189, 195, 202
Federation 17, 144–7, 151, 160–5, 166, 181, 182, 185, 186, 208
Feeley-Harnik, G. 13
Feierman, S. 13
fertility/fertile soil/fertilising 4, 10, 20–2, 25, 27, 30–2, 34–6, 45, 48, 51, 70, 83, 85, 88, 110, 122, 130, 133, 148, 154, 160, 232
Finland 78
fish/fishing 20, 33, 44, 195, 196, 201, 220, 233
floods 189–95, 202, 219, 229, 233
forest reserves 56, 78, 86, 108, 109, 110, 113, 120, 154, 155, 158, 162, 182, 198
forestry 3, 60, 62, 65, 70–9, 85, 102, 106, 108–11, 117, 156, 162, 181, 206, 226, 227, 237
Forestry, Department of 62, 63, 66, 70–4, 92, 94, 108–11, 113, 114, 117, 135, 153
France 78

G

game 37, 51, 52, 61, 62, 85, 86, 106–7, 117
Game, Department of/Department of Game, Fish and Tse Tse Control 66, 108
Gandhi 177, 180, 186
gender 7, 8, 9, 14, 17, 28, 29, 121, 187–214, 236
God 20, 44–6, 50, 79, 161, 165, 168–73, 176–9, 196
Gold Coast 78
grass/grasses 20, 23–6, 29, 31, 34–8, 44, 51, 75, 76, 85–8, 123, 124, 134, 139, 150, 153, 154, 224
grazing 85, 88, 89, 109, 112, 132, 170, 172, 206, 219
Great Depression 84
Great Plains 5, 65, 68, 85, 231

Index

Green, Robert 151
groundnuts 4, 22, 24, 27, 156, 209, 222
Grove, Richard 35, 37, 45–7, 57
Gudu, Wilfred 16, 157, 166–79, 186
gully erosion – *see* erosion

H

harvest/harvesting 6, 14, 20 25–9, 32, 34, 113, 124, 134, 148, 149, 154, 195, 202, 209, 226
health 42, 44, 54, 63, 79, 173, 191, 225
Hemingford, Lord 180
Hemingway, Ernest 15, 41
Hirschmann, D. 29
HIV/AIDS 230
Holland 78
Homewood, K. 217
Hornby A.J.W. 1, 10, 18, 19, 37, 48, 65, 69, 71, 122
hunting/hunters 33, 37, 50, 52–3, 106–8
Huxley, Elspeth 15, 41

I

immigrants/immigration 15, 18, 26, 30, 31, 55, 87, 125, 140, 141, 146, 155–8, 161, 185, 186, 208, 229, 235
Imperial Forestry Institute (IFI) 5, 16, 61, 69, 72–80, 236
imperialism 48, 58
imprisonment 81, 95, 102, 104, 107, 119, 147, 166, 172, 173, 174, 186
improvement 58, 90, 93, 101, 103, 140, 198, 208, 212, 218
India 69, 76, 77, 177, 180, 186
inheritance 9, 159, 188, 213, 214
inter-cropping 12, 26, 27
interdisciplinarity 13
interviews 12, 13, 18, 31, 38, 41, 44, 163, 204
irrigation 27, 35, 225, 226
Isaacman, A. xii, 13
Italy 78

J

Jeanes Training School 200
Jehovah's Witnesses 54, 168
Jesus 170, 186
Johannesburg 222

K

Kadewere, Chief 162
Kalahari desert 220
Kalipeni, Ezekiel 227
Kalulu 56
Kambuwa, A. 177
Kamwana, Elliot 167
Kanduna, H. 94
Kanthack, F.E. 68
Kapichi (village) 134, 196, 202, 204, 205, 207
kapitaos 129, 131, 137, 160
Kaponda, VH 171
Kaponda (village) 169–73, 186
Karonga (district) 112–13
Katchenga, Mr 152, 175
Kaulu, Raiti 205
Kawinga, Chief 183
Kennedy, D.M. (Governor) 159, 171, 173
Kenya 13, 49, 50, 68, 88, 107, 180, 186, 217, 231
Kettlewell, R.W. 48, 69–73, 83, 84, 93, 223, 224
Khwethemule (Village Headman) 170–1
Kilimanjaro 197
Kimbangu, Simon 167
Kincaid-Smith (Capt) 158–9
Kittermaster, H. 62, 176
Kumakanga, Stephenson 94
Kumbikano, Clement 165, 204, 207
Kuntumanji (Traditional Authority)192

L

labour 4, 6–9, 13, 14, 17, 24, 25– 31, 34, 38, 53, 54, 58, 96, 103, 105, 112, 118, 121, 128, 129, 131, 132, 140, 143–8, 153–61, 168, 172, 173, 178, 188, 200, 201, 210, 213–14, 217, 227, 235, 237

Index

Lancaster Conference 164
land husbandry 113, 221, 226
land tenure 4, 8, 9, 17, 51, 53, 73, 74, 119, 120, 136, 140, 159, 202, 211, 212, 236
land use systems/production systems 6, 9, 12, 13, 15–17, 18, 21–8, 34–8, 40, 43, 46, 48, 50, 53, 83, 88, 105, 140, 166, 177, 209, 217, 218, 221, 226, 236
Leach, M. 217
legislation 13, 56, 67, 68, 83–6, 93, 94, 99, 100, 107–9, 117,213, 215, 216, 218
Legum, C. 180
leguminous plants 24, 27, 32
Leopold, Aldo 66
Lesotho 13, 88, 89, 123, 218
level (agricultural implement) 148–50, 224
Likwenu valley 208
Lilongwe 90, 110, 111, 176, 219, 222
Limpopo River 85
livestock 34, 44, 53, 86, 88, 94, 107, 112, 182, 201, 202
Livingstone, D. 21–3
Livigstone, W.J. 159
Livulezi valley 89, 182
Liwonde 108, 198, 205
Lockhart-Smith, W.J. 85, 86
Lomwe 18, 87, 121, 140, 141, 146, 155, 156, 158, 198
London 68, 77, 163–5, 166, 180, 181, 183, 185

M

Macdonald, Duff 15
Machinjiri 205
Mackenzie-Kennedy, Governor 159
Magomero 158–60
maize 4, 22–4, 26–7, 29, 35, 50, 64, 76, 127, 155, 159, 160, 163, 169, 174, 177, 179, 209, 220, 222, 231–2
Malabvi 32, 56, 162, 196

Malawi Growth and Development Strategy (MGDS) 226
Malemia (Traditional Authority) 150, 152, 192, 203
Chief 201–4, 207
malimidwe 7, 56, 71, 143–53, 160–1, 163, 170, 175, 186, 203, 205–10
Malosa 74, 198, 200, 203
Malthus(ian) 83, 219, 231
Mambala 127, 162
Mangwende and the Trees 88
Maonga, Headman 173
Mapemba, Lawrence 164, 183
Mathews, B.W. 183
matrilineage 9, 17, 159, 189, 211–13, 236
Matuta, Abiti 205
Mau Mau 181
Mbona (spirits; cult) 32, 56–7, 95, 196
McCracken, John xi, 9, 48, 59, 68
Mchoma, Stapleton 203
Mgwede, Richard 203
Michiru 58, 229
Estate 70, 127
millet 22, 24, 25, 27, 38, 41, 48, 50, 116–17
Ministry of Agriculture 221, 223, 224, 226
missionaries 12, 14, 16, 22, 23, 39–49, 51, 53, 54, 57, 107, 120, 168, 170, 176, 193, 197, 201, 212, 235, 236
Misuku Hills 113–17
Mitchell, J. Clyde 9, 197, 211–12
Mmanga, Lawrie 203
M'Mbelwa, Inkosi ya Makosi 94, 116
Moffat, Robert 47
Moore, H. 13, 25, 217
mounds 24, 31, 38, 44
Mphande Hills 155, 157
Mposa, Ellerton K. 94
Mulanje (district) 36, 45, 122, 125, 138, 141, 155, 195
Muwamba, E. Alex 94
Muyere, Snowden 203
Mwana Lesa movement 167
Mwase, Chief 163–5, 170, 183

Index

Mwase, G.S. 55, 64, 153–4, 176
myths/mythology 44–6, 189, 193–4, 197, 236

N

Namibia 216–17
Namikhate Estate 134
Namvula 32, 56, 196, 229
napolo 189–95, 202
Natal 167
National Environmental Action Plan (NEAP) 1, 225
national parks 107–8
National Rural Development Programme 221
Native Development and Welfare Fund 128, 162
Natural Resources Board 16, 61, 69, 81–105, 118–19, 126–41, 160, 174, 175, 181, 203, 219
Natural Resources, Department of 104
Natural Resources Ordinance 83, –7, 91–7, 99, 100, 102, 104, 106, 125–8, 135, 147, 158, 174, 203
Natural Resources Rules 97–9, 130–2, 135, 147, 160, 162
Nazis 76, 79
Nchoma, Che 205
Ndirande 229
New Zealand 77
Ng'ombe (village) 202, 205
Ng'ombe (Village Headman) 201, 204–7
Nigeria 71, 77
Nkalo, Chief 162
Nkula 228
North Nyasa 112
Norway 78
Nsabwe, Chief; Nsabwe's area 137, 153–7, 170, 175, 229
Nswadzi River/Estate 132–3
Ntondeza, Chief 156, 157, 171
Ntondeza (Traditional Authority) 169, 171
Nyanja
 language 18, 22, 28, 36

people 23–4, 27, 31, 38, 52, 159, 169, 198
Nyasaland African Congress (NAC) 145, 164, 182, 183, 185, 207
Nyasaland Fauna Preservation Society 108
Nyasaland Railways 132–3, 140
Nyirenda, Loti 167

O

Oliphant, J.N. 74, 75, 77
Omari, C.K. 55
oral accounts/oral evidence 23–4, 27, 31, 38, 52, 159, 169, 198
oral traditions 19, 41, 191–2

P

Pakistan 77
paradise 15, 45, 46, 48
Parekh, Muljibhai Chaturadas 127
Parker, Capt. 159, 173
pastoralistm 28, 217
Pegler, S.J. 155, 156, 171, 174, 178
Perham, Margery 180
Petani, Headman 171
Phillips, John 78, 173
plant succession 75
policy framework 16, 82, 84, 125, 215, 225
population 2, 3, 8, 10, 12, 1, 30, 31, 49, 56, 57, 70, 71, 83, 96, 100, 103, 108, 120, 140, 151, 155, 163, 167, 178, 198, 201, 215, 216, 219, 222, 226, 229–31, 234
Portugal 78
post-colonial
 conservation 4, 17, 215–34
 economy 87
 period 3, 4, 87, 215–34
 society 234
 state 1, 2, 17, 215, 218, 226, 227, 237
post-dictatorship period 3, 17, 216, 233
Postwar Development Committee 69, 82–3, 208

Index

postwar period 71, 78, 81–4, 106, 109, 126, 128, 143–4, 178, 188, 197, 200, 235
Potter, J.R. 55
Potts, D. 230
poverty 1, 3, 216, 230, 237
power relations 1, 3, 8, 13, 98, 105, 137, 144, 146, 170, 190, 203, 210, 217, 235
pre-colonial
  conservation 12, 18–39, 40, 52, 117, 235
  cults 196
  economy 52
  environment 15, 18–39
  farming methods 18–39
  period 7, 12, 13, 15, 18–39, 40, 52, 117, 196, 235
Pretoria 75, 223
private estates 16, 89, 92, 96–8, 118–42, 155, 157, 158, 218, 233, 235
protective grasses 31, 38, 44
Protestants 58

Q

Quakers 180
Queen Elizabeth II 161, 164, 165

R

racial issues 14, 19, 64, 78–9, 118, 125, 126, 141, 145, 146, 186, 234
rains 26, 31–3, 56, 57, 87, 132, 139, 150, 191–6, 220, 229
rainwater 10, 100, 226
Rangeley, William 126, 130, 174, 175
reclamation 123, 124
religion (*see also* individual denominations) 41, 55, 167, 179
resistance 4, 6, 15, 17, 56, 71, 80, 81, 82, 91, 99, 102–5, 118, 121, 137, 144–5, 147, 151, 153, 154, 157, 162, 163–5, 168–86, 187–214, 221, 227, 234–6
Rhodes, Cecil 68

Rhodesia 60, 68, 77, 85, 88, 92, 122, 128, 144–6, 166, 180, 181, 185, 186, 208, 219, 229
Rhodes-Livingstone Research Institute 197
ridges 28, 53, 56, 87, 92, 95, 97, 102, 117, 119, 122–4, 148–50, 154, 156, 209, 224
Rodgers, W.A. 217
Rose, W.V. 156
Rotberg, R. 176
Roux, Edward 63, 78
Rumsey, E.J. 174–5

S

Sambankhanga Estate 136
Sangala, J.F. 207
Schoffeleers, M. 55–6
Scott, Michael (Rev.) 16, 164, 166–8, 179–86
Seretse Khama, Prince 180
Seventh Day Adventist Church 169, 176
Shaxson, T.F. 219, 220
sheet erosion – *see* erosion
Shembe, Isaiah 167
shifting cultivation/slash-and-burn 24, 25, 30, 38, 48, 49, 50, 53, 54, 87, 88, 102, 108, 116, 117 153–5, 217, 229
Shire Highlands 7, 10, 12. 13, 18, 21–9, 32, 34, 36–8, 43, 52, 56, 58, 100, 118–42, 146, 151, 154, 155, 157, 163, 165, 195, 210, 227, 235, 236
Shire River 227–8
Showers, K. 123, 218
slash-and-burn – *see* shifting cultivation
slave trade 12, 22, 23, 30, 42, 49, 106
slavery 152, 165
smallholders 104, 218, 221, 222, 223, 233
Smith, Eric 171
Smuts, Jan Christian 63, 78
Social Darwinism 14, 19
social engineering 4, 81, 188, 197, 213
Soil Conservation Service 68–70, 74, 85

Index

Soil Conservation Teams 132, 137, 139
soil erosion (*see also* erosion) 1, 2, 7, 10, 13, 16, 24, 25, 27, 28, 30, 31, 34, 35, 38, 50, 51, 61–6, 68–73, 82–9, 95, 98, 103, 104, 106, 110, 113, 118–26, 127, 130, 133–4, 138–9, 141–2, 147–51, 154–5, 158, 162, 194, 210, 215, 218–21, 224–6, 228, 231, 233–5
soils (types; qualities) 10, 20, 21, 30, 32, 34–7, 64, 70, 74, 85, 117, 160, 196, 209, 232
Songani 201, 207, 208
songs 13, 55, 150, 160, 189, 202
Sons of God sect 16, 54, 166, 168–70, 178
sorghum 22–5, 41, 160, 209
South Africa 47, 53, 68, 119, 146, 180
storm water 88, 97, 124, 175
stream bank (protection; cultivation) 88, 113, 124, 129, 130, 132, 150, 154, 156, 162, 237
subsistence 4, 35, 213
Sudan 77
Sullivan, Sian 61, 216
sustainability 1, 2, 7, 8, 9, 218, 237
Sweden 78

T

Tahiti 46
Tangadzi 107, 229
Tanganyika 78
Tangri, Roger 210
Tansley, Arthur George 78
Tanzania 55, 88, 197
taxes/taxation 52–3, 117, 121, 141, 147, 156, 158, 164, 166, 170–3
tchire 56
tenants 89, 96, 97, 118, 119, 121, 122, 126, 127, 131–2, 134–7, 140–1, 155, 157–9, 235
tenure – *see* land tenure
terracing 4, 13, 38, 54, 58, 66, 81, 88, 92, 104, 113, 122–4, 206, 218, 221
thangata 121, 141, 144, 146–7, 158–9
Thomson, T.D. 148, 197, 203–8

Thondwe Estate 134, 135
tobacco 4, 22, 24, 38, 49, 57, 58, 64, 71, 89, 110, 111, 121, 123, 127, 139, 158, 159, 160, 222, 230, 231, 232, 234
Topham, P. 1, 68–70, 72–4, 76, 83, 84, 154, 155, 157, 229
Townsend, R.G. 73, 74
Traditional Authorities 55, 112, 166, 169, 170, 192, 197, 202, 206, 207, 229
tragedy of the commons 217
training 5, 61, 65, 68, 69, 72–5, 77, 80, 91, 99, 100, 129, 131, 135, 149, 197, 200, 221, 236
Transvaal 75, 107
travel accounts 14, 18, 19, 28, 34, 41, 46, 49, 51, 60, 67, 71, 104
trees 4, 20, 23, 25, 26, 31, 33, 35–7, 40, 44, 45, 48, 51, 53, 55, 58, 76, 85, 87, 88, 102, 109–10, 112, 116, 153–4, 182, 190, 191, 194, 196, 227–9, 232, 234
Troup, R.S. 69, 73, 75–7
trusteeship 62, 145
Trust Land (African; Native) 16, 64, 96, 103, 106–17, 118–21, 125, 127–8, 130, 132, 134, 135–7, 141, 155, 157–60, 163, 218, 235
tsetse-fly 60, 63, 85

U

Uekötter, F. 79
Uganda 78, 180
United States 5, 65, 66, 68, 69, 74, 77, 80, 87, 231
Universities' Mission to Central Africa (UMCA) 42, 43
urban
  areas 201, 207, 227
  people 222
  settlement 200
uxorilocal marriage 9, 211
  system 211

Index

V

Vail, Leroy 49
Vaughan, M. xi, 12, 13, 25, 29, 33, 52, 55, 217
Vereeniging 76
Veterinary Department 62, 63, 72, 93, 94, 114
Victoria Falls 163
village forest area 108–11
village headmen (*see also* individual names) 37, 65, 110, 111, 112, 134, 136, 171, 202, 203, 204, 211

W

Walker, Peter 227
Watch Tower (Movement) 64, 167, 170, 179
watershed 109, 148, 155, 220, 224, 228, 229
Watts, M. 13
Werner, A. 21, 24–7, 29, 52
wet season 24, 27, 29, 31
White, Landeg 160
White, Louise 13
wildlife resources 40, 62, 106–8
Willan, R.G.M. 73–4
Wood, Rodney 107

Y

Young, Anthony 231

Z

Zambezi 146, 227
Zambia 8, 25, 38, 167, 217
Zimbabwe 119, 129, 140
Zion za Yehovah 166
Zomba xii, 9, 13, 17, 21, 22, 32, 36, 43, 47, 56, 58, 72, 87, 90, 111, 122, 123, 133–6, 141, 148, 150, 159, 161, 170, 173, 187–214, 221, 229, 135, 136

www.ingramcontent.com/pod-product-compliance
Lightning Source LLC
Chambersburg PA
CBHW020911020526
44114CB00039B/268